Studies in Natural Language Processing

Machine translation
Theoretical and methodological issues

Studies in Natural Language Processing

Executive Editor: Aravind K. Joshi

Sponsored by the Association for Computational Linguistics

This series publishes monographs, texts, and edited volumes within the interdisciplinary field of computational linguistics. Sponsored by the Association for Computational Linguistics, the series represents the range of topics of concern to the scholars working in this increasingly important field, whether their background is in formal linguistics, psycholinguistics, cognitive psychology or artificial intelligence.

Also in this series:

Machine translation
Theoretical and methodological issues

Edited by
SERGEI NIRENBURG
International Center on Machine Translation,
Carnegie-Mellon University

The right of the
University of Cambridge
to print and sell
all manner of books
was granted by
Henry VIII in 1534.
The University has printed
and published continuously
since 1584.

CAMBRIDGE UNIVERSITY PRESS

CAMBRIDGE

LONDON   NEW YORK   NEW ROCHELLE

MELBOURNE   SYDNEY

Published by the Press Syndicate of the University of Cambridge
The Pitt Building, Trumpington Street, Cambridge CB2 1RP
32 East 57th Street, New York, NY 10022, USA
10 Stamford Road, Oakleigh, Melbourne 3166, Australia

First published 1987

Printed in Great Britain at the University Press, Cambridge

British Library cataloguing in publication data
Machine translation: theoretical and methodological issues. –
(Studies in natural language processing)
1. Machine translating
I. Nirenburg, Sergei   II. Series
418'.02   P308

Library of Congress cataloguing in publication data
Machine translation.
(Studies in natural language processing)
Bibliography.
Includes index.
1. Machine translating.   I. Nirenburg, Sergei.   II. Series.
P308.M34 1987   418'.02'028   86-23207

ISBN 0 521 33125 0 hard covers
ISBN 0 521 33696 1 paperback

Contents

v

Contributors

Douglas Arnold, University of Essex
Jaime Carbonell, Carnegie-Mellon University
Richard Cullingford, Georgia Institute of Technology
Roderick Johnson, University of Manchester Institute of Science and Technology
Richard Kittredge, University of Montreal
Steven L. Lytinen, Cognitive Systems, Inc.
David McDonald, University of Massachusetts
Alan Melby, Brigham Young University
Makoto Nagao, Kyoto University
Sergei Nirenburg, Carnegie-Mellon University
Boyan Onyshkevych, 12025 Dove Circle, Laurel, MD 20708
James Pustejovsky, Brandeis University
Victor Raskin, Purdue University
Louis des Tombe, State University of Utrecht
Masaru Tomita, Carnegie-Mellon University
Allen Tucker, Colgate University
Donald E. Walker, Bell Communications Research,
Ralph Weischedel, Bolt Beranek and Newman, Inc.
John S. White, Box 7247, Siemens Corp.
Peter Whitelock, University of Manchester Institute of Science and Technology

Preface

The demand for computer systems that can translate texts among various languages, or at least help human translators, is high and growing in our information-saturated world. Research and development activities directed at building such systems can be united under the headings 'machine translation' and 'machine-aided translation.' The state of the machine translation art in the mid-1980s is encouraging but not yet satisfactory. Speaking plainly, we don't have systems that can adequately translate texts devoted to a reasonably broad domain of discourse, even between two specific languages. At the same time, technological and especially conceptual advances are evident in this renascent field of study.

During its early years machine translation research was viewed as primarily an engineering task. Advances in linguistic theory and repeated failures of the first-generation systems to achieve their stated goals have united to discredit this attitude. Machine translation has come to be understood as an application domain of both linguistics and computer science. It was then demonstrated that fully-automated high-quality machine translation is possible only when the meaning of the input text is taken into account, in addition to its syntax and a version of a bilingual dictionary at the word or even phrase level. As a result, knowledge representation has become an important facet of machine translation work, and artificial intelligence has been recognized as another field of which machine translation can be considered an application.

Machine translation researchers understand the goals and the methodology of their research in numerous different ways. Some of the machine translation activity is predominantly product-oriented. But even if one restricts oneself to discussing the more basic research projects, either in academia or in industry, the above diversity is still significant. There are two major areas of differences among research workers in machine translation. One of them concerns the kinds of systems that are being built, designed or even only contemplated (especially, the extent to which humans are supposed to intervene in the translation process as performed by those systems). The other has to do with the necessary and appropriate amount of knowledge that various researchers put into their systems. The two points above are not independent, since it is assumed that the greater the amount of knowledge put into a machine translation system, the smaller the need for human involvement in the translation process, and *vice versa.* This book contains discussions of all theories and methodologies currently prominent in machine translation. It also includes descriptions of tools used (or usable) for developing machine translation systems as well as firsthand accounts of successes, difficulties and failures of particular machine translation projects. A special emphasis is given to presenting the potential benefits to machine translation of using methods developed in artificial intelligence, the latest addition to the list of 'parent' disciplines of machine translation. To make this book readily usable as a text, the first two chapters set the conceptual stage for discussing machine translation and briefly survey the current picture of machine translation research and development, respectively. The book is meant to be used either as a text, as a reference source for those who become machine translation researchers, or as a potential source of definitive statements about the various theories and methodologies currently employed in the field.

Most of the contributions are revised versions of papers that were read at the *Conference on Theoretical and Methodological Issues in Machine Translation* which was held on August 14-16 1985 at Colgate University, Hamilton, NY, USA, where I was a member of the Computer Science Department. However, Chapters 1, 9, 12 and 13 were commissioned specifically for the book, and Chapter 2 is a much revised and updated version of a paper that appeared in the 1984 *Annual Review of Information Sciences and Technologies.*

The Colgate Conference was sponsored by the ACL and the NSF, and I would like to thank Don Walker and Paul Chapin for their encouragement and advice and the anonymous referees that made the grant to support the conference possible. Allen Tucker's friendship and insight helped and supported me throughout the entire cycle from coming up with the concept of the conference to the actual appearance of the book. The research environment at the Colgate University Computer Science Department, which is of an unusual quality for an undergraduate institution, has helped in setting up and developing our machine translation project. The department and the university as a whole provided various kinds of assistance with the logistics of organizing the conference and preparing this book.

I am grateful to Aravind Joshi and anonymous reviewers of this book's manuscript for their support. It has been a pleasure to work with Penny Carter of Cambridge University Press. I would also like to acknowledge the help I received in preparing the camera-ready copy of the manuscript. Patricia Ryan was a constant source of help throughout the stages of conference organization and book preparation. In particular, she typed into the computer all the submissions that were not received electronically. Ellen

Peletz supplied the graphics. Lindsey Hammond helped with the bibliography, and Sabine Bergler, with the index. Victor Raskin read through the entire manuscript and made many suggestions concerning both the style of the presentation and the ways of clarifying many conceptual points. I am specifically grateful to him for his insistence that I actually make decisions and make them irrevocable. Finally, I would like to thank Irene Nirenburg, my principal associate. She wrote the computer programs that specify and maintain the book layout, actually supervised the production of the camera-ready copy and successfully fought against the numerous malfunctions of the printers and the inadequacies of the standard typesetting systems. Her energy, the sense of responsibility and emotional support have made the entire experience much more pleasant, even in its most mundane moments.

Sergei Nirenburg

1   Knowledge and choices in machine translation

SERGEI NIRENBURG

The field of machine translation (MT) has a long and turbulent history. Indeed, it may have been the first nonnumerical application suggested in the 1940s for the then nascent field of computer science, and it seemed a very attractive application to try to develop. This opinion was bolstered by the following considerations. First, in the era of information explosion translation becomes a very critical business. As in every other business, automation is developed to enhance efficiency. Second, because translation is a common task regularly performed by humans, the specification of the task is relatively straightforward: the conceptual design of a potential MT system can be modeled after the organization of the translation process performed by humans. Third, the dictionary look-up, which may account for a very significant part of the time spent on translation, can be reduced to an insignificant level when on-line dictionaries are used. Feasibility considerations tended to be influenced by the belief that since translation is such a common everyday task, performed with relative ease by humans, it must be easy to automate. This was the rationale behind the exciting development of MT research from the late 1940s till the early 1960s.

It is common knowledge that the early MT projects failed to reach their stated goal of building systems of good-quality fully automated translation in broad domains. A number of good surveys of the history of machine translation (notably, Hutchins, 1978, 1986 and Zarechnak, 1979) discuss the reasons for the failure of MT research to achieve this goal. One must not forget, however, that the early MT efforts provided insight into the study of language and its processing by computer. They yielded many positive results by contributing to the development of modern linguistics, computational linguistics and, eventually, artificial intelligence (AI).

The principal mistake of the early MT workers was that of judgment: the complexity of the conceptual problem of natural language understanding was underestimated. It soon became clear that both the variety and the sheer amount of knowledge that must be used in any solution to this problem are enormous. In Section 1.1 we will discuss the types of knowledge needed to understand natural language text. As soon as it became obvious that the good-quality fully automated translation in broad domains was not immediately feasible, MT workers started to develop alternative methodologies, with the aim of rendering their systems more readily useful. A number of such methodologies coexist in the field now, and we will discuss

1

their strategies and achievements in Section 1.2. Section 1.3 contains brief overviews of the rest of the chapters in this book.

1.1. Knowledge in MT

The task of MT can be defined very simply: the computer must be able to obtain as input a text in one language (SL, for source language) and produce as output a text in another language (TL, for target language), so that the meaning of the TL text is the same as that of the SL text. It is clear that finding a way of maintaining invariance of meaning is the crucial problem in MT research. Indeed, the differences among the existing machine translation efforts can be summarized in terms of the solutions that they propose for the problem of finding means of expression in TL for the various facets of meaning of the input text units.

A number of important questions are raised at this point.

1.   What *is* the meaning of the text?
2.   Does it have any component structure?
3.   How does one represent the meaning of a text?
4.   How does one set out to extract the meaning of a text?
5.   Is it absolutely necessary to extract meaning (or at least *all* of the meaning) in order to translate?

Question 1 is a basic problem in linguistics and philosophy of language. We cannot even circumscribe all of its facets here. This book is devoted to the theory and methodology of one of the application areas of linguistics and AI. Therefore, we will take a more operational approach to discussing the problem of meaning, as made manifest in the rest of the above questions. Components of meaning that have to be taken into account include morphological, syntactic, lexical-semantic and contextual (inferential-semantic and pragmatic) facets of meaning. Question 3 relates to the problem of knowledge representation, either in the style it is done in AI or in a more traditional sense, as in lexicography. Question 4 highlights the computational problems of such an enterprise as MT. Question 5 strongly implies the negative answer which reflects the hopes of many MT researchers and the practical limitations of the state of the art in MT.

All of the above problems are difficult. No definitive solutions have been suggested for them at this moment in the development of the field of computational linguistics and AI. It is in this light that one must interpret Question 4. Is there a possibility that success in a particular application area, such as MT, is not contingent on producing workable solutions for the above problems? The rest of this section is devoted to a discussion of the depth of meaning analysis necessary for determining the translation of a text.

Human translators use dictionaries as sources of information about SL and TL. The type of dictionary that is most used by humans is the bilingual dictionary that connects units of SL and TL. By design, this SL-TL mapping seeks to preserve meaning. And since meaning is the invariant between the SL and TL texts in translation, such dictionaries must serve the purpose adequately. An important point to remember, however, is that bilingual dictionaries, as we know them, are designed for human use. People possess a great ability to 'make sense' of language units. This makes the task of the lexicographer simpler in that not all aspects of meaning have to be absolutely laid out; people will able to understand even a flawed explanation. The situation is quite different when the dictionary is used by a computer program. Let us illustrate the types of dictionaries and processing modules that will become necessary in this case.

Suppose the system obtains the German text (1) as input.

(1)   Das Buch liegt auf dem Tisch.

The English translation of (1) is (2).

(2)   The book is on the table.

The dictionary necessary to perform this translation is as follows:

German	English
auf	on
Buch	book
das	the
dem	the
liegt	is
Tisch	table

The translation program is supplied that substitutes the English words for their German counterparts, one by one. Do we have an MT system? Yes, a system of machine translation of the German sentence (1) into the English sentence (2). Can we use the same system to go from English into German? No, because we have a one-to-many relationship from *the* to *das* and *dem*. Our knowledge, as recorded in the dictionary, is insufficient to resolve this ambiguity, and we have no additional knowledge to help us make the proper choice.

This is the first time we observe that MT research can be viewed as a process of accumulating knowledge that facilitates making correct choices of output.[1]

---

[1] It is interesting to note, in passing, that the problem of disambiguation can be reduced to the general problem of *search*, as it is known in AI. The most important and pertinent property of this problem is that the average time of search is in inverse proportion to the amount of knowledge that the system is able to use to establish priorities at every choice point.

Now, to translate (2) into Russian, we will need the dictionary as follows:

English	Russian
book	kniga
is	#
on	na
table	stole
the	#

Sentence (2) will be, therefore, translated into Russian as (3).

(3)   Kniga na stole.

Interestingly enough, (3) is also the translation of (4):

(4)   The book is on a table.

The above suggests, somewhat unexpectedly, that articles do not have meaning in English. This, of course, is not true. We will return to the question of how the articles influence the translation later. Note also that the Russian word *stole* is in fact one of 10 different words (corresponding to different case and number values) that will each correspond to the English *table* meaning a piece of furniture. We will not, however, discuss morphological analysis here. Morphological analyzers have been built for many languages, including such morphologically rich ones as Hebrew (Nirenburg and Ben Asher, 1984) and Finnish (Koskenniemi, 1984).

Once again, we can see that it is impossible to use the same dictionary for a back translation of (3) into English. There is no indication where to put (if at all) the words that correspond to empty strings (marked '#') in Russian. This example shows that more knowledge has to be introduced into the system. For instance, class nouns, when used in their singular forms in English sentences, must be preceded by an article (e.g, *a, the*), a demonstrative (e.g., *this, that*), a possessive (e.g., *my, their*), a question-word (e.g., *what, which, whose*), or the quantifier *one*. This is a part of the knowledge about the syntax of English which an automatic translation system must possess.

Another type of syntactic knowledge used in the disambiguation process relates to lexical categories of words.

(5)   The coach lost a set.

Without the knowledge of the syntactic structure of (5) it is impossible to decide whether *coach* is a noun or a verb; *lost*, a verb or an adjective; *set*, a noun, a verb or an adjective. The knowledge of English syntax is sufficient to eliminate this 12-way ambiguity and choose the correct reading. This type of knowledge is recorded in a *grammar* of English (or any other SL in an MT system). A special processing unit (a syntactic *parser*) applies this knowledge to the input text and produces its syntactic structure. The dictionary can now have a separate entry for every distinct syntactic reading of an SL word (that is, *set* will appear as noun, adjective and verb).

Unfortunately, in some cases, syntactic knowledge is not sufficient for complete disambiguation. Thus, on purely syntactic grounds it is impossible to determine whether in (6a) the conjunction connects two nouns or a noun and a noun modified by an adjective (in other words, whether the chairs are also white). Note that one cannot neglect to extract this type of knowledge, because the form of a potential translation may depend on the intended meaning. Thus, (6a) will be translated into Hebrew as either (6b) or (6c).

(6) (a) White tables and chairs
     (b) *shulhanot levanim vekisaot* (white tables) and (chairs)
     (c) *shulhanot vekisaot levanim*: white (tables and chairs)

Further types of ambiguities that syntactic knowledge fails to take care of include prepositional phrase attachment and decomposition of noun compounds in English.

Even more profound evidence of the insufficiency of syntactic analysis for MT is presented by the commonplace lexical-semantic ambiguity of natural language. Thus, in a standard English-Russian dictionary (Halperin, 1972) the words *coach*, *lose* and *set*, in their correct syntactic meanings, detected by the syntactic analysis, have six, ten and thirty-four readings, respectively. This is a 2040-way ambiguity. Incidentally, even though syntactic disambiguation leaves us with this multiple ambiguity, syntactic analysis is still very useful. After all, if the correct parts of speech are not detected, the number of readings for the three words is eleven, fifteen and ninety-six, respectively, producing a 15840-way ambiguity.[2]

	coach	lost	set	total
ways ambiguous, syntactically and semantically	11	15	96	15840
ways ambiguous, syntactic ambiguity eliminated	6	10	34	2040

As another example, consider the Russian sentence (7).

(7)   *Novaja partija byla luchshe vo vsex otnoshenijax*

Taken out of context, this sentence does not contain any clue as to the meaning of *partija*. The texts in (8) illustrate the correct translations when the context is provided.

(8) (a) [The old Liberal Center was too doctrinaire for his taste.]
         The new *party* was better in all respects.

---

[2] It certainly says something about the disambiguating powers of humans that in actual discourse we can assign a single meaning to this sentence effortlessly.

(b)   [The previous consignment contained substandard supplies.]
       The new *batch* was better in all respects.

(c)   [In the previous game he did not notice a fork that cost him a rook and lost.]
       The new *game* was better in all respects.

The choice of the appropriate TL correlate was facilitated for humans by the context. A Russian-English dictionary that would be able to distinguish the alternatives will have to have special context identification markers, as in (9). These context markers are semantic in nature, and they suffice for human translators. MT systems should, however, possess special means of identifying the semantic context. This task has been a central concern of the subfield of natural language processing within AI.

(9)   *Partija*, noun, feminine. 1. (political) party; 2. (commerce) batch; 3. (chess) game.

It has been soon recognized that in order to automate semantic analysis one has to devise a principled way of representing the meaning of the input text with the help of a complete system of semantic markers and then provide rules of using such a representation to extract the necessary knowledge about the context. The large number of semantic markers necessary to describe a reasonably rich subworld, the fact that they stand in well-defined relationships to other markers, and the total absence of the material of a natural language in the representation are characteristics of AI-oriented approaches to meaning extraction. The notations used in AI systems are rich enough to be called semantic interpretation languages. In AI they are called knowledge representation languages; in MT they are traditionally called *interlinguae*.

One of the first attempts to use semantic analysis, that is, to use a knowledge representation language in MT, was made within the Yale AI school. The Conceptual Dependency knowledge representation language (e.g., Schank, 1975) was used to represent the meaning of the input sentence. The experimental MT systems that were built in this school used background knowledge about the world to infer information not explicitly mentioned in the input sentence, in order to be able to disambiguate it. This background knowledge usually described typical event sequences, called *scripts*, that are common in certain subworlds. Thus, the knowledge that the event described in (5) belongs to the TENNIS script helps disambiguate this sentence completely by suggesting the appropriate readings for the words *coach* and *set*. The bilingual dictionaries in such systems take the form of discrimination nets with choice points marked by particular units of semantic knowledge. These nets were used at the generation stage of the system and connected *meanings* and TL units. Of course, the meanings to be used in a particular generation instance were first obtained through semantic analysis of the input text.

Schematically, the process of translation in such systems can be illustrated as follows (we use an example from Carbonell et al., 1981). Suppose, for instance, that the sentence (10) has been supplied as the input to the translation program. (10) will be analyzed (translated into the conceptual dependency language) as (11). The dictionary that the analyzer will use connects the English verb *hit* with a *frame* in which there will be a slot for *action*, occupied by the marker PROPEL (which is *not* an English word but rather an interlingua concept!) and a slot for *force*, which will be filled by the marker ABOVE-AVERAGE. The slots for *agent, object* and *instrument* will be listed in the dictionary without fillers. It is the responsibility of the analyzer to create the representation of a new event with the representation of *hit*, taken from the dictionary, as its nucleus and to find fillers for the slots that are unoccupied. It is predominantly for the purpose of identifying these slot fillers that the system uses scripts and other background knowledge.

(10)   Mary hit John.

(11)   (event EV001
                (action PROPEL)
                (agent MARY)
                (object JOHN)
                (instrument *UNKNOWN*)
                (force *ABOVE-AVERAGE*)
                (intentionality *POSITIVE*))

In order to translate (11) into Spanish, a discrimination net such as that in Figure 1 has to be used. The aim is to choose the appropriate Spanish verb to render the English *hit.*

In this particular case *pegar* will be chosen.

The type of analysis performed by this type of system is, however, far from sufficient. A number of choices still remain unresolved even at this level of semantic processing. It appears that the script information is insufficient to resolve all the text ambiguities. Additional types of choices remain unaccounted for. Let us briefly illustrate them.

(12)   Will you please start working on the project?
(13)   Bud'te dobry, nachnite rabotu nad proektom.
(14)   Ne mogli by vy nachat' rabotu nad proektom?

If (12) is uttered by a boss in a conversation with a subordinate, it should be translated into Russian as (13); if it is uttered in a conversation between a homeowner and a reluctant housepainter, it should rather be translated as (14). This example highlights the influence of the *speech act* character of the utterance (an order in the first case; a plea in the second) on the representation of its meaning and, therefore, its eventual translation.

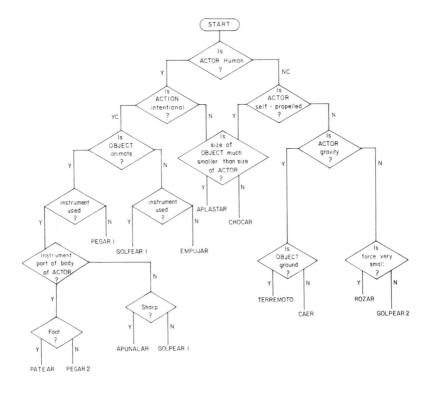

Figure 1. An example of a generation dictionary structured as a discrimination net.

(15) (a) *Chelovek voshel v komnatu.*
      (b) *V komnatu voshel chelovek.*
      (c) *Voshel chelovek v komnatu...*
      (d) *Voshel v komnatu chelovek.*
      (e) *V komnatu chelovek voshel.*
      (f) *Chelovek v komnatu voshel.*

(16) (a) The man came into a/the room.
      (b) Into the room came a man.
      (c) Came the man into the room...
      (d) A man came into the room.
      (e) It was a man that came into the room.
      (f) It was into a/the room that the man came.

In a standard conceptual analysis system all six Russian sentences in (15) will be assigned the same meaning. The word order permutations are, however, significant in that they contribute to the meaning of the sentence. (16) lists the English translations of the nonemphatic readings of the sentences in (15). The sentences in (16) differ in what is considered (by the speaker) already known and what is considered new information in them. Establishing these distinctions is known as thematic analysis of text or the functional sentence perspective. Note that, while in Russian these distinctions are marked by word order, in English word order is accompanied by the choice of indefinite and definite articles (indefinite articles typically introduce noun phrases that are new). Thus, we find that English articles do, after all, carry a meaning. Note that in (15a) the new information can be either the prepositional phrase *v komnatu* or the entire verb phrase *voshel v komnatu*. In the former case the indefinite article must be used; in the latter, the definite.[3]

Sometimes it is difficult or impossible, while processing a text, to evoke a standard script or even a more general *memory organization packet* (MOP; Schank, 1982) that relates texts to typical abstract settings and events remembered from past experience. But it may help enormously if just the *subworld* to which the text belongs can be determined. Thus, (17) (from Anderson et al., 1977) will be translated in two clearly distinct manners depending on whether the text belongs to the subworld of *jail* or *prizefighting*. Of course, it is not an easy task to detect the subworld automatically.

(17)   Rocky slowly got up from the mat, planning his escape. He hesitated a moment and thought. Things were not going well. What bothered him most was being held, especially since the charge against him had been weak. He considered his present situation. The lock that held him was strong, but he thought he could break it.

One must also have means of understanding elliptic constructions. Ellipsis is an ordinary and necessary feature of all input texts, not an aberration. Thus, one has to be able to understand (18) if it appears in a text after (19). Special types of knowledge and processing arrangements are necessary for this task.

(18)   Six, to be precise.
(19)   There are several flights from Atlanta to Pittsburgh on Tuesday.

The problem of anaphoric reference also involves a number of knowledge-based choices. Knowledge is needed for the computer to be able to find the referents for *there* and *they* in (20), as well as the beginning of the list of problems referred to there. Note that one cannot in the general case translate (20) without understanding, that is, simply using corresponding pronouns in TL. This is because in some languages additional choices have to be explicitly made. For example, translating (20) into Hebrew, one will have to make a choice between the masculine and the feminine gender form of *they*. In order to do this, one has to determine the anaphoric referent for the pronoun. Anaphoric phenomena cover not only pronouns but also definite noun phrases. In order to translate (21) (the example is from Brown and Yule, 1983, p. 56) one has to understand that all the italicized noun phrases in this text refer to one concept token. Indeed, a

---

[3] The remaining ambiguity in (15f) is of a different origin: the new information in it is that the man came into a/the room *and not into some other place*.

straightforward translation of this passage into, say, Russian would be difficult. Thus, a human translator would not use *ispanec* (Russian for *Spaniard*) to translate the noun phrase in the last sentence. It will be similarly quite difficult to render in Russian the indefinite noun phrase *a man...* if complete understanding of coreference relation in this text is not achieved.

(20)   There they found many additional problems.

(21)   *Priest* is charged with Pope attack (Lisbon, May 14)
        A *dissident Spanish priest* was charged here today with attempting to murder the Pope.
        Juan Fernandez Krohn, aged 32, was arrested after *a man armed with a bayonet* approached the Pope while he was saying prayers at Fatima on Wednesday night.
        According to the police, *Fernandez* told the investigating magistrates today *he* trained for the past six months for the assault. *He* was alleged to have claimed the Pope 'looked furious' on hearing *the priest's* criticism of his handling of the church's affairs.
        If found guilty, *the Spaniard* faces a prison sentence of 15-20 years.
        The Times, May 15, 1982.

It is approximately at this level of understanding of the input text meaning that the number of legal readings becomes comparable with that recognized by human translators. The state of the art in the MT field is such, however, that no actual or even experimental MT system at present can detect all or even much of semantic, contextual and rhetorical meaning.

Potentially, however, there are additional levels of sophistication that can be added to an MT system. For instance, style considerations will often be important during the generation stage of the operation of an MT system. The study of these factors (one can call it computational stylistics) has not yet fully gained the attention of the research community. Natural language generation as such has been extensively studied in the context of dialog, question-answering systems (most often, to generate computer responses in the natural language front ends of database systems). The general problem of generation of texts has been studied to a much lesser degree.

Another example of a possible avenue of research which is still *terra incognita* is the study of the craft of the human translator as an expert task. Translators are experts. In this age of expert systems it is surprising that no thought has been given to studying the process of translation from this point of view. Some difficulties arise, of course. One important question is, whether the expertise of the translator transcends the knowledge of the two languages and the knowledge of the subject area of the translation. If the answer is yes, then the expert system approach may prove interesting, because it will provide a way of extracting this additional knowledge and learning to use it in a computer system. Naturally, it may prove impossible to extract that knowledge efficiently. It seems, however, that such knowledge exists: we intuitively believe that experienced translators know how to do translations better than novices. This may have to do with their ability to express their understanding of the SL text better. Indeed, it is the case that the translation agencies consider it more important for a (human) translator to know TL better than SL.

1.2. The choices

In recent years the MT activity in the U.S., Europe, and Japan has markedly intensified. Many new projects appear on the map, and a number of existing projects both amplify their activities and attempt to change to newer models of MT research. In each such case there are a number of strategic and tactical decisions to be made with respect to the nature of the MT system(s) that will be the result of proposed research and development. In this section we will briefly discuss the spectrum of possibilities in MT research.

The deeper the desired level of analysis, the more difficult it is to achieve and therefore (given the state of the art in the field) the less feasible it is at present to build an MT system that would benefit from that depth of analysis. Indeed, even syntactic parsers and grammars of sufficient generality cannot be taken off the shelf and used without major modifications. Semantic analyzers are scarce and provide at best a partial coverage of the world of concepts necessary for translation. Modules capable of analyzing the rhetorical content of an utterance or, say, its discourse structure are even more remote. A significant amount of research is currently underway on the problems of semantic and pragmatic analysis of natural language. But this research is predominantly theoretical at the present time.

Is it possible to simplify, or avoid having to produce, systems of complete automatic analysis and still achieve tangible results in MT? The answer is a qualified yes. One can do it, at the expense of decrease in both the linguistic and conceptual coverage and the degree of automation of the translation process.

There are two major avenues of circumventing the problem of completely automatic disambiguation. First, one can restrict the grammar and the vocabulary of the input text in such a way that most of the ambiguity is eliminated. This is the *sublanguage,* or *subworld,* approach to MT. Second, one can drop the requirement of complete automation and allow humans to get involved in the translation process. As we will see, there are a number of ways in which this process of machine-*aided* translation can be organized. The difference between these approaches is not only in the tactics of interspersing automated and manual steps in the process of translation, but also in the nature of the subtasks for which humans are responsible.

Those who contemplate building an MT system must weigh the particular requirements in terms of quality, allowed development time and breadth of coverage of their projects before deciding what level of automation is the most appropriate for them. A simplified rule of thumb is: the less time allowed for research and development, the shallower the analysis module and, therefore, the deeper the involvement of humans in the translation process.

1.2.1. Restricting the ambiguity of SL text

The star example of the sublanguage approach is the operational MT system TAUM-METEO, developed at the University of Montreal and delivered to the Canadian Weather Service for everyday routine translations of weather reports from English into French. The system operates very successfully, practically without human intervention. Its vocabulary consists of about 1,500 entries, about half of which are place names. The syntactic constructions that occur in the variant of English used as SL in TAUM-METEO are a very proper subset indeed of the set of English syntactic constructions. There is very little semantic ambiguity in the system, since it is always expected that ambiguous words are used in that of their meanings which belongs to the subworld of weather phenomena. This project is further described in Chapter 2 of this book. Finding such well-delineated, self-sufficient and useful sublanguages is a very difficult task in general.

1.2.2. Partial automation of translation

The demand for MT is high and growing. Most of it occurs in subject areas whose corresponding sublanguages are much richer, and, consequently, less feasible, than that of weather forecasts (as the Montreal group quickly learned when they tried, with quite limited success, to extend their system to the subject area of aircraft maintenance manuals). To deal with the demand for automation of translation *today* one has to think of ways of using the knowledge and know-how already available in the field to provide a certain *degree* of automation of the translation process. Practically all operational and experimental MT systems require some human involvement, and it is safe to say that, in the immediate future, this involvement will decrease but not disappear completely.

There are two major classification dimensions for MT systems featuring partial automation. They may be classified according to

- the actual share of work performed by the computer (the degree of automation);
- the strategy of human involvement: whether the humans work on the text before, during, or after the computer deals with it (there is, of course the possibility of combining some or all of these three strategies);

In accordance with the degree of automation involved, MT systems range from relatively simple interactive editing and dictionary look-up tools for the use of human translators (this type of activity is known as *machine-aided human translation*, MAHT) to quite sophisticated systems, most of them still experimental, that involve syntactic and sometimes even semantic analysis and provide a much higher level of automation of the translation process (these systems perform *human-aided machine translation*, HAMT). The achievement of fully automated good-quality translation remains a distant but, for some projects, persistent goal.

Examples of MAHT systems are various products from such companies as LOGOS, Weidner and ALPS. The philosophy of this approach is best expounded by Alan Melby (cf. Chapter 9 of this book). He recognizes three levels of interaction between man and machine in developing what he calls a translator workstation. Level One Workstation, the least sophisticated one, essentially presupposes a complete and convenient word processing environment with convenient means of accessing on-line dictionaries and encyclopaedias. Level Two Workstation adds the spelling checks, concordances and text dictionaries and presupposes that the text to be translated is in machine-readable form. Level Three Workstation involves a degree of automatic processing, possibly including some analysis. Melby is not specific about what particular means are available at this level, but it is clear that such a workstation is somewhere in between MAHT and HAMT.

With respect to the strategy of human involvement, the three basic possibilities have come to be known as *pre-editing*, *post-editing* and *interactive editing*. A human pre-editor reads the input text and modifies it in such a way that the MT system is able to process it automatically. Difficult and overly ambiguous words and phrases are replaced with those that the editor knows the program will handle. A human post-editor, conversely, obtains the output from an MT system and eliminates all inaccuracies and errors in it. An interactive editor engages in a dialog with the MT system, in which the human resolves ambiguities that the machine is not capable of resolving itself. It is, of course, necessary to build a special interface to maintain this kind of dialog. In it, the types of questions asked can vary: the computer may ask the human to provide a TL correlate for an ambiguous SL unit or may ask to be provided with the meaning of an SL unit, in the language in which the meanings are represented in the system.

Interactive editing is among the topics discussed in Chapter 5 of this book. It is suggested there that the dialog can include interactions as follows:

```
The word 'pen' means:
1) a writing pen
2) a play pen
NUMBER > >
```

To resolve referential ambiguity, a system can ask in the following manner:

```
The word 'she' refers to
1) 'Cathy'
2) 'my mother'
3) 'the sailboat'
NUMBER > >
```

The interactive word sense disambiguation can indeed be accomplished relatively easily. The referential ambiguity, though, will present a problem, because the program will have to be able to find the candidate (pronominal and other) referents, which is a non-trivial task in itself. The design of the interactive component to perform syntactic disambiguation may be difficult and the component itself cost-ineffective, simply because it is not an everyday task for a human to compare syntactic structure trees. Semantic analysis, however, has a stronger disambiguating power and, therefore, syntactic disambiguation can be rendered unnecessary in an interactive editing system that relies on human intervention to choose the appropriate word senses.

Until very recently human intervention came almost exclusively in the form of *post-editing*, whereby the product of an MT system is submitted for editing by a human editor, exactly as human translations are in better translation agencies. The important feature of this approach is that the post-editor is not required to know SL. In practice, however, many of the outputs of such systems are so garbled that it becomes a major problem to edit them without dipping into the SL text.

In the systems that espouse the HAMT strategy with post-editing (and a majority of current experimental systems belongs to this group) feasibility and cost-effectiveness become the major criteria for success. The post-editing approach is based on the premise that MT can (and should) be performed without a complete understanding of SL texts by the computer. This belief is justified in terms of feasibility. What this approach means is that an MT system is essentially an aid in human-controlled translation.

The quality and depth of the disambiguation process, as determined by the quality of underlying conceptual models of language and world used in an MT system, is an alternative criterion for judging MT systems. If one accepts the position that the nature of human involvement should be not in correcting the (erroneous) texts produced by the system but rather in providing the system with additional disambiguation knowledge that was not recorded in its knowledge base, one becomes able to judge an MT system in terms of this latter criterion. The methodological basis for this approach is interactive editing, with the dialog aimed at gaining disambiguation knowledge, not the actual TL correlates that will be eventually obtained based on this knowledge. This approach is compatible with the research strategy of gradual movement toward fully automated translation and, therefore, its success depends on significant advances in basic research. The former approach is more of the engineering variety in that it aims at partial automation within the realm of what is feasible today. The tension between proponents of these two approaches enlivens the MT research scene of the 1980s.

1.3. About this book

This book can be naturally divided into six parts:

Part I   (Chapters 1 and 2): 'The State of the Art in Machine Translation'

Part II   (Chapters 3 and 4): 'Machine Translation and Linguistic Theory'

Part III (Chapters 5 through 9): 'Methodologies for Machine Translation'

Part IV (Chapters 10 through 12): 'Machine Translation and Artificial Intelligence'

Part V   (Chapters 13 and 14): 'Research Tools for Machine Translation'

Part VI (Chapters 15 through 17): 'Case Studies of Machine Translation Projects'

A brief outline of these parts and their constituent chapters follows.

Part I sets the stage for all the subsequent discussion. This chapter introduces the problems of MT and presents the variety of research and development avenues that the workers in the field can opt for.

Chapter 2, *Current strategies in machine translation research and development*, by Allen B. Tucker, summarizes the situation in the field today. It starts with a description of the methodologies that have been used in MT over the years. The direct translation strategy that sought to juxtapose the elements of SL and TL with very little analysis is discussed first. The transfer approach, which involves more analysis steps than the direct approach, makes the connection between SL and TL more indirectly, by comparing, typically, both lexical units and syntactic structures of the two languages. Finally, the interlingua strategy presupposes the connection between the languages of translation via a language-independent representation. Chapter 2 goes on to discuss the types of analysis modules employed by current MT systems, the problem of the choice of translation domains and the important question of evaluating performance of MT systems.

The rest of Chapter 2 is devoted to brief surveys of a number of representative MT systems, both operational and experimental. The seminal early work at Georgetown University is evaluated, together with the systems, like SYSTRAN, based on that effort and built later. The TAUM-METEO operational system is then described, and the METAL system developed at the University of Texas. The section on MT projects currently in the research stage includes entries devoted to the EUROTRA project of the European Economic

Community, the Japanese government MT project, the SUSY project at the University of the Saarland in Germany, the DLT (Distributed Language Translation) project in Utrecht, The Netherlands, and the TRANSLATOR project at Colgate University, U.S.A.

Part II of this book discusses the influence that the study of linguistic theory must have on the research in such an applied area as machine translation. Theoretical results in linguistics are known not to be directly transportable into applications. Many workers in MT (as well as other computational linguists) made repeated attempts to import the theoretical constructs and the way of reasoning about language developed within various linguistic theories, notably the transformational grammar paradigm and the systemic grammar paradigm. Such attempts have been only partially successful. As a result, computational linguists set out to develop their own views of language and language use (which, naturally, stressed the discovery, *parsing*, procedures and, more recently, the reconstitution, *generation*, procedures for meanings of utterances in natural languages).

Chapter 3, *Linguistics and natural language processing*, by Victor Raskin, makes a case for the indispensability of using linguistic theory and especially the expertise of a well-trained linguist for any application that involves analysis of natural language. It describes the spectrum of phenomena in morphology, syntax and semantics that the linguists have knowledge about and explains why it is rarely possible to apply this knowledge without modifications in systems for automatic language processing. A special discussion is devoted to the necessity of developing an explicit theory and methodology of linguistic applications. MT is taken as one example of a linguistic application, and specific problems in translation are discussed. Another linguistic application illustrated in this chapter is that of the study of sublanguages. This last topic is the bridge to a more dedicated discussion in Chapter 4.

Chapter 4, *The significance of sublanguage for automatic translation*, by Richard I. Kittredge, is devoted to the following three questions:

> What is sublanguage?
> Why is sublanguage analysis important for automatic translation?
> How can a translation system take advantage of sublanguage properties?

The discussion of the first question is necessarily concise, because it is only recently the study of sublanguages has become a focus of attention in the field, and no definitive theory of sublanguages has been proposed as yet. This chapter is a step in that direction. The chapter describes three examples of sublanguages: the language of weather reports, the language of stock market reports and that of aircraft maintenance manuals. It proceeds to discuss the influence of the size and type of sublanguages on the nature and computational tractability of various processes of automatic analysis and dictionary augmentation and maintenance.

Part III of this book is devoted to an in-depth discussion of the methodologies for MT research. The emphasis here is not on the well-established approaches and techniques but rather on the new opinions and proposals that have not yet been fully implemented but represent the way MT will be done in the years to come. It is safe to say that the concerns and suggestions highlighted in this part will remain prominent in the field in the year 2000 and beyond.

Chapter 5, *Knowledge-based machine translation, the CMU approach*, by Jaime G. Carbonell and Masaru Tomita, starts by surveying the variety of MT paradigms in existence and goes on to suggest that the most appropriate directions for practical MT research are the knowledge-based and the interactive strategies. Each of these is discussed in some detail, and the particular proposal for an MT system at Carnegie-Mellon University is presented.

Chapter 6, *The structure of interlingua in TRANSLATOR*, by Sergei Nirenburg, Victor Raskin, and Allen B. Tucker, describes the design of the knowledge representation medium used for representing concepts and assertions in the subworld of the knowledge-based MT project TRANSLATOR. The chapter's main methodological thrust is the opinion that it is unrealistic to expect to achieve good-quality translation in a system with shallow analysis. It is claimed that decision-making during translation must be based on a large number of meaning components. Thus, the knowledge to be extracted from the input text must include not only the syntactic and compositional-semantic data, but also information about the discourse structure of the input text, its speech-act character, thematic relations, and more.

Chapter 7, *Basic theory and methodology of EUROTRA*, by Doug Arnold and Louis des Tombe, describes the methodological position of the EUROTRA MT project. The methodological approach described in this chapter is quite different from that presented in Chapter 6, in that it seeks to eliminate the need for an involved analysis of the input text. EUROTRA is a multinational effort, in which a number of research groups in different EEC member states are responsible for producing the grammars of their (usually native) languages and the bilingual dictionaries from these languages to the rest of the EEC languages. Logistically, it is a very ambitious enterprise and, therefore, its results are expected to have a strong impact on the state of the field of MT. This chapter presents results of the work in the 'kernel' group of EUROTRA and concentrates on the overall methodology (the four *levels* of specificity in MT research) and the particular proposal for the grammar formalism to be used by all the various teams within the project.

Chapter 8, *Machine translation as an expert task*, by Roderick L. Johnson and Peter Whitelock, contains further methodological observations concerning the current non-feasibility of the fully-automated high-quality automatic translation. A case is made here for studying and eventually simulating the behavior of a human translator in an automatic translation system. Specifically, the concept of *contrastive knowledge* that the translators have about the two languages they work with is highlighted. It is claimed that there is more to this concept than the information one obtains in a typical bilingual dictionary. The chapter goes on to discuss the distribution of work between people and machines in MT and concludes by proposing improvements to existing interaction strategies.

Chapter 9, *On human-machine interaction in translation*, by Alan Melby, discusses the methodology for translation systems at the lower end of the automation scale. He considers the ways of enhancing the technology and methodology of human-machine interaction and ways of their application to the specific problem of MT. Some of the possibilities here were mentioned in 1.2 above.

Part IV of this book deals with the new horizons for automation in MT. A sampling of conceptual problems in the field of artificial intelligence (processing ill-formed natural-language input; analyzing the discourse structure of a text; generating a natural language text from speakers' intentions and conceptual representations) is presented here, together with some current ideas about the ways of solving them. If MT research is not facing these problems in their entirety now, it will have to tackle them before long. Therefore, it is very important for a person contemplating an MT effort or thinking about augmenting an existing one to be aware of the work done in AI.

Chapter 10, *Reflections on the knowledge needed to process ill-formed language*, by Ralph M. Weischedel and Lance A. Ramshaw, makes the case that processing ill-formed language requires contributions from morphological, syntactic, semantic and pragmatic knowledge. The particular kinds of knowledge required from each area are discussed, as well as the nature of the problem of combining those multiple knowledge sources. Various recent systems have made good starts at handling ill-formed input using knowledge from some of the above areas, but a substantial amount of fundamental work must still be done if the AI systems are to understand language as robustly as humans do. This chapter concentrates on the pragmatic knowledge necessary for understanding information-seeking dialogs. Based on this discussion, the chapter offers important perspectives on the knowledge and architecture needed in any task that involves understanding natural language.

Chapter 11, *An integrated theory of discourse analysis*, by James Pustejovsky, is devoted to an increasingly intensive area of research in computational linguistics that deals with the laws of the rhetorical structure and meaning of texts. A number of difficult questions related to various specific topics in discourse analysis are discussed in this chapter. Critical surveys of existing approaches are followed by suggestions with respect to partial solutions of certain discourse analysis problems. Thus, the chapter argues that, in order to attain a sufficient depth of discourse analysis, one must distinguish between the syntactic and semantic components of the rhetorical meaning. The chapter also discusses CICERO, a knowledge-based system for discourse analysis that incorporates some of these theoretical ideas.

Chapter 12, *Natural language generation: complexities and techniques*, by David D. McDonald, describes the progress in this area over the last fifteen years. It discusses the conceptual differences between the tasks of natural language comprehension and generation. Next, it analyzes the popular misconception (of which MT workers are also typically guilty) that generation is a simple process. It then goes on to discuss the succession of generation techniques, from the early direct replacement paradigm to the modern grammar- and knowledge-oriented approaches. It concentrates on the multi-level description-directed generation approach used in the Mumble generation system. The chapter concludes with some thoughts about the relevance of the current generation research in AI to the task of machine translation.

Part V is devoted to more practical problems than the other parts of this book — the ways to establish and maintain an optimum research environment for an MT project and the use of information resource tools that can be made available for an MT project.

Chapter 13, *The research environment in the METAL project*, by John S. White, describes the working environment that has been developed over the years at the Linguistics Research Center at the University of Texas. It discusses the difference of the software maintenance problems in small experimental projects and large, production-oriented MT efforts, such as METAL. The importance of software maintenance in the latter type of projects becomes infinitely higher, with the accumulation of language and world knowledge. The chapter describes in some detail the software development tools in METAL, starting with those facilitating development of grammars and continuing to those used for augmentation and maintenance of dictionaries. It also describes the translation tools, such as the sophisticated trace and statistics packages that help to test the system 'in action.'

Chapter 14, *Knowledge resource tools for accessing large text files*, by Donald E. Walker, provides an overview of a research program under development at Bell Communications Research. The objective of this program is to develop facilities for working with large document collections in order to provide more refined access to the information contained in these 'source' materials than is possible through current information retrieval procedures. The tools being used for this purpose include machine-readable dictionaries, encyclopaedias and other sources of knowledge. A distinction is made in the chapter between the texts (*sources*) and tools (*resources*), and the relationship between them is discussed. Two specific systems (both under development) are described as illustrations of this overall approach: one aiming at extracting the overall subject from the text; the other, at concept elaboration while reading text. The chapter concludes with a discussion of implications of this type of research for MT.

The final part of the book, Part VI, contains Chapter 15, *The role of structural transformation in a machine translation system*, by Makoto Nagao; Chapter 16, *An experimentl in lexicon-driven machine translation*, by Richard E. Cullingford and Boyan A. Onyshkevych; and Chapter 17, *Integrating syntax and semantics*, by Steven L. Lytinen. This part will allow the workers in MT to make use of the experience accumulated in these three projects with respect to the implementation of various theoretical proposals as well as practical 'everyday' problems that inevitably pop up in developing large software systems.

Chapter 15 describes the state of the MT project at Kyoto University in Japan, which is one of a significant number of projects supported by the Japanese government. It describes the experience of building an actual MT system that is based on the transfer methodology and is augmented by semantic processing. It goes on to show how the basic transfer approach has to be augmented by the pre-transfer and post-transfer processing 'loops,' and how a phrase structure transformation component has to be added to the process of generation. The chapter presents a number of examples of Japanese-to-English translation.

Chapter 16 describes a system of automatic translation from Ukrainian into English in which the focus of processing is at the level of the *lexicon*, rather than the grammar. The approach expects the analyzer to map SL language units into an interlingual form, which then is mapped into the surface structures of the TL (optionally, after a certain amount of inferencing activity takes place to *annotate* the interlingual form). The particular representation language used for describing the world knowledge in the system (ERKS, for Eclectic Representations for Knowledge Structures) is presented and illustrated.

Chapter 17 argues that one has to use both syntax and semantics in the analysis stage of an MT system and suggests an approach to this type of integration. It provides a good operational example of how one can reconcile positions that can seem to some to be quite opposite. Indeed, the early conceptual analyzers attempted to disregard as much of the syntactic knowledge as was possible without hindering the extraction of meaning. At the same time, some of the natural language processing (including MT) paradigms disregarded semantics altogether. This paper argues for the integration of syntactic and semantic *processing* in such systems, while maintaining a separate body of syntactic (a grammar) and semantic (a world knowledge base) knowledge. An experimental MT system is described that performs this type of analysis, including even the construction of a separate syntactic representation during the parsing process.

2 Current strategies in machine translation research and development

ALLEN B. TUCKER

2.1. Introduction

This chapter identifies several major theoretical and methodological strategies that are helping to guide contemporary research and development projects in machine translation (MT). Rather than attempt a complete survey, I focus instead on three key operational systems and five active research and development projects; the latter are chosen for their strong commitment to underlying theoretical considerations, rather than the need to reach an operational system in a short period of time. The three operational systems are Georgetown's GAT (and its recent derivatives), TAUM-METEO, and METAL. The first is the classical example of the 'direct' approach to MT, while the second and third are modeled after the 'transfer' approach. The five experimental projects are divided into two classes, the transfer-based systems (EUROTRA, Japan, and SUSY) and the interlingua-based systems (DLT and TRANSLATOR). I will identify major principles and problems that surround MT research, and assess fundamental differences and avenues for future research and development.

I therefore skip past most of the early history of machine translation, roughly from 1945 to 1970, because it is well-documented elsewhere (Hutchins, 1978, 1982; Zarechnak, 1979; Tucker and Nirenburg, 1984). Here, I focus on emerging and lasting principles of MT research and development, rather than on the operation, cost, efficiency, and other (more-or-less bureaucratic) considerations which tend to dominate discussions of 'production' MT systems.

Three prevailing strategies have governed the design of MT systems over the last two decades; the so-called 'direct' translation strategy was historically the first, followed by the 'transfer' and 'interlingua' strategies. These are discussed individually in the following three sections.

2.1.1. The direct MT strategy

The direct translation strategy passes each sentence of the text to be translated through a series of principal stages (usually about 10), in which the output of each stage is the input to the next. A direct translation system is designed, from its outset, for a specific source and target language pair.

22

No general linguistic theory or parsing principles are necessarily present for direct translation to work; these systems depend instead on well-developed dictionaries, morphological analysis, and text processing software to gain credible translations of the source text into a series of reasonably equivalent words and phrases in the target language. A minimal series of stages in direct translation is summarized below:

1. Source text dictionary lookup and morphological analysis
2. Identification of homographs
3. Identification of compound nouns
4. Identification of noun and verb phrases
5. Processing of idioms
6. Processing of prepositions
7. Subject-predicate identification
8. Syntactic ambiguity identification
9. Synthesis and morphological processing of target text
10. Rearrangement of words and phrases in target text

Different systems differ slightly in the order and use of these stages, but the general approaches are similar among all direct translation systems. For instance, some versions of the SYSTRAN system (Toma, 1977) include an ability to use semantic case information to assist in subject-predicate identification and other disambiguation tasks. The classical example of direct translation is the Georgetown system, whose origins and influence in the development of later systems are discussed below.

2.1.2. The transfer MT strategy

Today a major strategic decision for workers in MT is choosing between the transfer and interlingua strategies. (The direct strategy now serves researchers more as an historical benchmark, rather than as an intellectual basis for research and design of future MT systems.) In the transfer strategy, a source language (SL) sentence is first parsed into an abstract internal (usually, some sort of annotated structure) representation. Thereafter, a 'transfer' is made at both the lexical and structural levels into corresponding structures in the target language (TL). In the third stage, the translation is generated. A model of this process is pictured in Figure 1. Three dictionaries are needed for transfer: an SL dictionary, a bilingual transfer dictionary, and a TL dictionary. The approach is an improvement over direct translation systems, in which no structural information was used — i.e., the transfer was lexically driven and not differentiated from the analysis or generation phases.

The level of transfer differs from system to system — the representation varies from purely syntactic deep structure markers to syntactico-semantic (compositional semantics, case frame information, and so forth) annotated trees. Note that the transfer stage involves a (usually substantial) bilingual component, i.e., a component tailored for a specific SL-TL pair. This adds a relatively significant level of complexity in a multilingual environment, since a transfer block will have to be written for every such pair. The tactical decisions necessitated by the transfer approach thus include: 1) choosing the level of transfer (cf. Figure 1), and 2) determining the relative 'weight' of the monolingual vs. bilingual parts of the process — by trying to shift part of the work of the transfer block out to the SL analysis and TL synthesis stages one can improve the cost-effectiveness of possible extensions to multilinguality. In Figure 1, the extent and complexity of the transfer module ranges from TRANSFER-2 (maximum) through TRANSFER-0 (minimum).

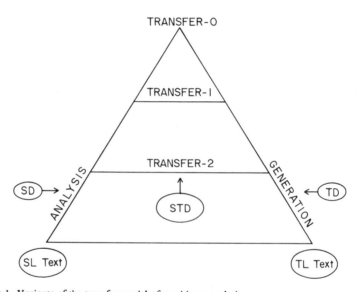

Figure 1. Variants of the transfer model of machine translation.

The transfer approach has been developed, maintained and popularized by such well-known MT groups as GETA in Grenoble (Vauquois, 1975; Boitet et al., 1985) and SUSY in Saarbrücken (Maas, 1984).

2.1.3. The interlingua MT strategy

An alternative to the transfer approach is to develop a universal, language-independent representation for text, known as *interlingua.* In effect, an interlingua permits the size of the transfer module in Figure 1 to be reduced to zero, and the MT model thus has two phases: analysis and generation. What makes this approach attractive? First, we can in principle dispense with bilinguality. Indeed, for a multilingual system with n SLs and m TLs the transfer approach will require mn (on the order of n^2) transfer blocks (if the sets of SLs and TLs are disjoint), in addition to n analyzers and m generators. In the interlingua approach, only n parsers and m generators will be needed (but, of course, of a different sort).

The 'true' interlingua projects fall into two classes: the early syntactic approaches and those inspired by artificial intelligence (AI). The former (e.g., the early efforts at the University of Texas and at Grenoble (Lehmann and Stachowitz, 1972; Vauquois, 1975)) came chronologically before the advent of the transfer and provided valuable practical experience with the complexity of the interlingua concept. The main idea was very attractive: the (syntactic) structure obtained after parsing an SL text was declared universal (interlingual) and was supposed to be used directly by the generator. The bilingual dictionary for transferring lexical components remained intact in these systems, so that the separation of SL and TL was not complete. 'In retrospect, the interlingua approach was perhaps too ambitious at that time (1960s)' (Knowles, 1982, p.29), mostly because the expressive power of the syntactic representation was hardly sufficient to support the interlingua concept.

A genuine interlingua must be able to express the *meaning* of the text to be translated. This type of research can proceed despite the debate as to whether it is possible to capture and formalize the human encyclopedic knowledge that is a necessary part of language understanding. This is because one can work with 'subworlds' and sublanguages in the hope of producing a translation scheme which can later extend beyond the experimental stage.

The methodology used in this type of project is borrowed almost exclusively from the field of AI, for which MT could be (but curiously enough has not yet become) a major application. It is quite understandable historically that in the 1960s concepts on which to base MT were borrowed from linguistics. Today, workers in MT often look to AI to provide added insight into solutions for their problems. Therefore it is not surprising that, for example, Sawai et al. present their Japanese-English MT system, ATLAS/I, as featuring 'knowledge representation.'

There has been *some* interest in MT as an application within the AI community itself (Carbonell et al., 1981; Lytinen and Schank, 1982; Wilensky and Morgan, 1981). The main strategy of such efforts is to equate utterances in an interlingua with formulas of a knowledge representation scheme (in practice, a version of the conceptual dependency representation language augmented with higher-level structures — e.g., scripts, plans, goals, memory organization packets [MOPs]). The process of translation is assumed to proceed along the following lines. 'First, the source text is analyzed and mapped into a language-free conceptual representation. Inference mechanisms then apply contextual world knowledge to augment the representation in various ways, adding information about items that were only implicit in the text. Finally, a natural-language generator maps appropriate sections of the language-free representation into the target language' (Carbonell et al., 1981, p.376).

These authors say that their computer programs 'technically speaking ... do not perform strict translation, but rather retell or summarize the source text in the target language, (p. 377). It is clearly necessary to provide a theory of what sections are appropriate or what to retell and what to include in a summary and what to leave out: a theory of 'salient features' of the text. The AI practitioners' interest in MT is a very positive development, even though 'practical MT has not been a primary working goal with...the...understanding systems built within the conceptual dependency/knowledge structure framework' (Carbonell et al., 1981, p.376).

An important methodological question is whether the particular knowledge representation schemata used can be applied directly to MT or whether it must be customized. For example, it is reasonable to investigate augmenting a typical AI knowledge representation scheme with explicitly presented linguistic (syntactico-semantic) knowledge as well as a representation of the expert behavior of human translators, so that it can become effective in the MT domain. In my opinion, the current AI-based techniques of knowledge representation for natural language understanding systems are not immediately applicable to natural language translation. Further customization of interlingua for the purposes of MT is required on its own merits; and thus direct research and development of interlingua for MT should be viewed as an ongoing task.

2.1.4. Grammars and parsing

It was recognized early in MT that a systematic analysis of the input text is an indispensable part of the translation process. Morphological analysis, the determination of word class and word form to which an input word belongs, has since become a theoretically uninteresting task. However, the approach to syntactic analysis, which seeks to identify constituent and/or dependency structure of input text sentences, has not yet been agreed upon: different approaches coexist, and none has emerged as the definitive method.

Parsing natural language was probably the most important and one of the most widespread topics of research in linguistics and AI from roughly 1968 to 1978. For an excellent review of syntactic parsing systems readers should see Winograd, 1983 (Chap. 7). The most widely used grammar formalisms on which the various current parsing systems are based include generalized phrase structure grammars, various functional grammars, and 'situation-action rule' systems that do not use a grammar in the traditional linguistic and computational sense.

The form of the structures assigned to sentences varies in accordance with the underlying grammatical formalism. Typically, parsers in natural language processing systems produce variants of annotated surface structures (immediate constituent, dependency or functional structure, or a combination of the three), or various systematic nonsyntactic structures, such as conceptual dependency representations produced by the conceptual parser ELI (e.g., Birnbaum and Selfridge, 1981).

At present most of the MT systems parse SL text into a structure that provides: 1) sentence constituent information, and 2) case frame information for verbs and nouns. In the terms of Charniak (1983), these processes belong to a parallel (intermingled) application of syntactic and 'non-inferential-semantic' rules. If an MT system strives to obtain a true interlingua representation, the process must be augmented by 'compositional semantics,' the rules of which permit the construction of the 'logical form' of the input, as suggested by Charniak. Only at this stage, when the process of parsing ends, can the full advantages of knowledge representation (interlingua) be fully felt. With the help of the rules of 'inferential semantics' one may augment, through a chain of knowledge-based deductions (inferences), the system's understanding of the meaning of the input, and thus provide a high level of reliability to the generator. Examples of 'deeper' parsers are the members of the ELI family that produce conceptual dependency (one type of 'logical form') structures. As of now there is no reasonable-scale MT system that uses knowledge representation for inference making in this way. Despite their use of a frame-based approach, Sawai et al. (1982) actually implement a transfer system and claim no inferencing capability. A thoughtful discussion of the properties necessary for an MT parser and of design choices can be found in Johnson et al., (1985).

The computational peculiarities of parsers are seldom addressed in reports about MT systems. A notable exception is the LRC project, in which the choice of the parser was given specific attention. 'The current METAL parser is a variation on the Cocke-Kasami-Younger bottom-up algorithm...augmented with top-down filtering...This parser was shown to be highly efficient during an extensive series of experiments comparing a dozen parsers on the basis of their practical performance characteristics' (Bennett and Slocum, 1985).

2.1.5. *Sublanguages*

In general, MT systems limit their domain of usefulness to a particular field or area of discourse. For example, the TAUM-METEO system (Isabelle, 1984) is applied only to weather reports and thus has a very limited vocabulary, while the Georgetown system (Zarechnak, 1979) concentrates on nuclear physics. Current developers are also aiming their MT systems at well-defined and highly stylized text, such as auto repair manuals, computer science publications, and the like.

Such a focus generally gives the MT system a stronger chance for success because the development of a highly specialized and complete dictionary in a specific field is needed to enable the system to penetrate effectively the substance discussed in the text. Such text tends to have much more manageable semantics because it has a relatively high frequency of technical terms, each of which renders only a single interpretation, and a relatively low frequency of ambiguous terms and difficult style.

It remains to be seen how much the introduction of 'understanding' to MT can widen the translation domain. Even the recent AI experiments (Carbonell et al., 1981) are not particularly ambitious in this respect, sticking to examples about visiting restaurants and reports about automobile accidents.

2.1.6. *Performance and evaluation*

Performance of operational MT systems is usually measured in terms of their cost per 1,000 words and their speed in pages per post-editor per hour vs. the relative cost and speed of human translation. Specific cost and speed information appears in many publications, and will not be repeated here. In my opinion, it is becoming increasingly uninformative to compare the performance of MT systems with that of human translators, even though many organizations tend to do that to justify their MT investments. In the long run, MT and human translation will probably not be viewed in competition with each other; humans will tend to concentrate on the more 'creative' translation tasks, while machines will concentrate on the more routine, high-volume tasks.

More important is the question of translation quality — i.e., the fidelity of the translation to the original source text and the legibility of the translated text itself. Although much discussion of quality also appears in the literature, no effective, universally applicable, quasi-objective measure of translation quality — either human or mechanical — has yet been discovered. An inroad on this problem has been made by the Japanese government MT project (see below). It is to be hoped that other MT projects will embrace this model as an acceptable quality measure in the future.

The need for such a measure will become increasingly important, not so much for comparing mechanical with human translations but rather for comparing the output of various types of MT systems with one another to determine the relative effectiveness of different translation strategies.

2.2. Operational machine translation systems

Three classes of operational MT systems are reviewed here, primarily from historical and methodological perspectives. They are the Georgetown system and its derivatives (as operational examples of direct MT), the TAUM-METEO system (as an operational example of transfer-based MT in a limited subject matter domain, but with no appreciable reliance on post-editing), and the METAL system (as an operational example of transfer-based MT using contemporary computing and linguistic technology, in a broader subject matter domain). These three are discussed in turn in the following sections.

2.2.1. Georgetown and its derivatives

The Georgetown MT system (Zarechnak, 1979) is the first truly successful effort to develop an operational MT system. Its approach, labeled as 'first generation' or 'direct translation,' was later emulated by various incarnations of the SYSTRAN system (Wheeler, 1984; Toma, 1977) and the SPANAM system (Tucker, 1984; Vasconcellos and Leon, 1985). The Georgetown system became productive, translating Russian to English, in 1964 at Oak Ridge National Laboratory. The SYSTRAN system has been in use for Russian-English translation at Wright-Patterson Air Force Base since 1970 and at the European Economic Community Headquarters in Luxembourg since 1976. SYSTRAN is used to translate into French, Italian, and German from English and into English from French and German. The SPANAM system, in use since 1980, translates between Spanish and English.

Effectiveness of these systems relies principally on three factors: 1) highly developed dictionaries and morphological analysis routines, 2) human post-editing of the raw translation before distribution of the results, and 3) well-developed word- and text-processing tools to aid the post-editor and the dictionary officer. The expectation for such systems to deliver high-quality MT is limited, and there is no expressed goal for these systems substantially to eliminate their present dependence upon post-editing.

The productivity and volume of output for operational MT systems varies widely. The Georgetown system, oldest of all, has produced virtually hundreds of thousands of (250-word) pages of Russian-English translations since 1970. Its various derivatives have also produced thousands of pages of translations since their respective beginnings. The productivity of a post-editor has been measured in these systems, and varies from three to eight pages of text per hour. This compares favorably with human translation speed. Actual cost per page of post-edited MT is difficult to estimate accurately, even though organizations claim significant cost and time savings over manual translation.

2.2.2. *TAUM-METEO*

The MT group at the University of Montreal (TAUM) was active between 1968 and 1980, and produced a number of experimental systems (TAUM-71, TAUM-73, TAUM-76 and TAUM-AVIATION) and one operational system (TAUM-METEO). TAUM-METEO may be the closest approximation to fully automated high quality translation among currently operational systems. The methodology of the TAUM project as a whole is transfer. The transfer component involves two subcomponents: lexical and structural. A number of formalisms and programming environments have been developed and/or applied and tested in this project: Q-SYSTEMS (Colmerauer, 1971) facilitate the linguist's work on specifying the grammar rules; SISIF (Morin, 1978) aids pre- and post-processing of the text; REZO (Stewart, 1978) is a modification of the augmented transition network grammar system for syntactic analysis. The analysis phase in the TAUM system is syntactic, and it involves a number of semantic features (subject-verb agreement; semantic features on verbs, and so forth) as well. Synthesis is performed on a sentential basis, so that the problems of focus and anaphora are largely unsolved.

The major practical success of TAUM was in the TAUM-METEO application. Faced with the necessity of developing an operational system, the members of the TAUM group chose in 1974 to build a system to translate weather reports issued by the Canadian Environment Department from English into French. 'The feasibility studies, design, development and on-site implementation of an operational version of the system took less than two years (approximately 8 person/years)' (Isabelle, 1984, p.27). The most striking peculiarities of TAUM-METEO are its overt semanticity and the lack of the transfer module.

Analysis in TAUM-METEO is based on a semantic grammar in which the nonterminal vocabulary includes not only the familiar set of syntactic labels like NP, VP, and so forth, but also domain-specific semantic markers. For instance, one such marker can be 'atmospheric_condition' which 'consists of a weather condition optionally modified by a locative or temporal specification; but the condition itself cuts across syntactic categories: 1) *mainly sunny today*; 2) *a few showers this evening*' (Isabelle, 1984, p. 29).

Transfer in TAUM-METEO is effectively incorporated into analysis. The few operations not covered in analysis (e.g., the correct placement of

French adjectives) are dealt with in the synthesis stage, which is essentially trivial due to the peculiarities of the sublanguage of translation.

Unlike any other TAUM efforts, or, for that matter, any other transfer system, TAUM-METEO was from the outset designed to operate in an extremely narrow sublanguage (1,500 dictionary entries, including several hundred place names; input texts containing no tensed verbs). It therefore uses unabashedly *ad hoc* measures to improve efficiency. The decision to use a semantic grammar was made with efficiency in mind. The same applies to the decision to disregard morphological analysis (indeed, in so small a dictionary the space efficiency gained with the help of morphological analysis is negligible).

TAUM-METEO has been operational since 1977, translating about five million words annually at a rate of success of 80% without post-editing. This is a uniquely high level of quality among operational MT systems. Moreover, many of the remaining errors are caused by noise in the communication lines and misspellings.

The study of sublanguages and subworlds seems to be a most important theoretical topic for MT. The success and the experience of TAUM-METEO in this respect should attract the attention of other MT groups (cf. Kittredge and Lehrberger (1982) for a discussion of the sublanguage issue). In my opinion, it will require only a relatively small shift of emphasis to present the semantic grammar of the sort used in TAUM-METEO in terms of a knowledge representation scheme and operations on it. The result of input text analysis will be an expression in this representation language; synthesis will take this representation as input and produce a TL sentence. It is not an unreasonable task to build a representation based on semantic primitives for 1,500 objects. Therefore, TAUM-METEO is potentially a precursor of sublanguage-oriented interlingua MT systems.

2.2.3. METAL

The MT project of the Linguistics Research Center at the University of Texas at Austin has been active, in one form or another, since 1961. The current project, called METAL, attempts a large-scale MT system from German into English, in the field of telecommunications (Bennett and Slocum, 1985). The project is sponsored by Siemens Corporation, and an operational system was turned over to the sponsor for market testing in January, 1985. The system is now being extended to add Spanish and Chinese as target languages, and English as an additional source language.

The LRC approach uses the transfer method, but adding a fourth phase called 'integration' between analysis and transfer. At the present time (Bennett and Slocum, 1985), this phase is used to perform inter- and extra-sentential anaphora resolution. The entire system is implemented in

Lisp. Transfer dictionaries consist of approximately 10,000 'canonical word pairs,' which connect the stems in the source and target languages. Context restrictions on such pairs can be both syntactic and semantic in nature. The grammar used is a version of phrase structure grammar with a transformational component. Currently, approximately 600 phrase structure rules comprise the grammar. Case frame constraints are used as well. The result of parsing is a syntactic structure tree with some semantic information (class membership of lexemes, case information, and so forth) attached. Grammar rules are augmented with tests, which makes them similar to ATN arcs. Transformations can be applied to any of the three parts of the grammar rules.

The fact that syntax and semantics are not formally demarcated in parsing is a distinguishing point of METAL. The system uses several parsers (cf. White, this volume). The parser operation depends strongly on the preliminary lexical and morphological analysis. It generates (presumably, slot-filler type) in-process definitions for non-words and unknown words, and treats parentheticals through a recursive call to the parser itself (a clever idea).

A special routine within the parser assigns scores to the variant parses with respect to their applicability. This is another point at which the knowledge of the world and the expert knowledge of the type possessed by translators about their craft can potentially be added to the system. A most important feature of the parser is that it is robust; it will attempt to parse and eventually to translate a sentence that either contains an unknown word or is ungrammatical.

The METAL system does not seem to use any significant AI methodology in a functional way; the algorithm exhibits no level of 'understanding,' in the sense that it cannot add implicit information to what is said or answer questions about the content of the text. Moreover, no attempt is made by the system to emulate the expert behavior of the translator in making critical morphological, syntactic, or semantic choices when alternatives are possible.

By 1985, the METAL system had been used to translate over 1,000 pages of German text into English (Bennett and Slocum, 1985), running on a Symbolics Lisp machine. Prior experiments were performed on translating 43,000 words of German technical manuals into English. In an earlier experiment, the DEC 2060 implementation had translated 330 pages of texts over a two-year period.

In terms of translation quality, the METAL system is reported to have achieved between 45% and 85% 'correct' translations, using an experimental base of 1,000 pages of text over the last five years. These figures vary widely as the nature of the text varies, and depend upon whether the test is a 'blind' test or not (Bennett and Slocum, 1985). It is clear from this information that the METAL system, when put into production, will not escape the near-universal need for extensive post-editing of its output.

In terms of the amount and quality of support tools for the translating program, the working environment of the LRC system is probably the most complete and best designed among the existing MT systems, both production and experimental ones. Adequate attention has been paid to auxiliary tasks, such as optimizing the process of compiling dictionaries using the advances in database theory and practice, introducing a spelling correction module, benchmark tools, and text processing support. The attitude toward the translation program as the innermost routine in a complex software system seems to be a fruitful approach from the software engineering standpoint.

2.3. Experimental machine translation projects

In this section, we turn to examine the features of selected research and development projects that aim at improving the quality of contemporary MT systems, and in some cases moving MT strongly into the domain of true multilinguality. By their nature, these systems are more strongly grounded in contemporary linguistic and AI theory than are the production MT systems. Free from the need to meet cost and time deadlines, these systems can experiment more deeply with the underlying intellectual issues that surround the theory and practice of translation.

2.3.1. EUROTRA

The European community has, for the last five years, supported a new and ambitious concept in machine translation. Dubbed EUROTRA (King 1981; 1982; Johnson et al., 1985; Arnold et al., 1986), it is a project to develop a multilingual MT system that will translate any of the seven 'official' EEC languages into any other. These languages are English, French, German, Dutch, Danish, Italian, and Greek. The project involves approximately 100 linguists working in the cooperating countries. A first working system is to be produced on a pilot basis, using a corpus of approximately 2,500 lexical entries in each of the seven languages. A 'real' prototype system is expected to follow, with an expanded lexicon of about 20,000 entries per language. No firm date is officially given for the eventual delivery of a working production system, but informal estimates project this to occur in the early 1990s.

The framework for translation is proposed as a generalization of the basic transfer approach, as described above. However, the multilingual capability for seven languages requires seven analysis modules, $7x6 = 42$ transfer modules, and seven generation modules.

The rationale for this approach is both practical and theoretical. Its practical implication is that the effort required to develop the 56 modules for seven languages will be significantly less than that which would be needed for developing a separate MT algorithm for each of the 42 different language pairs. This conclusion also assumes that the size and complexity of the 42 transfer modules will be minimal. The theoretical motivation for this model is that it permits, even encourages, separation of methodology among the different language working groups. Thus, for instance, one language may be analyzed using a phrase structure grammar while another may use ATNs for the same purpose. Considering the diversity of current opinion on parsing natural language, this kind of flexibility is very important.

To date, technical descriptions of EUROTRA have been brief. Perhaps the most complete description appears in this volume (Chapter 7), although much more descriptive information will emerge as the prototype system is unveiled. Moreover, the EUROTRA project appears to be a uniquely difficult task, not only from the theoretical/implementation point of view but also from the organizational/management point of view. If successful, EUROTRA will certainly set a new standard for comparison in machine translation, and will distinguish itself from current production systems in many ways.

2.3.2. The Japanese government's MT project

The Japanese Fifth Generation project places strong emphasis on natural language translation as a major technical goal. Within this framework, the Japanese government supports a project entitled 'Research on Fast Information Services between Japanese and English for Scientific and Engineering Literature.' Basically, this is an MT research and development project, and (as its title implies) aims at developing MT capabilities for scientific and technical documents (Nagao et al., 1985).

The project, headed by Makoto Nagao at Kyoto University (Nagao, 1983b; Nagao et al., 1985), aims at building a good-quality broad-based Japanese-English system. The University is responsible for developing the software system for the MT process. Three other organizations are participating in the project as well: the Electrotechnical Laboratories (responsible for the text processing support), the Japan Information Center for Science and Technology (for developing the noun dictionary and compiling the technical terminology bank), and the Research Information Processing System (for completing the man-machine interface, including pre- and post-editing support, dictionary maintenance, etc.).

The system is basically a transfer system, but each of the stages — analysis, transfer, and synthesis — has conservative first generation components. The system is based on the premise that most linguistic phenomena can be handled by lexical rules rather than syntactic rules.

Thus, the linguistic method is highly dependent on the lexicon. The analysis phase consists of seven steps: 1) morphological analysis, 2) noun phrase analysis, 3) simple sentence analysis, 4) relative clause analysis, 5) analysis of (intra)sentence relationships, 6) outer case analysis, and 7) contextual processing. This analysis phase finally produces dependency tree structures, which show the semantic relationships between the words in the input sentence. However, no extrasentential analysis is performed in this stage, or either of the other two stages.

The transfer stage then converts the Japanese dependency tree structure into a corresponding English dependency tree structure, again as a series of (eight) elementary steps. Two of these steps are denoted as 'apply heuristic rules' steps, leaving one to wonder if this is where some of the 'translator's expertise' comes into play in the translation process. The output of transfer is a phrase structure tree, which is then used by the generation stage to synthesize the English target sentence.

One of the valuable byproducts of this MT project is the development of a powerful grammar-writing system, called GRADE (Nagao et al., 1985). Such a system allows linguists and translators continually to refine the underlying grammars that govern analysis, transfer, and synthesis by adding, deleting, and changing individual grammatical rules.

The system was recently evaluated, for intelligibility and accuracy, using a sample of about 1,600 Japanese sentences (Nagao et al., 1985). Half of the sentences chosen were those used in development of the system, and the other half were chosen more-or-less blindly from a technological journal. Accuracy was measured on a scale of 0 to 6 (0 being the best score), and intelligibility was measured on a scale of 1 to 5 (1 being the best score). About 15% of the sample sentences received the highest score for intelligibility, while about 12% received a score of 0 for accuracy. About 65% received scores of 2 or 3 for accuracy and the remaining 20% received scores of 4 or 5. For intelligibility, 46% received scores of 1 or 2, 25% received scores of 3 or 4, and the remaining 16% received scores of 5 or 6.

This particular evaluation is commendable because it objectively assesses the quality of MT output, without post-editing and without a particular vested interest to protect. Moreover, this appears to be the only such evaluation of MT quality that has been published in the open literature. The proponents of other production-level and experimental MT systems should be encouraged to submit their outputs to a comparable evaluation process, so that accurate and objective assessments of such systems can be obtained, disseminated, and compared.

2.3.3. SUSY

The MT project SUSY (Saarbrûcker Ubersetzungssystem) was derived from a Russian-German prototype system that had been developed in the 1970's (Maas, 1984). It attempts to generalize that system by adding multilingual capabilities (German, Russian, French, English, and Esperanto), but the main goal of SUSY is MT research rather than development of an operational system. The basic MT methodology of SUSY is transfer.

The analysis stage of the system has eight subprocesses: 1) word identification, 2) morphological analysis, 3) homograph disambiguation, 4) clause-level parsing, 5) noun group analysis, 6) verb group analysis, 7) combining noun and verb groups, and 8) semantic disambiguation. The homograph disambiguation subprocess uses a weighted heuristic to estimate the likelihood of word class, based on the word classes of surrounding words in the sentence. The semantic disambiguation subprocess uses semantic dictionaries, which allow assigning features to nouns and transformations on syntactic structures.

The transfer stage uses the bilingual dictionary to replace source words with target words, and has the following subprocesses of its own: 1) input, 2) translate using bilingual dictionary, 3) handle negations, 4) handle noun groups, 5) consistency check for generation, 6) predicates—reflexives and cases, 7) another consistency check, 8) adjectives and adverbs.

The synthesis stage of SUSY has three parts; one which produces idioms and 'artificial' words, one which generates a string of stems in the target language, and one which performs morphological generation from these stems. The second part actually has several tasks, including the generation of compounds and determination of pronoun referents.

Although quite developed, the SUSY system is particularly focused on the details of syntactic, rather than semantic or pragmatic, processing of text. Little information is available in the literature about any experimental results of the system, or even about the domain of texts which the system might be designed to process. In some ways, SUSY's characteristics are reminiscent of the direct MT systems that evolved out of the Georgetown approach during the early 1970's.

2.3.4. DLT

Distributed Language Translation (DLT) is a project underway in Utrecht, The Netherlands (Witkam, 1983). It aims to develop multilingual MT using an interlingua model. A pilot study is planned to take two years (and 12 man-years), and the subsequent development stage is to take three more years. The availability of the product is planned for the early 1990s.

The pilot study expects to include work on a system of interlingua-to-German translation, with only a simulation of a source language parser (through a dialog system). The pilot project will involve: 1) the specification of the intermediate language (interlingua, or IL) kernel which involves writing an IL grammar in the ATN form, devising a parse tree structure, compiling an IL monolingual dictionary, testing, and implementation; 2) the development of the TL part including the interlingua-to-German transfer dictionary, the German synthesis dictionary, which is borrowed from SUSY (Maas, 1984); and 3) the accumulation of a compendium of terminology on international business and law (to enrich the system's vocabulary).

Although DLT is claimed to be interlingual, it appears to be 'double transfer' because it includes a full translation module between the source language and the interlingua and a full translation module from the interlingua into the target language, complete with parsers, transfer modules, and generators. The differences between this approach and the traditional types of transfer are summarized by Witkam.

The most unusual feature of this project is its decision to use Esperanto as the interlingua. Witkam proposes three criteria for the choice of an interlingua — unambiguity, compactness, and inspectability — and claims that BCE (binary coded Esperanto) is an optimal choice.

I find this choice questionable for several reasons, especially the following. First, the advantages of Esperanto over framelike or annotated tree data structures are not obvious. The latter also exhibit unambiguity, compactness, and inspectability, and, moreover, hierarchical data structures are superior to the string representations that characterize an Esperanto sentence, from the computational point of view.

Second, the real problem in the choice of a representation language is its expressive power and the extent to which it facilitates inference making, which is in MT the process of augmenting the incoming information with information implied in the input text. In other words, a representation language must facilitate a level of understanding that is significantly deeper than syntactic. The only theoretical alternative to this premise is to show that such a deeper level of understanding is not necessary for high-quality translation. No such nontrivial result has been shown to date.

The process of translation in DLT is twofold: it involves a (transfer-based) translation from a source language into Esperanto and a (transfer-based) translation from Esperanto into the target language. The efficiency of this approach must be judged in comparison with the other two valid alternatives: 1) the conventional transfer approach, and 2) the use of a different kind of interlingua.

If a translation system is aimed at a single pair of languages, the Esperanto-based approach is less efficient than the transfer method because an extra analysis/synthesis step is involved. If the system is multilingual, the efficiency of any interlingua-based approach will improve with the number of languages added. On the other hand, if an interlingua is a natural language such as Esperanto which requires separate parsing and generating stages to extract latent semantic and pragmatic features, it will be more difficult to adapt as efficiently as an interlingua that is based on a system of internal meaning (knowledge) representation of the AI variety.

The linguistic part of the DLT project has largely been done in the feasibility study; major lexical and syntactic structure classes of Esperanto and their coding have been discussed there. An ATN scheme is chosen for the formal specification of the interlingua grammar. Selectional restrictions and case markers are added to the grammar, making it syntactic/semantic.

Although the report proposes DLT's interlingua design as an 'excellent platform for AI enhancements,' no specific AI methodology (inferencing capabilities, expert system technology or other knowledge-related matters) is mentioned as an *essential* part of the initial design.

2.3.5. TRANSLATOR

The present author has participated in developing an MT model called TRANSLATOR, which is also based on an interlingua design. Here, the interlingua is designed to express the various facets of meaning of the text. Unlike all the other interlinguas, the TRANSLATOR interlingua accommodates the pragmatic and discourse-structure information contained in the source text. Moreover, the system has provision for representing the expert knowledge of a human translator and using it in the translation process, thus making the system an experiment in modeling human translation as well (Nirenburg et al., 1985; 1986).

In its most general form, the model has the major elements shown in Figure 2. The Inspector is the embodiment of the expert translator. It thus examines the alternative parses in interlingua for the source text and determines which is the most plausible in the context of its understanding of the translation domain, as represented in the knowledge base (KB). Initially, the Inspector is designed as an interactive program. The challenge here is ultimately to simulate the behavior of the human expert. The Inspector should be able to assess the completeness and the appropriateness of the final translation as well as results of intermediate stages in the translation process. It will assess, for instance, how well the pragmatic ambiguity of a text has been resolved, including the quality of anaphora resolution, and so forth.

The operation of the Inspector requires the use of a knowledge base (KB). The first approximation of the form of this KB is shown in Figure 3. It is important that a common representation scheme for all the types of knowledge be found, since the exact boundaries among them are not firm. For example, in the analysis of a specific text, certain 'facts' may be discovered that will initially be placed in short-term memory. However, their relevance may extend to future texts in the subject matter area, in which case these facts should be allowed to 'migrate' from short-term memory to long-term memory (where the rest of the world knowledge about that subject area resides). Similarly, the graceful migration of linguistic knowledge to long-term memory and vice versa should also not be prevented.

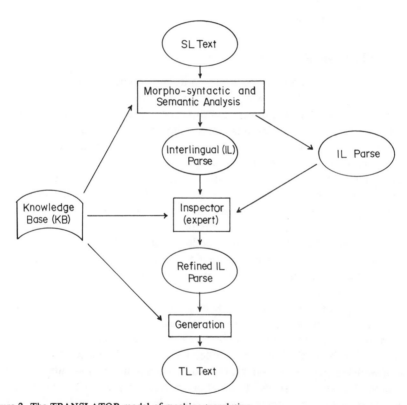

Figure 2. The TRANSLATOR model of machine translation.

Another distinguishing feature of this design is its commitment to uncover intersentential semantic connectivity, by way of discourse analysis techniques (Tucker et al., 1986). Briefly, this proposal seeks to use discourse connectives to help resolve intersentential pronoun references and other semantic ambiguities in text which is assumed to be 'well-connected' semantically.

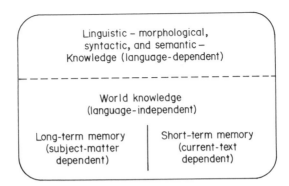

Figure 3. Knowledge-base components of TRANSLATOR.

2.4. Conclusions

Research in MT has received new vitality and optimism in the past several years. Current systems are productive, but they all require post-editing. Contemporary projects promise multilingual capabilities by the early 1990s, yet three fundamental questions continue to be unanswered.

First, although most current projects use the transfer approach, there is no convincing evidence that this approach will yield the kind of fully automatic high quality MT that is distinguished from current production systems. Although some preliminary research has examined the question of interlingua, only one or two research projects have been committed to the development of an adequate interlingua for MT. Moreover, many feel that such a development is impractical or impossible at the present time. While the design of an effective interlingua for MT continues to be elusive, I believe that such an achievement is an essential element in achieving the necessary quality of MT.

Second, although AI experiments have demonstrated the potential for machines to 'understand' natural language text by incorporating large knowledge bases and inferencing algorithms, their effective adaptation to the specific 'world' of MT has not been achieved. The TRANSLATOR project represents a step in that direction, but it too has uncovered substantial fundamental research issues in its short period of existence. Similarly, AI advances in expert systems have yet to be adequately adapted to simulate the particular expert behavior of the human translator.

Third, although human translators have an intuitive sense of what makes a 'good' translation and although various efforts have been made to evaluate the quality of MT, no quantitative standard has been defined or demonstrated. However, the careful methods displayed by the Japanese government's evaluation of MT output may represent a beginning toward the development of this standard.

Machine translation is, truly, one of the most profound and intrinsically interdisciplinary research problems in the history of scientific inquiry. Its effective solution will not be realized until scholars from several fields (linguistics, software engineering, artificial intelligence, and psychology) can effectively merge their creativity to achieve this common goal.

Acknowledgement

This material is based upon work supported by the National Science Foundation under Grant DCR-8407114.

3   Linguistics and natural language processing

VICTOR RASKIN

3.1. Introduction

This chapter addresses the issue of cooperation between linguistics and natural language processing (NLP), in general, and between linguistics and machine translation (MT), in particular. It focuses on just one direction of such cooperation, namely applications of linguistics to NLP, virtually ignoring any possible applications of NLP to linguistics, which can range from providing computer-based research tools and aids to linguistics to implementing formal linguistic theories and verifying linguistic models.

Section 3.2 deals with the question why linguistics must be applied to NLP and what the consequences of not doing so are. Section 3.3 provides a counterpoint by discussing how linguistics should not be applied to NLP and, by contrast and inference, how it should be. Section 3.4 narrows the discussion down to one promising approach to NLP, the sublanguage deal, and the interesting ways in which linguistics can be utilized within a limited sublanguage. Section 3.5 is devoted specifically to what linguistics can contribute to MT.

3.2. Why should linguistics be applied to NLP?

Linguistics is the discipline which is supposed to know about the organization of text. The primary goal of linguistics, according to an enlightened view, is to study the mental mechanisms underlying language. Since direct observation of these mechanisms is impossible, linguistics is trying to match, or model, the native speaker's language competence by observing the indirect consequences of his/her speech output and by discovering and presenting formally the rules governing this output.

What the native speaker is competent about as far as language is concerned boils down to matching sounds and meanings. However, this is done not on a one-to-one basis but rather with the help of a heavily structured medium, consisting of quite a few interrelated levels of interrelated elements. These levels include phonetics and phonology, morphophonology and morphology, syntax, semantics and pragmatics, and text linguistics/discourse analysis.

At each level, linguistics tries to discover and/or postulate the basic units and rules of their functioning. Contemporary linguistics does things formally, which means utilizing one or more — and frequently all — of the various manifestations and/or interpretations of **linguistic formality** listed in (1).

(1) (a) using mathematical notation

(b) relying entirely on the forms of the words and word combinations in linguistic analysis

(c) adhering to the mechanical symbol manipulation device paradigm

(1c) is the strongest and most serious commitment to formality, having far-reaching consequences, free from concern for the cosmetic factors involved in (1a), and less constrained in its heuristics than (1b). What the **mechanical symbol manipulation device** (MSMD) **approach** amounts to is all of the factors listed in (2).

(2) (a) collecting all the relevant information without any rigorous method and denying any possibility of formal heuristics

(b) summarizing the findings as a formal mathematical object, most frequently as a set of rules forming a calculus or a formal grammar

(c) applying the formal object from (b) to describe, or generate, a set of linguistic entities sharing a property or properties

(d) assuming (practically without ever trying to prove that experimentally) that the native speaker has a natural intuitive ability to distinguish each linguistic entity having the property (or properties) in question from any entity lacking it (or them)

(e) claiming (or, more realistically, trying to perfect the formal object in (b) to achieve a situation, such) that the set of entities described or generated in (c) contains all the entities, to which the native speaker assigns the property (or properties) in question, and nothing but such entities.

Chomsky's transformational grammar is, of course, the best known example of an MSMD linguistic theory, and the problematic property it is built upon is **grammaticality**. However, recently most formal proposals in linguistics, including the anti-Chomskian ones, have followed the MSMD format and aimed at discovering and/or postulating a set of rules.

It might seem, and may have seemed for a while, that the MSMD format brings linguistics tantalizingly close to computer science and that the rules and sets of rules proposed by the former can be directly implemented by the latter for NLP. It will be shown in Section 3.3 that 'it ain't necessarily so.' This, however, should not at all lead to the opposite reaction, displayed by quite a few NLP experts and groups, that linguistics is practically totally useless for NLP.

Everybody who has had some practical experience in NLP knows that at a certain point one has to describe the morphology, syntax, and semantics of a natural language. Not only does linguistics possess most, if not all, of the knowledge one would need in this situation, but much of it is already preformatted and preformalized for the NLP person, though never in his/her favorite format or convenience language. The alternatives to tapping this resource are listed in (3).

(3) (a) using published grammatical descriptions, which are often imperfect and always inconvenient to use

(b) resorting to monolingual dictionaries, which are nothing short of disaster in coverage, methodology, selection, and consistency (bilingual dictionaries are even worse)

(c) doing introspection, i.e., using one's own (or an associate's) native competence (which invariably leads to the reinvention of the wheel, and quite often the wheel does not even come off quite round)

In many projects, ignoring linguistics and not employing active research linguists or defectors from linguistics, some combination of (3a-c) is utilized, and a price is paid for that in efficiency and quality.

Typical examples of linguistic wisdom, necessary for NLP and immediately available to a linguist but not easily accessible, though certainly known in principle, to the native speaker, are listed in (4) - (19), roughly according to the level of language structure. Almost all of the examples are related to ambiguity, easily the thorniest issue in NLP.

As far as phonetics/phonology is concerned, unless an NLP system contemplates the acoustic input/output, which is hardly ever the case and not quite realistic at this point, this level does not have any significance for NLP. Its written correlate, **orthography**, does not have much to offer either, though a sophisticated system might list permissible spelling variants, such as in (4a). Another possibility of utilizing the linguistic knowledge at this level would be treating spelling as self-correcting codes and devising a robust program which would correct a misspelling to the nearest correctly spelled word in the lexicon. However, in most languages and certainly in English, there are too many pairs of words, such as in (4b), the distance between which is 1. Treating spelling as an error-detecting (but not self-correcting) code is more realistic if it is based on what might be termed **graphotactics**, similarly to its known oral correlate phonotactics. The latter deals with permissible sequences of sounds in a language; the former would deal with permissible sequences of letters (or other graphemes) in the orthography of a language. A simple program based on graphotactics would rule out strings like the ones in (4c). However, this would be taken care of also by looking up — and not finding — a word in the system's lexicon if unfamiliar words are unlikely to occur.

(4) (a) fulfil : fulfill, antisemitic : anti-semitic : anti-Semitic, stone wall : stonewall

(b) read : lead : bead, lane: lake: lace, lace : lack, tie : tee, tie : tip

(c) *rbook, *tfa, *bkate, *stocm, *haa

Morphemes, the minimal language entities which have meaning, are in fact the lowest level of language structure which concerns NLP directly, simply because NLP is interested in what the processed text means. Morphonology and morphology are the two levels dealing with the morpheme. **Morphonology** knows that some morphemes have different spellings (and pronunciations) but remain identical otherwise — some obvious examples are listed in (5a). **Morphology** contains data and rules on the various exceptions from seemingly obvious rules, along with the rules themselves. Thus, while thousands of English nouns are pluralized by adding *-(e)s* to their singular form, quite a few are not — see some representative examples in (5b). On the other hand, a noun having the standard plural form can in fact be in the singular and require the singular form of a verb to agree with it, e.g., *is* (5c); then again, a noun may have the plural form and require the plural form of a verb, e.g., *are*, but still denote a single object (5d).

The concept of the zero morpheme is not trivial either — in (5e), the lack of an additional form in the first word of each group is as meaningful as the italicized additional morphemes in the other words. The zero morpheme in the three listed cases means 'noun, singular, nonpossessive,' 'verb, present, nonthird person singular,' and 'adjective, positive (noncomparative, nonsuperlative) degree,' respectively. One also needs to know that the same morpheme in a language can have multiple meanings, each determined by its position and function. Thus, in (5f), the same English suffix *-s* means 'verb, present, third person singular,' 'noun, plural, nonpossessive,' and the apostrophe has to be counted as a regular character in order to distinguish either of these two forms from the two possessive forms, plural and singular.

(5) (a) cap*able* : cap*ability*, *serene* : *serenity*, *in*credible : *im*polite

     (b) many child*ren*, sheep, syllab*i*, formul*ae*, addend*a*

     (c) news, linguistics, statistics

     (d) scissors, trousers

     (e) boy, boy*s*, boy*'s*, boy*s'*; walk, walk*s*, walk*ed*, walk*ing*; white, whit*er*, whit*est*

     (f) walk*s*, book*s*; student*'s*, student*s'*

A linguist also knows, without having to figure it out, that there are parts of speech, such as Noun, Verb, Adjective, etc., and that each of them has a typical paradigm of word forms, listed in (5e) for the three parts of speech in question. Somewhere on the border of **morphology and syntax**, another piece of wisdom, potentially of great interest for NLP, looms large, namely that the same morpheme in English can signify a different part of speech as in (6).

(6)   (a)   John saw a big *stone*

    (b)   In some countries they *stone* adulterous women to death

    (c)   This is a *stone* wall

Only a syntactic analysis of each sentence or at least a part of it — and not a simple morphological characteristic in the lexicon — can determine whether the word in question is a noun, a verb, or an adjective.

In **syntax**, the available wisdom is even more varied and complex. A few less obvious examples are listed in (7). (7a) - (7c) are typical cases of syntactic ambiguity, paraphrased as (8a), (8b), (9a), (9b), and (10a) - (10c), respectively. (7d) and (7e) are two sentences which have a different surface structure but the same (or very similar) deep structure. (7f) and (7g) are examples of the opposite — the surface structure is the same but the deep structures are different; (10d) and (10e) illustrate the difference. (7h) - (7j) contain a verb which must be used with maximum one noun phrase (the subject only), minimum two noun phrases (the subject and the direct object), and minimum three noun phrases (the subject, the direct object, and the indirect object), respectively.

(7)   (a)   flying planes can be dangerous

    (b)   old men and women

    (c)   time flies

    (d)   the dog bit the man

    (e)   the man was bitten by the dog

    (f)   John is eager to please

    (g)   John is easy to please

    (h)   John snores

    (i)   John sees Mary

    (j)   John reminds Mary of Bill

(8)   (a)   it is possible that flying planes *is* dangerous

    (b)   it is possible that flying planes *are* dangerous

(9)   (a)   old men and old women

    (b)   old men and age-unspecified women

(10)   (a)   one does not notice how much time has passed

    (b)   you there, measure the performance of flies with regard to time

    (c)   a breed of flies called 'time'

    (d)   John pleases somebody

    (e)   somebody pleases John

In **semantics**, the most important item for NLP is the homonymy of words and ambiguity of sentences. Dealing with the written language, NLP has to be concerned not only with full homonyms (11a), which are spelled and pronounced the same way and have different and unrelated meanings, but also with homographs (11b), whose pronunciations are different, and with polysemous words (11c), whose meanings are different but related.

(11) (a)   *bear₁* 'give birth' : *bear₂* 'tolerate' : *bear₃* 'wild animal'
      (b)   *lead* 'be the leader' : *lead* 'heavy metal'
      (c)   *bachelor* 'unmarried man; academic degree; subservient knight; etc.'

Homonyms, homographs, and polysemous words are the usual source of purely semantic ambiguity (12a), as opposed to the purely syntactic ambiguity in (7a-b). (7c), however, was an example of a mixed, syntactico-semantic ambiguity, which is very common, because both the syntactic structure of the phrase and the meanings of the two words are changeable (*time* is polysemous, and *flies* homonymous). Semantics is connected with syntax and morphology in other ways as well: thus, the animal meaning of *bear, bear₃* in (11a), is excluded from consideration for (12a) because it is a noun, while the syntactic structure of the sentence determines the slot as a verb.

(12b) exhibits a much more sophisticated kind of referential/attributive ambiguity, which tends to be overlooked by non-linguists almost universally and which is important for NLP, for instance, from the point of view of whether a token in the world of the system needs to be actualized or not. (13) - (14) paraphrase the ambiguous sentences of (12a) and (12b), respectively.

(12) (a)   She cannot bear children
      (b)   John would like to marry a girl his parents would not approve of

(13) (a)   She cannot give birth
      (b)   She cannot stand children

(14) (a)   There exists such a girl that John would like to marry and his parents would not
            approve of her (referential)
      (b)   John would only like to marry such a girl that his parents would not approve of
            her (attributive)

While almost any sentence can be ambiguous, hardly any is intended as ambiguous in normal discourse. What it means is that disambiguating devices are available to the speaker and hearer. Some of them are in the text itself, others are in the extralinguistic context, and linguistics is supposed to know about both but, in fact, knows much more about the former. (15a) contains a well-known example of a sentence containing a homonymous word, *bill*, with at least three meanings, namely, 'invoice,' legal, and bird-related, and in (15b) it is disambiguated with the help of another word, *paid*, which corroborates only the invoice meaning. Priming procedures in NLP are based on this and similar kinds of corroboration.

(15) (a)   The bill is large
      (b)   The bill is large but does not need to be paid

Two words corroborate, or prime, each other's meanings if they share one or more semantic features, and the concept of semantic feature is central to contemporary semantics. In various ways, it has been incorporated into a number of formal semantic theories and into quite a few NLP lexicons. Thus, *bill* and *paid* in (15b) share the feature of 'money related' or whatever else it might be called.

The processing of a text by the native speaker and, therefore, by the computer as well depends heavily on a number of even more complicated meaning-related items which are studied by pragmatics, the youngest and least developed area of linguistics. It is known in **pragmatics** that the same sentence can play different roles in discourse (known as the illocutionary forces — see Searle 1969), and pragmatics studies the factors which determine the roles in given situations. (16) can be perceived as a promise, a threat, or a neutral assertion, depending on whether the hearer would rather the speaker came home early, would rather the speaker did not come home early, or does not care when the speaker comes home.

(16)   I will be back early

(17) contains an example of a sophisticated and little explored role-related ambiguity. The same sentence (17c) in a dialog can signify agreement and disagreement, depending on whether it is uttered in response to (17a) or (17b), respectively. The resulting polysemy of *no* is not obvious to most native speakers.

(17) (a)   The weather is not too nice over there
      (b)   The weather is nice over there
      (c)   No, it isn't

Pragmatics is also interested in situations in which sentences are not used in their literal meanings, i.e., as implicatures — see Grice (1975). Thus (18a), which is phrased and structured as a question, is in fact typically used as a polite request. (18b) may be used sarcastically about an idiot. (18c), though ostensibly laudatory, may be a sexist putdown.

(18) (a)   Can you pass me the salt?
      (b)   He is a real genius
      (c)   She cooks well

The examples in (17) involve two-sentence structures, (17a) followed by (17c) or (17b) followed by (17c). The structure of such sequences of sentences, of paragraphs, which are supposed to be logically organized sequences of sentences, and of whole texts, which are sequences of paragraphs, is the major concern of **text linguistics/discourse analysis** (with the second term, extremely homonymous in its use, usually emphasizing the structure of dialogs, or conversational strategies). This discipline is somewhat older than linguistic pragmatics but even less definite about its facts or methods. Some of the simplest examples of sentential structures

are such sequences as the enumeration in (19a), the temporal sequence in
(19b), and the causal one in (19c) — the italicized words are the connectors, which provide explicit clues as to the type of the structure.

(19)   (a)   The English verb paradigm contains four basic forms. *First,* there is the infinitive
               form, which doubles up as the nonthird person, nonsingular form of the present.
               Secondly, there is the third person, singular form of the present. *Thirdly,* there is
               the past form, which doubles up as the past participle form, with the regular
               verbs. *Fourthly and finally,* there is the gerund form, which doubles up as the
               present participle form.
       (b)   In the morning, I get up at 6. *Then* I take a shower and have breakfast.
       (c)   I cannot fall asleep as easily as other people. *Because of that,* I try to avoid drink-
               ing strong tea or coffee after 6 p.m.

All of the examples listed in (4) - (19) and many similar pieces of
linguistic knowledge are more or less immediately accessible to a linguist,
though some do require more sophistication, e.g., (12b) and (17) - (19).
All of them are related to ambiguity and therefore (at least potentially)
important for NLP. One serious problem for NLP is that all of these facts
cannot be found in any one published source and certainly not in any
acceptable form, and the only way to obtain them all when they are needed
is to have a linguist around on a permanent basis. Now, the reason the
written sources do not exist is not because the linguists keep the knowledge
to themselves so as to sell it — and themselves — to the highest bidder but
rather because of serious theoretical problems, some of which are inherent
only in linguistics while others are shared with the other human studies. It
is essential, therefore, for any NLP project with some concern for adequacy
and efficiency, to have a linguist on the staff. A much more serious problem for NLP is that having a linguist on the staff is not enough.

3.3. How not to apply linguistics to NLP

A linguist on the staff of an NLP project should have an immediate and
errorless access to all the linguistic facts of the kind listed in Section 3.2
and of potential or actual importance to the project. Now, much of this
information comes packaged as part of a formal grammar, i.e., as a set of
rules. The linguist should be smart enough to know that the packages are
not ready for use in NLP. Much of the negative attitude to linguistics on the
part of NLP researchers stems from their obtaining such a package by themselves and trying to implement it directly, without the benefit of a qualified
linguist's advice, simply because it looked formal and even algorithmic
enough.

Qualified linguists differ from regular linguists (even good ones) in that
they know the rules of correct linguistic application. These consist of general rules of applying a theory to a problem and specific rules of linguistic
application.

Generally, when a source field is applied to the target field, it is essential that the problem to be solved come entirely from the latter, while the concepts and terms, ideas and methods, and the research design as a whole may be borrowed from the former. If the problem comes from the source field, the application is not likely to yield any insight into the target area, nor will it be of any value to the source field either because, in most cases, it does not need any additional proof that a certain method works. Thus, it is clear that statistical methods can be applied to anything that can be counted. It may be perfectly possible to determine, with a great degree of reliability, which country in the world has the greatest number of Jewish-Gypsy couples, who have two or more children and an annual income over $21,999, and by how much, but unless this answers a real question in demography, ethnography, and/or economics, the research will be a statistical exercise in futility.

Similarly, linguistics can, for instance, analyze any sentence syntactically and do it pretty well. It would be rather unwise to hope to get a handle to poetry and to claim that linguistics is being applied to poetics if all one did was to analyze every sentence of a poem syntactically. On the other hand, if poetics comes up with a real question concerning the role of syntactic structure in achieving a certain kind of rhythm or effect, the same syntactic methods can be used fruitfully, and a correct application of linguistics to poetics will be taking place.

In other words, as far as linguistics as the source field and NLP as the target field are concerned, no purely linguistic problem should be imposed on NLP and substituted for a real NLP need. No linguistic method should be used or linguistic description attempted to be implemented unless this is necessary for the realization of the project. Now, all of this is different if the project is, in fact, about a research model in linguistics and the computer implementation aims entirely and deliberately at verifying a linguistic model or description or checking the linguistic formalism. This is the only situation in which a straightforward implementation of, for instance, Chomsky's transformational grammar would make any sense. It is quite possible that some useful results may be obtained in the course of this kind of work for regular, non-linguistic-research-model NLP, but these gains are likely to be indirect and almost tangential. The linguistic-research models will be ignored here for the rest of the chapter.

For a real-life, non-linguistic-research project in NLP, aiming at a working system, the typical dilemma is that a good linguistic description is needed but without the forbidding-looking, cumbersome, and inaccessible packaging it typically comes with. The weathered linguist should unwrap the package for his/her NLP colleagues, separate the gems of wisdom from the wrapping which, at best, answers some purely linguistic needs, and let the group utilize the 'real thing.' In order not to perform that kind of operation from scratch and on an *ad hoc* basis every time it is needed, the NLP-related linguist should be able to rely on an applied linguistic theory, specially adapted for NLP. This is exactly what computational linguistics should be about but for the most part is not.

An applied linguistic theory for NLP should contain formulae of transition from linguistic theories and models to models and descriptions practically digestible for NLP. It should be able to distinguish between elements of language substance and the purely linguistic representation of them, not necessarily of much use for NLP. It should be able to take into consideration the state-of-the-art methods and tools of implementation in NLP and the convenience of implementing various kinds of linguistic information with their help. In other words, such a theory should have the beneficial effect of repackaging the linguistic goods NLP wants in the way which is the most convenient for NLP to use.

As an example, Postal's classic and sophisticated treatment of the English verb *remind* (1970) will be compared with what NLP is likely to need to know about it. Focusing on just one meaning of the verb as used in (20a) and deliberately excluding the meaning in (20b) from consideration, Postal comes up with a number of sharp even if at times controversial observations about the verb, briefly summarized in (21). He then proceeds to propose a transformational treatment for the sentences containing the verb in the like-ness meaning, again briefly summarized in (22). The sentences triggering and/or resulting from the transformational process are listed in (23).

(20) (a) Harry reminds me of Fred Astaire
      (b) Lucille reminded me of a party I was supposed to attend

(21) (a) The verb *remind* must be used with exactly 3 NP's in one particular syntactic structure, viz., NP$_1$ Verb NP$_2$ *of* NP$_3$
      (b) *remind* differs syntactically from the very few other English verbs which can be used in this structure
      (c) *remind* is unique in that no two of its three NP's can be coreferential
      (d) Sentences with *remind* in the likeness meaning are typically paraphrased as, for (20a), (23a)

(22) (a) The standard transformational generative processes are assumed to have generated a structure like that of (23a)
      (b) A transformation, called 'the psych movement,' interchanges the subject and object of the higher sentence in the structure, yielding a structure like (23b)
      (c) A transformation, called 'the remind formation,' changes (23b) into (20a)

(23) (a) I perceive that Harry is like Fred Astaire
      (b) Harry strikes me like Fred Astaire

(24)   Harry is like Fred Astaire

Typically for the best transformational work and very elegantly, the choice of transformations is determined primarily by the unique feature of *remind* (21b). It is demonstrated that each of the three non-coreferences involved is not unique and is, in fact, derived from one of the transformations applied to generate (20a). One non-coreference follows from presenting the sentence as a two-clause structure with (24) as the lower clause, with similarly non-coreferential NP's. Another follows from the psych formation, motivated independently on other English material. And the last and most problematic non-coreference is shown to follow from the remind formation, which is, of course, postulated specially for the task and thus not independently motivated as a whole but, in its components, related to various other independently motivated rules.

The point of the description is that the verb *remind* is derived transformationally and therefore does not exist as a surface verb. That was supposed to prove that the claims of interpretive semantics concerning deep structure and lexical insertion were false.

NLP will ignore both the theoretical point of the previous paragraph and the entire contents of the one before it. What NLP, or the applied theory catering to it, should extract from the entire description and discussion can be briefly summarized as (25).

(25) (a)   *remind* has (at least) two distinct meanings illustrated in (20)
      (b)   = (21a)
      (c)   = (21d), elaborated as (d)
      (d) NP_1 *reminds* NP_2 *of* NP_3 = NP_2 *perceive(s) that* NP_1 *is (are) like* NP_3 = *it strikes* NP_2 *that* NP_1 *is (are) like* NP_3

The difference between what linguistics wants to know about the English verb *remind* and what NLP must know about it has a deep theoretical foundation. Linguistics and NLP have different goals, some of which are presented schematically — and necessarily simplistically — on the chart in (26).

(26)	*Linguistics wants:*	*NLP needs:*
(a)	to know all there is to know about the complex structure mediating the pairings of sounds (spellings) and meanings in natural language	to use the shortest and most reliable way from the spellings to the meanings in the text(s) being processed
(b)	to structure linguistic meaning and relate it to context	to understand the text and make all the necessary inferences
(c)	to distinguish the various levels of linguistic structure, each with its own elements and relations	to use all the linguistic information which is needed for processing the text(s) without much concern for its source
(d)	to draw a boundary between linguistic and encyclopedic information to delimit the extent of linguistic competence and, therefore, the limits of the discipline	to use encyclopedic information on a par with linguistic information, if necessary for processing the text(s)

(e)	to present its findings formally, preferably as a set of rules in an axiomatic theory	to implement the available information in a practically accessible and convenient way

The situation is complicated by the fact that, in most cases, linguistics cannot offer a definite, complete, and conclusive knowledge of the facts. Thus, in spite of the enormous and concentrated effort in transformational grammar since the early 1960's, no complete transformational grammar of English or any other natural language has been written — a fact which often surprises and disgusts NLP researchers but should not. If, for instance, linguistics had fulfilled (26b), the processes of understanding in NLP could follow the resulting structure of meaning. In reality, NLP can only incorporate the abundant but fragmentary semantic findings as 'ready-made' descriptions but the qualified linguist will help to extrapolate those to the rest of the linguistic material NLP needs to handle.

To ignore linguistics in this situation may be simpler than to use it, but it would also be extremely wasteful and self-defeating. To apply linguistics fruitfully and correctly, one has to be both a well-trained and weathered linguist and an accomplished NLP-er. More realistically, a working tandem of a linguist, knowledgeable about NLP and willing to shed some of his/her theoretical arrogance, and a person in NLP, enlightened enough about linguistics to be respectful but firm enough to be demanding, would be a good solution to the dilemma presented in this and the previous sections. (If everything else fails, they can at least have an interesting discussion along the lines of Nirenburg (1986).) One particular form of linguistic application is briefly discussed in the next section.

3.4. Sublanguage

One significant difference between linguistics and NLP is that while the former is concerned with language in general, the latter deals with a(n often extremely) limited part of it. In fact, the difference is much less pronounced when one realizes that, on the one hand, in practice, a linguist also deals with the descriptions of very limited fragments or manifestations of language while, on the other hand, serious NLP research always aims at significant generalizations about the whole problem. The difference is more in the emphasis on what is typically done in either field. If the linguist had to describe a particular language or its part every time he or she wanted to publish something, the problems would be at least partially very similar to the practical headaches and hard choices faced by NLP when working on a parser and a lexicon. If, on the other hand, an NLP researcher could get away with simply theorizing about the problem, he or she would probably move much closer to linguistics — in fact, those scholars who do, do.

Typically, an NLP project deals with a limited sublanguage of natural language, such as the language of a narrow area of science or technology. By doing that, NLP puts linguistics even further on the spot because to be useful, it would have to shed its most important, though for the most part unconscious idealization, namely that one native speaker's competence is identical to any other's. It is true that there are areas in linguistics, such as dialectology, sociolinguistics, and — recently and most unsurely of itself — linguistic pragmatics, which do not subscribe to the idealization. However, the bulk of linguistics ignores the obvious fact that, in a certain empirical sense, the Chinese, English, Spanish, Hindi, Swahili, Russian, etc., languages do not exist. What exist instead in reality are the 700 million or so Mandarin Chinese idiolects, 400 million or so English and Spanish idiolects, etc. What follows is that the rules formulated for a language may not be true of many of its dialects and idiolects; the lexicon of the language is not utilized in its entirety by any of its native speakers; the syntactic inventory available in the language is used only partially in any dialect, and so on and so forth.

It is obvious, nevertheless, that the national language exists in some less empirical and more abstract way in spite of all that. However, theoretically this situation is not easy to resolve, and linguistics has largely ignored it. Raskin (1971) seems to remain the only monograph on the subject, and even that effort was geared towards a computational aim. In more practical terms, some recent efforts in NLP are characterized by a growing realization of the predominantly if not exclusively sublanguage orientation in NLP (see, for instance, Kittredge and Lehrberger 1982) and of the need to take advantage of the situation without shooting oneself in the foot.

What happens practically when dealing with texts from a limited sublanguage is listed in part in (27).

(27) (a) the lexicon of the sublanguage is often limited to just a few hundred words, which is a mere fraction of 500,000 or so words in the maximum dictionary of a full-fledged multi-register national language

(b) the amount of homonymy and polysemy is reduced drastically because many meanings of potentially troublesome words go beyond the sublanguage in question

(c) the amount of extralinguistic knowledge about the world described by the sublanguage is many orders of magnitude smaller than the global knowledge of the world

(d) the inventory of syntactic constructions available in the language is used only in small part in the sublanguage

Thus, none of the words in (28a) is likely to occur in textbooks or research papers on NLP, except in examples. The words in (28b) will lose all of their numerous computer-unrelated meanings. The piece of common-sense knowledge in (28c) will never be used. The syntactic structure in (28d) is unlikely to occur in any text of the sublanguage.

(28) (a) beige, whore, carburetor, serendipity
      (b) operate, data, user, insert, memory
      (c) a person considered good-looking is likely to attract sexually other persons, primarily of the opposite sex
      (d) that bad — what a shame — oh, all right, what can one do?

There are two undesirable extremes in dealing with sublanguages. The first one is to ignore their limitedness and deal with each as if it were the entire language. It would seem that nobody would be likely to do that, especially given the fact, mentioned at the end of the previous section, that linguistics typically does not furnish complete descriptions of the entire languages. It is surprising, therefore, to discover many traces of the (largely unconscious) language-as-a-whole approach, manifesting itself usually as the descriptions of phenomena which cannot occur.

The other extreme is much more widespread because it is tempting and, in the short run, efficient. Following it, one tends to describe only what is there in the texts being processed, in a highly *ad hoc* fashion, which makes it impossible to extrapolate the description beyond the sublanguage and which makes the system extremely vulnerable in case of the occurrence of any slightly nonstandard text or even individual sentence within the same sublanguage. Thus, it would be foolish to process the word *xerox* in a sublanguage entirely on the basis of its being the only word in the lexicon beginning with an *x*. More plausibly, it would be nearsighted, in the computer sublanguage of English, to take advantage not only of the fact that the verb *operate* has lost all of its computer-unrelated meanings, such as the surgery meaning, but also of the fact that its only direct object in the sublanguage is *computer*. A non-*ad hoc* solution would be to define it in this meaning as having something like *machine* as its direct object and to make *computer* the only child of *machine* in the sublanguage. Then, in case of an extrapolation, it may be easier to add children to the concept *machine* than to redefine the verb. In general, an extrapolation is much simpler to bring about with the help of a mere addition than by restructuring the description.

A wise approach to sublanguage in NLP requires, therefore, not only that information elicited from linguistics be mapped onto NLP needs but also that it be reduced in size, as it were, to ensure an economical but non-*ad hoc* description of the linguistic material.

It appears that theoretical research on sublanguage has also the most to offer to MT as a specific problem in NLP.

3.5. Linguistics and MT

Linguistics should be able to contribute to MT in two ways. First, within its general contribution to NLP as outlined above, since MT is primarily NLP, albeit with its own specific problems not necessarily shared by other areas of NLP. Secondly, MT should profit from an application of linguistics to a general theory of translation, no matter whether human or automatic. Only the latter aspect will be briefly commented upon in this section.

Unfortunately, linguistics has had very little positive to say about translation. In fact, in the early literature on MT in the 1950's, those who claimed to be speaking for theoretical linguistics (or for the philosophy of language — see Quine 1960) argued against the feasibility of any MT and deplored any practical endeavors in this direction as impermissible short cuts, having nothing to do with the way language was. While they may have been right most of the time then, the unhelpful, standoffish attitude, resulting in virtually no attempt to look at the problem of translation from a serious linguistic perspective, was surprising. One explanation of that phenomenon could be the very limited constraints on linguistics at that time and the antisemantic attitude of the then dominant structural linguistics.

A much broader view of linguistics at present and the wealth of semantic and pragmatic wisdom accumulated in the last two decades or so should have changed the situation, and it is true that these days, one notices more literature on translation appearing. However, most of the effort comes not from linguists but rather from philosophers and philosophically minded literary scholars (especially, from the more formal schools of literary criticism) and practitioners. Much of the literature remains anecdotal, and the concerns expressed are usually of a stylistic and/or aesthetic nature.

It is true that translation is not a linguistic problem — it is extraneous to the discipline. However, to the extent that translation involves the use of one or more natural languages, what linguistics knows both about language in general and about the involved language(s) cannot be ignored. Similarly to the reasoning in Section 3.3, the only chance for linguistics to contribute to translation is via an applied linguistic theory catering to the needs of the field.

What is the main problem of translation? It can be presented as the ability to determine whether some two texts, each in a different language, are translations of each other. In order to be translations of each other, the texts should probably satisfy the following linguistic conditions (29):

(29)   Two texts in different languages are translations of each other if they have the same:

    (a)   meaning
    (b)   illocutionary force and perlocutionary effect
    (c)   inferences

Obviously, (29a-c) are interrelated, while focusing on general and specific facets of meaning. The term 'perlocutionary' (see Austin 1962, and Searle 1969) is used here as an extension beyond linguistics of the notion 'illocutionary,' i.e., the role of an utterance in discourse.

Perlocution covers the extralinguistic effect of the text on the hearer and his/her resulting actions, moods, attitudes, etc. Perlocution is determined also by the additional factors in (30) but those go definitely beyond linguistics and into stylistics, rhetoric, and composition, respectively (to each of which linguistics can also be profitably applied, though again on a carefully limited scale).

(30) Two texts in different languages are translations of each other if they have the same:

  (a) stylistic status (e.g., scholarly style)
  (b) rhetorical effect (e.g., persuasive)
  (c) aesthetic effect (e.g., well-written)

(It is interesting to note that the conditions in (29) - (30) are equally applicable to two texts in the same language, i.e., paraphrases of each other.)

Given the goal of linguistics to match the native speaker's competence, the applied linguistic theory of translation should aim at matching the bilingual native speaker's translation competence, which, of course, can only be done practically by observing and studying their performance. These observations will yield interesting results. It will become clear immediately that there is a many-to-many correspondence between texts in one language and their translations in the other. The differences between any two alternative translations will be primarily due to syntactical and semantical variations. The word-for-word translation is ruled out by morphological differences as well, and the more sophisticated morpheme-for-morpheme approach will not work out either. In decreasing degree of triviality, (31) lists various deviations from the morpheme-for-morpheme approach in translation, and (32) illustrates them with English/Russian examples.

(31) (a) there is no one-to-one correspondence between morphological forms in two different languages
     (b) syntactic structures cannot generally be copied from one language to another
     (c) due to differences in semantic articulation, the same word may be translated differently in two sentences
     (d) an element of meaning may have to be lost in translation
     (e) an element of meaning may have to be added in translation
     (f) significant changes in translation may be due to the necessity to control the 'given-new,' or 'topic-focus' information
     (g) a significant rephrasing may be necessary for illocutionary reasons
     (h) additional information of a sophisticated pragmatic kind, e.g., the different systems of honorifics, i.e., forms of address depending on the speaker/hearer's (relative) status, may determine the outcome of translation

(32) (a) walk (V) = xodit', xozhu, xodish', xodim, xodite, xodjat; walk (N) = progulka, progulki, (o) progulke, progulku, progulkoj; he walked, had walked, was walking, had been walking = on guljal

(b)   the train being late, he missed the meeting = poskol'ku poezd opozdal, on pro-
pustil zasedanie [because the train was late...]

(c)   they are romantically involved = oni neravnodushny drug k drugu [they are not
indifferent to each other]

Russia is heavily involved in Nicaragua = Rossija sil'no zameshana v delax
Nikaragua

(d)   I washed **my** hair - ja vymyl golovu [I washed head]

(e)   the sky was blue - nebo bylo goluboe [**light** blue]

are these shoes black or blue? = eti tufli chernye ili sinie? [**dark** blue]

(f)   a man came into the room = v komnatu voshel chelovek [into room came man]

the man came into the room = chelovek voshel v komnatu [man came into room]

(g)   can you pass me the salt? = bud'te dobry, peredajte sol' [be (so) kind, pass salt]

(h)   'I love you,' Count X whispered to Princess Y = 'ja ljublju vas [polite **you**],'
prosheptal graf X princesse Y

'I love you,' said Evdokim the shepherd to Agraphene the dairy maid = 'ja tebja
[familiar **you**] ljublju,' skazal pastux Evdokim dojarke Agrafene

The best contribution linguistics can make to translation, besides merely
alerting translators to the factors in (31) and the other similar ones, is by
providing, via the applied theory, the format for translation-oriented
descriptions and by filling this format with information for each language.

One would think that linguistic universals should also play an important
role in translation by facilitating it. It is true that translating into a nonhu-
man language, i.e., an artificial or space alien language, is likely to be
much harder. However, most universals are of a highly formal nature and
a very limited practical use (e.g., the universal specifying that each natural
language uses entities of three levels, sound, word, and sentence).

The transition from a linguistic contribution to translation in general to a
linguistic contribution to MT involves primarily the selection function.
While many translations of the same text are possible, they are usually
weighted on the scale from optimal to barely acceptable. The selection
function assigning the weights is determined by the factors in (30) and
other factors concerning, for instance, the special purpose of the text, e.g.,
to have a poetic effect. In MT, due to the limited nature of most projects,
the selection function may often be allowed to stay strictly within the basic
requirements in (29). It has been demonstrated in earlier work (Raskin
1971, 1974) that in addition to that, in limited sublanguages, some of the
factors in (31) do not apply or at least not to the same extent. Thus, as far
as (31b) is concerned, all the permissible syntactical transformations of the
same sentence — and in a limited sublanguage, the inventory is greatly
reduced — can be treated as identical, and therefore, any variant will do, at
least as long as (31f) is not affected. (31c) may be dropped altogether
thanks to the limited lexicon. (31g-h) are extremely unlikely to play any
significant role, either.

4 The significance of sublanguage for automatic translation

RICHARD I. KITTREDGE

4.1. Introduction

This chapter addresses three questions:

- What is sublanguage?
- Why is sublanguage analysis important for automatic translation?
- How can a translation system take advantage of sublanguage properties?

The first of these questions appears to have a simple answer. Natural languages clearly have specialized varieties which are used in reference to restricted subject matter. We speak, for example, of the 'language of chemistry' to mean a loosely defined set of sentences or texts dealing with a particular part of reality, or — more precisely — the set of linguistic entities and relations underlying these texts.

The attempt to write grammars for special-purpose sublanguages raises a number of theoretical and practical problems, which are only now being intensively discussed. Since the most promising path to high-quality automatic translation seems to lie through sublanguage (at least during the next decade or two), we must attempt a definition of sublanguage as a coherent, rule-based system, i.e., as a language.

4.2. What is sublanguage?

4.2.1. Two definitions

For the purposes of this chapter we can informally define a 'sublanguage' to be any subsystem of a language which has the following properties:

- the language subsystem is used in reference to a particular domain of discourse, or family of related domains,
- the set of sentences and texts in the language subsystem reflects the usage of some 'community' of speakers, who are normally linked by some common knowledge about the domain (facts, assumptions, etc.) which goes beyond the common knowledge of speakers of the standard language,
- the subsystem has all the 'essential' properties of a linguistic system, such as 'consistency,' 'completeness,' 'economy of expression,' and so forth,

●   the language subsystem is maximal with respect to the domain, in
      the mathematical sense that no larger system has the same proper-
      ties.

This definition is vague on a number of points, but serves to indicate some
of the important theoretical dimensions from which sublanguage can be
viewed.

A more mathematical definition of sublanguage has been given by Harris
(1968): 'certain proper subsets of the sentences of a language may be
closed under some or all of the operations defined in the language and thus
constitute sublanguages of it.'

In Harris' theory, the important grammatical operations are mappings
between sets of sentences. Thus, for example, if the sublanguage of
analysis in mathematics contains sentence (1a), it also contains sentences
(1b-f):

(1a)   This theorem provides the solution to the boundary value problem.
(1b)   It is this theorem that provides the solution to the boundary value
        problem.
(1c)   What this theorem does is provide the solution to the boundary
        value problem.
(1d)   The solution to the boundary value problem is provided by this
        theorem.
(1e)   Does this theorem provide the solution to the boundary value prob-
        lem?
(1f)   This theorem does not provide the solution to the boundary value
        problem.

In essence, Harris' definition guarantees that a set of sentences will be
considered a sublanguage only if it is grammatically complete and maximal
with respect to the subject matter. But it does not tell us directly how to
identify sublanguages, or how to determine their boundaries.

The search for a better theoretical definition of sublanguage should not
overly concern us here (theoretical questions are treated in some detail in
Harris (1968), Raskin (1971, 1974), Sager (1982), Kittredge (1982) and
Lehrberger (1982, 1986), among others). If we are mainly interested in
the engineering design of machine translation systems, we should look at
some cases of sublanguages which have proven to be 'computationally tractable.'

4.3. Sublanguages in the real world

4.3.1. Weather bulletins

Figure 1 gives a typical weather bulletin of the kind translated by the Canadian METEO system.

```
FORECASTS FOR YUKON AND NORTHWESTERN BC
ISSUED BY ENVIRONMENT CANADA AT 5:30 AM PDT
FRIDAY JULY 11 1980 FOR TODAY AND SATURDAY
KLONDIKE
BEAVER CREEK
STEWART RIVER
RAIN OCCASIONALLY MIXED WITH SLEET TODAY
CHANGING TO SNOW THIS EVENING. HIGHS 2 TO 4.
WINDS INCREASING TO STRONG NORTHWESTERLY THIS
AFTERNOON. CLOUDY WITH A FEW SHOWERS
SATURDAY. HIGHS NEAR 6.
```

Figure 1. Typical text in weather bulletin sublanguage.

Weather bulletins are highly 'formatted,' and written in a telegraphic style. Well-formed bulletin sentences have no tensed verbs, very few articles, etc. In fact standard English grammar is of little use in describing the sentences of weather bulletins, so that a completely new grammar must be set up. In this specialized bulletin grammar, the 'head construction' of the sentence is a string of words describing the primary weather condition, such as 'partly cloudy,' 'rain,' 'clearing,' etc. If we construct a grammar for this sublanguage, we find it necessary to set up a *syntactic* class (i.e., < weather condition >) in which there is great *semantic* homogeneity, but no syntactic homogeneity in terms of the standard grammar of English. We are required to put adjective phrases, noun phrases and gerundive phrases into the same *syntactic* class as far as weather sentence patterns are concerned. Thus, the syntactic patterning of words and word groups in this sublanguage:

1. does *not* correspond to the syntactic classes of general English,
2. but *is* a direct reflection of the important conceptual categories and relations used in the world of meteorological observation.

4.3.2. *Market reports*

Figure 2 shows a representative text from a second sublanguage, daily stock market reports of the kind published in most North American newspapers.

> Stocks were narrowly mixed in the early going on Canadian exchanges today as the pace-setting New York market slumped on news of a higher-than-expected rise in July's producer prices.
>
> The MSE industrial index after the first hour of trading was down a fraction while the TSE composite index of 300 key stocks held a small gain. Financial service and metal issues sagged while oil, paper and utility stocks edged ahead. ...
>
> Dom Stores edged up 1/4 to 19 after posting higher profits. CP, a recent high flyer, was off 1/8 at 33 5/8. Gaz Metro, which posted lower profits and filed for a rate increase, was unchanged.

Figure 2. Stock market summary (*Montreal Star*, August 9, 1979.)

Reports from stock exchanges, commodities markets, agricultural markets and the like often belong to relatively well-behaved sublanguages. In stock market summaries, even though a large variety of words may be used to describe changes in the value of stocks, they fall into a very small number of classes. It is possible to write a very precise grammar for the reports in terms of the word classes that can be discovered using distributional analysis (Harris, 1963). A very good correspondence can be established between the data contained in the reports and the linguistic patterns used to convey that data (Kittredge, 1983a). The correspondence is in fact so good that some market reports have been generated directly from the data.

4.3.3. *Aircraft maintenance manuals*

One of the most complex sublanguages which has been described in some detail is that of aircraft hydraulics manuals. Figure 3 gives a text fragment which illustrates the two distinct varieties of text in such maintenance manuals: (1) system description and (2) maintenance instructions.

PRESSURE SWITCH

22   Two identical pressure switches, one in each system, are electrically connected to
         lights on the warning light panel. When the system pressure drops to 1250 (0,-150)
         psi, the switch closes the circuit to the hydraulic pressure warning light.

REMOVAL AND INSTALLATION OF PRESSURE SWITCH - NO. 1 SYSTEM

23   Removal procedure:
         (a)   Depressurize hydraulic system (refer to Paragraph 13, preceding).
         (b)   Disconnect electrical connector on pressure switch.
         (c)   Disconnect line at pressure port.
         (d)   Disconnect line at drain port elbow.
         (e)   Loosen the two mounting bolts and remove switch.

Figure 3. The aviation hydraulics sublanguage.

The two types of text found in hydraulics manuals share a very large vocabulary (estimated to be on the order of 40000 words). Despite the lexical size and syntactic complexity of this sublanguage, hydraulics manuals use fairly predictable sentence structures. What is more important, these structures can best be described in terms of sublanguage-specific word classes. Instead of stating sentence patterns in terms of major syntactic classes such as 'noun phrase,' 'manner adverbial,' etc., they can generally be stated in terms of specific word classes such as < fluid>, < instrument>, < replaceable component>, etc.

4.4. Why is sublanguage important for automatic translation?

We are now in a better position to see just why and how the study of sublanguage is useful for automatic translation. Let us first summarize the major points about sublanguage.

First, in a sublanguage, the rules for constructing meaningful sentences can be made much more precise than in the language as a whole. These rules can be related in terms of word classes which are discovered by studying the distributional properties of words in texts.

Second, in a sublanguage the rules for constructing sentences may be quite different from (and even contrary to) the rules for sentences in the 'standard' language. The grammar of standard English does not 'contain' the grammars of all English sublanguages, because some structures or operations exist only in particular sublanguages and have no role in standard English grammar.

Third, sublanguages may be rather small (e.g., weather bulletins), or very large (e.g., texts in aircraft hydraulics or organic chemistry). What qualifies a variety of language as a sublanguage is not its size or complexity, but its adherence to systematic usage. The 'well-behaved' sublanguages of science and technology may use terminology from the everyday world, but this 'seepage' from general language is usually possible only in specific grammatical positions. We must admit that some sublanguages appear to be more systematic than others. It is in fact the *degree* of systematicity which will determine how appropriate a sublanguage is for automatic translation.

4.5. The importance of sublanguage grammar during analysis

Adequate analysis of input text is a key to successful machine translation. If a source language analyzer is based on a sublanguage grammar, instead of (or in addition to) a grammar of the 'whole' language, then a significant gain in efficiency is possible.[1] First, the parsing time is reduced, since sublanguage grammars are always smaller than the grammars of whole languages. Second, the problem of structural and lexical ambiguity is greatly reduced, since many interpretations or analyses which are possible in the standard language are not 'legal' (i.e., they are meaningless) in the sublanguage, and therefore can be ruled out. In cases where technical or scientific language contains reference to the outside world, a good sublanguage grammar will also state where in the sentences or texts this intrusive language can be expected.[2]

---

[1] Slocum (1985) reports on experiments conducted to this end; Isabelle (1984) summarizes this approach as used at the TAUM project; Sager (1981) presents an English analyzer which uses a general grammar, but filters parses with a sublanguage-specific 'restriction grammar.'

[2] Sager (1982) reports on how metascience predicates embed science predicates. Kittredge (1983a) deals with grammatical subordination used for embedding reference to a secondary domain.

4.6. Help from sublanguage grammar during lexical translation and structural transfer

There is now strong evidence that languages are more similar in sentence and text structure within scientific and technical writing than in nontechnical writings (e.g., newspaper editorials). Examination of English and French sublanguages for a variety of structural features shows that corresponding sublanguages of English and French are often structurally more similar than are two dissimilar sublanguages of the same language (Kittredge, 1982). It is thus important to write transfer grammars as mappings between corresponding sublanguage grammars, both on the level of sentence and text. The functional equivalence of sentences can then be computed with respect to the particular sublanguage, and not to the whole language. Furthermore, when an analyzed sentence carries the word class labels assigned by the sublanguage grammar, word translation equivalence is much easier to compute. This is because a word is translated as a function of its position in the analysis tree; since the syntactic labels of the tree have semantic import, this means that a word can be translated as a function of its semantic relations to its neighbors.

4.7. Preparation for sublanguage-based automatic translation

Building a translation system which depends partly or entirely on a sublanguage grammar is a painstaking process (even if much simpler than for the entire language). It can pay off handsomely in terms of translation quality, but only in the long run, and when the volume of texts justifies the development investment. In the case of the Canadian METEO system, the investment has already paid for itself many times over. In the case of the AVIATION system, the development time proved to be too long to meet the practical needs of the user. It is therefore of crucial importance to choose a sublanguage of the right size and complexity. Given the small number of sublanguage-based systems now working, any new system inevitably involves a significant component of basic research, both in linguistic description, and in strategies for optimizing analysis and transfer.

4.7.1. Comparing candidate sublanguages

Before picking a particular sublanguage for system design, it may be advisable to compare candidate sublanguages and estimate the computational tractability of the most likely choices. Methods for doing this are still experimental, but certain guidelines can be given.

The simplest measure of sublanguage size and complexity involves only its vocabulary. One can plot a curve of vocabulary growth against the number of running text words in a corpus which is considered representative of the sublanguage. Figure 4 gives these growth curves for nine separate sublanguages based on a recent study carried out for the Canadian Translations Bureau (Kittredge, 1983b).

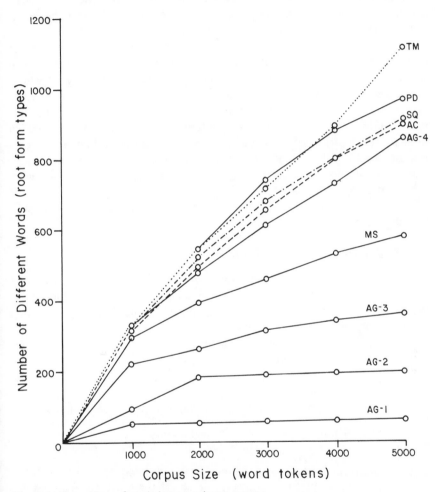

Figure 4. Comparison of vocabulary growth rate curves.

To the extent that these curves flatten out after a certain point, one may assume that the sublanguage word usage is relatively constrained. From the slope of the curve and the maximal value of different words found in the largest corpus used, one can estimate the total size of the vocabulary. Thus in Figure 4 the agricultural market reports marked AG-2 used fewer than 200 different root words (lexemes) in a 5000-word corpus, and showed a marked tendency to vocabulary closure. In contrast, the technical registry describing foreign trademarks approved for use in Canada, marked TM, showed no sign of lexical convergence, with over 1100 distinct words used in 5000 words of running text. Although several thousand words of representative texts may give a rough indication of closure tendencies, large sublanguages will require many times that sample size for reasonably accurate estimates of convergence and vocabulary size to be made.

Vocabulary growth curves are easy to compute and present only minor problems of methodology, but they do not give the most accurate picture of sublanguage closure. What is more important than vocabulary growth is the degree of closure of the grammar itself. One recent attempt to measure grammatical closure (Grishman et al., 1984) has used the number of grammatical production rules of a general English grammar which were applied in analyzing a corpus of sublanguage texts. It would be still better to measure the specific sublanguage grammar rules (assuming that no other grammar exists) needed to account for a growing corpus. This requires rewriting the sublanguage grammar several times for a growing corpus, which is very hard work, but should give the most accurate prediction of sublanguage closure.

4.8. Estimating computational tractability

Estimating the computational tractability of sublanguage texts goes beyond the question of sublanguage closure. In the case of machine translation, the feasibility of correctly analyzing the source language texts is somewhat separate from the transfer problem.

For predicting the difficulties of analyzing English texts, some of the following questions are relevant:

- Is there ellipsis of articles, copula, object noun phrases, etc. (this is frequent in many sublanguages and often a factor in sentences which are structurally ambiguous, even within the sublanguage)?
- Is there frequent conjunction using 'and' (which raises problems in determining the scope of its arguments)?
- Are there quantifier words and negation (which raise still other scope problems)?
- Does the sublanguage use long nominal compounds (the bane of the TAUM-AVIATION project)? If so, these must be analyzed for scope of modification and often paraphrased using domain language before translation can be attempted;
- Are there parenthetical expressions (which raise questions concerning points of attachment in the syntactic structure)?
- Is a text grammar possible for the sublanguage? If so, can it be made precise enough to help in structural and lexical disambiguation?
- Do co-referential pronouns link consecutive sentences? If so, what are the problems of determining co-reference within the sublanguage?

- What sort of cohesion devices does the sublanguage use to link consecutive sentences? Are synonyms frequently used (as in stock market reports) or avoided (as in technical manuals)? How much can be inferred from the use of a given cohesion device?

For predicting the problems of making correct translation correspondences, much less is known of a general nature. The experience of the University of Montreal's TAUM project, which concentrated entirely on English-to-French translation, showed that some of the following grammatical and semantic phenomena were generally problematic in establishing correspondence between the two languages. In most cases, the restriction of the correspondence problem to a technical sublanguage allowed fairly good rules to be set up:

- tense and aspect: most English sublanguages use a subset of possible forms, and their functional equivalents in French are both idiosyncratic for the French sublanguage, and simpler than in general French;
- verb modality: translations of English 'can,' 'must,' 'should,' etc. present many problems for general language that can be solved in specific sublanguages;
- passive: although English passive has at least six possible renderings in French, within aircraft hydraulics manuals the correspondence algorithm is far simpler;
- lexical choice: there is a complex interaction between structural transfer rules and the valency (i.e., semantic case slots) of available verbs in the target language; this complexity is usually much reduced within the limits of a given sublanguage;
- textual constraints: this is one area where corresponding technical sublanguages of English and French were found to share many of the same features; thus, textual constraints of the target language must be used properly to give a natural-sounding output text.

5 Knowledge-based machine translation, the CMU approach

JAIME G. CARBONELL and MASARU TOMITA

5.1. Approaches to machine translation

5.1.1. A historical perspective

Researchers in machine translation have aspired for three decades to develop highly accurate, practically useful, fully-automated translation systems. This ultimate objective remains as elusive today as it was in the late 1950s, although the field has seen considerable progress ranging from theoretical advances in computational linguistics to useful partially-automated translation systems. In the early heyday of machine translation, the rallying cry was '95% accurate, fully automatic high quality translation!' (cf. Locke and Booth, 1957; Bar-Hillel, 1960). However, little attention was paid to fundamental issues such as: exactly what does 'high quality translation' signify? what does it mean for a translation to be '95% accurate'? And, most importantly, little thought was given to the requisite theoretical underpinnings — linguistic and computational — that must be established and understood before fruitful system engineering can begin.

As discussed in Carbonell et al.(1981), there are multiple dimensions of 'quality' in the translation process, namely:

- *Semantic invariance* — Preserving invariant the meaning of the source text as it is transformed into the target text.
- *Pragmatic invariance* — Preserving the implicit intent or illocutionary force of an utterance. The manner in which a proposition is stated may convey intent, urgency, politeness, etc., and the translated text should convey the same implicit information to preserve pragmatic invariance.
- *Structural invariance* — Preserving as far as possible the syntactic structure of the text under translation.
- *Lexical invariance* — Preserving a one-to-one mapping of words or phrases from source to target texts.
- *Spatial invariance* — Preserving the external characteristics of the text, such as its length, location on the page, etc.

Whereas early MT systems sought to preserve lexical invariance in the hope that all other invariances would follow, modern approaches take a somewhat more realistic view. Semantic invariance, for instance, is becoming a more dominant criterion — with other invariances preserved only in the service of conveying the appropriate meaning. Given this criterion for accuracy, the 95% approach rings rather hollow. First, it doesn't address the severity of the 5% errors — are they simply misinterpreted nuances, or can they completely change the meaning and intent of the text? Second, can the MT system localize the errors, or must a human translator review both source and target texts in their entirety to determine the location of such errors? Unfortunately, errors committed by most MT systems span the gamut from innocuous to severe, and current systems seldom realize when they commit severe errors. Thus, a 95% system in the worst case produces a translated text that is analogous to a jar of cookies, only 5% of which are poisoned. Such a cookie jar is useless without a complete professional analysis to localize the poisoned ones.

Accurate translation was found to require some degree of text comprehension (cf. Bar-Hillel, 1960; The ALPAC Report, 1966; Carbonell et al., 1981). As the MT problem proved to be much more complex than originally envisioned, the once lavish government funding programs were reduced to a trickle. At this point the MT community bifurcated into those who chose to address the fundamental problems of language understanding, helping to found the field of computational linguistics, and those who persevered in building MT systems. The latter group abandoned the unrealistic goal of developing fully automated translators and focused on the more pragmatic objective of building systems that increased the throughput efficiency of human translators. Several distinct approaches were taken; the most significant ones are discussed in the following section. More recently, newer technological developments are giving rise to qualitatively different methods. Section 5.1.3 discusses knowledge-based machine translation, the re-unification of the more theoretically motivated language processing methods with the objective of fully automated accurate translation. Section 5.1.4 outlines highly interactive, symbiotic human-computer approaches that promise to yield practical systems for low-volume, real-time translation.

Recent results indicate that the time may finally be coming to strive once again for the promise of true automated translation, fulfilling the aspirations of the early pioneers of the field.

5.1.2. Existing approaches

Current MT systems range from translation aids that facilitate the job of a human translator to 'best-effort' MT programs that require human intervention only after the fact — in order to isolate and correct any errors committed in the automated translation phase. This section outlines the three major paradigms, assessing current and future potential.

5.1.2.1. Translation aids

Much of the time of a human translator is wasted in manual lexicographic searches, and in document editing and formatting. Time consuming as they may be, these are the simplest tasks that a translator must perform, and therefore the easiest to automate effectively. Hence, one approach to improving the efficiency of a valuable, experienced human translator is to provide him or her with high-powered computational tools for the more mundane, time-consuming tasks. Such tools range from split-screen editing systems, to document formatters and graphic layout modules, to on-line technical dictionaries and grammar checking programs. Figure 1 outlines the basic flow of information in a machine-aided human translation approach.

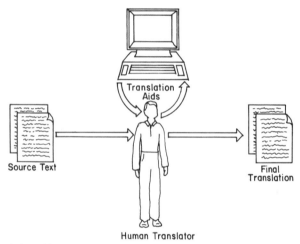

Figure 1. Translation aids.

Multiple versions of these tools are in existence (cf. Kay, 1982), but much more productive sophisticated translation aids could be built, such as the following:

- *Context-sensitive searching utilities* — A human translator requires fast access to accepted technical terminology. To meet this need, on-line dictionaries have been implemented. However, context-sensitive searching programs would make these far more effective. For instance, if a term has multiple meanings, these could be presented in rank order based on the topic of the text under translation, or based on previous terminological choices. Also, the ability to search for all occurrences of a technical term (or phrase) in the source text is very helpful. The translator may then decide to translate all occurrences identically, or to vary depending on local context.

- *Automated dictionary update interfaces* — No technical dictionary is ever complete, largely due to the rapid evolution of technical vocabularies vis-a-vis the slower evolution of general-purpose language. Thus, a dictionary needs to evolve with the language in an incremental manner. The most effective way to track and stay abreast of a continuous but gradual lexical evolution is to enable the translators themselves to augment or modify dictionary entries. Such entries to local dictionaries can later be examined for eventual inclusion in the master dictionaries. However, experience has shown that building robust software to guide the translator in providing all the relevant information in the proper format is far from an easy task.(The ALEX facility of the LOGOS translation system is an example of a utility that provides a large fraction of the requisite functionality.)
- *Morphological analysis tools* — The simplest aspect of automated language processing is morphological analysis (often coupled with secondary functionality such as spelling correction, etc.). Dictionary systems are far more effective when entries are stored in their basic form, and all inflections and other morphological variants are computed automatically. Of course, each language would require its own set of morphological analysis and composition rules, as well as exception tables.

The essence of all translation aids is that the human translator remains the central player, orchestrating all aspects of the translation process. The automated aids function only to increase efficiency (and possibly accuracy) by automating subsidiary tasks that would either be ignored or performed manually (such as searching several terminology banks for a possibly better translation of an obscure technical phrase, rather than manually searching several paper documents or simply accepting the translator's first guess). In contrast with the translation aids paradigm, all other approaches discussed in this chapter place the automated system in the central role, with the human checking results, correcting errors, preprocessing the input, or answering questions too difficult to be resolved automatically.

5.1.2.2. The post-editing approach

Since fully-automated machine translation of unrestricted text has proven an elusive goal (as discussed earlier), several compromises have been made in automating as large a fraction as possible of the entire translation task. The most prevalent paradigm has been one of allowing an automated MT system to do its best to translate unrestricted source text, and subsequently have a human translator (i.e., the post-editor) clean up the result. As illustrated in Figure 2, systems requiring human post-editing of the translated output operate in the following manner:

- The source text is converted to computer readable form.
- The text is then sent to a batch-processing MT system, which produces a rough translation several hours (or days) later.
- The original source text and the rough translation are presented to a human translator (the post-editor), who cleans up the translation, fixing any errors or other difficulties.

Since post-editing requires significantly less time than complete translation, there is a potential for major gains in human efficiency. But, a knowledgeable human translator is still required. The post-editing approach has, until recently, predominated in MT research and development. This domination had reached the extent that adherents of the post-editing paradigm have on occasion considered all other approaches as temporary aberrations from the true path.

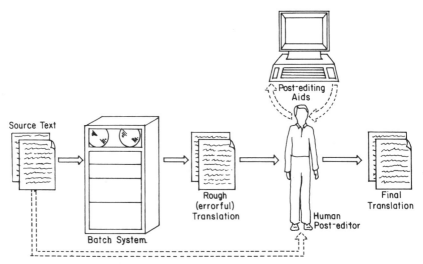

Figure 2.   Post-editing systems.

5.1.2.3. The pre-editing approach

The intervention of a human translator is required because current MT systems are unable to interpret all of the source text correctly. Errors in interpretation manifest themselves as incorrect translations. Thus, the post-editing approach recognizes the problem and attempts to minimize its impact by *post-factum* human corrections. An alternative is to ameliorate the problem at the interpretation phase by pre-editing the source text, eliminating difficulties such as complex grammatical structures, ambiguous words, and problematic semantic nuances. The pre-editing method is illustrated in Figure 3.

The practicality of a machine translation system is a function of accuracy and efficiency — human efficiency being more significant than machine efficiency. Adherents of the post-editing approach have claimed that pre-editing is a time-consuming manual task, one that can also alter the meaning and intent of the source text in subtle ways. Thus, the general belief has been that pre-editing is less practical than post-editing on both counts: efficiency and accuracy. The veracity of this claim is difficult to ascertain in the general case, but for specific domains, such as translation of weather forecasts, pre-editing has proven quite viable (cf. Kittredge et al., 1976). The primary reason for the effectiveness of pre-editing in narrow domains is that source texts in such domains are usually written in their own jargon, in essence a fairly restricted sublanguage (cf. Kittredge and Lehrberger 1982). Owing to the relative simplicity of sublanguages, pre-editing can be held to a minimum, thus avoiding the problem of inefficiency and minimizing the problem of unwitting alteration of meaning. Nagao (1983a) suggested a Japanese sublanguage called 'Machine Acceptable Language' where structural ambiguity is eliminated by extensive use of punctuation marks. In that system, pre-editing consists of manually inserting all the disambiguating punctuation into the source text.

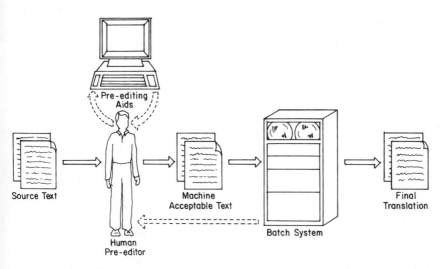

Figure 3. Pre-editing systems.

5.1.3. *The knowledge-based approach*

In order to address the semantic invariance criterion head on, a new approach to MT was developed, namely:

- PARSE — Map the source text into a language-free meaning representation.
  - □ Use a semantic knowledge base to disambiguate source text utterances, and to resolve other linguistic problems such as anaphoric referents.
  - □ Encode only the meaning of the utterance, not its syntactic structure or source-text lexicon, in the semantic representation.
- ELABORATE — (Optionally) run a domain specific inferencer to fill in situational details left implicit in the source text.
- GENERATE — Map the semantic representation into one or more target languages.

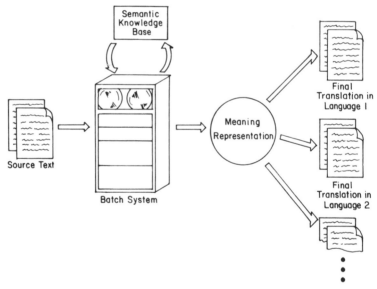

Figure 4.   Knowledge-based systems.

Knowledge-based machine translation (KBMT), depicted in Figure 4, has been implemented in a pilot system called SAM, 'Script Applying Mechanism.' It was a multifaceted project originally conceived by Schank and Cullingford to explore the role of stereotypic domain knowledge in automated text understanding. Machine translation occurred when several natural language generators were added to render its internal meaning representation into multiple languages (cf. Carbonell et al., 1981; Cullingford, 1977;

Schank and Abelson, 1977). SAM proved successful in translating brief newspaper accounts of vehicular accident stories from English into Spanish, Russian, French, Mandarin Chinese and Dutch. SAM established the technical feasibility of KBMT — as well as helping to reintegrate translation research as a mainline activity into the study of automated natural language processing. Newer and more robust semantic-based parsing techniques (cf. Hayes and Carbonell, 1981; Carbonell and Hayes, 1983) and better natural language generators (cf. Carbonell et al., 1985) argue in favor of converting the KBMT approach from a laboratory exercise to production-quality translation systems in the very near future.

The semantic analysis required to build a language-free meaning representation has both advantages and drawbacks over earlier approaches. A clear advantage is that KBMT creates the possibility of true multilingual translation by the abandonment of transfer grammars in favor of more principled parsing and generation techniques. A transfer grammar (cf. Kittredge et al., 1976; Boitet, 1976) is a large, amorphous, ad hoc set of rules, referencing specific lexical entries, that map phrases in one language into corresponding phrases in another language. Thus, a complete transfer grammar needs to be created for each pair of languages — over 5,000 gargantuan grammars to translate between the 72 most active languages. The KBMT approach, however, requires only a parser to map the source language into the semantic representation and a generator to map that representation into the target language (72 parsers and 72 generators for any pair of languages in the example above). Moreover, if one text is to be translated into several languages, it need be parsed only once, and the resulting meaning representation generated in each target language. Generation is the simpler, less computationally demanding process. Thus, KBMT makes the process of multilingual translation far more computationally tractable — as well as reducing significantly the amount of development work required to reach eventual closure in the number of grammars needed to translate among all commonly spoken human languages.

Perhaps the major disadvantage is that the KBMT process produces a paraphrase of the source text in the target language, rather than performing 'exact' translation — in the sense that it does not strive to achieve lexical or syntactic invariance. Thus, KBMT would be singularly inappropriate for translating poetry or other literary forms where the very structure of the text conveys a central message. Moreover, KBMT requires general semantic information and domain-specific knowledge roughly proportional to the semantic knowledge base that a human translator would bring to bear. With this caveat, KBMT could become highly practical for domains where a large volume of material must be translated swiftly and accurately, but less practical for low volume domains where it is more difficult to amortize the cost of building the domain-specific knowledge bases.

Finally, we should stress that if a meaning representation can be constructed automatically and unambiguously, the poisoned-cookie problem does not arise. Unlike the older post-editing approach, no human translator is needed to read carefully both source and target texts to determine where the meaning was radically altered. If KBMT can translate at all, meaning remains invariant.

5.1.4. The interactive approach

The interactive approach illustrated in Figure 5 is particularly suitable in systems in which an input text is provided directly by the user. In this approach, the user types a sentence (or a text) in his language; the system asks him questions in his language whenever needed; the user answers those questions; and finally the system produces a sentence (or a text) in the target language which does not require post-editing.

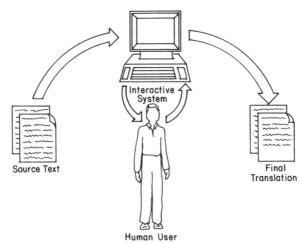

Figure 5. Interactive systems.

The interactive approach is especially desirable when:

- A text is so small and personal that the user cannot afford calling a translation service, or the urgency of the task precludes waiting days for the result.
- A text is to be translated into several languages (as with the KBMT approach).
- A text is so technical that even professional translators require help from domain experts.

The first situation is discussed in detail by Tomita (1985a). The second and third situations were advocated by Kay (1982).

Unlike conventional post-editing systems, the interactive approach exhibits the following characteristics:

- The user does not have to know the target language.
- The user need not have any special knowledge of linguistics, software, translation, etc.
- The system's final output requires no post-editing.
- Thus, everybody can use the system and generate target language texts without assistance of a translator or post-editor.

In designing and implementing an interactive translation system, the following characteristics are highly desirable:

- Because the system must run in real time rather than as a batch job, its response time should be reasonably quick.
- Because the system's input can be typed in from the terminal and not provided as a polished text file, the system must be reasonably robust against ill-formed sentences.
- The system, being particularly well suited for small, rapid turn-around, but possibly infrequent tasks, must run on affordable general purpose machines (such as high-end micros), so that it can be used at home or office on demand.

5.1.4.1. *Interactive sentence disambiguation*

This subsection describes how to resolve sentence ambiguity by asking the user focused questions. The essence of the interactive approach is to bypass the massive semantic knowledge requirements of KBMT by querying the user to disambiguate troublesome sentences. Such disambiguation, however, should not presuppose any formal linguistic, computer science or target language knowledge on the part of the user.

To resolve word-sense ambiguity, a system can ask questions such as the following:

```
The word 'pen' means:
1) a writing pen
2) a play pen
NUMBER? >
```

To resolve referential ambiguity, a system can ask in the following manner:

```
The word 'she' refers to:
1) 'Cathy'
2) 'my mother'
3) 'the sailboat'
NUMBER? >
```

Those two kinds of interactive disambiguation can be implemented relatively easily by simply enumerating alternatives on the screen. However, resolving syntactic ambiguity is not that easy. It is clearly not acceptable simply to enumerate all possible parse trees on the screen, because:

• the user may not be familiar with tree structures, and
• the number of alternatives can amount to the hundreds (cf. Church and Patil, 1982).

Therefore, we need a little more intelligent mechanism as in the following example:

> I saw a man and a woman with a telescope.
> 1) 'a man' and 'a woman'
> 2) 'a man' and 'a woman with a telescope'
> NUMBER? > 1
>
> 1) the action 'saw' takes place 'with a telescope'
> 2) 'a man and a woman' are 'with a telescope'
> NUMBER? >

The algorithm for this interactive disambiguation was developed recently by Tomita (1986a), and is described in Chapter 8 of Tomita, 1985b as well.

Tomita et al. (1984) built an experimental interactive system, modifying Nishida and Doshita's English-Japanese machine translation system (cf. Nishida and Doshita, 1983) so that the system is capable of asking questions interactively to disambiguate its input sentences. Experiments show that, in general, the syntactic ambiguity of a sentence can be resolved by a couple of questions, assuming that a little semantic knowledge is available (so that the system can resolve the simpler ambiguities by itself) (cf. Tomita, 1985a).

5.1.4.2. Bypassing source text

This subsection describes a different kind of interactive system that generates a target language text by interactive dialog with the user, requiring no source text. Of course, such systems are more 'automated text composition systems' than true MT systems. In these systems, questions are asked to construct the 'semantic content' which contains enough information to generate the target text, as illustrated in Figure 6.

This paradigm can be thought of as one extreme variation of the interactive method in which the system obtains semantic content directly from the user without parsing any source text. Saito and Tomita (1986) built a prototype system that enables the user to generate formal letters in several languages, solely by interacting with the user in his language. Although the system can handle only stereotypic topics such as moving notification, the quality of its output is so good that the user might want to use the system to produce letters in his own language as well.

First the user is asked his language and the language of the target letter :

```
Your language ?
1 English
2 Japanese
3 Spanish
4 French
5 German
1 — 5 ?  1

Target language ?
1 English
2 Japanese
1 — 2 ?  2
```

Next the user is asked the topic of a letter he is writing:

```
The topic of a letter ?
1 Moving
2 Thanks for Gift
3 Invitation
4 Happy New Year
1 — 4 ?  1
```

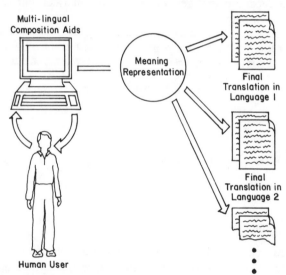

Figure 6. Multilingual composition aids.

The system then asks the user questions to acquire enough information to generate a moving notification letter in Japanese.

```
What's your old address ?
Type → Amberson

What's your new address ?
Type → 5600 Munhall Rd, Pittsburgh, Pa 15217

What's your new phone number ?
Type → (412)-682-8242

To whom are you writing ?
```

```
1  Business acquaintance
2  Superior
3  Friend
1 — 3 ?   2
```

What month is it now ?
```
1 — 12 ?   6
```
Have you finished moving ?
Y / N ?   *y*

The completed semantic content is illustrated below in a simple frame representation:

```
[ Moving
    [ writetowhom: superior ]
    [ nowseason: june ]
    [ fromwhere: Amberson ]
    [ towhere: 5600 Munhall Rd, Pittsburgh, Pa15217 ]
    [ tel: (412)-682-8242 ]
    [ done: yes ]
]
```

The final Japanese text generated by the generator out of the semantic content is shown below.

拝啓　　風薫る好季節を迎えましたが、いかがお過ごしでいらっしゃいますか。
さて、この度住み慣れたAmbersonから、下記に移転いたしました。お近くまでお
越の際は、ぜひお立ち寄り下さいませ。
まずは取り急ぎ書中をもって御挨拶申し上げます。
                                                            拝具

移転先
5600 Munhall Rd. Pittsburgh Pa15217

電話番号   (412) - 682 - 8242

5.1.5. Concluding remarks

Whereas this chapter has so far focused on well-defined paradigms for machine translation, we do not mean to rule out hybrid approaches. In fact, the combination of two or more approaches may prove superior in many circumstances. For instance, the knowledge-based and interactive approaches may be combined as illustrated in Figure 7. For most routine semantic decisions, the combined system queries its knowledge base. On the rare occasions when that query proves insufficient (e.g., the topic of the text strayed from its expected domain to one where the system lacks knowledge, or the system's knowledge is otherwise incomplete), the interactive component formulates a focused question to the user. Such compromises may prove to be the key to practicality, if neither extreme proves feasible.

Having surveyed the major approaches to machine translation, we observe that the established post-editing technique has received the most commercial attention, despite some of its more obvious weaknesses. Some of the newer approaches, such as KBMT, are based on recent developments in computational linguistics and artificial intelligence, such as semantic analysis and knowledge representation techniques. Thus, they could not emerge from the laboratory to be tested in a production environment. The interactive approach requires sophisticated interactive computers for practical application; such machines are just recently becoming widely available. Hence, in the near future we should be able to produce practical systems based on these newer, more powerful techniques. Section 5.2 describes the CMU approach to the next generation MT systems based on the latest advances in computational linguistics and artificial intelligence.

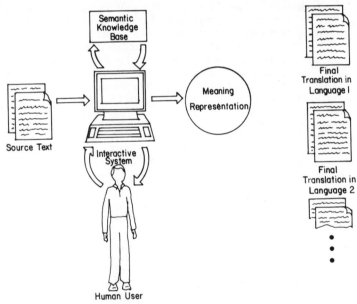

Figure 7. Knowledge-based interactive systems.

5.2. Efficient knowledge-based translation

5.2.1. The new generation MT systems at CMU

Carnegie-Mellon University has begun a project for the development of a new generation of MT systems whose capabilities range far beyond the current technology. The design criteria for the new MT technology can be summarized as follows:

- *Accurate* : Translations in well-defined domains should be error-free, requiring no human supervision. Accuracy implies the preservation of both meaning and style in the translation process.
- *Real-time* : It should take no more time to translate a letter or telex message than it takes to type it into the system.
- *Multilingual* : Translations to many different languages should be possible from one source text.
- *Interactive* : Our MT systems should be interactive and user-friendly, pausing to ask questions of their user if a word is not understood or a passage in the text is ill-formed.
- *Stand-alone* : Unlike current MT systems, no human translator should be required to check and correct the translated text.
- *Capable of operating on low-cost hardware* : The systems should in principle be able to run on computers that will be commonplace in the office environment in 2 or 3 years, such as the new generation of powerful 32-bit micro-computers.
- *User extensible* : The dictionary, the grammar, and the knowledge base of each system should be incrementally extensible without requiring post-factum alterations to previous data. Moreover, the extensions should be guided by knowledge-acquisition tools so that non-programmers can extend and customize their own systems.
- *Integrated* : Eventual integration with word-processing software, electronic mail, and application programs on the same computer is crucial to enhance the practical utility of MT.
- *Multifunctional* : The natural language interpreter and the language generator — integral components of all the new-generation machine translation systems — should be available for several other purposes, such as:
    - ☐   Multilingual data-base query, where questions to a data base can be phrased in any language the system understands, for instance: permitting Japanese queries and formulating Japanese answers to a data base whose contents are written in English (or vice versa).
    - ☐   Multilingual composition aids for stylized texts, such as certain kinds of business letters, purchase orders and invoices.
    - ☐   Automated production of concise summaries of lengthy texts in one or more target languages.
- *Speech-compatible* : A long-term objective is the automated simultaneous translation of spoken language. The MT systems should be designed to couple with speech-recognition hardware as the performance of the latter improves to the point of reliable practical usage.

In order to achieve the performance objectives set forth, several new technological directions must be pursued. We identify the following directions as particularly significant for our first step towards the next generation MT systems. These are:

- *Modularization of knowledge* — Syntactic and semantic knowledge required for accurate translation is compartmentalized into separate, well-defined knowledge sources, all of which are brought to bear in the translation process. Modularization provides a two-fold advantage: First, as new semantic domains are added to the system (such as banking telexes, purchase orders, travel requests, etc.) all previous linguistic knowledge remains applicable and need not be replicated. Second, as new languages are added to the system, all previous semantic domain knowledge may be brought to bear to translate texts in any known domain into the new language.

- *Very efficient parsing* — To achieve real-time translation on low-cost hardware, very efficient methods are required for parsing (and generation). In order to satisfy our criteria of modularity-of-knowledge-sources and efficiency-of-parsing, we are developing means of compiling complex declarative grammars and knowledge bases (understandable to humans) into a very efficient run-time version (analogous to object code, understandable and efficient for machines).

The following section describes the system structure in a more concrete fashion.

5.2.2. System overview

Figure 8 shows the overview of our system. We intend the system to be a first step toward the next-generation systems. First, we modularize domain-specific semantic knowledge and domain-independent (but language-specific) syntactic knowledge. Semantic knowledge is represented as an *entity-oriented grammar*, and syntactic knowledge is represented as a *functional grammar*, both of which are recent advances in the area of computational linguistics. They are described further in the following sections.

To achieve the real-time efficiency, we precompile these two kinds of grammar into a single large grammar which is less perspicuous but more efficient. This merged grammar is further precompiled into a parsing table, and input sentences are parsed in a very efficient manner using the parsing table. More on this issue will be discussed in section 5.2.5.

Section 5.2.6 describes other techniques which we intend to integrate with our system in the future, such as an *inferencer* and *speech recognition.*

5.2.3. Entity-oriented grammar formalism

The entity-oriented approach to restricted-domain parsing was first proposed by Hayes (1984) as a method of organizing semantic and syntactic information about all domain concepts around a collection of various entities (objects, events, commands, states, etc.) that a particular system needs to recognize. An entity definition contains information about the internal structure of the entities, about relations to other entities, about the way the entities will be manifested in the natural language input, and about the correspondence between the internal structure and multiple surface forms for each entity.

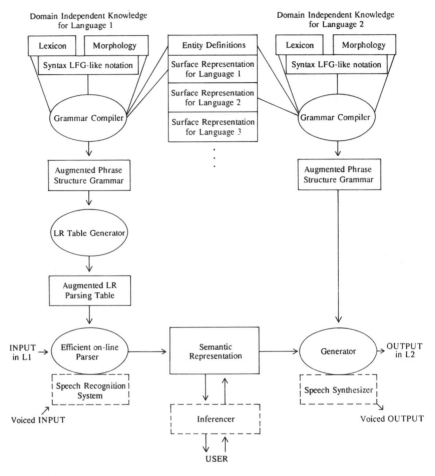

Figure 8. System structure.

Let us consider the domain of doctor-patient conversations; in particular, the patient's initial complaint about some pain. Entities in this domain include an event entity PATIENT-COMPLAINT-ACT and object entities PAIN, HUMAN and so on. An example entity-oriented grammar is shown in Figure 9. The notation here is slightly simplified from that of Hayes. Sentences of different surface form that should be recognized as instantiations of this entity include:

> I have a head ache
> I have a burning pain in the chest.
> I don't feel any pain.
> Did you have a dull ache in your head?
>
> [EntityName: PATIENT-COMPLAINT-ACT
> Type: STRUCTURED

```
Agent: HUMAN            ; Semantic restriction on the agent.
Pain: PAIN
SurfaceRepresentation:
  [SyntaxType: SENTENTIAL
  Head: (have | feel)
  Subj: ($Agent)        ; $Agent refers to the semantic case 'Agent'
  DObj: ($Pain) ] ]     ; $Pain refers to the semantic case 'Pain'

[EntityName: PAIN
Type: STRUCTURED
Location: BODY-PART      ; Semantic restriction on the location.
PainKind: PAIN-FEEL
SurfaceRepresentation:
  [SyntaxType: NOUNPHRASE
  Head: (pain | ache)
  PP: ( [Prep: in
         Comp: ($Location) ])
  Adj: ( [AdjPhrase: (sharp | stabbing | acute)
          Component: PainKind
          Value: SHARP ]
         [AdjPhrase: burning
          Component: PainKind
          Value: BURN ])
  ]
]
```

Figure 9:   Example entity definition.

The final semantic representation of the sentence

'I have a dull ache in my chest'

produced by instantiating entities is shown in Figure 10.

```
[cfname: MEDICAL-COMPLAINT-ACT
type: SENTENTIAL
agent: [cfname: PERSON
        name: *speaker*]      ;Whoever is the 'I' who has the chest ache.
pain: [cfname: PAIN
       location: [cfname: BODY-PART
                  name: CHEST ]
       pain-kind: DULL]
]
```

Figure 10:   Sample semantic representation — instantiated entities.

The 'Surface Representation' parts of an entity guide the parsing by proving syntactic structures tied to the semantic portion of the entity. As the
result of parsing a sentence (see figure 10), a composition of the semantic
portion of the instantiated entities is produced. This knowledge structure
may be given to any backend, whether it be a language generator (for the
target language), a paraphraser, a data-base query system, or whatever may
be required.

The biggest advantage of the entity-oriented grammar formalism is its
clarity of sublanguage definition (see Kittredge and Lehrberger 1982) for a
discussion of sublanguages). Since all information relating to an entity is
grouped in one place, a language definer will be able to see more clearly
whether a definition is complete and what would be the consequences of any
addition or change to the definition. Similarly, since surface (syntactic) and

structural information about an entity is grouped together, the surface information can refer to the structure in a clear and coherent way. This advantage is even more valuable in the application to multilingual MT. Because the semantic portions of the entities are totally language independent, we can use one set of entity definitions for all languages — merely requiring that each entity have a multiple number of surface forms; one or more for each language. In this way, it can be ensured that the semantic domains that each language can handle are identical.

In addition to clarity and its multilingual extensibility, an advantage of the entity-oriented approach is robustness in dealing with extragrammatical input. Robust recovery from ill-formed input is a crucial feature for practical interactive language systems, but is beyond the immediate scope of this chapter. See Carbonell and Hayes (1983) for a full discussion on entity-based robust parsing.

5.2.4. *Functional grammar formalism*

In addition to the entity-oriented grammar formalism for semantic knowledge described in the previous section, we adopt the functional grammar formalism to define the language-specific (but domain-independent) syntax.

The functional grammar formalism is presented in Kay (1979). Two well-known functional grammar formalisms are Functional Unification Grammar (UG) (cf. Kay, 1984) and Lexical Function Grammar (LFG) (cf. Kaplan and Bresnan, 1982). In this chapter, however, we do not distinguish between them and use the term 'functional grammar' for both. Application of the functional grammar formalism to machine translation is discussed in Kay (1984). Attempts are being made to implement parsers using these grammars, most notably in the PATR-II project at Stanford (cf. Pereira, 1985; Shieber, 1985). However, these efforts have not been integrated with external semantic knowledge bases, and have not been applied to KBMT.

There are two main advantages to using the functional grammar formalism in practical MT systems:

- A system implemented strictly within the functional grammar formalism will be reversible, in the sense that if the system maps from A to B then, to the same extent, it maps from B to A. Thus, we do not need to write two separate grammars for parsing and generation. We merely apply the grammar (in parsing mode) for the source language, and a different grammar (in generation mode) for the target language. The same two grammars would be applied in reverse order to translate in the opposite direction.
- Functional grammar formalisms such as UG and LFG are well-known among computational linguists, and thus linguists who

write a syntactic grammar tend to prefer those existing formalisms to system-specific local grammar formalisms.

On the other hand, the general problem of functional grammar formalisms is implementation inefficiency in practical applications. Although a reasonable amount of work has been done to enhance efficiency (cf. Shieber, 1985; Pereira, 1985), functional grammar formalisms are considered far less efficient than formalisms like ATN (cf. Woods, 1970) or context-free phrase structure grammar. We resolve this efficiency problem by precompiling a grammar written in the functional grammar formalism into an augmented context-free grammar, as described in the following section.

5.2.5. *Grammar pre-compilation and efficient on-line parsing*

The previous two sections have described two kinds of knowledge representation methods: the entity-oriented grammar formalism for domain-specific semantic knowledge and the functional grammar formalism for domain-independent syntactic knowledge. In order to parse a sentence in real time using these knowledge bases, we precompile the semantic and syntactic knowledge, as well as morphological rules and dictionary, into a single large morph/syn/sem grammar. This morph/syn/sem grammar is represented as a batch of augmented context-free phrase structure rules, each of which is associated with a Lisp program for test and action as in ATN. (To be exact, each rule has two Lisp programs; one for parsing and the other for generation.) A simplified fragment of an example morph/syn/sem grammar is shown in figure 11.

```
have-a-pain-1-S → patient-NP have-a-pain-1-VP
  ((cond ((equal (not (getvalue '(x1: agr:)))
                 (getvalue '(x2: agr:)))
          (return nil)))
   (setvalue '(x0: semcase:) (getvalue '(x2: semcase:)))
   (setvalue '(x0: semcase: agent:) (getvalue '(x1: semcase:)))
   (setvalue '(x0: syncase:) (getvalue '(x2: syncase:)))
   (setvalue '(x0: syncase: subj:) (getvalue '(x1:)))
   (return (getvalue '(x0:))))

have-a-pain-1-VP → have-a-pain-1-V
  ((setvalue '(x0: semcase:) (getvalue '(x1: semcase:)))
   (setvalue '(x0: syncase: pred:) (getvalue '(x1:)))
   (setvalue '(x0: agr:) (getvalue '(x1: agr:)))
   (setvalue '(x0: form:) (getvalue '(x1: form:)))
   (return (getvalue '(x0:))))

have-a-pain-1-V → ACHE
  ((setvalue '(x0: semcase: cfname:) 'HAVE-A-PAIN)
   (setvalue '(x0: agr:) (getvalue '(x1: agr:)))
   (setvalue '(x0: form:) (getvalue '(x1: form:)))
   (return (getvalue '(x0))))
```

Figure 11:   A Fragment of Precompiled Grammar.

Once we have a grammar in this form, we can apply any efficient context-free parsing algorithm, and whenever the parser reduces constituents into a higher-level nonterminal using a phrase structure rule, the Lisp program associated with the rule is evaluated. The Lisp program handles such aspects as construction of a semantic representation of the input sentence, passing around attribute values and checking semantic and syntactic constraints such as subject-verb agreement. It should be remembered that those Lisp programs are generated automatically by the grammar precompiler. Note also that those Lisp programs can be further compiled into machine codes by the Lisp compiler.

We adopt the algorithm introduced by Tomita (1985b, 1985c) as our context-free parsing algorithm to parse a sentence with the morph/syn/sem grammar. The Tomita algorithm can be viewed as an extended LR parsing algorithm (cf. Aho and Ullman, 1972). We precompile the morph/syn/sem grammar further into a table called the LR parsing table, with which the algorithm works very efficiently.

The Tomita algorithm has three major advantages in the application of real-time MT systems:

- The algorithm is fast, due to the LR table precompilation; perhaps faster than any other existing general context-free parsing algorithm. The experiments with several English grammars and sample sentences have shown that it is 5 to 10 times faster than Earley's standard algorithm.
- The efficiency of the algorithm is not affected by the size of its grammar, once the LR parsing table is obtained. This characteristic is especially important for our system, because the size of the morph/syn/sem grammar will be very large in practical applications.
- The algorithm parses a sentence strictly from left to right, allowing the parser to be *on-line*, which is described below.

The *on-line* parser starts parsing as soon as the user types in the first word of a sentence, without waiting for the end of a line. There are two main benefits from on-line parsing:

- The parser's response time can be reduced significantly. When the user finishes typing a whole sentence, most of the input sentence has already been processed by the parser.
- Any errors, such as mistyping and ungrammatical usages, can be detected almost as soon as they occur, and the parser can warn the user immediately without waiting for the end of the line.

More discussion of on-line parsing can be found in Chapter 7 of Tomita (1985b).

5.2.6. *Long-term technological directions*

The architecture of our MT system is in the process of being refined and implemented. Although we have had considerable success with earlier knowledge-based MT experiments (cf. Carbonell et al., 1981) with our efficient parsers, and with the entity-oriented approach (cf. Hayes, 1984), other parts of the architecture rest on a smaller experience base. At present we are starting to focus on multilingual generation, which demands that our grammar definitions be flexible and non-directional. The system should be capable of generating and comprehending a language from a single well-structured grammatical LFG-like specification, together with domain-specific (but language-independent) entity definitions.

A sampling of our longer-term research directions includes:

- Exploring the integration of our direct translation system with sophisticated domain inferencers, capable of providing default or implicit information absent from the source language proper, but capable of enhancing the quality of the translation. For instance, in translating the sentence 'Juan estaba enojado' from Spanish to English, one can choose to say 'John was angry,' or 'upset,' or 'unhappy,' or 'disgruntled,' or 'enraged.' Some knowledge of the degree of his anger, inferred from its cause or from John's subsequent action, could lead to improved lexical selection. In more complex cases, appropriate domain inference can color the entire tone of a translated text.
- Integrating the parsing process with a speech recognition system and the generation process with a speech synthesis system could lead to translation of spoken language, or multilingual transcription. Although speech-recognition technology, especially for real-time, speaker-independent, connected speech is very much an unsolved active research problem, we have started integrating our parsing technology with the CMU speech recognition project (cf. Hayes et al., 1986; Tomita, 1986a). Initial results indicated that linguistic and semantic constraints can significantly improve the accuracy of the acoustic recognition, but practical results in the MT area are still many years away.
- In natural language projects parallel to our MT research, we have built several interfaces to data bases, expert systems, and other software utilities (cf. Carbonell et al., 1985). Someday, we foresee the integration of such systems with our MT technology, to produce multilingual interfaces. For instance, such an interface to large scale data bases could allow a user to query using his or her own language, and have the output of the search translated back into the source language of the query.

Thus, although we foresee very useful applications of our knowledge-based approach in the medium-term, the MT project is also dedicated to a longer-term vision, where MT, speech, domain inference, and natural language interfaces based on a common underlying technology form a family of useful and integrated natural language processing capabilities.

6 The structure of interlingua in TRANSLATOR

SERGEI NIRENBURG, VICTOR RASKIN and ALLEN B. TUCKER

6.1. Delimiting the problem

The TRANSLATOR machine translation (MT) project explores the knowledge-based approach to MT. The basic translation strategy is to extract meaning from the input text in a *source language*, SL, represent this meaning in a language-independent semantic representation and then render this meaning in a *target language*, TL. The knowledge representation language used in such a set-up is called, for historical reasons, *interlingua* (henceforth, IL).

TRANSLATOR's ultimate aim is achieving good quality automatic translation in a non-trivial subworld and its corresponding sublanguage. The philosophy of TRANSLATOR aims at the independence of the process of translation from human intervention in the form of the traditional pre- and/or post-editing. Interaction *during* the process of translation can be accommodated by this philosophy, but only as a temporary measure. Interactive modules will be plugged into the system pending the development of automatic modules for performing the various tasks as well as more powerful inference engines and representation schemata. This methodology facilitates early testing of a system (even before all the modules are actually built) and enhances its shorter-term feasibility.

This strategy is an extension of one of the approaches discussed, for example, by Carbonell and Tomita in Chapter 5 of this volume since it implies knowledge acquisition during the exploitation stage and also involves a broader class of texts as its input. Johnson and Whitelock (Chapter 8) are also proponents of the interactive approach, but their motivation is different, in that they perceive the human to be an integral part of their system even in its final incarnation. In any case, interactivity is not the central design feature of TRANSLATOR. The background of the TRANSLATOR MT project is presented in Tucker and Nirenburg (1984).

6.2. Configuration of TRANSLATOR

There are three procedural modules in TRANSLATOR: the analyzer, the augmentor and the synthesizer. The analyzer obtains the input text and produces a representation of it as a set of IL frames. A number of slots in these frames will remain unfilled, because a text practically never has all the

90

information about objects and events it describes spelled out — it is
intended that the rest be inferred by the hearer (reader). In a computer
model these inferences are made through the operation of the augmentor.
This additional information is instrumental in narrowing the choice of TL
correlates for an input text (see Chapter 1 for a discussion of choices).
Finally, the synthesizer obtains the augmented IL text and produces a TL
text.

Each of the procedural modules is supported by a number of
TRANSLATOR's static knowledge clusters, as shown in Figure 1.

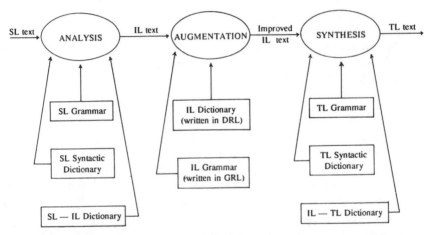

Figure 1. Knowledge and processes in TRANSLATOR.

In this chapter we will describe the design of TRANSLATOR's IL and illustrate how its grammar is used to represent the meaning of SL texts with the
help of the knowledge of the ontology of the TRANSLATOR subworld, stored
in the IL dictionary. In other words, the illustration will concern only the
knowledge structures for the analyzer. The augmentor and the synthesizer
will necessarily require significant additions to the IL dictionary (including
representations of typical groupings of objects and events in a subworld).
We see the compilation of the subworld knowledge base as a prolonged and
incremental empirical process.[1]

---

[1] It is clear that in order for this process to succeed one has to come up with an appropriate
methodology for the effort. It is common knowledge that people tend to be idiosyncratic in the
ways they perform semantic analysis (which is exactly the type of work involved in IL dictionary compilation). Interactive aids, as described in Chapter 9, must be developed, and the experience of working with large dictionaries, even of a different type, as discussed in Chapter 14
must be taken into account.

IL is, in fact, a set of two knowledge representation languages: the Interlingua Dictionary Representation Language (DRL) and the Interlingua Grammar Representation Language (GRL), respectively. DRL is a language for describing the types of concepts that can appear in the subworld of translation. GRL is a language for representing the assertions about tokens of those types that actually appear in texts. DRL is used for writing the IL dictionary, while GRL is used for writing the IL grammar. The distinction between these two languages is similar to that between the description and assertion languages in KL-ONE (cf. Brachman and Schmoltze, 1985). The ontology of the translation subworld is expressed in DRL, while the results of analyzing an SL text take the form of a set of GRL frames that incorporate instances of DRL frame types. Note that GRL is not used for representing the grammar of any SL or TL.

After discussing these languages we will very briefly sketch the structure the SL — IL dictionary to help us through an illustration of how the IL dictionary is used during the analysis stage.

6.3. DRL

The IL dictionary is a source of information for representing the meanings of SL texts. In it, one does not find any information pertaining to any particular SL or TL. Thus, it is only for reader convenience that most of DRL concepts as well as most of the members of the property sets used to describe properties of IL concepts were made to look like English words. This choice was made with the dictionary writers in mind. The other possibility would have been to assign non-suggestive identifiers to DRL concepts. This would have slowed down the process of dictionary compilation. The dictionary writers must do their best not to mix the semantics of an entry head in the IL dictionary with that of an English word whose graphical form is identical.

There are two kinds of entities in DRL: concepts and properties. Concepts are, roughly speaking, IL 'nouns' (*objects*) and IL 'verbs' (*events*). IL 'adjectives,' 'adverbs' and 'numerals' are represented by properties. These are organized as sets of property values indexed both by the name of the property set (e.g., 'color,' 'time' or 'attitude') and by the individual values, to facilitate retrieval. Property values pertain to specific concept types. Their tokens do not appear on their own in IL texts, but only as fillers of slots in the frames for concept tokens. Thus, for example, 'red' will be a potential filler for the 'color' property of a token of every physical object. The proper choice of primitive concepts in a real subworld is a notoriously difficult problem (cf. Hayes, 1979). We approach it as an empirical task and are prepared to revise our system when new insights and information are gathered. An explanation of the relationship between IL word types and tokens follows. An illustration of the ways members of various natural language lexical classes are treated in the SL-IL dictionary may be seen in Table 2.

The IL dictionary is organized as a set of entries (concept nodes) inter-connected through a number of link types (properties). However, the structural backbone of the dictionary is the familiar *isa* hierarchy with property inheritance. Note that most of the time the translation system will be working with terminal nodes in this hierarchy. But the nonterminal nodes play a special role in it. By representing sets of entries, thereby providing a link among a number of (related) concepts, they serve as the basis for a variety of inference-making procedures. Even more importantly, these 'nonterminal entries' constitute, together with the sets of various property values, the *schema* of the dictionary, the set of terms that are used to describe the semantics of the rest of the dictionary entries.

Like all other nodes in the hierarchy, nonterminal nodes represent dictionary entries, which means that they can also have tokens. This device comes handy when, on analyzing a segment of input, we conclude that a certain slot filler is unavailable in the text. At the same time, if we know the identities of other slot fillers in the frame, we can come to certain conclusions about the nature of an absentee. For instance, if the Agent slot of a certain mental process is not filled, we, by consulting the 'agent-of' slot of the nonterminal node 'mental-process,' can infer (or, rather, abduce) that, whatever it is, it must be a 'creature.' This knowledge helps in finding referents for anaphoric phenomena.

The dictionary entries represent IL concept and property *types*; IL texts consist of IL concept *tokens* (as well as IL clause and sentence tokens), organized in accordance with the IL syntax postulated by GRL. Every token of an IL concept stands in the *is-token-of* relationship to its corresponding type. Structurally both IL concept types and IL concept tokens are represented as frames. The frame for a type and the frame for a corresponding token are not identical in structure, though the intersection of their slot names is obviously non-zero. One must note, however, that even in this case the semantics of the slots in the dictionary frames is different from that of the corresponding slots in the text frame.

Some of the slot names in the type frames refer to the paradigmatic relationships of this concept type with other concept types. These are the *type parameters* of an IL dictionary entry. The rest of the information in an entry describes syntagmatic relationships that tokens of this particular type have with tokens of other types in an IL text. These are the *token parameters*. Among the type parameters one finds, for example, pointers in the *isa* hierarchy and such relationships as *part-of.*

The token-parameter slots in the dictionary entries contain either *default* values for the properties (the 'no-value' *nil* value is among the possible default choices) or acceptable *ranges* of values, for the purpose of validity testing. IL concept tokens, which are components of IL *text*, not its dictionary, have their slots occupied by actual values of properties; if information about a property is not forthcoming, then the default value (if any) is inherited from the corresponding type representations.

We now turn to the actual description of DRL. We will do this by presenting the top levels of the *isa* hierarchy of concepts in our subworld and listing the frames for high-level nodes. Next, we'll present examples of IL dictionary frames, including one complete path in the *isa* hierarchy, from the root to a terminal node.

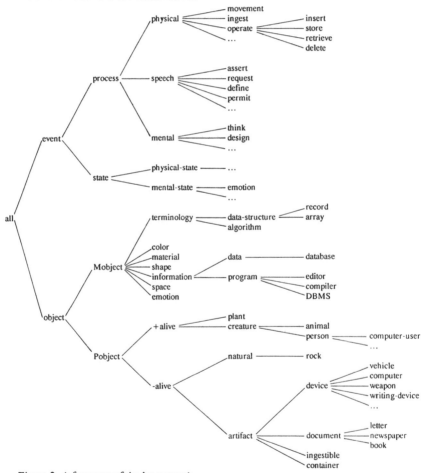

Figure 2. A fragment of the **isa** network.

The hierarchy of Figure 2 depends on the subworld for which it is designed. It may be overdeveloped in some of its branches and under-developed in many others. This state of affairs corresponds to the strategy of working within a subworld.

6.3.1. Frames

```
all :: = ('all'
         ('subworld' subworld*))
```

This is the root of the *isa* hierarchy. The slots in this frame mean that every node in the tree represents a concept that belongs to one or more *subworlds*.

```
event :: = ('event'
           ('isa' all)
           ('patient' object))
```

At this level we meet the 'isa' slot for the first time. This is the pointer to a node's parent in the hierarchy. Events, as one can see from Figure 2, are subdivided into processes and states. The only property common to all events is the conceptual case of 'patient.'[2]

```
process :: = ('process'
             ('isa' event)
             ('is' process-sequence)
             ('part-of' process*)
             ('agent' creature)
             ('object' object)
             ('instrument' object)
             ('source' object)
             ('destination' object)
             ('preconditions' state*)
             ('effects' state*))
```

In addition to the conceptual case slots, the process frame contains information about preconditions and effects. These are states that must typically hold before and after the process takes place, respectively. A process can also be a component of other processes. Thus, for instance, *move* is a component of *travel, fetch, insert*, etc. The 'is' slot of a process frame contains either the constant *primitive*, if the process is not further analyzable in DRL, or the description of the sequence of processes which comprise the given process. The *process-sequence* is a list of process names connected by the operators *sequential, choice* and *shuffle*. In other words, a process may be a sequence of subprocesses (*sequential*), a choice among several subprocesses (*choice*), a temporally unordered sequence of subprocesses (*shuffle*) or any recursive combination of the above. This treatment of processes is inspired by Nirenburg, Reynolds and Nirenburg (1985). For the purposes of

---

[2] This reflects our opinion that in the sentence *John is asleep John* is not an agent, but rather a patient. Note that 'patient' in DRL subsumes the semantics of 'beneficiary.'

machine translation it seems unnecessary to introduce a more involved temporal logic into consideration for the 'is' slot.

```
physical-process :: = ('physical-process'
                       ('isa' process)
                       ('object' object))
mental-process   :: = ('mental-process'
                       ('isa' process)
                       ('agent' creature)
                       ('object' object | event))
```

Only creatures can be fillers for the 'agent' slot. Mental processes classify into reaction processes (cf. the English 'please' or 'like'), cognition processes ('deduce') and perception processes ('see'). Objects of mental processes can be either objects, as in (1) or events, as in (2).

(1)   I know John
(2)   I know that John has traveled to Tibet

```
speech-process :: = ('speech-process'
                     ('isa' process)
                     ('agent' person)
                     ('patient' person* | organization*)
                     ('object' event | object)
                     ('source' 'agent')
                     ('destination' 'patient'))
```

Some of the varieties of speech processes recognized by DRL are listed in Figure 2. The 'agent' slot filler has the semantics of the speaker. The 'patient' is the hearer. Note that there is a possibility for the hearer to be a group or an organization, as in (3). The 'agent' is the 'source' and the 'patient' is the 'destination' of a speech process.

(3)   I promised the band to let them have a ten-minute break every hour

```
state :: = ('state'
            ('isa' event)
            ('part-of' state*))
```

The actant in states, which is the patient rather than the actor, is inherited from the event frame.

```
object :: = ('object
             ('isa' all)
             ('part-of' object*)
             ('consists-of' object*)
             ('belongs-to' creature | organization)
             ('object-of' process)
             ('patient-of' event)
             ('instrument-of' event)
             ('destination-of' event)
             ('source-of' event))
```

The '...-of' slots are used for consistency checks.

6.3.2. Properties

Property values are primitive concepts of IL used as values for slots in concept frames. We give here just an illustration of these. Many more exist and will be used in the implementation.

```
size-set     :: = infinitesimal | ... | huge
color-set    :: = black | ... | white
shape-set    :: = flat | square | spherical ...
material-set :: = (gold (specific-gravity 81) (unit-value 228)) | ...
subworld-set :: = computer-world | business-world | everyday-world ...
boolean-set  :: = yes | no
texture-set  :: = smooth | ... | rough

properties :: = ('properties'
                 'none'
                 ('size' size-set)
                 ('color' color-set)
                 ('shape' shape-set)
                 ('texture' texture-set)
                 ('belongs-to' creature | organization)
                 ('part-of' object | event)
                 ('consists-of' object | event)
                 ('power' real)
                 ('speed' real)
                 ('mass' real)
                 ('edibility' boolean-set)
                 ('made-of' material-set)
                 ...)
```

6.3.3. From the root to a leaf

A path of concept representations from the root to a leaf node is presented below.

all → object → pobject → +alive → creature → person → computer-user

Frames for 'all' and 'object' see above.

```
pobject :: = ('pobject'
             ('isa' object)
             ('object-of' (+ (Take Put))
             ('size' size-set)
             ('shape' shape-set)
             ('color' color-set)
             ('mass' integer))
```

The ' + ' sign in slots means all inherited information plus the contents of the current slot.

```
+alive :: = (' +alive'
            ('isa' pobject)
            ('edibility' boolean-set))

creature :: = ('creature'
              ('isa' +alive)
              ('agent-of' (Eat Ingest Drink Move Attack))
              ('consists-of' (Head Body))
              ('object-of' (+ (Attack))
              ('power' real)
              ('speed' real))
```

```
person :: = ('person'
              ('isa' creature)
              ('agent-of' (+ (Take Put Find Speech-process Mental-Process)))
              ('source-of' Speech-process)
              ('destination-of' Speech-process)
              ('consists-of' (+ (Hand Foot ...)))
              ('size' medium)
              ('shape' oblong)
              ('power' 50)
              ('speed' 50)
              ('mass' 55))
computer-user :: = ('computer-user'
                     ('isa 'person)
                     ('agent-of' (+ (Operate)))
                     ('subworld' computer-world))
```

The complete frame of the leaf of this path, 'computer-user', including all inherited slots and default values is listed below. In reality frames like this do not exist, because the tokens of this type do not contain all the possible slot fillers.

```
(computer-user
  ('isa' person)
  ('agent-of' (Operate Take Put Find Speech-process Mental-Process
             Eat Ingest Drink Move Attack))
  ('object-of' (Find Mental-process Speech-process Attack Take Put))
  ('destination-of' Speech-process)
  ('size' size-set)
  ('shape' shape-set)
  ('color' color-set)
  ('edibility' boolean-set)
  ('source-of' Speech-process)
  ('consists-of' (Hand Foot Head Body))
  ('size' medium)
  ('shape' oblong)
  ('power' 50)
  ('speed' 50)
  ('mass' 55)
  ('subworld' computer-world))
```

6.4. GRL

In the previous section we dealt with the IL dictionary. This section is devoted to the syntax of IL 'text.' Unlike a natural language text, an IL text is not linear. It is a (potentially) complex network of IL sentences, interconnected by IL *discourse markers*. An IL sentence is represented as a frame with slots for each of any number clauses (that are represented as frames themselves) as well as for speech act and focus information. The IL clause is the place where event tokens are put into the modal and spatio-temporal context. The tokens for events and their actant objects that appear in IL texts are produced by obtaining tokens of the appropriate concept types in the dictionary and augmenting them by various property values identified during SL text analysis. It follows that the slots whose values depend on contextual meaning (e.g., negation and modality) appear only in GRL frames for event and object tokens, and not in DRL.

At the same time, there are regular correspondences between units of GRL and DRL. The values of the properties in entity tokens typically correspond to the data types listed as fillers for the corresponding slots in DRL frames. Thus, for instance, the *color* property slot in the DRL frame for 'flower' can be occupied by a list *(white yellow blue red purple pink,* etc.), the one for 'snow,' on the other hand, will contain only the one-element list *(white).* At the same time, 'rose11' will have the value 'red' as the contents of its 'color' slot. This underscores the difference in the semantics of similarly named slots in DRL and GRL.

6.4.1. Text

text :: = sentence | (discourse-structure-type text text+)

The above means that an IL text is either an empty string, a single sentence, or a number of sentences interconnected through discourse structure markers.

6.4.2. Sentence

```
sentence :: = ('sentence-token'
              ('clauses' clause*)
              ('subworld' subworld)
              ('modality' modality)
              ('focus' focus)
              ('speech-act' speech-act))
```

Every sentence is declared to contain a speech act. Thus, we will represent (4) as (5), provided we can infer the identities of the speaker and the hearer, as well as the identity of the process:

(4)   I'd rather not do it.
(5)   The boss ordered Employee X not to agree to the terms of Sales Offer Y.

Both direct and indirect speech acts are represented with the help of speech process tokens. With direct speech acts, the information to be put into the sentence frame is present in the text, while with indirect speech acts it has to be inferred.

Thematic information about the sentence includes the values for the 'given' and the 'new' (or focus) slots in the sentence frame. Both values can be pointers to a concept, a property of a concept, or an entire clause. The value of the modality slot for the IL sentence is chosen from the set of modalities. The subworld slot is a marker that shows that the sentence belongs to a certain 'semantic field.' In TRANSLATOR the designated topic for translations is the world of technical texts about computers. In broader environments the subworld information will be helpful to prune unneeded inference paths.

6.4.3. Clause

```
('clause-token'
    ('discourse-structure' discourse-structure)
    ('focus' focus)
    ('modality' modality)
    ('time' time)
    ('space' space)
    ('event' event)
    ('quantifier' quantifier2)
    ('subworld' subworld))
```

The major difference between the interlingua clauses and events is that clauses contain information that actually appears in the input text (augmented by anaphora resolution), while events can be either contained in the input or *inferred* from it.

A clause may be connected discourse-wise not only with another clause but also with an object or an event, as well as with a sentence, a paragraph or even a whole text; also note that discourse structure assigns the given clause as one of the two arguments in the discourse structure; one clause can be an argument in more than one discourse-structure expression.

6.4.4. Process

```
('physical-process-token-id'
        ('is-token-of' string)
        ('agent' object-token)
        ('object' object-token)
        ('patient' object-token)
        ('instrument' object-token)
        ('source' object-token)
        ('destination' object-token)
        ('negation' negation)
        ('quantifier' quantifier2)
        ('phase' phase-set)
        ('manner' manner-set)
        ('space' space)
        ('time' time)
        ('subworld' subworld-token))
```

An actual process token is represented as follows:

```
(move21
        ('is-token-of' move)
        ('is' primitive)
        ('agent' person12)
        ('object' person12)
        ('source' (in house2))
        ('destination' (in house3))
        ('negation' nil)
        ('quantifier' nil)
        ('phase' static)
        ('manner' easily)
        ('part-of' travel5)
        ('time' (before 1700))
        ('subworld' everyday-world))
```

6.4.5. State

```
('state-token-id'
    ('is-token-of' string)
    ('negation' negation)
    ('quantifier' quantifier2)
    ('patient' object-token)
    ('phase' phase-set)
    ('part-of' state-token*)
    ('space' space)
    ('time' time)
    ('subworld' subworld))
```

Events in IL have a property of 'phase:' they are either 'static,' 'begin-ning' or 'end.' This device is needed to represent changes of state. Changes of state are sometimes represented as a separate class of processes. The solution in IL may be more economical.

6.4.6. Object

A typical frame for an object token in GRL is as follows. The 'string' in the 'is-token-of' slot stands for the name of the corresponding object type.

```
('object-token-id'
    ('is-token-of' string)
    ('subworld' subworld)
    ('negation' negation)
    ('quantifier' quantifier1))
```

An example object token follows:

```
(person23
    ('is-token-of' person)
    ('subworld' everyday-world)
    ('negation' no)
    ('quantifier' any)
    ('power' 50)
    ('speed' 50)
    ('mass' 55))
```

Note the difference from DRL object frames. No '...-of' slots here. More emphasis on syntagmatic relationships and default overriding.

6.4.7. Time

```
time :: = absolute-time | relative-time

absolute-time :: = ('time'
                    ('quantifier' quantifier2)
                    ('point' integer) |
                    ('interval-begin' integer)
                    ('interval-end' integer))

relative-time : = ('time'
                    (temporal-operator event)
                    ('quantifier' quantifier2))

temporal-operator :: = simultaneous | before | during | around | always | none
```

Relative time markers will predominantly appear in texts.

6.4.8. Space

```
space :: = absolute-space | relative-space
absolute-space :: = ('space
                     ('quantifier' quantifier2)
                     ( 'coordinate1' real)
                     ( 'coordinate2' real)
                     ( 'coordinate3' real))

relative-space :: = ('space'
                     (spatial-operator object)
                     ('quantifier' quantifier2))
spatial-operator :: = left-of | equal | between | in | above | near | none
```

As in the case of time, relative (topological) space specifications will predominate in texts.

6.4.9. Slot operators

```
quantifier1 :: = all | any | most | many | some | few | 1 | 2 | ...
quantifier2 :: = hardly | half | almost | completely
```

6.4.10. Modality

```
modality    :: = ('modality' modality-set)
modality-set :: = real | desirable | undesirable | conditional | possible |
                  impossible | necessary
```

6.4.11. Focus

```
focus :: = ('given'
             ('object' obj) |
             ('event' event) |
             ('clause' clause) |
             ('quantifier' event-quantifier | quantifier))
           ('new'
             ('object' obj) |
             ('event' event) |
             ('clause' clause) |
             ('quantifier' event-quantifier | quantifier))
```

The thematic information, together with the discourse structure and speech act information, explicitly represents the rhetorical force of SL texts. It is the lack of this type of knowledge in most IL-oriented systems that led many MT researchers to declare that SL traces are necessary in the internal representation. Table 1 illustrates the influence of the focus information on distinguishing between sentences (all of them paraphrases of the sample sentence (6), see below) that have the same propositional content and would have to be judged indistinguishable by an analysis system that did not tackle rhetorical meaning.

Entity in Focus	Form of Input Sentence
Object: 'Database'	Data such as the above, that is stored more or less permanently in a computer, we term a DATABASE
Object: 'Data'	What is stored more or less permanently in a computer and what we term a database is DATA; for an example of such data see above
Clause: '[data that is] stored more or less permanently in a computer'	Data, such as the above, which we term a database, is stored more or less permanently in a computer
Clause: '[data is] such as the above'	It is data such as the above, stored more or less permanently in a computer, that we term a database

Table 1. An illustration of focus distinctions.

6.4.12. Discourse structure

```
discourse-structure :: = (discourse-structure-type
                          (clause1 clause-n | sentence | text) |
                          (clause-n | sentence | text clause1)* )

discourse-structure-type :: = none | temp | equiv | + expan | -expan |
                              condi | + simil | -simil | choice
```

For a more detailed description of the discourse cohesion markers in TRANSLATOR see Tucker et al., 1986.

A clause may be connected discourse-wise not only with another clause but also with a sentence, a paragraph or even a whole text; also note that discourse structure assigns the given clause as one of the two arguments in the discourse structure; one clause can be an argument in more than one discourse-structure expression.

6.4.13. Speech act

```
speech-act :: = ('speech-act'
                ('type' speech-process)
                ('direct?' yes | no)
                ('speaker' object)
                ('hearer' object+ )
                ('time' time)
                ('space' space))
```

Every IL sentence features a speech act, irrespective of whether it was overtly mentioned in the SL text. If it was, it is represented through a token of a speech process. Otherwise, it is inferred. The time and space of the speech act can be quite different from that of the proposition which is the information transferred through this speech act.

6.4.14. Other slots and slot fillers

```
negation    :: = boolean-set
referent-set :: = above | below | object-token
manner-set  :: = difficulty | attitude
difficulty  :: = easily | ... | difficultly
attitude    :: = caring | ... | nonchalantly
phase-set   :: = static | beginning | end
```

6.5. Knowledge about SL

A word in the SL text potentially contains clues for a number of types of meaning: syntactic, semantic or pragmatic. The analysis modules require a number of dictionaries for operation. One of them is syntactic and contains information necessary for the syntactic parsing modules to operate. Another is semantico-pragmatic and contains information to be used by the semantic, discourse, anaphora and speech act parsers. Table 2 illustrates what IL categories correspond to sample categories of English grammar.

SL (English) Category	IL Representation
NOUN	object frame
ADJECTIVE	slot in object frame; state frame
VERB	action or state frame
MODAL	modality marker in clause and sentence frames
ADVERB	slot in action or state frame (time, space, ...); state marker ('he moved nonchalantly'): may introduce a separate clause frame
DETERMINER	marker in given/new; directs generation of new instances of objects vs. reference to existing instances
CONJUNCTION	marker of sentence type; marker of cohesion
PREPOSITION	case marker; state marker: may introduce a separate clause frame
DEMONSTRATIVE	marker of deixis
NUMERAL	a quantifier operator on IL NPs
PRONOUN	marker of deixis; reference to object

SL (English) Category	IL Representation
NP	marks boundaries of case slot values
VP	helps mark boundaries
PP	helps mark boundaries
CLAUSE	fills clause frame
S	fills sentence frame
PARENTHETICALS	discourse markers; connector clues for sentences

Table 2. Selected categories of English with their IL counterparts.

A number of analysis modules will be employed by TRANSLATOR for extracting the above meanings from SL texts. We will not discuss them in any detail in this chapter, but will assume their existence in order to perform a manual trace of TRANSLATOR's analysis.

6.6. A sample analysis

Given the IL dictionary and grammar, we can now sketch the process of using these knowledge structures for analyzing an SL text. The system makes use of a number of analysis knowledge sources, as shown in Table 3. The emphasis in the discussion that follows is not on a particular control structure for analysis, but rather on the identity of the sources of knowledge that are used to derive IL representations (texts). Therefore, the central point is the expressive power of the interlingua.

KS name	input	output	background knowledge
morphological analyzer	SL word token	SL word type + form specification	SL form formation paradigms + exception lists
syntactic constituent detector	SL sentence	boundaries of constituents in SL sentence	SL grammar and syntactic dictionary
dependency structure detector	SL sentence	syntactic dependency structure of SL sentence	SL grammar and syntactic dictionary
functional structure detector	SL sentence	functional structure of SL sentence	SL grammar and syntactic dictionary
event detector	SL sentence	IL frame token	SL-IL dictionary + results of syntactic analysis + IL dictionary

KS name	input	output	background knowledge
case detector	SL sentence	IL frame token	SL-IL dictionary + results of syntactic analysis + IL dictionary
time detector	SL sentence + event token	filler for the time slot of event token	SL-IL dictionary + IL dictionary + IL grammar
space detector	SL sentence + event token	filler for the space slot of event token	SL-IL dictionary + IL dictionary + IL grammar
clause builder	event token	clause token	IL grammar
modality detector	SL sentence + clause token	filler for the modality slot of clause token	SL-IL dictionary + results of syntactic analysis + IL dictionary + IL grammar
focus detector	SL sentence + clause token	filler for the slots in the focus subframe of clause token	SL-IL dictionary + results of syntactic analysis + IL dictionary + IL grammar
discourse detector	SL sentence + clause token	filler for the discourse slot of clause token	SL-IL dictionary + results of syntactic analysis + IL dictionary + IL grammar + IL representations of previously translated sentences
sentence builder	a set of clause tokens	sentence token	IL grammar
speech act detector	SL sentence + clause tokens + sentence token	fillers for the subslots of the speech-act slot of a sentence token	IL grammar + IL representations of previously translated sentences
subworld detector	SL sentence + clause tokens + sentence token	filler for subworld slot of a sentence token	IL grammar + IL representations of previously translated sentences
ellipsis augmentor	SL sentence + clause tokens + sentence token + world knowledge base	inferred fillers for various clause, object or event slots reference to which was omitted in SL text	IL grammar + IL representations of previously translated sentences

KS name	input	output	background knowledge
anaphora resolver	SL sentence + clause tokens + sentence token + world knowledge base	inferred fillers for various clause, object or event slots reference to which was indirect in SL text	IL grammar + IL representations of previously translated sentences
augmentor	IL text with some frame slots unfilled	IL text with fewer slots unfilled	world knowledge base + IL grammar

Table 3. Analysis knowledge sources in TRANSLATOR

The background knowledge for the analyzer includes 1) the IL dictionary; 2) the IL grammar; 3) the SL-IL dictionary and 4) the SL grammar.

The input to the analysis is an SL text; its output is an IL text. The aim of the processing is to make the IL text 'mean' the same as the SL text.

Consider the example sentence (6). We assume that this sentence is the first input to the system in a translation session.

(6)   Data, such as the above, that is stored more-or-less permanently in a computer, we term a database.

The system starts by evoking a *morphological analyzer* for SL and a *dictionary look-up* knowledge source which is responsible for retrieving the entries for all the words in the input text. Only a fraction of the SL words in (6) will cause the instantiation of new tokens of IL concepts.

The *syntactic constituent* detector knowledge source determines boundaries of syntactic constituents in (6). Another knowledge source is entrusted with augmenting the representation by eliminating *elliptical phenomena*, so that the clauses acquire the fullest possible complement of arguments. A special knowledge source deals with the *anaphoric reference*, as, for instance, seen in the first of the relative clauses of (6). Thus, the three clauses are identified (cf. (7)).[3]

(7)   Data is such as the above.
         Data is stored more or less permanently in a computer.
         Data is a database.

Additional knowledge sources come into play at this point, in order to perform the following tasks:

●   extract the event names from the SL text and, for each event
●   translate it into IL
●   augment the representation by inserting the IL translations of the event actants and other relevant property slots (thus bringing it up to the IL clause level)

---

[3] The clauses are listed in their 'reconstructed' form, for simplicity.

- embellish the representation by specifying the modality, focus, IL sentence-level discourse structure and speech act information (thus reaching the IL sentence level of representation) and, finally,
- connect this representation through IL text-level discourse connectors (thus reaching the level of IL text).

The three events present in (7) are identified by the event-detector knowledge source, as the following state tokens.

```
(state1
    (is-token-of be-example-of)
    (phase ?)
    (patient ?)
    (counterpatient ?)
    (time ?)
    (space ?)
    (subworld ?))

(state2
    (is-token-of be-in)
    (phase ?)
    (patient ?)
    (counterpatient ?)
    (time ?)
    (space ?)
    (subworld ?))

(state3
    (is-token-of be-defined-as)
    (phase ?)
    (patient ?)
    (counterpatient ?)
    (time ?)
    (space ?)
    (subworld computer-world))
```

Independently of the event detector operation, the case detector knowledge source produces object tokens for all the candidates present in the input. Three objects are involved in sentence (6). These objects are: *data, computer* and *database*. The representations for the corresponding tokens are as follows. Note the difference in the information contained in the object type frame in DRL and the following GRL frames. No default values for DRL object slots are overruled in these particular tokens.

```
(object1
    (is-token-of data)
    (subworld computer-world)
    (negation nil)
    (quantifier nil)
    (properties none))

(object2
    (is-token-of computer)
    (subworld computer-world)
    (negation nil)
    (quantifier any)
    (properties none))

(object3
    (is-token-of database)
    (subworld computer-world)
    (negation nil)
```

```
(quantifier any)
(properties none))
```

The specialized knowledge sources dealing with additional clause properties (subworld, phase, time and space in our example) produce the necessary fillers for their slots. After the event representations are augmented by
the translations of their actants and additional properties they look as follows.

```
(state1
      (is-token-of  be-example-of)
      (phase static)
      (patient object1)
      (counterpatient (referent above))
      (time always)
      (space none)
      (subworld computer-world))
(state2
      (is-token-of  be-in)
      (phase beginning)
      (patient object1)
      (counterpatient (computer any))
      (time always)
      (space none)
      (subworld computer-world))
(state3
      (is-token-of  be-defined-as)
      (phase beginning)
      (patient object1)
      (counterpatient (object3 any))
      (time always)
      (space none)
      (subworld computer-world))
```

Note that since this is the first sentence in a text, there is no hope of restoring the referent of the counterpatient slot in the token of 'be-example-of.'
Once the events are analyzed, TRANSLATOR proceeds to assemble the
clause representations. The knowledge sources active at this stage are the
focus, modality and discourse structure detectors. The time and space
values are inherited from the representation of the corresponding event.
The three clauses are represented as follows.

```
(clause1
      (discourse-structure ( + expan clause1 clause3))
      (event state1)
      (focus state1.counterpatient)
      (modality real)
      (subworld computer-world)
      (time always)
      (space none))

(clause2
      (discourse-structure ( + expan clause2 clause3))
      (event state2)
      (focus time)
      (modality conditional)
      (subworld computer-world)
      (time always)
      (space (in object1 object2)))
```

```
(clause3
    (discourse-structure none)
    (event state3)
    (focus object3)
    (modality real)
    (subworld computer-world)
    (time always)
    (space none))
```

When the IL clauses are ready, the IL sentence knowledge sources can finish their activity. A number of slot fillers propagate to the level of the sentence from the clause level. The main clause detector and the speech act detector are the typical knowledge sources at the sentence level. Also note that the focus information at the sentence level is not necessarily inherited from the clause level. The sentence token produced by the TRANSLATOR analyzer for (6) is as follows.

```
(sentence1
    (main-clause clause3)
    (clauses clause1 clause2)
    (subworld computer-world)
    (modality real)
    (focus object3)
    (speech-act (type definition)
        (direct? no)
        (speaker author)
        (hearer reader)))
```

The text frame is at this point trivial: the text is just one sentence long so far. Therefore, there are no discourse markers to be detected by the main text level knowledge source: the text discourse marker detector.

The sentence (6) has been represented in IL as a network of frames. The process will be repeated for all the rest of the sentences in an input text.[4] Then the IL text will be given as input to the generator group of knowledge sources. The design of the generator will be reported elsewhere. Suffice it to say now that for the above IL representation of (6) we will allow a number of possible TL translations that we will consider equally acceptable. For English as TL consider the translations (8) in addition to the original SL sentence (6). All of these are, naturally, acceptable paraphrases.

(8) (a) Data of the type described above is called a database if it is stored for significant periods of time inside a computer.

(b) Such data, stored in a computer for a long time, is a database.

(c) A database is defined as data, similar to the above, stored relatively permanently in a computer.

(d) Databases are collections of such data stored for long periods of time in computer memory.

---

[4] Or a section of the input text, when it is too extensive. The questions of engineering-oriented appropriateness, such as deciding where to put the cutoff point for accumulating analyzed text before going to the generator module, are postponed till implementation time.

(e)   We define a database as data of the kind illustrated above, stored inside a computer.

Many more variants are possible.

6.7. Conclusion

IL-based MT projects seem to be the most scientifically challenging in the family of approaches to MT. They aim at fully automatic translation, and therefore do not promise immediate feasibility. We would like to conclude this chapter by presenting a number of critical opinions about IL-based projects, with our comments.

Opinion. It is unnecessary to extract the full meaning from the SL text in order to achieve adequate MT.

Comment. With a large portion of input sentences, especially in carefully selected subworlds, an MT system can do without an involved semantic analysis. Many sentences, however, will involve at least the ambiguities for word choice in synthesis, and this will necessitate either semantic analysis or post-editing. Machines, unlike humans, cannot on demand produce interpretations of an input text at an arbitrary depth exactly sufficient for understanding. Therefore, if one aims at fully automatic translation, one has to design the system so that it performs semantic analysis to the maximum necessary depth for all sentences involved. One can, of course, think of designing a system that can decide how deeply each sentence can be analyzed semantically in an attempt to minimize semantic analysis. We maintain that the decision making involved in such an enterprise is as complex as the initial problem of uniformly deep semantic analysis.

Opinion. It is not necessary to finish processing the input sentence before starting the translation. Indeed, people very often do this (consider interpreters) with very good results.

Comment. This opinion is based on introspection. The real thought processes that go on in the heads of translators and interpreters have not been studied scientifically. It seems highly probable that this behavior is knowledge-based. Also, the decision to start translating before finishing the processing of input is a function of the translator's belief about the cost of a possible error. Indeed, the more 'important' the translation is, the more one would be disinclined to indulge in this type of activity.

What makes such preemptive moves possible is the translators' extensive knowledge about the subject matter of the text (speech), about the speech situation as well as their expert knowledge about the process of translation in general. A subproject of TRANSLATOR is devoted to building an expert system that embodies the knowledge about translators' craft, to be used as the main troubleshooter of the system.

Opinion. Approaches to MT based on AI (such as the interlingua-based approach described here) do not pay sufficient attention to the syntactic analysis of SL, while syntactic information is important for MT. Instead of translating one ends up with paraphrasing. The structure of the SL text, when used in addition to IL in MT, governs the choice of one of the paraphrases. Therefore, one needs to retain information about SL till the stage of TL synthesis.

Comment. Syntactic structure of texts in SL conveys meaning. This meaning is extracted by the analyzer in a knowledge-based system, with the help of knowledge about the syntax of SL. This is done, commensurately with the general scope of the effort, in all knowledge-based MT systems. The difference is that no results of syntactic analysis are stored by most of such systems (cf., however, Lytinen, 1984). This decision stems from the conviction that the syntactic structures of SL do not need to play a role in determining the syntactic structures to be used in generating a TL text.

If one accepts the premise that it is not reasonable to expect the syntactic structures of an SL sentence and its TL translation to be similar, then attempting to catalog the relations among the various syntactic structure trees in SL and TL seems to be redundant, if possible at all. Instead, one should devise a representation for meanings conveyed by the syntax of SL and then provide (SL-independent) rules for building syntactic structure of TL from this representation. The information about the thematic structure of SL text and its discourse parameters are good examples of what can be expressed by syntax in SL.

If we assume that the common (invariant) core of a set of paraphrases is their Θ-structure (set of conceptual case slots with values filled), together with such verbal properties as tense, aspect and modality, then, indeed, the current experimental knowledge-based MT systems are producing a sentence which is a(n unmarked) paraphrase of an SL sentence. If, however, one extracts from the SL text the information about speech acts, discourse and topic/focus, one obtains additional constraints that help distinguish between the paraphrases and choose the most appropriate one. We claim that the above constraints have at least the same power as the systems in which meanings in SL and TL are put in correspondence through extensive enumeration (in the bilingual dictionaries) of possible combinations, augmented by syntactic information. In other words, a system like TRANSLATOR does not produce paraphrases any more than a transfer system that uses the syntax of SL in translation proper.

Opinion. IL-based approaches lead to an overkill because no peculiarities of SL (and of the relationship between, or contrastive knowledge of, SL and TL) can be used in translation. Some languages have quite a lot in common in their syntax and meaning distribution. It is wasteful not to use this additional information in translation.

Comment. While such insights can sometimes be detected and used, most of them come from human intuition, and cannot be taken advantage of in MT systems, which are not typically built as models of human performance. We also believe that it is wrong to imply that discovery, representation and manipulation of these pieces of contrastive knowledge can be simpler or, in fact, distinct from involved semantic analysis.

Opinion. Interlingua reflects the semantics of just one language, English. It will not be automatically extensible to describe the semantics of other languages, because they have different perceptions of the world.

Comment. Indeed, the interlingua dictionary will be updated and revised even during the exploitation phase of a knowledge-based machine translation system. It would be nice to be able to come up with a language of atomic units of sense, à la Hjelsmlev's *semes*, but we cannot hope to. Therefore, IL will at any given moment provide a semantic analysis of limited grain size.

Opinion. Generation of TL is a relatively simple problem for which very little or no knowledge other than lexical or syntactic is needed.

Comment. Generation requires non-trivial decision making, for instance, in the light of the discussion in the previous paragraph, or, for that matter, as regards the computational stylistics, which will have to be a part of the choice-making mechanisms in building TL texts.

Acknowledgement

The authors wish to thank Irene Nirenburg for reading, discussing and criticizing the numerous successive versions of the manuscript. Needless to say, it's we who are to blame for the remaining errors. This chapter is based upon work supported by the National Science Foundation under Grant DCR-8407114.

7   Basic theory and methodology in EUROTRA

DOUG ARNOLD and LOUIS des TOMBE

7.1. Introduction

The aim of this chapter is to describe some aspects of the methodology and theoretical basics of the approach to Machine Translation (MT) taken in the EUROTRA project. At the heart of the chapter is a description of the so called <C,A>,T framework, which embodies a number of ideas about the nature of translation in a special purpose notation, describing in effect the syntax and semantics of a family of abstract 'translation machines.' The background to this is the attempt to develop a general framework for research and development work in MT. In particular, we hope this framework provides an environment which facilitates thinking about the relationships between representations that are necessary for automatic translation between natural languages.[1]

The chapter is in five sections. The introduction gives some background about the project; section 7.2 introduces the basic methodological position taken within this framework, and gives an informal introduction to main theoretical issues. Section 7.3 gives a rather more precise and formal account of these ideas, and section 7.4 gives some exemplification of how they can be applied in practice. The final section notes some of the limitations of the approach, and the direction of some of the work in progress. The chapter reports work in progress, and is thus somewhat programmatic and speculative: the ideas presented are generally in the form of hypotheses rather than conclusions or practical results. This is not particularly satis-

---

[1] The ideas in this chapter are a development of those set out in the papers presented at the 1985 Colgate Conference on MT: Arnold et al. (1985), and des Tombe et al. (1985). Developing the theory and methodology described here has been the work of a large number of people in the project, and the ideas described here are certainly not the intellectual property of the present authors alone. Our colleagues in the EUROTRA Central Team, the other authors of the papers just mentioned, and the various authors of the EUROTRA Reference Manual (Krauwer, 1986) have particular claims in this respect. The last mentioned document contains a fuller and more formal presentation of these ideas, including details of many matters not discussed here (e.g., description of the implementation and 'friendlier' versions of the notation). Further background discussion about EUROTRA, and an idea of the evolution of the ideas presented here can be found in Johnson et al., 1984, 1985; Arnold et al., 1985, 1986; Cecchi et al., 1985.

factory, but we hope it is appropriate in a volume on methodology and theory.

The following may be useful background to begin with. EUROTRA is a research and development project of the European Economic Community (EEC), with two basic aims:[2]

(i)   construction of a pre-industrial prototype MT system for the official EEC languages;
(ii)   development of expertise in MT and related areas in the Community.

The prototype system is intended to be multilingual (capable of handling the official EEC languages: originally Danish, Dutch, English, French, German, Greek, and Italian; the precise implications for the project of the addition of Spanish and Portuguese are not yet clear). It is to provide reasonable-to-good quality translations without significant human involvement, for texts from limited subject domain (information technology) and text type (official community documents such as EEC Council decisions). An indication of the overall size of the prototype is given by dictionary size (ultimately 20,000 items for each language). The system is to be easily extensible and repairable, and to be reasonably robust in operation. Since the system is only 'pre-industrial' the emphasis is to be on quality of output, and extensibility rather than on speed of performance.

These aims are extremely ambitious, both from the point of view of pure development, and in terms of the basic research they presuppose. To date, the intellectual effort of the project has been directed towards basic research developing the methodological and conceptual apparatus required to fulfill the aims.

The second purpose of the project is to promote the development and spread of expertise in MT and related fields through the Community. Consistent with this, and for a number of quite practical reasons, the project is highly *decentralized* organizationally: the basic theory and implementation is provided centrally, but the bulk of the linguistic work (both research and development) is done by 'language groups,' each responsible for work relating to one language, and consisting of about 10 people. This, combined with the sheer size of the project (in excess of a hundred researchers in 16 different locations: several of the language groups are themselves decentralized) naturally leads to practical and organizational problems, but it has some interest from a methodological point of view. First, it places an emphasis on the need to develop a common framework of clear, general and

---

[2] These aims are defined in the EEC Council Decision setting up the project. They have been described and discussed elsewhere, e.g., King & Perschke, 1982. For discussion of organizational aspects of the project see EUROTRA report ETL-6 (King, 1985).

rather strong theoretical and methodological principles. Second, it motivates a model that minimizes communication amongst languages, and generally places a stress on modularity of design. The methodological interest of this decentralized organization is that the requirements it imposes seem to be those appropriate for practical MT generally.

7.2. Methodology and basic ideas

From the perspective of a project like EUROTRA, MT is fundamentally an engineering enterprise, i.e., an enterprise oriented towards solving some practical problem. In the case of MT this practical problem is normally to do with constructing programs which describe the translation relation for some language pairs. Despite this description, however, the problem is not simply one of programming. The problem is sufficiently difficult, so that finding reasonably adequate solutions requires descriptive apparatus which is genuinely *problem-oriented* and *appropriate* for the task — properties which conventional (general purpose) programming languages clearly lack. The apparatus required is a notation (or set of notations) which is appropriate for describing the 'translation relation,' with an interpreter which will execute programs written in the notation. Essentially, the syntax and semantics of this notation define a family of abstract 'translation machines' which are in some way oriented towards the problem of MT. Since no such apparatus exists, it must be developed, and given this current state of knowledge about the problem itself, the practical MT problem develops into a fundamentally theoretical and methodological problem.

As regards the methodology, ideas like appropriateness and problem orientation presuppose an analysis of the problem, i.e., theoretical commitment supported by experimentation. Experimentation, in its turn, is productive only in proportion to the generality, strength and clarity of the hypotheses tested. For these reasons, we take such properties, which are required in the special EUROTRA context for quite practical reasons, to be requirements in practical MT generally.

These requirements are just the properties normally required of scientific theories, of course. There are some differences, however. For example, given its practical orientation, there is often room for considerations of practicality and feasibility in MT, which might be out of place in a purely scientific enterprise. Likewise, whatever kind of strength may be appropriate to theories in pure science, it seems clear that for purposes like MT it should not be a kind that yields only monolithic 'package deal' theories. To begin with, one would like one's theory to be such that it is possible to entertain and compare some alternative proposals within it: in this way it will be possible to improve the theory, by comparing alternatives, and selecting the one that appears better on the basis of experimentation. One would also like the theory to have some internal structure, to be modular, and 'parameterized' in some way so that, for instance, it could be possible to modify the theory in a controlled way when it turns out to be inadequate. There is clearly some tension, but not necessarily a contradiction, between this and the need for theoretical strength. What it means is that the strength will come from the theory allowing a number of classes of alternative hypotheses, together with some evaluation of them, rather than allowing a single class to the exclusion of all others.

The most obvious aspect of the theoretical commitment required in MT relates to the nature of the translation relation itself. Here we make two basic assumptions. The first is that it is not feasible to devise a notation for relating texts directly, and that consequently some decomposition of the translation relation, into a sequence of relations between representation languages (and representation languages and texts), is appropriate. The second is that the translation relation is fundamentally and irreducibly a relation between *linguistic* objects. The representation languages must be linguistic in nature, and cannot therefore be completely neutral with respect to different natural languages, in the way that a genuine interlingua would be. Consequently, the claim is that quite apart from being the only practically feasible architecture, a transfer architecture is also the *appropriate* architecture for MT systems.

The following diagram provides a useful reference point for discussing transfer based MT systems:

(1)

$$
\begin{array}{ccc}
\text{AN} & \text{TRF} & \text{GEN} \\
\end{array}
$$

$$
\text{TL}_S \text{------------} \text{RL}_S \text{------------} \text{RL}_T \text{------------} \text{TL}_T
$$

where TL$_S$ and TL$_T$ are (source and target) text languages (i.e., ordinary natural languages such as French, Greek, Danish, etc.), and RL$_S$ and RL$_T$ are representation languages, or *levels*, and AN, TRF, and GEN are the relations (analysis, transfer and synthesis) between them.

As regards the representation languages RL$_S$ and RL$_T$, three properties seem important. The first is the obvious property implied by the general idea of problem orientation: the representation languages should make the description of the translation relation easier. It should be easier to describe the sequential composition of the relations AN, TRF and GEN, than it is to describe the translation relation directly in terms of texts. The second is equally obvious: the representation languages must provide an appropriate degree of 'resolution' (so that at least non-translationally equivalent texts are 'differentiated' — paired with distinct representations; the representation languages should express whatever the properties are that are preserved by valid translation).

The third property involves the 'learnability' or 'specificity' of the representation languages. By this we mean that the theory of representation must be such that given some text t, it is possible for a linguist to decide on the representation(s) of t that the theory provides, and it must be possible for different linguists to converge on the same representation(s) for t. The theoretical basis of the representation languages should be such that their intuitive semantics, and their relation to text languages, are accessible to the linguists who must describe the various relations. This requirement emphasizes the need for representation languages that are theoretically coherent, and 'natural' in some way.

A straightforward way of achieving this is to impose a 'constructivism' requirement on the system as a whole.[3] We require each RL_i to be explicitly defined by means of a generative device G_i which recursively enumerates the expressions in RL_i. The picture of translation now becomes (2), where a 'vertical' relation between Gs and representation languages has been added to normal horizontal translation relations. We will return to the ways this extra dimension can be exploited below.

(2)

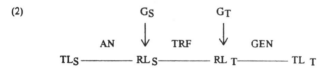

Turning now to the relations AN, TRF, and GEN, adopting a transfer design replaces the problem of translating text languages with the problem of translating between texts and representation languages of some kind.

The notation should be such that the relations (AN, TRF, and GEN) should be in some sense 'simple to describe.' This need is particularly pressing in the case of TRF in the context of multilingual MT systems, given the number of transfer components (n languages gives on the order of n^2 transfer components), and the special knowledge and ability needed for their construction (knowledge of two text languages plus two representation languages and their interrelations). But the requirement holds generally. For TRF, simplicity of description is a matter of choosing appropriate representation languages, minimizing the difference between RL_S and RL_T for any text. For AN and GEN, the difficulty of providing a simple description in any notation motivates a further decomposition, introducing further levels of representation inside these relations, yielding a 'stratificational' model.

---

[3] A limited form of this sort of requirement was described in Krauwer & des Tombe, 1984, where it was called the principle of 'isoduidy.'

Thus, the overall translation is decomposed into a sequence of primitive translations giving a picture such as (3), where each R_i is a representation language and each '$\rightarrow$' is a 'translator,' one of which is TRF.

(3)

$$
\begin{array}{ccccccc}
G_1 & G_2 & & G_{n-1} & G_n & \\
\downarrow & \downarrow & & \downarrow & \downarrow & \\
TL_S \longrightarrow RL_1 \longrightarrow RL_2 \longrightarrow & \cdots \longrightarrow & RL_{n-1} \longrightarrow & RL_n \longrightarrow & TL_T
\end{array}
$$

In keeping with the aim of simplicity of description, we impose two conditions on all primitive translations. They must be (i) 'compositional,' and (ii) 'one-shot.'

When applied to translation, the idea of compositionality is the intuitively natural one that the translations of expressions are normally related to the translations of their parts in a systematic way. The condition we impose is that the rules that make up a translator must operate in such a way that the translation of an expression E at some level is some (reasonably straightforward) function of the translation of (i) the parts of E, and (ii) the way these parts are combined in E. We will discuss some of the ways this can be made precise in the following sections. For the moment, it is enough to notice that some restrictions on the complexity of this function are necessary if the idea is to have any content beyond just imposing some systematicity. For this reason, we also impose the 'one-shot' requirement.

The idea of the 'one-shot' requirement is that a primitive translation should always yield a well-formed target language expression 'in one step,' without resort to further intermediate representations. The translator from R_i to R_j must be a set of rules such that application of a rule to an expression in R_i yields an expression in R_j. Essentially, this eliminates interactions between the rules that make up a translator, and means that translators cannot have any internal 'strategy.'

The ideas of 'constructivism,' 'compositionality,' and 'one-shotness' are closely related. For example adopting the 'constructivist requirement' means that it is always possible to give a precise sense to these conditions. The way the parts of an expression are combined is always explicitly defined by some G_i, which also gives a precise sense to the notion 'well formed expression of a representation language.' On the other hand, the one-shot principle serves to guarantee the constructivist requirement, by ensuring no 'illicit' intermediate representations are introduced.

More precise formulations of these idea will be given in the next section, where we will also discuss their implications.

7.3. The <C,A>,T notation

In the previous section, we outlined a methodology for MT, and introduced three basic ideas: the ideas of 'constructivism,' 'compositionality,' and 'one-shotness.' The purpose of this and the following section is to exemplify the methodology, and make these basic ideas more precise and concrete by describing a family of abstract 'translation machines' which embody these ideas. This family of machines is defined by the syntax and semantics of the so-called <C,A>,T notation. This notation has two components, which are the subjects of sections 7.3.1. and 7.3.2. respectively:

(i)   A set of 'generative devices,' or Gs, each of which is a pair <C,A> — a set of 'constructors' and a set of 'atoms.' These provide the independent definitions of the representation languages, satisfying the constructivism requirement.

(ii)   A set of translators, or Ts, which satisfy the compositionality and one-shot requirements.

7.3.1. Generative devices: Gs

A central idea of this approach is the 'constructivist principle' that each representation language R should be explicitly defined by means of some generative device G.

We take each representation language to be a set of expressions (or 'objects'), and a generative device G to be a pair, <C,A>, where A is a finite set of *atoms*, the basic expressions or objects of the language generated by G, and C is a finite set of *constructors*, or rules, which will take a number of expressions as arguments, and return a new expression. Each constructor in G is associated with a specific arity, identifying the number of expressions it takes as arguments; atoms can be thought of as just a special class of constructors with arity zero.

Given this, we can define for each G the language of *derivation trees* D(G) which it generates. For this we assume the simplest possible syntax:

(i)   every atom a in A is a member of D(G); and
(ii)   if c is a constructor in C with arity n, and u1....un are in D(G) then <c, u1, ..., un> is in D(G).

Intuitively, a derivation tree is a tree where each terminal node is an atom, and each non-terminal node is labeled with a constructor, and has a number of other derivation trees (or atoms) as daughters. For example, if c1 and c2 are constructors of arity 2, and a1, a2, and a3 are atoms, then the derivations tree (4)

(4)   <c1, a1, <c2, a2, a3>>

can be represented graphically as (5):

(5)

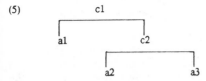

Syntactically, atoms are of the form:

atom ::= (<Cname>, <name>, <fd>)

where <Cname> is the unique name of the atom, <name> is the value of the privileged or distinguished feature for the relevant G, and <fd> represents the rest of the atom's feature description. We use '_' for the anonymous variable:

    <Cname> ::= <constructor name> | _
    <name> ::= <value> | _
    <fd> ::= { <feature>*}
    <feature> ::= <attribute> = <value>

For example, the following might be atoms corresponding to the definite article and the noun *bicycle* for a constituent structure representation language, where the 'leading idea' is that of syntactic category.

(6)   (the, det, {definiteness = plus})
         (bicycle, noun, {number = sing})

Constructors are of the following form:

    <constructor> ::= (<Cname>, <name>, <fd>) [<argspec>*]
    <argspec> ::= (<Cname>, <name>, <fd>) | <constructor>

where <Cname> is a unique identifier; <name>, and <fd> describe the type of construction that the constructor is to build, and the argspecs describe the type of arguments it is intended to take; the number of argspecs must equal the arity of the constructor. For example:

(7)   (cnp, np, { person=3 }) [(_, det, {}),
                                   (_, noun, {})]

might be a constructor for constructing simple NPs for a constituent structure language, assuming (wrongly) that all determiner noun NPs are third person. The following is an example of a derivation tree:

(8)   < (cnp, np, { person=3 }) [(_, det, {}),
                                      (_, noun, {})],
           (the, det, { definiteness= plus }),
           (bicycle, noun, { number= sing }),   >

However, since their Cname uniquely identifies atoms and constructors, the following is an acceptable shorthand:

(9)   <cnp, the, bicycle>

The evaluation of a derivation tree to a representation proceeds as follows:

(i)   An atom in a derivation tree evaluates to a copy of itself. (Note that while this copy is apparently identical to the derivation tree atom, it belongs to another set: an atom in a derivation tree is in $D(G)$, the set of derivations; the result of evaluating it is in $R(G)$, the set of representations.)

(ii)   For non-atomic derivation trees the essential idea is that what the evaluation produces is the result of *unifying* the constructor with its arguments. More precisely, the general form of a derivation tree is: $<c, u1,..., un>$. Call the list of $u1,..., un$ the *argument list.* Evaluation involves applying the constructor c to the result of evaluating each argument i in the argument list (i.e., constructors apply to representations (members of $R(G)$)). Application of c to its argument list requires the number of argspecs of the constructor to equal the number of arguments in the argument list. If each u_i in the argument list unifies with the corresponding argspec$_i$ in the constructor, then the result is the object created by making a copy of c, and substituting for each argspec$_i$ the unification of argspec$_i$ with the corresponding member of the argument list. Otherwise, the evaluation yields nothing.

For example, evaluation of the derivation tree (8) and (9) will yield the representation (10):

(10)   (cnp, np, { number=sing })
        [(the, det, { definiteness=plus })
            (bicycle, noun, {number=sing})   ]

The result of evaluating the derivation tree $<cnp,$ the, the$>$, on the other hand, yields nothing, since the second actual argument in the argument list will not unify with the second argspec of the cnp constructor. Both the $<C,A>$ notation and the representation languages themselves are 'machine languages,' and may not be particularly 'user friendly' from the perspective of normal linguists. For this reason, we allow the possibility of syntactically sugared versions. The sugared version of the basic notation is sometimes called a 'user language,' and the sugared version of the representation language is sometimes called an 'inspection representation' in EUROTRA. The idea is that linguists developing the actual system may prefer to express themselves in the user language, and check the operation of the system by looking at the inspection representation it produces. The general requirement is that such user-directed languages must be very similar (e.g., isomorphic) to the formal 'machine' versions.

7.3.2. Translators: Ts

A translator T is a set of rules, called *t-rules*, which relate expressions of one language to expressions of another language in a way that is: (a) 'one-shot,' and (b) compositional. The basic form of a t-rule is the following:

<t-rule> ::= <lhs > → <rhs >

However, it is not clear what the most appropriate formulation of the ideas of 'one-shotness' and compositionality is, or consequently what precise restrictions should be placed on the form and interpretation of t-rules. Given that each G defines two languages, a language of derivation and a language of representations, t-rules could operate in one of four ways:

(i)   < derivation >   → < derivation >
(ii)   [representation] → [representation]
(iii)   < derivation >   → [representation]
(iv)   [representation] → < derivation >

We expect to experiment with a number of different formulations. Here we will present the main issues that arise, and describe our current hypothesis.

An intuitive and fairly neutral formulation of the idea of compositionality would be the following. Suppose a language consists of a set of basic expressions E, and a set of complex expressions with various properties from a set P, reflecting their internal make-up. Then the relation T between languages L1 and L2 would be compositional when:

(i)   T maps from E1 into E2, (giving the translations of atoms directly); and
(ii)   There is a mapping t from P1 into P2 such that if Exp is an L1 expression [p1: e1,...,en,] then T(Exp) is [t(p1): T(e1),...T(en)]. (i.e., t maps from properties of complex expressions in the source language to corresponding properties in the target language in such a way that if Exp is a source language expression, made up of basic expressions e1,...,en, and p1 describes the properties of Exp as a whole, then the translation of Exp contains the translations of e1,...,en, and has the property that corresponds to p1 according to t).

Typical t-rules might be of the form:

(11)   <(bicycle, _, _) > → <(bicyclette, _, _) >
        <c36, ... > → <c42, ... >

meaning, translate the atom 'bicycle' as the atom 'bicyclette,' and translate any expression Exp built by c36, by applying c42 to the translations of the parts of Exp.

In effect, this approach makes t-rules operate on, and produce, derivation trees. Given that one knows the derivation tree for a representation, then translating the representation involves (a) building, and then (b) evaluating the derivation tree containing the corresponding target language atoms and constructors. This is the formulation assumed and exemplified in Arnold et al. (1985) and des Tombe et al. (1985),[4] and one could picture it as

---

[4] This is also roughly the formulation assumed in the 'Isomorphic Grammar' or the Rosetta

something like (12). Notice that this approach observes the 'one-shot principle' in that the result of successfully applying a t-rule will be an expression of the target derivation language. The role of the representations in this would be to 'filter' some overgeneration that may occur in translation (recall that only a subset of derivations evaluate to representations: the subset which make linguistic sense, according to the feature descriptions in constructors).

(12)

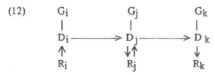

The major drawback of this approach is its inflexibility. One aspect of this is that it makes no allowance for source and target language expressions differing in the number or order of their subexpression. This seems unreasonable: languages typically differ in the order of elements. Thus, going from syntactic to semantic representation languages will involve deleting 'formal' items such as function words. It can be remedied by allowing t-rules of the form:

(13) $<c34, 1, 2, 3> \rightarrow <c42, 2, 1>$

with the meaning: if a source representation Exp is built by applying $c34$ to three arguments, then its translation is the result of applying $c42$ to arguments 2 and 1, in that order. This relaxes the definition of compositionality to allow for deletions, re-orderings, and copyings, in a fairly natural way.

However, the approach is also inflexible in a more radical way. It requires both the translator(s) into a language, and the translator(s) out of a language to use the same description of the language, the same classification of expressions in the language (the one provided by the constructors and atoms in the relevant G). This requirement is extremely strong. A partial solution to this problem was incorporated in Arnold et al. (1985), and des Tombe et al. (1985), in the form of a relaxation of the above formulation of compositionality.

We will now describe this formulation of compositional translation in more detail. A translator is a set of t-rules, each of which consists of a lhs and a rhs. On this view, the lhs of a t-rule describes the kind of representation the rule is to apply to. Its main component is the *pattern*, which is said to *match* any representation of the source language with which it

Project (Landsbergen to appear). To our knowledge, this was the first work in MT to take an explicit compositionality requirement seriously; it has exerted an obvious influence on the approach presented here.

unifies. Since constructors are also partial descriptions of representations, t-rule lhs and constructors are formally very similar (though, of course, the lhs need not be an actual source language constructor). The only difference between lhs and an actual constructor is that the former can mark some of the argspecs with indices, which can then be referenced on the rhs. For this, the syntax is:

<index> : <argspec>

where the index is simply an integer. Intuitively, the purpose of this is to allow t-rules to delete, reorder and duplicate. The rhs of a t-rule is similar to a derivation tree according to the target generator, but with the addition that it can contain indices as well as subexpressions.

For example, suppose there is a level of representation whose leading idea is syntactic dependency, and where expressions like 'the bicycle' are analysed as containing a governing nominal, and a modifying determiner, giving representations like:

(14)   (cnom, _, {cat=np}) [(bicycle, gov, {cat=n})
                                (the, mod, {cat=det})]

(cnom is the constructor which builds such representations; the dependency relation of the expression is anonymous because it cannot be determined for expressions in isolation). Translation from this level to a constituent structure level might involve t-rules such as:

(15)   (_, _, {cat=np})
                [1:(_, gov, {})
                  2:(_, mod, {cat=det})] → <cnp, 2, 1 >

where cnp is roughly as stated in section 7.3.1. This rule will translate nps containing a governor and a modifying determiner (irrespective of which constructor actually built the np). The translation will be found by applying the cnp constructor of the constituent structure level to the translation of the determiner and the governor, in that order.

What happens is this. Given a source representation S, the translator searches for a relevant t-rule (i.e., one whose lhs matches S). If it finds one, the subexpressions S_i ... S_n of S are translated by recursive application of the translator. A copy is made of the rhs side of the t-rule, and each of the S_i which has an index is substituted for the corresponding index in the copy of the rhs. The derivation tree that results is then evaluated in the normal way. Of course, the translator may find no lhs to match a representation, in which case the representation gets no translation; or it may find several, in which case the representation will receive several translations.

7.4. Contents of linguistic representation levels

The purpose of this section is to provide some exemplification of the ideas discussed in the previous sections, and to outline the main ideas behind current linguistic research in EUROTRA. However, the results of this research are not very clear yet, and the example given below will contain some analyses which are obviously wrong, and whose only motivation is to exemplify the basic framework in the simplest way.

7.4.1. Overview

Given the framework outlined above, one can start thinking about representation languages. These must satisfy two essential requirements:

(i)   They must be chosen so that the translator steps are 'simple to describe:' compositional, and 'one-shot,' as discussed above.
(ii)   They must be independently defined, which means that linguists must have some 'feeling' for them, i.e., they must refer to known linguistic concepts.

The practical methodology is that we examine certain 'plausible' ideas about representation in terms of the possibility of translating between them by the mechanisms described above. Here, by 'possible,' we mean something in the way of 'expressible in a natural way,' which is itself a somewhat vague and ill-understood notion. In the case of a negative result, there are two options:

(i)   modify the representation theory in some way, e.g., by adding extra levels of representation in order to reduce the differences between adjacent representations;
(ii)   modify the translation mechanism (the notation), so that it becomes strong enough to handle the differences between levels.

At the moment, experimentation is still in its early stages. Thus the representational theories are still not very well worked out or motivated in terms of translation, and it is likely that quite radical changes will occur in the future.

The current 'standard' hypothesis is that there are five representational levels for each language briefly described below (see (16) for a graphical representation).

1. IS: case frame structure..   This is the most abstract representation language: the input to and output from transfer (hence 'IS,' for 'interface structure'). The basic idea is that of semantic dependency. Hence it represents 'semantic' cases ('Θ-roles:' agent, patient, time, place, etc.) and some semantic typing (semantic features: animate, human, abstract, etc). Since it is a dependency structure, every construction contains a lexical 'head.' This is conventionally represented as a member of the construction alongside its dependents (rather than their mother, as in traditional dependency), and is labeled 'gov.'

2. ERS: relational syntax ('E' stands for 'EUROTRA'). ERS represents surface grammatical relations like subject, object, etc, together with some typing to indicate syntactic category. The level is intended to be broadly similar, with respect to its basic ideas, to LFG's f-structure (Bresnan, 1982). For example, constructions at this level are supposed to be complete and coherent (i.e., contain all and only the syntactic dependents of the element that governs the construction — the lexical head). As with IS, the lexical head is represented as a member of the construction alongside its dependents. Both relational syntactic and case frame structures abstract away from the surface order of constituents.

3. ECS: configurational syntactic structure. ECS for a language represents the superficial distributional categories of the language: its surface syntactic constituency structure, with typing to indicate syntactic categories. Various conceptions of this are being compared at the moment, with particular reference to the issue of distributing work between this level and ERS: clearly, given a sufficiently rich configurational structure, along the lines of GPSG (Gazdar et al., 1985), or even a more limited version of X-bar theory, surface syntactic relations can be expressed directly in a configurational representation. However, we will not pursue this issue here, and the version of ECS we assume now is extremely impoverished: encoding little more than basic syntactic categories (np, s, vp, n, number, person, etc.) and surface order and hierarchical structure.

4. EMS: morphological structure. The basic idea of EMS is that of word structure. Words can be represented as built from words and morphemes, and both words and morphemes can be labeled by features. A text is represented as a sequence (concatenation) of labeled word trees and punctuation marks (though there are no serious proposals about the latter in the project). However, the whole idea of 'morphological structure' and the role of morphological analysis in MT is somewhat controversial in the project, and this level may disappear (e.g., by being subsumed under some theory of the lexicon).

5. ENT: normalized text. ENT is a representation of actual text in a normalized form. This level has not received much attention yet, and at the moment, normalized text is equivalent to ASCII file.

Not much EUROTRA research has gone into the parsing steps (normalized text → morphological structure → configurational structure), i.e., from the shallow 'concatenation' levels to the fully structural levels of ECS, ERS, and IS. This is basically because important and relevant work has already been done elsewhere. In any case, the ideas of compositional translation are most clearly applied between representation languages where structure is explicitly represented. This is also the main motivation behind the very impoverished ECS: it was felt to be important to gain experience with translation between structural levels as soon as possible because this is the kind of translation relevant to transfer. For this reason, the examples that follow concentrate on the definition of syntactic and semantic structures and their mutual relationships.

(16)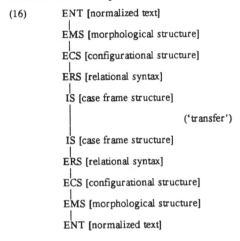

7.4.2. An example

The basic example will be (17), and we will suggest ECS, ERS, and IS representations, and discuss some typical constructors and t-rules.

(17)   The council adopted the proposal.

For the sake of simplicity, we will take atoms at all these levels to be abstractions of words, and ignore all questions of word internal structure. We will assume that some part of the parsing process translates the string of characters (the normalized text of (17)) into a sequence of atoms, performing some morphological analysis. This process might analyze 'the' and 'council' as a single atom (a singular proper noun), assign features such as number, person, and tense to the atom corresponding to 'adopt,' and assign singular number to the atom corresponding to 'proposal.'

Thus, one might get representations as in (18) as the terminal items of ECS representations.

(18)   (adopt, v, {number=sing, person=3, tense=past})
         (the, det, {})
         (proposal, n, {number=sing})

Since ECS is a level of surface constituent structure, it is natural to think of constructors as corresponding to phrase structure rules, and use the 'name' slot of both atoms and constructors to indicate the syntactic category. Thus, the following would be example ECS constructors:

(19)   (Cs, s, {}) [(_, np, {})
                        (_, vp, {})]

(20)   (Cvp, vp, {}) [(_, v, {})
                          (_, np, {})*
                          (_, pp, {})*]

(21)   (Cnp1, np, {person=3})[(_, det, {})
                                 (_, n, {})
                                 (_, pp, {})]

(22)   (Cnp2, np, {} [(_, np, {})]

These are intended to assign np-vp structure to sentences, and to deal with nps with det-n structure, and those containing simply proper nouns. The vp rule and Cnp2 allow unlimited numbers of prepositional phrases under np and vp; the vp rule will overgenerate by allowing unlimited numbers of 'object nps.'

Some of this overgeneration will be filtered by other levels of representation. For example, ECS takes no account of subcategorisation (valency) restrictions, and so will contain representations which violate these restrictions (e.g., it will assign a representation to *The council adopted the proposal the idea*). The idea is that these will be 'filtered' by receiving no representation at ERS where subcategorization facts are taken into consideration. Similarly, overgeneration at ERS caused by ignoring semantic valency will be filtered by IS.

Other kinds of overgeneration at ECS can be reduced by a number of A-type constructors. For example (23) percolates number from n to np; given a similar rule for percolation from v to vp, then (24) will enforce agreement on np and vp (hence on head noun and verb). Of course, it is an open question whether one would like to account for agreement at a level like ECS, or at ERS, or at both.

(23)   (_, np, {person=X, number=Y}) [(_, n, {person=X, number=Y})]

(24)   (_, s, {}) [(_, np, {person=X, number=Y}),
                       (_, vp, {person=X, number=Y})]

These atoms, constructors, and A-type constructors will produce representations like (25):

(25)   (CS, s, {})[
             (Cnp2, np, {number=sing, person=3}) [
                 (the-council, pn, {number=sing, person=3})]
             (Cvp, vp, {number=sing, person=3}) [
                 (adopt, v, {number=sing, person=3, tense=past})
                 (Cnp1, np, {number=sing, person=3}) [
                     (the, det, {})
                     (proposal, n, {number=sing, person=3})]]]

For readability, we can introduce an 'inspection' representation which omits C-names, abbreviates feature descriptions, and represents the hierarchical structure of the representation in normal tree form. Corresponding to (25) might be (26).

(26)

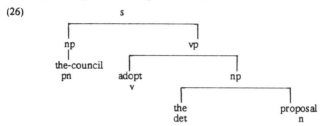

The leading idea at ERS is that of syntactic dependency. Thus, the name slot of atoms and constructors is used to identify the syntactic relation the corresponding representation holds to its governor, and constructors are taken to correspond to characteristic patterns of syntactic dependency — to the syntactic valency frames of governors. For example (27) might be the constructor for sentential constructions with np subject, np object with pp modifiers. Notice that the requirement that each construction have a lexical head means that there is no vp at ERS.

(27)   (Cs7, _, {cat=s}) [
          (_, gov, {syn-frame= 7}),
          (_, subj, {cat=np}),
          (_, obj {cat=np})
          (_, modifier, {cat=pp})*]

(28) might be the constructor for nps containing a governing noun, a determiner and any number of pp modifiers.

(28)   (Cnp2, _ {cat=np}) [
          (_, gov, {cat=n}),
          (_, mod, {cat=det}),
          (_, mod {cat=pp})*]

(We have used the same C-name for the constructor in (28) as for that in (22). This is because each constructor and atom would normally be associated with an indication of the level it relates to, which would make these names unique. For exposition we have omitted this level indication whenever the context makes it obvious.)

Atoms at ERS will be similar to those at ECS, except that (i) instead of filling the name slot (as at ECS), the syntactic category will be part of the feature description; and (ii) where appropriate there will be an indication of the subcategorisation of the atom, in terms of the environment of dependents it expects. This is stated in the feature syn-frame, which relates directly to the particular constructor that builds constructions with this environment of dependents.

Thus, one expects atoms such as:

(29)   (adopt, _, {syn-frame=7})

atom t-rules such as (30) from ECS→ERS, where the rhs uses the short-hand form of the atom in (29):

(30)   (adopt, v, {}) → <adopt>

and type A t-rules such as (31), capturing the invariance of number and person across ECS and ERS, and the fact that the name of representations at ECS is expressed as the value of the feature cat at ERS:

(31)   (_, X, {number=Y, person=Z}) → (_, _, {cat=X, number=Y, person=Z})

For constructors, some ECS→ERS correspondences are straightforward: for common-noun nps the only important change is that required to produce canonical gov-modifier order, (32), which applies the ERS constructor in (28) to the translations of the noun, determiner, and any pps, in that order:

(32)   (_, np, {}) [1: (_, det, {}),
                    2: (_, n, {})
                    3: (_, pp, {})*] → <Cnp2, 2, 1, 3>

Others are slightly more complex. In particular, eliminating the ECS vp requires a set of t-rules translating (non-deterministically) constructions of type s into the various ERS constructors which, like C7 in (27), describe the frames of verbal governors. For example:

(33)   (_, s, {}) [1: (_, np, {})
                    2: (_, vp, {}) [
                    3: (_, v, {})
                    4: (_, np, {})
                    5: (_, pp, {})*]] → < Cs7, 3, 1, 4, 5 >

(This kind of rule will be involved in many of the structural changes that occur because of the simplification and flattening of structure that occurs; items are moved so as to be in the same construction as their syntactic governors, as required by the coherence and completeness conditions on ERS.) (33) will translate representations such as (25) by applying C7 to the translations of the verb *adopt*, the np *the council*, and the np *the proposal* in that order. Notice that an attempt to translate an ECS representation for something like *The council adopted* will fail, since it will produce an ERS derivation tree like (34), which will fail to yield any ERS representation, given the definition Cs7.

(34)   <Cs7, [the-council], [adopted] >

Similarly, attempting to translate the ECS representation for 'The council adopted the decision' (i.e., (17)) by any of the other t-rules translating ECSs constructions will fail, since 'adopt' can only occur in the environment created by Cs7.

This will give ERS representations such as (35), for which (36) might be inspection.

(35)   (Cs, _, {cat=s}) [
    (adopt,gov,{syn-frame=subj-obj,number=sing, person=3, tense=past}),
    (Cnp1, subj, {cat=np}) [(the-council, gov, {cat=pn, number=sing})],
    (Cnp2, obj {cat=np}) [(proposal, gov, {cat=n}), (the, mod, {cat=det})]]

(36)   _, cat=s

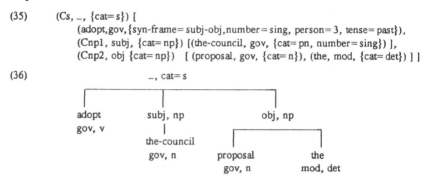

Finally, we will give an example interface structure (IS) representation (37), for which (38) might be inspection:

(37)   (Cage-pat, _, {cat=s})
    [(adopt, gov, {cat=v, case-frame=ag-pat, semfeat={activity} })
    (CF-np0, agent, {cat=np, semfeat={human, abstract})
        [(the-council, gov, {cat=n, semfeat={abstract, human, sing}})]
    (CF-np0, patient, {cat=np, semfeat={abstract, def, sing} })
        [(proposal, gov, {cat=n, semfeat={abstract}})]   ]

(38)   _, s

               adopt,   agent   patient
               gov   np   np
                       the-council   proposal
                          gov   gov

The leading idea of this level is the notion of 'semantic relation,' expressed in the second field of atoms and constructor headings (e.g., gov, agent, patient). Constructors at this level will correspond to the characteristic patterns of semantic relations. This representation contains two such patterns: the 'agent-patient' pattern of the head of the sentence, and the 'np-0' pattern that occurs in the representation of the agent and patient. The major differences between IS and ERS concern the 'geometry,' which is simplified at IS by elimination of 'formal' items (such as the articles, auxiliary verbs, and most prepositions) whose meaning is expressed by features, and the change from a syntactically based labeling to one with an important semantic component. Items at IS are categorized basically according to their syntactic category, but a set valued feature 'semfeat' has been introduced to hold all semantic features. However, the 'semantic' features and relations used in this example are rather arbitrary (and clearly incomplete). It is one of the most important tasks for the project to discover a basic set of such attributes and values that is motivated by translation between the EUROTRA languages.

A typical IS constructor would be (39), assigning agent, patient, and 'circumstantial' roles (the semantic relation for adverbials indicating location, time, etc.) of various kinds (depending, e.g., on their internal make-up, and the preposition their ERS translations contain).

(39)   (Cag-pat, _, {cat=s})
                    [(_, gov, {case-frame= ag-pat}),
                    (_, agent, {semfeat= {human}}),
                    (_, patient, {semfeat= {abstract}}),
                    (_, circumstantial, {})*]

Generalizations about the relationship of syntactic and semantic labeling can be captured by A-type t-rules. For example, suppose that there is some 'semantic' time labeling in the interface structure, including a label like h-a-n (for 'here and now').[5] Then one will find A-type rules such as:

(40)   (_, _, {tense= present}) → (_, _, {time= h-a-n})

This approach makes no essential difference between translations between levels within a language and translations between different ISs (i.e., transfer); though restrictions on the complexity of transfer rules are clearly desirable. Thus, leaving aside the adequacy of the IS representation itself, it should be clear from the preceding discussion how the approach will allow straightforward treatment of many of the contrastive phenomena that have to be treated in transfer. In particular, the approach seems to give elegant solutions to ambiguity in some cases. For example, in transfer between English and German, we can now simply have the rules:

(41)   (know, _, {}) → <wissen>
          (know, _, {}) → <kennen>

Application of the right hand sides yields the full German atoms for *wissen* and *kennen*, and in many cases only one of the two will be subcategorized for the actual German IS environment that results from translating the context of 'know.' (Roughly, *wissen* takes a sentential object, *kennen* takes a nominal object.) Note that if rules like these are a common type of transfer rules, then there could be a more sugared way of writing them;

---

5 For serious discussion of the treatment of time reference in MT, see van Eynde et al., 1985.

sooner or later. We expect to develop a number of 'user languages,' more friendly versions of the formalism we use here, so that the transfer writer might just write, e.g.,:

(42)   know → wissen
        know → kennen

This comes close to the optimal situation in a multilingual transfer-based project, where a leading idea is: keep transfer as simple as possible.

7.5. Work in progress

The purpose of this section is to note some of the outstanding problems with this approach, and indicate the main areas of work in progress. To begin with, however, it is worth summarizing what we take to be the advantages of the approach for practical MT.

The most important of these are methodological: the approach provides a very orderly environment for research and development work, and has a high degree of modularity (given the constructivist approach, at least each representation language is a module), with the usual benefits. It appears restrictive enough to aid experimentation and communication (it is relatively easy to compare representational proposals in terms of the complexity of the translators they require), but it also seems to allow scope for exploring an interesting space of variants, and for 'tuning' in response to improved perceptions of problems. The notation itself seems to provide a level of abstraction at which linguists and implementers can communicate easily about translation (cf. the level provided by conventional programming languages or traditional linguistic notations).

Some of the limitations of the approach are obvious. The notation is a 'machine language,' and though usable it is not especially friendly, and will need to be modified, by the addition of 'user languages' and in more serious ways, as substantive linguistic work motivates improvements to the representational theories.[6] The notation is also basically linguistic and not very natural for representing general 'real-world' knowledge. We think this is appropriate in MT, which is fundamentally about relating *linguistic* objects, but there is an important role for general knowledge in MT, as many examples indicate. Here what we hope to get from the approach is a proper understanding of the linguistic factors involved in translation, providing a basis for investigation of the role of non-linguistic factors.

---

[6] An obvious example of this is the treatment of coordinate constructions, whose properties are partly a function of the features common to all of the conjuncts: getting the correct feature description for a coordinate construction involves *generalization* (roughly self consistent intersection of feature descriptions) rather than unification.

A third obvious limitation is the lack of a principled account of the lexicon. Developmentally, the sheer size of MT lexicons is a problem. A simple view, given this approach, might be to identify the lexicon with the atom sets of all the levels. Clearly, this makes the problem worse, and unnecessarily so, since by and large the atom sets at different levels within a language will be very similar (cases such as function words and idioms where this does not hold are by far a minority). A number of solutions to this problem are being investigated: one approach would be to exploit the device of translator A-rules to capture the similarities by filling out 'schemas' for atoms at different levels. Alternatively, one might think of the monolingual lexicon as a data base, containing all the basic words of the language, together with the corresponding atoms at all the different levels. The atom set for a level could then be compiled automatically given a declaration of the features that occur at that level.

8   Machine translation as an expert task

RODERICK L. JOHNSON and PETER WHITELOCK

8.1. Introduction

The case against fully automatic high quality machine translation (FAHQMT) has been well-canvassed in the literature ever since ALPAC. Although considerable progress in computational linguistics has been made since then, many of the major arguments against FAHQMT still hold (a good summary is given by Martin Kay (1980)).

It is not our intention to reopen the case for FAHQMT here. Rather, we contend that, accepting that FAHQMT is not possible in the current state of the art, it is both feasible and desirable to set up research and development programs in MT which can both produce results which will satisfy sponsors and provide an environment to support research directed towards bringing MT closer to the ultimate goal of FAHQMT.

This chapter describes the rationale and organization behind one such program, the UMIST English-Japanese MT project.

8.2. MT as simulation of translator behavior

Since an ideal MT system will probably be expected by consumers of translations to exhibit the functional input-output behavior of an ideal human translator, it is not unreasonable to look to translators as a primary source of information about the problems of MT. Note that we are not saying here that an ideal MT system should necessarily be designed to model every aspect of the behavior of a human translator. We do believe, though, that important insights into the organization of MT systems can be gleaned from studying how translators operate — and, more importantly, what kinds of knowledge translators use — when they do translation.

What this claim comes down to is the assertion that translation as currently practiced is a task entrusted to experts — the translators. What we try to do when we build an MT system is to incorporate all or part of the translator's expertise into a computer program. If we were able to characterize all of the expertise of the ideal translator in such a way that the characterization could be expressed as an executable computer program then, presumably, we would have attained FAHQMT.

Since we do not yet know how to achieve such a characterization, we look for a model which partitions translation knowledge in such a way as to

136

maximize the efficiency of the human/machine collaboration, while at the same time facilitate transfer of responsibility from man to machine as our understanding of the act of translation improves.

8.3. Knowledge in translation

We postulate that the professional (technical) translator has access to five distinct kinds of knowledge: target language (TL) knowledge; text type knowledge; source language (SL) knowledge; subject area ('real-world') knowledge; and contrastive knowledge.

We assume that the first four of these are not contentious: a translator must know both the language in which the translation is to be produced and the language in which the source text is written; (s)he should have sufficient command of the subject area and its associated stylistic conventions to make sense of the source text and to produce a target text which is acceptable to a subject expert TL speaker. It is worth noting here, in passing, that a good translator is normally expected to be able to compensate for lack of expertise in all of these except (typically) the first two, by appropriate use of external sources like native (SL) informants, monolingual subject specialists and reliable reference works. We shall return to this question in section 8.6.

The question of contrastive knowledge is a little more delicate. Many workers in MT advocate a two-stage translation model in which source and target texts are mediated by a linguistically neutral 'interlingua.' In such a model there is clearly no place for contrastive knowledge, or rather the relevant contrasts are between SL objects and interlingual objects, on the one hand, and TL objects and interlingual objects on the other.

What we understand by contrastive knowledge is present typically in the so-called 'transfer' models of translation, where both SL and TL components map between texts and 'deep' representations or 'interface structures' (IS). An SL (respectively, TL) IS, although it abstracts away from superficial idiosyncratic properties of texts, is still recognizably an SL (respectively, TL) representation. The role of contrastive knowledge — which in the limit case may be restricted to simple lexical equivalence — lies in determining how a given SL IS 'translates' to the corresponding (set of) TL IS.

We do not want to enter here into the debate on the relative merits of interlingual versus transfer organization in models of MT. As will transpire from the rest of the chapter, it makes little difference to our organizational proposals whether contrastive knowledge mediates between abstract SL and TL representations or between some SL linguistic and some interlingua. The main difference lies in the ease and consistency of formulation of the necessary knowledge by experts in the domain (linguists, lexicographers, and translators).

8.4. A model of translation

The basic model we propose, in over-simplified form, is the familiar transfer scheme shown in Figure 1.

The idea is that some analysis device A applies SL knowledge to a source text to produce a source internal structure IS; a transfer device T applies contrastive knowledge to the source IS to produce a target IS; and finally a synthesis device S applies TL knowledge to the target IS to produce a target text.

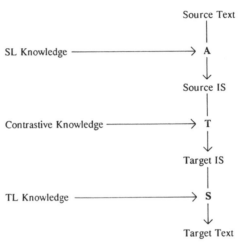

Figure 1. A model of translation.

In addition (not shown in the figure) all three of SL knowledge, contrastive knowledge, and TL knowledge may be enhanced by text-type knowledge.

In practice, as we all know, this model, even when enriched by text-type knowledge, is pathetically inadequate. For it even to have a chance of being useful, we should have to require that all of S, T, and A be total and functional. In practice, we know that this is unlikely ever to be the case with natural text.

Thus, we expect that the mapping computed by A (and its 'inverse' S) will be many-to-many (one text may have many corresponding IS, many texts may have the same IS). Similarly, T is likely to be many-to-many, even if T only involves lexical substitution (consider *wall* vs. the Italian *muro/parete*, or *veal/calf* vs. the Italian *vitello*). Moreover both A and T will almost certainly in practice turn out to be partial (some tests will be ill-formed with respect to available SL knowledge, contrastive knowledge). The only thing we can reasonably enforce is that S should be total, by placing the requirement on T that it produce only well-formed IS representation.

There is, however, an important difference between the non-determinism inherent in A and T, on the one hand, and S on the other. If A, for a given text, produces multiple IS representations, then we assume that choice between them is not arbitrary and may have significant consequences for the correctness of the translation, although the available SL knowledge is inadequate to distinguish them. Similarly, the available contrastive knowledge may be inadequate to disambiguate multiple IS representations, although again the disambiguation may be important for the adequacy of the translation. On the other hand, once we have a target IS, the assumption is that all texts generable from that IS within the constraints of a given text type will be equivalent with respect to translation. If it is possible to derive more than one text from the IS in principle we do not need extra information to choose between the possibilities and the choice can be purely arbitrary.[1]

Thus we come up against two kinds of situations where linguistic knowledge in the system is potentially inadequate to meet the requirement of acceptable translation: when SL knowledge cannot disambiguate SL texts or contrastive knowledge available to the system fails to produce any result at all.

In some cases we can remedy such failures simply by adding to the available stock of linguistic knowledge, as when the system fails to translate some text portion just because a word is missing from the dictionary. In many others there is no plausible linguistic solution; these are the cases where it is recognized that what is needed is an injection of subject-area or real-world knowledge.

Unfortunately, there does not exist, to our knowledge, any semantic or pragmatic theory which is sufficiently general and well-defined to allow incorporation into an MT model. Existing MT programs do what they can with what linguistics they have and leave the rest to human intervention. Our own view is also that practical MT should for the foreseeable future be a collaborative enterprise between human and machine. We want to claim, however, that current MT systems are generally not organized so as to make most efficient use of the human contribution. Moreover, we suggest that a

---

[1] Actually, the situation with respect to T is not so clear-cut. Louis des Tombe has pointed out (personal communication) that, under certain very reasonable conditions, for any lexical item which is apparently unambiguous in the SL but ambiguous in the TL (e.g., the *wall* vs. *muro/parete* case above) if the ambiguity is resolvable with respect to the source IS then the information for resolving it should also be present in the target IS. Under these circumstances there is no reason why 'disambiguation' should not be done by S, provided the available TL knowledge is sufficiently precise to rule out the inappropriate case. On this view we should also have to accept that S may be partial.

well thought out design for an MT system should not only allow more efficient use of human resources but should also provide a useful research environment aimed at enhancing our understanding of the knowledge needed for translation.

In the next section, we look at conventional ways of organizing the man-machine partnership, before going on to our own design.

8.5. The division of labor in MT

Suppose we have a machine which can perform some part of the translation task, assisted by a human expert. There are essentially three points in the translation process when the human can intervene: after the machine has finished, while the machine is operating, or before the machine starts. It is worth remarking that once human intervention has ceased and the machine is left on its own, the machine's knowledge of what remains of the translation task must be complete.

We look briefly at each of the three possibilities in turn.

8.5.1. After — post-editing

The safest way to organize man-machine cooperation in translation is to use a human post-editor to verify the output of an MT program, as is done in many large organizations using MT, especially where post-editing of work done by human translators is anyway the norm.

Post-editing is a highly skilled task; the post-editor needs to be an expert in:

- the subject area
- the target language
- the text-type
- contrastive knowledge.

In effect, the post-editor should be at least as skilled in all of these domains as the original translator. When the task of the translator is being done by a machine, it is not at all evident that we can claim that the machine is usefully extending expert capabilities to non-experts. At best, the computer is being used as a tool for the expert to increase productivity.

8.5.2. During — interactive MT

A number of systems currently in use display the source text in the screen and provide facilities to allow the operator to build up a translation interactively, usually in a second window. Typically, the facilities provided include a window-oriented word-processor and on-line bilingual glossaries. In addition, such systems tend to offer an interactive 'translation' mode, in which the machine attempts a sentence-by-sentence translation, pausing to prompt the operator to choose from among possible translation options; for example, the system might prompt:

Shall I translate 'party' as

1. partido
2. fiesta

This way of working does not really differ from the post-editing scenario above. The possibility of interaction is only used to reduce the size of text fragments to be post-edited from full texts to sentence-sized units. Thus, although it appears to increase productivity (Hundt, 1982), it does not relieve the operator of any responsibility for any part of the translation task. The human end of the collaboration still needs to be carried out by an expert operator, who needs to possess all the expert skills of a translator.

8.5.3. *Before* — *pre-editing*

In the pre-editing case there is at least some part of the translation task for which the machine is totally responsible (that part which happens after the last human intervention). Typically, in pre-editing environments, documents have to be specially drafted in a limited language using a restricted syntax and restricted vocabulary. The bargain is that the user guarantees only to submit input in the restricted language; the system guarantees that it will translate any valid text in that language.

The division of expertise here is quite different. Now the human needs only active, expert knowledge of the restricted language; all other aspects of translation expertise are supplied by the machine.

The neatness of this partition is somewhat illusory, however. The success of such an arrangement depends on being able to design a restricted language which ensures that all of the machine's inherent knowledge sources can operate infallibly: (passive) SL knowledge, subject-area knowledge, contrastive linguistic knowledge, text-type knowledge and (active) TL knowledge. As a consequence, these restricted languages tend to become so specialized and unnatural as to place unreasonable demands on the expertise of the pre-editor.

8.6. Distribution of knowledge in human and machine translation

None of these characteristics seems to us to offer a completely satisfactory framework for designing MT systems in such a way that they can be made to approximate more and more closely to the performance of an ideal translator.

To get closer to this goal, we look at the question of the use a human translator makes of available knowledge, with a view to finding a more productive basis for the sharing of expertise between man and machine.

A human translator is, first and foremost, a target language expert, as is evidenced by the practice of large organizations which require translators to translate only into their native language. It is rare for translators also to have expert knowledge of the subject area of the documents which they translate: they are normally expected to compensate for any deficiencies in their expertise by having extremely good contrastive knowledge and by consulting informed sources (reference works and/or subject types which they have to translate, since they largely bear the responsibility for the stylistic appropriateness of the translations they produce). Source language is also required, of course, but that knowledge need only be passive, and can be limited to experience of the written form in the relevant class of text types.

It is instructive to see how this use of knowledge compares to the presuppositions which seem to be built into the majority of commercial MT systems. In both the post-edited and the conventional interactive schemes, it appears that users expect to have to massage the machine's output to make it more acceptable stylistically. 'Style clearly seems to be the main problem in post-editing' (Lavorel, 1982). This view is certainly not consistent with the idea of an MT system as a target language expert.

MT systems with only pre-editing come much closer to treating the machine as an expert translator. Where they differ from human translators is in placing strong, even perhaps unreasonable, requirements on the originators of documents as a means of circumventing their own deficiencies.

8.7. Towards more productive interaction strategies

The model we propose is intermediate between the pre-editing and interactive styles of MT. If the machine is to behave functionally as far as possible like a human translator, then we would like to free the user from any need to know about the target language, so that the machine has to be a TL and a contrastive expert, as well as having text-type knowledge built in. On the other hand, while we anticipate that the system will be more or less deficient in knowledge of the user's SL and in subject-area knowledge, we assume that these deficiencies can be remedied in consultation with a (SL) monolingual operator. In terms of the model of section 8.4, we now have the picture in Figure 2.

It is, of course, one thing to say that the system makes up for its own shortcomings by consulting the operator. It is quite another to determine when and how such consultation should take place. Being able to determine when to trigger an interaction depends on an awareness on the part of the system that there is something which it does not know. We can distinguish two such situations:

(a)   the input is ill-formed with respect to either A (the analysis) or T (transfer);

(b)   the input is ambiguous with respect to either A or T.

These two situations may occur, respectively, in cases where (a) A (respectively, T) is partial, or (b) A (respectively, T) is not functional.

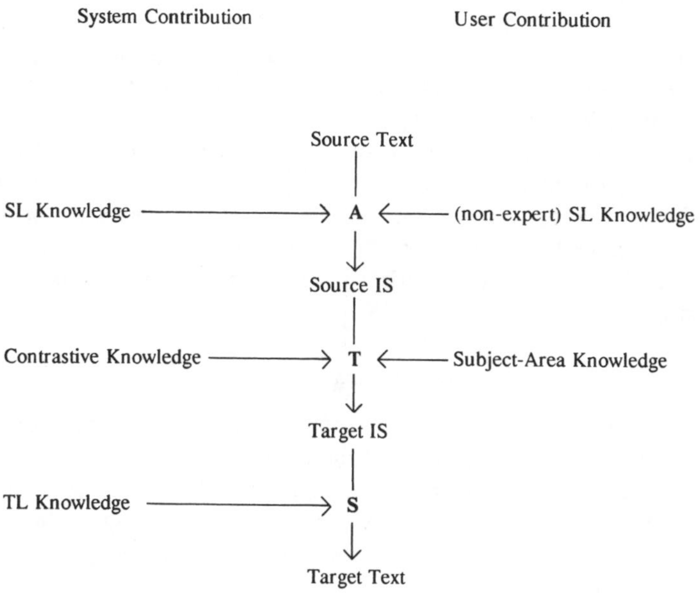

Figure 2. A modified model of translation.

Now we can (and should) arrange matters so that any construct produced by A can be transferred (i.e., T is total over the domain of outputs of A). This means that interactions triggered by ill-formed input (case (a)) can be localized within A only. We are not enthusiastic about attempts by the system to go it alone in 'repairing' ill-formed input (see Arnold and Johnson (1984) for discussion), although this does not rule out use by the system of its own SL knowledge to propose plausible reconstructions of the input as prompts to the user.

Case (b) is interesting, in that some apparent ambiguities in analysis may carry over to the TL (and so the system should not waste the user's time trying to resolve them). This observation suggests that this type of interaction should be handled as a part of transfer, utilizing contrastive information as criterion.

In cases of type (a), the system has a text fragment which it 'knows' at analysis time it is unable to translate. The aim is thus to prompt the user to rephrase the input in a form which the analyzer can recognize. Thus the system must indirectly use its contrastive knowledge (knowledge of what it can translate) to extract from the user, who has extensive, but non-expert, SL knowledge, an acceptable formulation of the input text.

In type (b) cases, what has happened is that the purely linguistic knowledge available to the system is insufficient to distinguish between translationally distinct 'readings' of the text. Hence the appeal to the user's 'real-world' or subject-area knowledge to resolve the ambiguity.

We believe the approach advocated in this chapter to have two advantages over more orthodox MT systems design: it encourages a more efficient and productive sharing of expertise between man and machine; and it provides a useful framework for MT research by allowing the role of the machine to be extended incrementally on the basis of systematic experimentation within an operational environment. Most of the ideas are not original — indeed, the basis principles go back at least as far as Kay (1973). The same principles also seem to have been applied to MT by Tomita (1984). In our case the application domain is an experimental English-Japanese translator for technical documentation.

Acknowledgement

The work reported in this chapter is supported by International Computers Limited and the UK Science and Engineering Research Council under the Alvey program for research in Intelligent Knowledge Based Systems. We are grateful to ICL and to SERC, as well as to our colleagues in UMIST and the University of Sheffield, for their help and support in putting our ideas into practice.

9   On human-machine interaction in translation

ALAN MELBY

9.1. Types of translation

Recently, while I was using a photocopy machine, an associate asked me a question similar to questions that many researchers in machine translation have been asked: 'When are you going to make a photocopier that has a language dial so I can put in an English original and have the "copy" come out in German?' Such an MT device would involve the minimum possible human-machine interaction—the operator would not even need to be able to read the source or target languages. But there is a theoretical problem with such a multilingual photocopy even if advances in AI allow MT to become indistinguishable from human translation or even if you hide a human translator inside the machine. The problem is that there is not just one correct translation for a given source document.

The translating machine would need at least one other dial for translation specifications (e.g., retain source culture or adapt for target culture; maintain the same register as the source document or shift to a simpler register; coin translations for new technical terms or leave them in the source language). Asking 'What is the translation of this text?' is like asking 'What is the product of this number?' Instead you ask, 'What is the product of this number and this multiplier?', and you ask 'What is a translation of this text according to these specifications?' Since translation specifications are relevant in discussing all translation, they are relevant, in particular, when discussing MT.

Indeed, translation specifications (and text type) are very important factors in MT. Weather forecast translation has been shown to be quite practically done using MT and a little cleanup by human translators. But automatic MT of advertising materials is not in great demand because, in advertising, a catchy, creative translation is needed, not a syntactically similar phrase with lexical substitution. Computers can be useful for any translation, but the type of interaction between the human and the machine will be quite different depending on the type of translation (i.e., text type and translation specifications).

Some well-known types of translation (besides weather forecasts and advertising) are technical, legal, and various forms of literary translation. In technical translation, the text is usually informative (e.g., how to install or maintain a piece of equipment), and the specifications are usually

145

consistent in terminology and simple in syntax. In legal translation, it is very important to assign equivalents to larger units than just words and phrases, and adjustments for differences in legal systems can be very important. In literary translation, style is all-important and there is no one set of specifications that all agree on. Sometimes, in a story, a papaya will be translated as an apple and other times (if source culture is specified) it will be left as a papaya. Sometimes, with poetry, the translation will rhyme and sometimes the specifications will be for free verse.

9.2. Types of human interaction

This essay will explore the connections between type of translation and type of human-machine interaction, using 'translator workstations' to refer to the device with which the human actually interacts. But first, we will briefly describe four types of interaction related to translation. The most common type of interaction is post-editing. Post-editing is a process of revising a translation after the draft translation has been completed. It can be done with red pencil on paper, but it is more efficient to use word processing.

Another type of interaction is pre-editing, which is a process of revising a source text before it is translated. This can be done manually with red pencil on paper, but it is hard to keep a set of writing rules in mind and apply them consistently, probably because the use of human language is not rule-governed but rule-influenced. An intriguing approach to pre-editing is to program a computer to analyze text and point out words and grammatical constructions that do not conform to the standard. Interactive pre-editing can also be part of the translation process.

A third type of interaction could be named 'intra-processing.' Pre-editing should not require the human pre-editor to know the target language; that is, all pre-editing interactions should be in terms of the source language. Intra-processing, on the other hand, involves bilingual questions, for example, 'How should this word be translated?' with several options given to the human to choose from. This interaction could be initiated by the human or by the machine.

A fourth type of human interaction involves text and dictionary studies outside the actual translation process which does not involve modifying the text. A common example of this type of interaction is a human evaluating a 'not found words' list generated by a computer program which scans a source text and compares it with a dictionary. The human decides on a case by case basis whether to upgrade the dictionary. This type of interaction could be called 'para-processing'.

9.3. Types of MT

So far this essay has made two claims: (1) that there are several types of translation, depending on text type and translation specifications; (2) that there are several types of human-machine interaction related to translation. The first claim is well accepted by translation theorists, and the second claim is merely an observation about what is happening in machine-assisted translation. Let us explore some implications. Since there are several types of translation, by analogy there should be several types of MT. The first type of machine translation is fully automatic translation in which there is no pre-editing, post-editing, or intra-processing. Fully automatic machine translation has been and is used successfully but only where there is a steady flow of technical texts for which 'indicative' translations are needed. Indicative translation is a specification which means that the translation need not completely conform to the target language grammar and need not be of publication quality. It need only give a rough idea of what the source text is about. Indicative translations from Russian to English have, for years, been produced fully automatically and are still used by the United States Air Force. Such translations are often used to decide whether or not to request a human translation of a given article. If publication quality is needed or if the source text is not a straightforward technical document one must currently back down from fully automatic translation. Then, a number of other types of machine translations are suggested by the types of interaction discussed above (pre-editing, post-editing, and intra-processing).

Pre-editing has been successfully applied at Xerox and in France (TITUS). At Xerox, studies of the SYSTRAN MT system led to rules for writers which helped them avoid troublesome constructions in the source text of manuals for photocopiers. In the French textile industry, a controlled language facilitates MT of abstracts. A new system currently under development (the DLT system in the Netherlands) uses on-line machine-assisted pre-editing to help the author conform to the system's grammar. Pre-editing obviously works best at the time of initial text creation if the text is to be modified. If the text is already created, pre-editing can be used to clarify the meaning without rewriting. This type of pre-editing was proposed in the 1960's by Martin Kay in his MIND system. Remember that according to our definition, any interaction that does not involve knowledge of the target language is classified as pre-editing.

All commercial MT systems (e.g., SYSTRAN, Logos, ALPS, Weidner) include a post-editing component. This may be done with standard word processing software (Logos uses Wang) or with a custom word processor (ALPS and Weidner). Several groups have attached workstations that include post-editing to SYSTRAN.

Intra-processing has also been implemented. The Brigham Young University (BYU) MT project used it, and so does ALPS (most of its programmers came from BYU). Intra-processing can take two distinct forms. In the ALPS CTS system (recently renamed TransActive), the machine is in control and the human waits for the machine to ask him or her a question. In on-line terminology access (e.g., Termium in Canada), the human is in control and the machine waits for the human to ask it a question. Kay has often used the acronyms HAMT (Human-Assisted Machine Translation) and MAHT (Machine-Assisted Human Translation) to make this distinction.

Para-processing has been implemented on many systems, with scans of text against dictionaries and generation of concordances being the most popular forms.

9.4. Factors in interaction

Once one has accepted several types of human interaction in various types of MT, then questions arise in such areas as human factors, quality, efficiency and cost effectiveness: How does a human feel when interacting with the machine in various ways? Which user interfaces are most friendly to the human? How convenient and practical are various types of interaction in terms of necessary data preparation? What is the quality of final output in various approaches? What about speed and cost? Obviously, with so many factors that may have different relative importance to various people, there is probably no one right solution for all circumstances. It would not be advisable or interesting to attempt a definitive description of workstations for implementing human-machine interaction in MT. Instead, the present chapter will describe one possible design for a translator workstation which allows for several types of interaction through an integrated user interface. This particular design was first proposed in Melby (1982). Only brief references will be made to other translator workstations but this is not meant to imply that they are inferior to or less important than the one emphasized. This chapter will present the author's viewpoint simply because it is the one with which he is most familiar.

9.5. A particular translator workstation

The author's design includes three levels: Level one consists of those software/hardware tools (such as on-demand dictionary lookup) which can be used to facilitate translation when the source text is not placed in machine-readable form. In other words, at level one, the translator produces a translation directly from a source text on paper (probably into a word processor or a dictaphone). Level two consists of simple software tools which can be used when the source text is in machine-readable form.

Level two may include morphological analysis and automatic lookup of words or phrases or even recurring entire sentences, but it stops short of full MT involving syntactic and/or semantic analysis, transfer, and generation. Level three adds full MT, installed either on the translator workstation itself or outside the translator workstation on a local area network or on a remote machine linked by telecommunications. The machine translation component may be fully automatic or produce intra-processing interactions. In addition, at level three the MT may be preceded by pre-editing and followed by post-editing.

Of course, in practice, not all translator workstations will include all options at all three levels, but whatever is included should ideally be integrated through a single user interface. This point cannot be overemphasized. One translator may prefer word processing software brand A and another translator may prefer brand B. Despite attempts, keyboards are not standardized. However, once a keyboard and word processor are chosen, it is inefficient to switch between two keyboards or word processors in the same day. So all tools that the translator uses should be available from the same keyboard and word processor. Violation of this principle has been shown to force users to choose one system and ignore the other.

Some options at each level will now be described, including the type of interaction used and types of translation they apply to.

9.6. Level one

Level one (and higher levels since they include level one as a subset) is based on word processing, telecommunications, and dictionaries. Admittedly, the following description is oriented toward the new generation of translators who are not 'keyboard shy' and does not apply as fully to dictaphone translators, although some elements (such as revision and telecommunications) may still apply. So whenever the human translator is translating, we will assume he or she will use the word processor. Of course, due to the nature of translation, in any but the most repetitive texts, there is often a need to access remote information sources. The most common are remote term banks, other colleagues (e.g., by electronic mail), and textual databases for monolingual research into the usage of certain terms. These are best accessed using the various packet-switched networks. The most common local information source needed is dictionaries. All these should be available without leaving the word processor, because otherwise too much time is wasted bringing the word processor up and down. The main type of interaction at level one is intra-processing with local and remote sources at the initiative of the translator, since the source text is not in machine-readable form and since there is not a machine translation component as in level three.

Level one does have the advantage of applying to all types of translation. Even advertising translation and literary translation can benefit from word processing, telecommunications, and a personal dictionary in which to record personal notes about lexical gems.

9.7. Level two

Level two includes all the options of level one and adds such options as dictionary scans, concordances, and text-related glossaries. A dictionary scan is essentially some form of spelling check, but it is tied to a bilingual dictionary and identifies missing terms. A concordance program can be a good tool for studying a text before translating it, or for looking at all occurrences of a troublesome word or phrase. A text-related glossary is simply a list of the words or phrases (in a certain segment of source text) that are found in a bilingual dictionary, along with their translation. Level two interaction is similar to level one interaction except that extended search options are available since the source text is in machine-readable form.

Level two text-related glossaries are most useful for technical texts for which the specification is that certain words and phrases should be translated consistently throughout the document. The ALPS AutoTerm system is similar to level two as just described.

9.8. Level three

At level three, there is an MT component, which provides the opportunity for post-editing, pre-editing and intra-process interaction. Most systems do use post-editing. But by then, the text may be so bad that normal post-editing is not effective. Only a small incremental improvement can be made in one post-editing session, whether the post-editor is revising human or MT. Automatic translation followed by post-editing has been found to be most effective when the texts are technical rather than persuasive or literary. There are several alternatives to traditional post-editing. One is selective post-editing. In this approach, the MT system grades its own output according to problems encountered during lexical, syntactic, or semantic processing. Then, the translator translates the text segment by segment until a segment is encountered for which there is a translation that received a grade above the translator's chosen threshold. Such a segment is likely to be worth post-editing and the translator evaluates it and inserts it into the text or ignores it and translates the segment. The idea is to avoid wasting too much time evaluating segments that are not worth post-editing. Another option at level three is to pre-edit the text interactively. This option is being pursued by several groups, including the DLT project of the BSO company in Utrecht, The Netherlands.

Interactive intra-processing is also an option at level three. Here, the computer initiates requests about the translation of certain words and phrases and then generates a target sentence. There are arguments for and against level three intra-processing. An advantage is that fewer mistranslations are used as a basis for inflecting other words. On the negative side, there are questions asked that may turn out to be unnecessary because the software would have defaulted to the proper choice. Also, the human must perform a significant amount of the work involved in translation just to answer the questions posed by the computer.

Level three certainly has the most potential for increasing efficiency but it is also the most restrictive in terms of types of translation to which it applies.

9.9. Conclusion

There are two lessons to be learned from the various options presented above. The first is that MT with post-editing is not in competition with manual translation but with levels one and two. The second is that MT designers need to include translation type, interaction type, and translator workstations in their initial plans, not as an afterthought.

When one writes an MT system it should be clearly kept in mind for which type of translation and which type of interaction it will be used.

If the system will be used for indicative translation, then it should always produce some output, no matter how bad the translation is. If it is to be used with selective post-editing then it need not translate everything from the source text, but what it does translate had better be done well. Interactive pre-editing and intra-processing obviously affect the basic design of an MT component. Even if the system is for research purposes only rather than practical results, the interaction with the researcher (who wants to know what went wrong and why) should be carefully planned from the beginning. For practical systems, as mentioned above, evaluation of the benefits of machine translation at level three should be calculated relative to the benefits of level two, not relative to manual translation. This places heavy demands on MT systems designed for producing cost effective translations rather than extending knowledge of linguistic structures.

SOURCE TEXT

↓

TRANSLATOR WORKSTATION
OPERATING AT LEVEL ONE, TWO, OR THREE

↓

TRANSLATION

Figure 1. The structure of a machine-aided translation system.

SOURCE TEXT

Les marchandises peuvent être vendues directement du fabricant aux consommateurs. Mais en général les services d'un intermédiaire sont nécessaires. Il dispose de moyens d'entreposage dont ne bénéficie pas un détaillant ordinaire.
La vente au grand public peut se faire par des démarcheurs à domicile, mais la plupart des gens font leurs courses dans les grands magasins.

↓

LEVEL ONE

Terminology Access Screen

The human translator sees 'fabricant' in the source text and decides to look it up in the dictionary. Once a translation (1 or 2) has been selected, it can be pasted into the output text window.

(Output text window) Goods may be sold direct from
(Dictionary window) fabricant (1) manufacturer (2) producer (src) Fred W. 26 March 1984

↓

TRANSLATION

Goods may be sold direct from manufacturers to consumers. But in general, the services of a middleman are required. He has warehousing facilities which an ordinary retailer cannot afford.
Sales to the general public may be done through door to door salesmen, but most people do their shopping in department stores.

Figure 2. A sample session with Level One Workstation.

SOURCE TEXT

Les marchandises peuvent être vendues directement du fabricant aux consommateurs. Mais en général les services d'un intermédiaire sont nécessaires. Il dispose de moyens d'entreposage dont ne bénéficie pas un détaillant ordinaire.
La vente au grand public peut se faire par des démarcheurs à domicile, mais la plupart des gens font leurs courses dans les grands magasins.

LEVEL TWO

Suggested Term Screen

(Output text window)

Sales to the general public may be done through door to door salesmen, but most people do their shopping in department stores.

(Current source segment)	**(Suggested translations of terms)**
La vente au GRAND-PUBLIC (1) peut se faire par des DEMARCHEURS-A-DOMICILE (2) mais la plupart des gens font leurs courses dans les grands magasins.	(1) grand public = general public (2) démarcheurs à domicile = door to door salesmen

---

TRANSLATION

Goods may be sold direct from manufacturers to consumers. But in general, the services of a middleman are required. He has warehousing facilities which an ordinary retailer cannot afford.
Sales to the general public may be done through door to door salesmen, but most people do their shopping in department stores.

Figure 3. A sample session with Level Two Workstation.

SOURCE TEXT

Les marchandises peuvent être vendues directement du fabricant aux consommateurs. Mais en général les services d'un intermédiaire sont nécessaires. Il dispose de moyens d'entreposage dont ne bénéficie pas un détaillant ordinaire.
La vente au grand public peut se faire par des démarcheurs à domicile, mais la plupart des gens font leurs courses dans les grands magasins.

LEVEL THREE

Suggested Translation Screen

(Output text window)	
Goods may be sold direct from manufacturers to consumers.	
(Current source segment)	**(Suggested translation of current segment)**
Les marchandises peuvent être vendues directement du fabricant aux consommateurs.	The goods may be sold directly of the producer at the consumers.

TRANSLATION

Goods may be sold direct from manufacturers to consumers. But in general, the services of a middleman are required. He has warehousing facilities which an ordinary retailer cannot afford.
Sales to the general public may be done through door to door salesmen, but most people do their shopping in department stores.

Figure 4. A sample session with Level Three Workstation.

10 Reflections on the knowledge needed to process ill-formed language

RALPH M. WEISCHEDEL and LANCE A. RAMSHAW

10.1. Introduction

Natural language understanding requires determining what is meant by a sequence of words in context. The key to understanding natural language is the use of constraints from language and from context to guide the search for the intended meaning by eliminating the plethora of alternative ways to group words. Those constraints make the problem tractable by reducing the size of the space that must be searched for an interpretation, but it is exactly those constraints that cannot be trusted when dealing with ill-formed input.

Natural language input may appear ill-formed to a system due to many causes. The input may violate some constraint of the language, e.g., a morphological, syntactic, semantic, or pragmatic constraint, in which case the input may be termed absolutely ill-formed. Absolutely ill-formed input is that which a native speaker judges to violate the rules of the language. Examples include misspellings; homonym confusions like that between *there, their,* and *they're*; omitted words, as in *Dump output to laser printer*; ungrammaticalities, such as agreement failures between subject and verb, agreement failure between determiner and noun, and resumptive pronouns (Kroch, 1981); selection restriction violations; and presupposition violation, as in *Is the greatest prime number 23?*

Alternatively, the input may violate some constraint of the machine's model, thereby appearing relatively ill-formed, even though a richer model would recognize it as an acceptable request. An example of relative ill-formedness is input containing a word that is not in the system's dictionary, or an expression that has meaning only outside the system's domain. In addition, it is often convenient to treat certain phenomena like figures of speech and ellipsis as relatively ill-formed, because the system will use the same mechanisms to handle them as it would to handle similar cases of true ill-formedness. For example, though contextual ellipsis is not absolutely ill-formed, many (Hendrix, 1978; Kwasny and Sondheimer, 1981; Weischedel and Sondheimer, 1982) have argued for treating both ungrammaticality and ellipsis via a meta-process on the grammar rather than embedding either within the grammar. Similarly, one could treat certain ungrammaticalities via relaxing syntactic classes of words; for example, *The*

155

student what is in my recitation section could be understood by relaxing the constraint on a personal relative pronoun to any relative pronoun. Semantic class relaxations could be employed to process figures of speech like *My car drinks gasoline,* where the class required by *drink* is relaxed from animate being to physical object (see Fass and Wilks, 1983; Weischedel and Sondheimer, 1983).

There has been growing interest over the past five years in processing ill-formed input, which has resulted in several implementations that handle various classes of ill-formedness. These include EPISTLE (Jensen et al., 1983), NOMAD (Granger, 1983), EXCALIBUR (Carbonell and Hayes, 1983), and a system based on meta-rules (Razi, 1985; Weischedel and Sondheimer, 1983). All deal with one or more classes of syntactic ill-formedness, and some work (Granger, 1983; Fass and Wilks, 1983; Weischedel and Sondheimer, 1983) even discusses certain classes of semantic ill-formedness. These systems have employed various kinds of knowledge to process input in the face of ill-formedness: only syntactic constraints (Jensen et al., 1983; Kwasny and Sondheimer, 1981), predominantly semantic constraints (Carbonell and Hayes, 1983; Fass and Wilks, 1983; Schank and Birnbaum, 1980; Waltz, 1978; Wilks, 1975), and both syntactic and semantic constraints (Charniak, 1981; Granger, 1983; Razi, 1985; Weischedel and Sondheimer, 1983).

Rather than describing another implementation, our reflections in this chapter consider the combination of knowledge sources necessary for any system to have a fairly complete, robust understanding of natural language, the combination which we believe will have to be exploited by those who extend the excellent beginnings made in these systems.

In this chapter, we consider the processing of ill-formed input from the perspective of the knowledge sources that must be used. Our aim is to demonstrate through examples that morphological, syntactic, semantic, and pragmatic knowledge are all necessary to interpret ill-formedness correctly, and since all classes of constraints may be violated, that ill-formedness is not a problem solely of ungrammaticality.

Recognition of the points above has implications for system design: the need to consult and combine those various knowledge sources. Consequently, we believe that this study offers important perspectives not just for ill-formedness work, but for all forms of natural language processing.

In section 10.2, we comment briefly on the relevance of ill-formedness work to various applications. Then sections 10.3 through 10.6 consider in turn the kinds of knowledge derived from morphology/phonetics, syntax, semantics, and pragmatics. Section 10.7 discusses the implications of combining knowledge sources, and section 10.8 concludes.

10.2. Ill-formedness and applications

There are some applications of natural language processing where locating errors in the input becomes an explicit goal. If the technique used for handling ill-formedness encompasses both a model of correct linguistic constraints and knowledge of ways that those constraints may be violated, then it can be used to identify errors in language use. Ill-formedness processing has been employed in this way in grammar and spelling checkers (Jensen et al., 1983) and in intelligent tutors for computer-assisted language instruction (Weischedel et al., 1978).

More generally, all natural language interfaces should be forgiving, doing what the user intends. In natural language access to information systems, the magnitude of the ill-formedness problem can be seen in several case studies; Thompson (1980) and Eastman and McLean (1981) indicate that as much as 25% of typed queries to question-answering systems are ill-formed. Consequently, ill-formedness processing is critical to natural language interfaces to data bases, expert systems, planning systems, etc.

Certain kinds of texts will make especially heavy demands on the ill-formedness component. Military messages and bank telexes are examples of short texts that contain many examples of ill-formedness. Processing them, whether for translation, data base update, routing, or summarization, seems to require a strong approach to understanding ill-formed input. Speech input also will require considerable attention to ill-formedness, due to the predominance of real-time generation errors, such as restarted sentences and spoonerisms.

Even in contexts like formal published texts where absolute ill-formedness is likely to be relatively uncommon, these techniques will still be essential for dealing with relative ill-formedness, for instance due to inadequate grammars or inadequate semantic models, and for handling those cases of ellipsis and figures of speech best treated as relatively ill-formed.

In the area of machine translation, it seems from the discussion above that ill-formedness processing will be especially important for military messages, telegraphic messages, and dialog. Furthermore, it may prove quite useful in translating inputs that exhibit relative ill-formedness.

10.3. Morphology and phonetics

Morphological and phonetic knowledge are helpful in those cases where there is doubt about the correct reading of the input words, either because an unrecognized symbol is encountered, or because what appears to be a known word is actually a misspelling. Current systems typically are able to correct some of the former class of problems, but do not attempt the latter.

Most systems that try to correct the misspellings that produce unrecognized symbols use a random permutation model of typographical errors to do so, but spelling errors are not completely random. There are several kinds of knowledge regarding true misspellings which have not, to our knowledge, been encoded in systems heretofore. For instance, there are many specific patterns of typical spelling errors of native speakers of English; the rule 'i before e except after c and in words like *neighbor* and *weigh*' reflects one such pattern of misspelling that is not the case of randomly transposing two letters when typing. Other such patterns of errors occur due to mistakes in spelling phonetically, such as confusing *ph* and *f*, or phonetically transcribing *Kane* for *Caine*. Correcting such spelling errors will require a model of phonetic similarity and other components.

It is also possible to use morphology to derive partial information about a word that is not in the system's dictionary, like suggesting that *grinds* in *Is CS 140 a course for grinds?* is probably a plural noun. Such partial information, when combined with that from other knowledge sources, may be enough to permit a suggested interpretation.

Misspellings or typographical errors that produce a symbol which is recognized as another word have generally been untouched, though there are exceptions (Trawick, 1983). Those errors are far more challenging, since there is no overt sign in the input regarding what is wrong. The system must mistrust the symbols actually present and determine which to revise, as in the phone message that one of my supervisors received, *Please call terminal main for insulation.* (What was intended was *Please call terminal man for installation.*) Once semantic processing has discovered that such an input is ill-formed, the repair process will require cooperation between semantics and pragmatics along with a measure of phonetic similarity. For instance, correcting *sources* in *Are any Computer Science sources offered in the evenings?* to *courses* would depend on knowledge from all three areas. Studies of examples like that may suggest both new kinds of knowledge that should be incorporated in natural language understanders and also new architectures for interactions among the kinds of knowledge.

10.4. Role of syntax

Even in considering only well-formed input, questions have been raised as to how much attention needs to be paid to syntax in parsing. Since language can be understood by humans in spite of very poor syntactic form, one might argue that syntax can be largely ignored. One need only look at transcribed spoken language or at headlines to see that syntactic rules are frequently violated. Employing as little syntax as possible in the analysis phase is attractive because of the simplicity that comes with ignoring a difficult component in the system. A loose use of syntax would also allow some forms of ill-formedness to pass without notice.

However, the argument that humans can understand language in spite of poor use of syntax does not imply that people do not have a syntactic model, nor that it is inapplicable to language processing by either humans or machines. On the contrary, there is quite strong evidence that humans have a very clear model of the syntax of their natural language. Humans can edit written language that exhibits poor syntax in order to correct it, and can rewrite correct grammatical structures to create a new form which is deemed to be clearer to the reader.

Furthermore, syntactic constraints, as well as morphological, semantic, and pragmatic constraints, are sometimes crucial to determining what interpretation is intended, so that ignoring syntactic constraints can lead to seeing ambiguity where there is none. For example, consider subject-verb agreement, which appears to be a very minor syntactic constraint in English and which is rather frequently violated; one case study (Eastman and McLean, 1981) found that 2.3 percent of natural language queries to a data base violated the subject-verb agreement constraint. Nevertheless, the constraint is a part of the language, and ignoring it would mean that a system or person could not distinguish between the following two forms:

1.   List all assets of the company that was bought by XYZ Corp.
2.   List all assets of the company that were bought by XYZ Corp.

As a consequence, we conclude that all syntactic constraints should be employed in natural language understanding systems; otherwise, forms that are perfectly clear to humans will not be correctly understood by machines. Ill-formed input tends to highlight the need for using all constraints including syntactic constraints, since relaxing or ignoring a potential constraint opens up the search space of possible interpretations, thereby making it even more critical to use all other constraints to prune the search and minimize the combinatorics.

10.5. Semantic knowledge

It is commonly agreed that for most applications semantic constraints such as selection restrictions must be applied in order to determine what is intended by an ill-formed input. (Exceptions to this include some applications where precise understanding is unnecessary, such as some checks for grammaticality and style (Cherry and Vesterman, 1980; Jensen et al., 1983).) Many systems, in fact, use the semantics of the concepts identified in an ill-formed input as the key to determining the intended meaning. For instance, Granger (1983) cites the following naval message, *Enemy SCUD-DED bombs at us*, where the verb is unknown to the system. The system proposes deriving the meaning of SCUDDED from the semantics of what actions the system does know about that can be done by an enemy, to a weapon, and at a reporting unit.

However, the limitations of such semantic constraints are not that well known. First, semantic constraints alone may still leave many possibilities. Suppose we are building a student advisement system which knows about courses, majors, degree requirements, registration, instructors, and policies. If the input is *Can I FROB Sociology 101?* then there are several verbs which might be known to the system having the case frame person <verb> *course*. These include *add, drop, transfer, pass, take,* and *fail,* which all also fit the syntactic context.

Furthermore, it appears that the same phenomenon occurs even in the most highly constrained of applications. For instance, natural language access to computer mail systems would seem to be one of the most highly constrained environments from the point of view of both grammar and lexicon (Hayes and Reddy, 1979). Entities in that domain are limited to messages, addresses, persons, sites, times, etc. Yet, if one says, *FROB the message to Jones,* almost any operation in the mail domain is a possibility, since *to Jones* could be dative or *the message to Jones* could be a reference. If both interpretations for *to Jones* are possible, then *send, resend, forward, delete, print, mark, edit, move,* etc. are all possible.

Second, selection restrictions or semantic constraints may be violated due to relative ill-formedness. For instance, in our experience with the RUS parser, the most frequent reason that a sentence fails to parse is not due to syntactic limitations but rather is due to limitations in the set of selection restrictions encoded or to limitations in their use.

Third, even when it becomes possible to have as general a model of selection restrictions and semantics as we have now for grammar, there will still be clear cases where selection restrictions are violated, such as metonymy, synecdoche, and metaphor.

Fourth, the constraining effect of selection restrictions may be weakened via relatively neutral noun phrases, such as pronouns, *stuff, thing,* and *gift.* Since they may refer to almost anything, they must be accepted almost regardless of selection restrictions.

Fifth is a related problem: the need for clear engineering and linguistic criteria for specifying an appropriate grain size for semantic classes (or semantic features) and for how to recognize from a given noun phrase what semantic class it is associated with. For instance, suppose our grain size dictates that we should have a semantic class, *commander,* as the logical agent of *deploy.* After all, only commanders can deploy a vessel. However, if one says *Foley deployed the Vinson,* Foley may be known only as a person; the fact that he is a commander would have to be assumed. As a second example, suppose one employs a semantic class, *weapon,* so that one could specify that the logical object of *fire* is a weapon. Then one has to determine whether it makes sense for *toy gun* and *fake gun* to be considered in the class of weapons. There are no clear answers to these questions; see Bobrow and Webber (1980).

These problems in formulating and applying semantic knowledge complicate the interpretation of even well-formed input, but they become even more serious when trying to make sense of ill-formedness. When we combine that with the fact that even successfully applied semantics does not always resolve ambiguity, we see that semantics alone is not sufficient either. We will need to combine it with all the other available knowledge, including pragmatics.

10.6. Prospects from pragmatics

Pragmatics is an important source of knowledge that has not yet been widely employed for understanding ill-formedness, though some recent work has begun to make use of it (Carberry, 1985a,b; Granger, 1983). While there are several kinds of knowledge that are pragmatic in nature and that could potentially be brought to bear on understanding natural language, whether well-formed or ill-formed, in this chapter we focus primarily on knowledge about the plans and goals of a speaker in the framework first proposed by Allen and Perrault (1980) and followed up by others (Carberry, 1985a; Litman and Allen, 1984; Sidner, 1985). Therefore, we can assume we have available a tree representing the goals and subgoals that a user may wish to accomplish. A particular path in that tree represents the stack of pending goals that the user may have. In such a tree, a child node is a subgoal that could be part of the means to achieve the goal of the parent node. We will represent a goal via the notation '(predicate $var_1:type_1$ ... $var_n:type_n$) such that proposition'; each var_i is a variable name, each $type_i$ is the type of the variable, and 'such that proposition' is a (possibly empty) additional constraint on the variables.

The expectations generated by such a context can add important constraints on the search space in a natural language processor. For instance, if the speaker says, *I've always wanted to learn how to play badminton*, the system could recognize an instance of the goal (Learn-Material < std >:student < subj >:subject), with the variable < std > matched to the speaker, and < subj > matched to 'badminton.' One of the plans for achieving that goal is (Take-Course < std >:student < crs >:course) such that (Covers-Material < crs >:course < subj >:subject). Thus, the system could set up the following tree of subgoals:

(Learn-Material <std>:student <subj>:subject)
|
(Take-Course <std>:student <crs>:course)
   such that (Covers-Material <crs>:course <subj>:subject)

If the user next asked, *Can I FROB Physical Education 145?*, while syntax could determine that FROB is a transitive verb and semantics could limit it to actions that students can do to courses, it would require this plan context for the system to deduce that FROB probably means to take a course.

10.6.1. The search space

This kind of use of plan context does require that the system be able to track the user's plans so as to be able to predict plausible next steps at the point of the ill-formedness. There are times, e.g., at the beginning of a new interaction, when only a very general default model of the user's plans is available, and there are also activities in which predicting the next step is difficult even in the midst of an interaction. However, people's ability to deal with ill-formedness also varies with their grasp of the pragmatic context.

Even in those situations where the plan context can be predicted, searching for the correct goal to use in interpreting an input can itself be expensive. Plan context models can be large and bushy trees, and the goal associated with the individual's next request need not be an immediate descendant of the current goal. For instance, suppose the discourse context is that provided by the user informing the advising system, *I still need to satisfy the distribution requirements.* If the user next asks, *Is there FROB in Biology 101?*, the system would have to expand and explore its model of the user's plan to find a predicate applying to courses that can help in interpreting the word FROB. Here is just one of the many branches that the system would have to explore:

(Satisfy-Distribution-Requirements <std>:student <dgp>:degree-program)
   such that (Is-B.A. <dgp>:degree-program)
|
(Satisfy-Lab-Science-Requirement <std>:student <crs>:course)
   such that (Is-Lab-Science <crs>:course)
|
(Earn-Credit <std>:student <crs>:course <sem>:semester)
   such that (Is-Offered <crs>:course <sem>:semester)
|
(Earn-Credit-Section <std>:student <sec>:section
                     <crs>:course <sem>:semester)
   such that (Section-Offered <sec>:section <sem>:semester)
        (Is-Section-Of <sec>:section <crs>:course)
        (Space-Available <sec>:section)

The matching predicate in the goal tree, namely (Space-Available <sec>:section), is located several levels below the original user goal. In general, the possible predicates and entities that need to be examined may need to be searched for many generations below the current goal.

Similarly, the path that needs to be searched may also include nodes higher in the tree than the original goal node, or descendants of such nodes. For example, suppose the student said: *Chemistry 103 is full. Is there FROB in Biology 108?* Here, the system might deduce that the student had the goal of taking Chemistry 103; such a goal would make the fact that it is full relevant, and could be motivated by the higher-level goal of taking a lab science. From that higher-level goal, it could build down to a goal that would include the predicate (Space-Available BIO-108-10).

Therefore, given a tree of subgoals representing a strategy to achieve a goal and the path in that tree representing the goals inherent in the last input, virtually any node in the tree, any new descendants of its leaves, a newly inferred supergoal, or (previously unexpanded) descendants of a newly inferred supergoal may arise as the goal of a new input, whether well-formed or ill-formed. The number of alternative subgoals which could contribute to interpreting correctly an ill-formed input is therefore large, though not all alternatives are necessarily equally likely.

In some cases, pragmatic context may at best be able to limit the number of alternatives sufficiently to report those alternatives to the user for his/her selection. Suppose we have the following input: *Last semester I was unable to get into CS 105. How many FROBS are in it?* If the system can recognize that the student is interested in adding the course, then it could predict that the student is asking either for the number of students already registered or the number of spaces available and present him/her with the alternative.

10.6.2. *An example*

Despite these difficulties in predicting the plan context of the ill-formed utterance, pragmatics can still provide helpful clues in conjunction with the other knowledge sources, allowing us to interpret examples that would otherwise be impossible. For example, as already noted, spelling errors that result in other known words are often especially hard, because it's not clear what portion of the input contains the problem. Consider the following two sentences: *I'm a part-time student who hasn't yet met the science requirement. Do any lab courses meet in Saturdays?* Since the typo of *in* for *on* violates no morphological or syntactic constraints, the second sentence would block during semantic processing due to the failed case assignment to the verb *meet*. If semantics were to attempt to repair this without the help of pragmatics, there would be many possibilities for it to explore. It would have to explore the possibility that there might be a metaphorical sense of meet-in which could connect courses with days of the week. Metaphorical senses do occur, as in the use of *carrying* in *What professor is carrying CS250?* Alternatively, lab courses or Saturdays here might be metonymies, references to entities associated with the literally described entity; an example of metonymy in information systems would be *Does Dr. Arnold meet on Saturdays?* in the sense of *Does Dr. Arnold's section meet on Saturdays?* Other hypotheses involve changes to the input, such as looking for errors in the content words: perhaps lab course should be some other entity that could meet in Saturdays, or Saturdays should be something (like September or Smith Hall) that courses could meet in, or *meet* itself should be some other relation that can connect courses and in Saturdays. The change in the function word *in* would be only one of the many possibilities that semantics would have to explore.

With the cooperation of pragmatics, however, a model of the user's possible plans can be used to suggest what was intended. Such a model in this case would include the following branch:

```
(Satisfy-Lab-Science-Requirement <std>:student <crs>:course)
such that (Is-Lab-Science <crs>:course)
                            |
(Earn-Credit <std>:student <crs>:course <sem>:semester)
such that (Is-Offered <crs>:course <sem>:semester)
                            |
(Earn-Credit-Section <std>:student <sec>:section
                     <crs>:course <sem>:semester)
such that (Section-Offered <sec>:section <sem>:semester)
          (Is-Section-Of <sec>:section <crs>:course)
          (Space-Available <sec>:section)
          (No-Schedule-Conflict <std>:student <sec>:section)
```

The No-Schedule-Conflict precondition to Earn-Credit-Section has subgoals of its own:

```
(No-Schedule-Conflict <std>:student <sec>:section)
                            |
(No-Conflict-Part-Time <std>:student <sec>:section)
such that (Part-Time-Student <std>:student)

              /——————— OR ——————\

(Meeting-Time <sec>:section     (Meeting-Day <sec>:section
<t>:time) such that             <t>:time) such
(Evening <t>:time)              that (Saturday <t>:time)
```

By referring to this plan model, the system could determine that lab courses, their meetings, and Saturdays are all relevant to the current plan context, thus ruling out the metaphorical and metonymical senses for those words that would otherwise have to be considered. Connecting those concepts from the partially understood input to the predicted user plan, the system could then identify

> (Meeting-Day <sec >:section <t>:time)
> such that (Saturday <t>:time)

as the relation to replace the anomalous *meet in Saturdays.* It takes a deft combination of pragmatic and semantic knowledge to identify and fix the problem in such cases.

Effective application of plan context to ill-formedness repair in the style of the example above is beyond what anyone has accomplished thus far. However, Carberry (1985b) has applied a model of user plans and goals to two problems related to ill-formedness: contextual ellipsis and pragmatic overshoot. (Pragmatic overshoot is displayed by requests that do not make sense in the underlying application system, such as requesting the grade points for an audited course.) Using rich pragmatic models is clearly a most important direction for future work, for it implies an ability to follow the intent of the user through a dialog at a level of detail that is useful not only for understanding ill-formed input but also for reducing ambiguity and for providing responses appropriate to those intentions.

10.6.3. Other types of text

Such models of plan context have been studied predominantly in information-seeking dialogs, which would arise in natural language interfaces to information systems. Such dialogs may be organized around the speaker's task-related domain goals and plans, which can be represented conveniently in the sort of tree described above. In working with other kinds of texts like expository prose, there may be a similar level of organization based on the structure of the developing argument (Cohen, 1984). For instance, even if it were ill-formed, this sentence could still be interpreted with the expectation that it was meant to communicate an example of the point made by the previous sentence. Such a level of organization in information-seeking dialogs is captured well by models of the speaker's plans, but in other contexts, rhetorical discourse strategies and general world knowledge could be more important, and should offer pragmatic knowledge for effective treatment of ill-formed language.

10.7. Combining knowledge sources

With an ill-formed input, an unsatisfied constraint preventing an interpretation from being found could arise from problems in the input or alternatively from deficiencies in the understanding system, as indicated in the table below. A natural language processing system has no foolproof way of knowing whether the problem is with the user's input or with its own limited model of language.

Input Error	System Problem
an error in an input symbol	inadequate lexical information
ungrammaticality	inadequate grammar
a semantic error	incomplete selection restrictions
a figure of speech	overly restrictive case frame constraints
non-felicitous input	incomplete dialog models

In the face of all the alternatives for what might prevent the system from understanding the input, all the knowledge and constraints available must be applied to determine what is intended.

For instance, consider an input containing an unknown word FROBBED in the form *Is History 101 FROBBED?* Case frame constraints give little indication of what FROBBED might mean, since a very large number of predicates can apply to courses. Syntax helps us little, since FROBBED could be either a noun, a proper noun, an adjective, or a past participle. Additional knowledge can limit the alternatives, however; if the word were capitalized, one could assume it to be a proper noun. Noticing the *ed* ending and repeated final consonant, the system could propose using the morphological information that FROB is a verb whose past participle is FROBBED. Pragmatic information can further limit the alternatives. For instance, if the input occurred in the context of the user saying *I need to take another Group 1 course*, the system could look at predicates associated with registration for a course such as being filled, the schedule of its being offered, etc. Using all the constraints together, the system could have a ranked ordering of the alternatives it believes likely and suggest them to the user; one would be *Is History 101 filled?*.

In a second example, phonetic knowledge and pragmatic knowledge play a crucial role. Though we have focused on models of user plans and goals as one kind of pragmatic knowledge, other kinds would also be very useful. For instance suppose the system knows of no Professor Chaminski. The request, *Does Dr. Chaminski teach any section of History 101?*, would then not make sense. Phonetic similarity might suggest two alternatives for Chaminski: Charinski and Kasinski. If the system knows that Charinski is in the EE Department and that Kasinski is in the History Department, then it might be able to reason that the student probably means Kasinski. The system could then answer appropriately, *Dr. Kasinski is teaching History 311 and History 620.*

The gain from this combined use of all available knowledge is two-fold: greater diagnostic precision regarding what the source of the problem is, as evidenced in the example regarding courses *meeting in Saturdays* and greater ability to predict what is intended, as in inferring the meaning of FROBBED in the example above.

10.8. Conclusions

Our first conclusion is that all forms of knowledge that may be used as constraints are potentially critical to understanding an ill-formed input. Though we have focused primarily in this chapter on examples regarding unknown words, the same principles seem to hold for the broad class of ill-formed inputs.

Our second conclusion is that work resulting in current implementations certainly has taken initial steps that should markedly improve the robustness and user-friendliness of applied natural language processors. Nevertheless, systems that hope to approach the performance of humans in understanding ill-formed language must incorporate far more knowledge than simply syntax and semantics. (At present, the approaches of Granger, 1983; Carberry, 1985b; and Weischedel and Sondheimer, 1983 have paid most attention to such extensions.)

Third, ill-formedness is not merely ungrammaticality. Morphological, syntactic, semantic, and pragmatic constraints may all be violated.

Fourth, the problems of ill-formedness appear to offer an important opportunity for studying knowledge sources and architectures for understanding natural language. Ill-formed input requires relaxing the rules that normally constrain search or requires doubting the symbols received as input. This suggests using all sources of knowledge, thereby exposing issues which might not surface so readily in studies of well-formed input in limited domains, where redundancy in the input, domain, and context may let one get by with fewer knowledge sources and simpler architectures.

Acknowledgement

This work has been partially supported by a grant from the National Science Foundation, IST-8419162.

11   An integrated theory of discourse analysis

JAMES PUSTEJOVSKY

11.1. Approaches to discourse analysis

A great deal of interest has been generated lately in the area of discourse analysis, motivated in part by the influence of researchers in Artificial Intelligence (AI), attempting to design 'natural language conversation systems.' As with many branches of AI, it at times appears as though it is reinventing the wheel, failing to take stock of past work done in related disciplines such as linguistics, philosophy, and psychology. However, much of the work has added new and complex dimensions to the study of discourse analysis (including speech act theory). I am thinking in particular of the works of Allen, Cohen and Perrault on the role of planning in speech acts; Wilks and Bien and the *Point of View* principle; and the recent work done on conversational moves and clue words, by Webber, Grosz, Sidner, Reichman, and others. The immediate uniformity between these approaches is that they are concerned with process oriented models of discourse understanding rather than claiming to be competence models, in the sense of Chomsky (1965).

In this section I will review the basic concepts that I think are crucial to discourse analysis. In section 11.2 I will survey the work done in the field of discourse analysis and discuss the limitations of existing approaches. In section 11.3 I outline an integrated theory of discourse semantics, building on the research discussed in the previous sections. Finally, in section 11.4 I discuss an implementation of a program, CICERO, which embodies much of the theory presented here.

11.1.1. Setting the stage

In what follows I will attempt to classify the different factors influencing the understanding of a discourse, and how these have been analyzed and dealt with in the field. Since discourse is a facet of the communicative aspect of language, it will be appropriate to start by defining the concept of the communicative content of an utterance, U:[1]

---

[1] I will follow Grice's classification as being essentially correct. See Grice (1971, 1968, 1969) for further discussion.

(1)   1.   Truth-conditional semantics for U.
        2.   Entailments from U.
        3.   Presuppositions from U.
        4.   Conventional implicatures from U.
        5.   Conversational implicatures from U.
        6.   Felicity conditions associated with U.

In this chapter we will concern ourselves with points 2, 3 and 4 from the above list. Unlike many workers in the field, we support the distinction between entailment and presupposition, which we understand in the sense of Strawson (1950). Thus, entailment is identified with logical consequence and defined informally as:

(2) α semantically entails β iff every situation that makes α true makes β true.

Presupposition, on the other hand, is defined as follows:[2]

(3) α presupposes β if:

     i.   if α is true, then β is true;
    ii.   if α is false, then β is true.

This is the standard negation test for distinguishing presuppositions from entailments, introduced by Strawson. It states that if a proposition α has a presupposition set, p, then $\text{NOT}(\alpha)$ will retain these presuppositions.

Some classic examples will illustrate this distinction. Consider the sentences below in (4) and (5).

(4)   a.   All of John's children are asleep.
       b.   John has children.

(5)   a.   John has stopped beating his wife.
       b.   John was beating his wife.

(6)   a.   John managed to stop the car.
       b.   The car stopped.

Sentence (4a) is said to 'semantically presuppose' (4b), but not entail it. For if sentence (4b) is false then we say that (4a) lacks a truth value.

With the sentences in (5) we see what is called 'pragmatic presupposition.' By the use of the aspectual modifying verb 'stop' we are eliciting the presupposition in (5b). As with the pair in (4), if (5b) is false, then there is something strange about (5a) (and in Strawson's theory, this translates to the lack of a truth-value for this statement). Sentence (6a) is said to entail (6b), however, since the negation of (6a) would also negate (6b).

---

[2] Strawson's view of presupposition states that this relation holds of 'statements,' whereas some take this to be a relation between sentences.

There are two other types of pragmatic presuppositions that should be mentioned here. One refers to certain conditions that must be met for a speech act to be 'felicitous' and appropriate in a specified situation. For example, (7b) is a reasonable assumption or presupposition for (7a) (the example is taken from Fillmore 1971).

(7) a.   John accused Harry of writing the letter.
     b.   There was something blameworthy about writing the letter.

Finally, there is the influence of the background knowledge (shared information) when making an utterance in a context, that can be thought of as presuppositional. Consider the sentences in (8).

(8) a.   It wasn't Mary that John married.
     b.   John didn't marry MARY (focused).
     c.   John married someone (and in fact someone else).

The assumed knowledge between the speaker and the hearer in this case, (8a) or (8b), is the proposition in (8c). The presupposition is determined by different means in each sentence, however. (8a) seems to have (8c) as a presupposition because it is in a cleft construction. (8b) has the presupposition in (8c) because it carries focus on the object position.[3]

Having reviewed the types of presuppositions, we should note what the role of conventional implicatures is in discourse analysis. These are non-truth conditional inferences that are associated with certain lexical items. For example, the word 'but' carries the conventinal conventional implicature that there is a contrast of some sort between the elements that are conjoined by this lexical unit. When we examine the work of Reichman and other structural analysts in the next section, the interpretation of clue words will determine just such inferences for the discourse.

In studying the conditions of language use, it is essential to discuss Grice's concept of conversational implicature. The major principle governing a person's behavior in a discourse is formulated as follows (Grice, 1975).

(9)   Cooperative Principle: Make your conversational contribution such as is required, at the stage at which it occurs, by the accepted purpose or direction of the talk-exchange in which you are engaged.

This subsumes the maxims of quantity, quality, relation, and manner which become major working concepts in Gricean theory. We will not

---

[3] The effect of focus on presuppositions has long been known. It received a significant amount of attention in the Prague school of linguistics, cf. Hajičova (1983). Recently Rooth (1985) has examined the issues surrounding focus and presupposition as well.

discuss these in any detail in this chapter (but see Bach and Harnish (1982) for a clear exposition of their role in discourse). Finally, consider the import of felicity conditions on the understanding of an utterance in discourse. These are the conditions that are required for successful, nondefective, communication. Felicity conditions are to be distinguished from the 'success conditions,' which are those conditions that are necessary and sufficient for the performance of an act. In our discussion, we will assume that the latter are necessary, but will have little to say about them here.[4]

Along with the semantic aspects of an utterance, we must include the deeper coherence relations in a discourse, such as causal, temporal, spatial, and definitional considerations (cf. sections 11.2 and 11.3 below).

It is difficult to address any of the components of the communicative content of an utterance without getting involved in at least one other. Therefore no clearly delineated classification is possible. Nevertheless, I would like to compare the work done on these topics by establishing what causal ('feeding') relationship exists between them.

Let us begin by identifying and discussing what appear to be the three major contemporary approaches to discourse analysis:

(10) a. Structural Analysis
     b. Goal Recognition
     c. Model Theory

11.7.2. Structural analysis

The major concerns of those working in this paradigm are to identify structural elements such as *topic, focus, discourse moves*, and *context spaces*. This approach is primarily concerned with how the structure of a discourse influences the interpretation (during analysis) as well as the linguistic realizations (during generation) of a text. Chief proponents of this view are Grosz, Webber, Reichman, and Sidner, as well as Mann and Thompson. I will use the work of Reichman as a representative example.

Early work by Webber (1978) and Grosz (1978, 1981) was aimed at identifying the contexts within which discourse anaphora was licensed. The concepts of *focus* and *topic* were adopted to delimit the search space for anaphoric bindings and coreference.

As Reichman (1985) puts it, the purpose of discourse analysis is to identify 'a conversation's deep structure in terms of the structural relations between the discourse elements.' In this view, discourse structure is defined by the conversational moves (CM) taken by the participants in the

---

[4] But see Austin (1962) and Searle (1969) for the best discussion of this issue.

discourse. Each move takes the discourse into a new stage; that is, each move has associated effects. Central to this model is the notion of *context space*, which is an 'abstract structure' with the following components:

(11) 1. The propositional representation of the discourse utterance.
2. The conversational move (CM).
3. The preconditions for the move.
4. Links to previous discourse spaces.
5. Focus level (strength) assignments for various elements in the context space.

According to Reichman's view, all discourse utterances obey certain rules, regardless of the type of discourse. A few of the more important ones are given below.

(12) 1. Conversation is a series of moves linked by functional relations.
2. Utterances in a single context space serve the same conversational move.
3. A move has preconditions and effects associated with the underlying discourse structure.
4. While in a subspace, the containing context space retains control over interpretation.
5. Inter-sentential anaphoric binding is possible only with strong-focus items.

Central to this model of discourse analysis is the belief that conversational moves (moves) are recoverable from the specific linguistic structure of the text. Thus, we have a taxonomy of possible moves and the clue words most frequently associated with them:

(13)	MOVE	CLUE WORD
1.	Support	Because; Like
2.	Restatement and/or conclusion of point supported	So
3.	Interruption	By the way
4.	Return to interrupted space	Anyway
5.	Indirect challenge	Yes, but
6.	Direct challenge	(No) but
7.	Subargument concession	All right
8.	Prior logical abstraction	But look
9.	Further development	Now

The 'deep structure' of a discourse consists of a sequence of the above moves, through which a conventional interpretation, that is, for Reichman, the understanding of the discourse, is accomplished. This essentially amounts to recovering the mutual knowledge between the participants in the discourse.[5]

---

[5] The important paper, Grosz and Sidner (1985), became available to me much too late to critique and review thoroughly. I would still like to say a few words about it, however.

Like Reichman, Grosz and Sidner are also conscious of the role that both the structure of

11.1.3. Goal recognition

A very different approach to discourse analysis is that which I will call *Goal Recognition*. This differs significantly from the structural analysis school in one important respect: the representation being recovered from an utterance or text involves information about discourse and is generally much deeper than the best representations one can hope to obtain using predominantly syntactic methods. Within this approach we can single out two major schools of thought: one is concerned with narrative form, coherence, and story understanding (Schank and Abelson, 1977; Hobbs, 1982; and Wilensky, 1982); the other stresses recognition of speech acts and intentions (Cohen and Perrault, 1979; Allen and Perrault, 1980).

For Schank and Abelson (1977), and much of the Yale school, understanding a text is a problem of inference generation and control. That is, a reader attempts to find the implicit connections between the sentences in the text. As a solution to the infinite search space problem of inferences, it was proposed that there are script-like knowledge structures which we can access in order to understand stories. Thus we form a coherent understanding of the text by recovering these prototypical event-sequences, the scripts.

Wilensky (1982) points out a number of problems with this approach, chief among them the fact that not all stories or texts can be characterized as stereotypical sequences of events. He proposes a theory of text coherence that incorporates the goals and plans that actors in a text may have. Thus, we try to recognize what the intention of the actor is and piece together the text on the basis of this goal.

Whereas Wilensky is concerned more with the underlying intentions and goals of the agents in a text, Hobbs (1979, 1982) attempts a general classification of coherence relations that may exist in a text. The two that he examines in detail (Hobbs, 1982) are *elaboration* and *occasion*. These relations are formal constraints on an inference mechanism which constructs

---

discourse and the clue words that help identify it. They propose a model of discourse structure with three interacting components:
1.   A linguistic structure: the utterance itself.
2.   An intentional structure; and
3.   An attentional state: an abstraction of the focus of attention of the discourse participants.

Central to their model is the notion of a *discourse purpose* (DP), which is the 'intention that underlies engaging in a discourse.' There is one discourse segment purpose for each discourse segment. Furthermore, the process of manipulating focus spaces, referred to as *focusing*, combines with the DP to control the emerging discourse.

a tree-like structure for a discourse containing all the asserted and presupposed propositions (cf. Hobbs, 1979).

Lehnert (1978, 1982) is also critical of the purely script-based and story grammar (Rumelhart, 1975) approach to understanding as being too topdown oriented. She proposes a system of text analysis and memory organization which has the features of bottom-up processing as well.

In this theory the underlying notion of text coherence is based on *affect states* and *plot units*. Affect states are a set of primitive predicates over states and events, with values *positive, negative*, or *neutral*. That is, an event is positive, etc. with respect to an object. These states are bound to objects.

In addition to these primitive predicates, the theory uses links between event/state pairs that describe causal coherence relations: *motivation, activation, termination*, and *equivalence*. These relations serve as the basis for Lehnert's definition of plot units as directed labeled links from one affect state value to another. The underlying coherence of a narrative, then, is captured in terms of these units.

It is important to note that in these approaches, the inference processes are spawned by the contents of knowledge structures (including plans, goals, and scripts) associated with propositions rather than linguistic or surface structural clues.[6]

Alterman (1985) proposes an interesting theory of text coherence based on the notion of *event concept coherence*. This property is part of the dictionary entry for an event/state description, and provides a way to group text into structured bundles, based on their relative coherence. Alterman makes three claims for his theory: (1) text is composed of structured chunks of conceptual event/state descriptions; (2) events can be bundled together without stating their complete causal connections; (3) the initial grouping and structuring of text can be done with simple augmentation of case relationships by inter-event relations.

The concept coherence relations assumed by Alterman are characterized as follows:

(14) a. Taxonomic—class/subclass
      b. Partonomic
          i.   sequence/subsequence
          ii. coordinate
      c. Temporal
          i.   before
          ii. after

---

[6] This is not completely true. Some researchers in this school make use of clue words first to detect the knowledge structures that must be connected with the propositions just as Reichman and Polanyi and Scha (1984) do.

Thus in an example such as (15), it is the relative proximity in the semantic field of the concepts *chop* and *drop* via the concept *hold* that establishes the coherence between the two sentences.

(15)   a.   The peasant was chopping a tree in the woods.
           b.   He dropped his axe ...

Another approach that addresses questions of goal recognition is taken by Cohen, Allen, and Perrault. These researchers have as their primary concern the recognition and modeling of the speaker's plans in a dialog.[7] According to this view, speakers' intentions can be thought of as plans, and speech acts are no different from any other actions. Hence, they can be planned and recognized with algorithms and heuristics already employed in AI for planning systems.

Cohen and Perrault (1979) treat actions as operators defined in terms of *preconditions* (applicability conditions), *effects,* and *bodies,* which explicate how to achieve the effects. The latter are evaluated relative to the speaker's models of their listeners. Thus discourse processing in this view has nothing to do with the structure of the discourse *per se* but rather with the intentions of the speakers.

The model that a speaker has of his listeners involves representing the beliefs and goals of those people. Belief is interpreted for Cohen and Perrault as a modal operator, A-BELIEVE, taking propositions as its argument. This formal treatment (cf. Hintikka, 1969) allows for infinite embeddings of belief contexts.

Recently Litman and Allen (1984) have extended the planning paradigm to allow plans about the planning process itself. This allows for tracking interruptions while still keeping track of the plans associated with the speech act being performed.[8]

---

[7] The work of Grosz (1978) deals with tracking a dialog topic in a task-oriented domain. She employed plan-tracking heuristics to this end, but did not embed speech acts into a general planning environment.

[8] Another important approach to belief (and goal) recognition is that taken by Wilks and Bien (1983). This 'least-effort' approach to language understanding and belief representation is to be contrasted with that just mentioned, such as Allen and Perrault (1980). Wilks and Bien argue that deep nestings of beliefs could not possibly be efficient from a psychological or computational perspective. They propose as an alternative a theory of what they call *belief percolation,* whereby temporary frames (pseudo-texts) indicating belief states can be propagated, if necessary for the understanding of a discourse.

11.1.4. Model theory

Discourse analysis has recently become a central topic within formal approaches to linguistics and semantics. I am thinking in particular of the discourse representation theories of Kamp (1981) and Heim (1982) and the recent work on situation semantics by Barwise and Perry (1983). These approaches take as their point of departure the formal framework proposed by Montague (1974) and Kaplan's work on indexicals and demonstratives (1977). There isn't room here to examine these works in detail, so only the major points of their theories will be reviewed.

Kamp's (1981) main concern is the correct interpretation and representation of discourse referents. Essentially, Kamp argues that deictic and anaphoric occurrences of pronouns are identical, and that identifying their antecedents involves selection from specified sets of previously available entities. Associated with an utterance is a discourse representation structure (DRS) containing the appropriate quantification over the entities in the proposition, as well as the propositional content. To illustrate, consider the DRS for (16a), shown in (17):

(16)   a.   Pedro owns a donkey.
        b.   He beats it.

(17)

```
 ┌──────────────────────────┐
 │  u          v            │
 │  .          .            │
 │  Pedro owns a donkey     │
 │  u = Pedro               │
 │  u owns a donkey         │
 │  donkey(v)               │
 │  u owns v                │
 └──────────────────────────┘
```

Now, the novel aspect of Kamp's proposal comes with the DRS for (16b). Because there are no possible referents within (16b) for the two pronouns, it does not license a separate DRS but must rather be embedded within (or bound by) another, satisfying structure; in this case, (17). Hence, we have the DRS for the discourse pair (16a) and (16b), shown in (18).

The proper linking is now possible between the pronominals and their antecedents, since there is a common scope delimiter, viz. the DRS, which contains both the binder and the variable.

Heim's (1982) approach is similar to Kamp's in many respects, but her concern is how to represent the presuppositions carried by utterances. Crucial to this theory is the notion of a *file*, a record on which descriptions of entities can be kept, and which is evaluated with respect to rules of *familiarity* and *file-change*.

(18)

```
u          v
.          .
Pedro owns a donkey
u = Pedro
u owns a donkey
donkey(v)
u owns v
He beats it
u beats it
u beats v
```

According to Heim, every sentence has 'file change potential.' That is, every utterance has the potential to change the set of contexts for the utterances following it. This is what Stalnaker (1979) terms the common ground between the speaker and the hearer, which is essentially the set of presuppositions common to both, and which, for Heim, is stored in a *file* of a context.[9]

11.8. Shortcomings of the current approaches to discourse analysis

It is clear from our discussion above that what counts as a representation of the discourse or as the understanding of the text differs wildly. In this section I would like to explore how these different representations interact and propose a model for discourse analysis incorporating some components from the above approaches.

11.8.1. Conversational moves versus coherence

Let us begin by examining the logical distinction between possible conversational moves in a discourse and possible types of coherence that tie a text together. Reichman and others, following Grice (1971), classify utterances according to the roles they play in the discourse, e.g., supporting, elaborating, interrupting, etc. Others working in goal recognition have classified the types of coherence relations that exist between sentences in a text or discourse. These include causation and temporal ordering, but also notions such as elaboration and occasion. The problem here is that what some are calling *moves* in a discourse others term *coherence relations.*[10]

---

[9] Another view that should be mentioned here is Lauri Carlson's game theory of discourse (Carlson, 1983). Space does not permit us to examine it here. However, we do discuss some of his ideas in section 11.3.

Barwise and Perry (1983) provide the groundwork for a theory of situations and attitudes that allows for partial models rather than being tied to the exhaustive models of Montague semantics. I will have nothing further to say here about this approach.

[10] Note that 'coherence' is distinct from 'cohesion.' The former notion is semantically motivated while the latter refers to syntactic properties.

Thus, as already mentioned, Hobbs (1982) describes the two coherence relations, *elaboration* and *occasion.* In the dialog shown in (19), (b) is said to elaborate (a).

(19) a.   John can open Bill's safe.
     b.   He knows the combination.

Similarly, (20) is said to be an instance of an elaboration.

(20) a.   Go down Washington St.
     b.   Just follow Washington St. three blocks to Adams St.

Although the (b) examples above clearly elaborate the (a) sentences, there is much more that can be said about the coherence relations between them than this. The notion of elaboration Hobbs is using here is *syntactic* coherence and is not significantly different from a conversational move for the structural analysts. In this sense I agree that both (19) and (20) are structural elaborations.

A deeper description, however, of the connectedness between the two sentences in (19) would involve something like a because-of relation; that is, the nonsyntactic coherence link here is *enablement* and not elaboration. The connectedness between (20a) and (20b), on the other hand, is one of identity.[11] Although structurally an elaboration, (20b) reflects a changed performative strategy by the speaker, due to his/her model of the hearer's beliefs.

The other coherence relation Hobbs mentions is *occasion,* which can be defined simply as follows: A occasions B if A creates a state so that B can occur. An example of this is a text involving direction giving:

(21) a.   Turn left.
     b.   Go to the corner.

By performing the action denoted in (21a) a change of location is effected that allows the action in (21b) to occur. The structural relationship between (a) and (b) is simply a continuation or further development, and I agree with Hobbs that the coherence link here is one of occasioning.

While Hobbs and others fail to make a careful distinction between conversational moves and deeper coherence relations, still others ignore the role of discourse moves entirely. Alterman (1985), for example, develops a taxonomy of concept coherence terms with which his system creates a complete representation of a narrative text without recourse to textual or conversational moves. The obvious problem with this approach, in my opinion, is that without the structural clues provided by a discourse or text (such as

---

[11] *Identity* is thus one of the possible values for connectedness. More examples are given below (cf. section 11.3).

topic and focus) it is impossible to adequately recover the interpretation of pronouns and deictic terms. For example, in the partial text mentioned in 11.1 *he* is bound by the NP mentioned in the previous sentence, *the peasant* (cf. (22)). But it is not the underlying coherence relation that licenses this as much as the structural positioning of the antecedent relative to the pronoun.

Determining such structural environments for discourse anaphora has been the concerns of researchers such as Sidner, Grosz, Webber, and Reichman. One such licensing context is the *domain of focus*, which accounts for the anaphoric behavior of the pronoun discussed in (22). These theories suffer, however, from the lack of any coherent representation of the deeper semantic relations between the discourse entities.

As discussed above, Reichman (1985) proposes a theory of discourse structure based on conversational moves. This model takes a surface representation (call it SS of an utterance) and maps it into a discourse representation (DR) using clue words as triggers for interpretation, because clue words act to signal when a shift in context is being made. Thus, an utterance such as (22b) is construed as a *support* for (22a).

(22) a.   I don't like John,
      b.   because he's rich.

Let the interpretation of (22a) be represented by P, and (22b) by Q. The derived DR for this pair is then,

(23)   P *because* Q → supports (Q,P)

Interestingly, however, there is another interpretation of (22) with the *because* connective (operator) inside the scope of the negative in (22a). The reading here can be paraphrased as 'That John is rich is not the reason I like him,' or formally: 'It is not the case that (P because of Q), but (P because of Q).' The function of *because* under this reading is not direct support, but rather to trigger an entirely different set of presuppositions. Namely, the fact that there is some other support to P that is not explicitly mentioned, and that Q does *not* support P.

This points to the problem of what to take as the input to discourse analysis. Reichman assumes that surface structure is the natural choice, as do most structural analysts. This example, however, seems to indicate that Logical Form (LF) may have a feeding role into Discourse Representation. Any presuppositions or discourse moves associated with the second interpretation would have to be derived from the LF, where the appropriate scope assignments are represented (cf. (24)).

(24)   [P *because* Q] → supports (Q, P)

Although this is an isolated example, I think it is important to study such interactions in order to establish the feeding relations between the various interpretation levels.

Another criticism that can be leveled at Reichman concerns her misunderstanding of the Toronto school's (Allen, Cohen and Perrault) meaning of 'understanding.' She points out that one must distinguish between a person's *intention for an utterance* and the *communicative effect* of the utterance in context: '[While] a speaker's intent may well be reflected by a communication, grasping that intent cannot be a necessary precondition for understanding' (Reichman, 1985). The confusion here is this: Reichman states that a hearer's interpretation is dependent on the communicative effect of the utterance in context, and this may or may not be identical to the speaker's intent. I agree with this, but I would not call this *understanding* the speaker. This is in fact the basis for *misunderstanding* in a communicative act. In order to fully understand the speaker, it is not a sufficient condition, but at least a necessary condition to recover the intent.

Finally the question arises as to where the model theoreticians fit into the discussion above. First, it is obvious that the major concerns are different for these researchers. Although questions of anaphora and reference are dealt with, Kamp's theory doesn't address the problems of inferencing or goal recognition and planning or computer modeling. Nor does he look at the structure or semantics of supra-sentential text and ask questions pertaining to coherence. Yet these are not his immediate interests. Heim addresses many topics related to Discourse Analysis as well, the emphasis being on the presuppositions from utterances, and the proper characterization of the *common ground*, the mutual belief space. Although this work highlights the importance of Logical Form (LF) for later interpretation strategies, her concerns do not extend to the deep coherence relations addressed by Hobbs and others.

11.3. Levels of discourse analysis

In this section I would like to outline a model for discourse analysis based on fairly strict levels of interpretation and establish what the relationships are among the different components. Some of the most important questions in discourse analysis are the following:

1.   What are the levels of analysis for Discourse Analysis?
2.   What is the unit of analysis for Discourse Analysis?
3.   How does Discourse Representation (DR) affect interpretation?
4.   If DR is not the final semantic interpretation, then what is?

In this section I will address mostly the first two questions. Although this model is obviously incomplete in the form outlined below, it seems to offer a new perspective which can contribute to the solution of some long-standing problems.[12]

Let us begin by separating the structural or syntactic aspects of a discourse from the coherence relations, which I will call the 'deeper semantics,' as distinct from the truth conditional semantics as typically employed for the interpretation of syntactic representations. First, it should be clear that the conversational moves discussed above in section 11.1.2 are structural descriptions for the constituent structure of the discourse itself.

A conversational move, following Carlson (1983), can be conceived as involving the following parameters.

1. The author of the move.
2. The addressee(s) of the move.
3. The audience of the move.
4. The utterance of the move.
5. The game rule(s) which justify the move.
6. The premises (preconditions) of the move.
7. The dialog(s) the move is in.

Perhaps most relevant to our discussion is the notion of structural admissibility which point (5) addresses. That is, a move is justified in the context of a larger structural unit, referred to as a game in Carlson's framework. We will return to this point later in our discussion of discourse syntax.

Also of a structural nature are the 'domain' notions, such as focus and topic, which have meaning (for interpretation purposes) only within a context, i.e., a discourse or a game. Constraints on the interpretation of anaphora and deixis are definable in terms of these notions.

Similarly, textual 'directives,' such as 'elaboration,' are syntactic rather than semantic in their function, since an elaboration of an expression may denote any number of semantic connections, from causation and noncausal explanation to simple description. Thus, a textual directive (or cohesion relation) establishes a certain 'inferential' connectedness without fully specifying what it is (cf. the comparison with coherence relations below).

The following possible structural relations in a discourse are thus formulated:

1. A conversational move (CM); e.g., support, interrupt, challenge, etc.
2. The parameters that act to constrain the evaluation of a discourse object, e.g., topic, focus, theme, rheme.
3. A textual directive (cohesion relation), e.g., elaboration.

While it is impossible to characterize all discourses in terms of a set of common *structural* properties, there may be semantic similarities that all

---

[12] Note that this is a proposal for a process-oriented model rather than a competence model (but this distinction will not be further discussed here).

dialog situations have (cf. Carlson, 1983 for such a view). Yet there are some text situations that lend themselves to a fairly straightforward analysis. These are the simple *monolog* structures, discourses involving one participant.

The complexity of a discourse can be characterized by the possible turns available at any stage in the dialog. It seems to follow from this that single participant speaking situations, then, will have fewer turns available at any state than those with two. The simplest structure in this view will then be a *directed monolog,* where the goal of the speaker is detected *by the manner in which the discourse is structured.*[13]

To say that directed monologs are the simplest discourse type is not to say that they lack complexity. Within this family of discourses several basic types can be distinguished, some still simpler than others:

Directed Monolog Types

1. Enumeration.
2. Elaboration
3. Definition.
4. Description.
5. Proof-form.
6. Narrative.

As an example of an enumeration, consider both texts below.

> The reasons we should hire John are as follows: A,B,C,...
> There are several reasons for hiring John. First A, secondly B, ...

An elaboration monolog is a textual directive of 'elaborate' for a larger text. For example:

(a)   John can open Bill's safe.
(b)   He has the combination,
(c)   which he got from Mary.

There are actually two types of elaboration in this example. The relationship between (a) and (b) is an *explanatory elaboration* while that between (b) and (c) is a *descriptive elaboration.*

Directed monologs are relatively simple. Therefore it can be suggested that there are useful structural generalizations that can be made about their form; namely, that a directed monolog is defined structurally as a text where one proposition acts as *head,* H, and at least one which acts as its *complement,* COMP.[14] Any other material in such a monolog can be

---

[13] Other types of text and discourse will also meet this criterion, of course. For example, rhetorical argumentation, dialectic discussion, and other dialogs, achieve the goal of the participant by the structure of the discourse itself. There is no space to discuss these here, however.
[14] These structural notions are borrowed from linguistic theory. Cf. Chomsky (1981) for further explanation.

analyzed as *adjunct* text. The text is said to be a projection of its head. Thus, a directed monolog, *M*, has the following minimal structure.

$M \rightarrow \{..., H, COMP, ...\}$

The specific type of text will specify further syntactic properties, for example, the position of the head, and the number of complements, etc. To make this clearer, consider the text structure of an enumeration.

$M_{enum} \rightarrow Head\ COMP$

$COMP \rightarrow p_1\ p_2\ ...\ p_n$

The only structural commitment being made here is that the listing acts as a unit, independent of the head, or theme. This approach differs, then, from 'systemic' classifications of text structure, in that only a minimal structure is attributed to the text, without any powerful functional labels. This is preferable on the grounds of the complexity of any eventual implementation of the approach.[15]

Moving on to discourses involving two participants one can quickly see the limitation of the syntactic model. Such texts are simply too rich to lend themselves to a simple, single-dimension grammar. The nature of more complex discourse will be discussed in a later work. In the next section, however, the data will be idealized in a two-participant text, and a conceptual generalization along lines similar to those outlined above for a monolog will be attempted.

Let us now consider the more interpretive aspects of discourse structure. The coherence relations discussed earlier in section 11.1.3 are less structural in nature than the above textual directives — although sometimes they are related to specific structural realizations. Relations such as enablement, or in general causation, or explanation are not uniquely or deterministically inferrable from the syntactic structure alone. The structure of a dialog can be characterized independently of coherence relations, but not of the cohesion relations and moves.

The major notion contributing to the semantics of an utterance in a given context is the intention of the speaker in performing the speech act. This will be termed, somewhat casually, the 'speaker's goal.' This might be compared to Grosz and Sidner's (1985) Discourse Purpose, and this similarity will be discussed below.

Let us now attempt to organize these various contributing factors (conversational moves, and thematic cohesion relations) into a model for discourse analysis (DA). In the previous section it was suggested that perhaps Logical

Form (LF) is the appropriate input for discourse analysis rather than the surface structure (SS) itself. This assumption will be continued with here.

It will be assumed that any adequate model of discourse analysis should represent the distinctions between properties and the semantic properties of the discourse. The former should be viewed as comprising a level of Discourse Representation (DR) distinct from the purely syntactic or semantic interpretation of the utterance. Let us then propose the following hypothesis as the first link in the model:

(25)   LF → DR

That is, the Logical Form of an utterance is seen as feeding Discourse Representation.

Establishing such a model, however, is meaningless without examining what the unit for discourse analysis is. Let the utterance, as defined by linguistics, be such a unit. One utterance may have several communicative effects, however, in terms of conversational moves and speech acts conveyed. If DR is the level at which moves and directives are represented in our model, then the mapping from LF to DR is not one-to-one, but rather one-to-many. For example, any non-restrictive relative clause can be thought of as (at least) an elaboration or further development of the NP it modifies. Yet for purposes of intrasentential anaphora and binding, one must treat it as one sentence.[16] Similarly, adjunct clauses containing temporal adverbial and other connectives may very often signal a conversational move on the part of the speaker, and will map to a separate subrepresentation.

In order to capture this mapping let us say that one of the primitives in DR is the clause, i.e., a simple proposition. The syntax of DR establishes the connectedness of these clauses in terms of the moves taken by the speaker (or inherent in the text). This is expressed as follows, where CF is the abbreviation for Clausal Form:

(26)   LF → $\{_{DR}CF_i\}$

The CF for the sentence 'John loves Mary,' for example, would be the standard logical representation 'TNS(loves(j,m)),' or the NP 'every woman' would have a representation $\lambda P(x)[woman(x) \longrightarrow P(x)]$. No particular Logical Form will be selected, however, as this is not a major concern in this chapter (but see Kamp, 1981, and references therein for discussion of logical form for discourse). Regardless of what logical formalism is assumed as input to DR, it is important to stress that DR contains

---

[16] Reinhart (1983) addresses some of the problems of anaphora between main clause constituents and adjunct phrases.

structural information that is beyond the scope of any general, context-independent linguistic formalism. The DR does not lose any information provided by the structural properties of LF.

We now define the structure of DR more completely. A Discourse Representation, DR, is the level of representation of the utterance derived from the logico-syntactic form, LF, which represents the cohesion relationships between clauses, the domain of topic and focus, and the moves associated with the utterance. The cohesion relations (the textual directives) relate clausal representations, and these are then bound to a particular move. A DR may be associated with one or more moves in the larger discourse structure, but there must be at least one move associated with it.

This gives us the following derived structure.

$$LF \longrightarrow \{_{DR}[_{M_1}CF_i] \dots [_{M_2}CF_j]\} \quad IF$$

where M stands for a conversational move. This level is the structure on which we interpret:

1. The bindings between discourse anaphora and deictic terms and their antecedents; that is , the domains of 'topic' and 'focus' mentioned above. If an NP is in focus, for example, the system allows for pronominal reference within a wider textual context than if it is not.

2. The relationship between moves in the context of higher order structures (i.e., games of discourse trees, cf. below), in other words, how these individual moves combine to make up a story-level or narrative discourse.

From the discourse structure one derives a level called Intentional Form (IF), by:

1. Establishing the deep coherence relations between clausal forms; and

2. Recovering the speaker's goal associated with the annotated discourse representation.

$$LF \rightarrow \{_{2DR}[_{M_1}CF_i \dots [_{M_2}CF_j\} \rightarrow IF$$

Two clausal forms may be connected by one of the following deep coherence relations:

1. Causal
2. Spatial
3. Temporal[17]
4. Definition

---

[17] Causality can be thought of as a covering term to include *occasioning, enablement,* and stronger senses of causation. For now, let us think of causation as an operator that limits or prunes the possible state space following an event. Thus, where b is *temporally subsequent* to a, we determine the strength of a causing b by examining b relative to the rest of the state space generated by a.

A textual directive which associates two clausal forms that are part of different moves is termed a move-directive. Move-directives are typically the clue words that signal a change in discourse space.

To illustrate how the above levels combine to form a model for Discourse Analysis, let us look at a simple discourse and the representations associated with the utterances.

A.   The economy of Houston, where most US oil is refined, is rapidly declining,
B.   Because the price of oil is falling.

Assuming an uncontroversial logical representation as input to our analysis, the DRs for A and B are given as follow:

DR_A [$_M$ type:statement &
        Exists (x)[economy(x) of (x,H & decline(x) &
        ELABORATE(H,λ x(most-oil-refined-in(x))))]

DR_B [$_M$ type:support &
        BECAUSE(m,the(y)(oil-price(y) &
        falling(y)))]

The nonrestrictive relative clause in sentence A is embedded in a cohesion relation with its head, 'Houston.' Since 'because' relates propositions in different moves, it acts as a move-directive, and is analyzed similarly to clue words in Reichman's approach.

The IF associated with each utterance will establish coherence relations between clauses, and will recover the speaker's goal. Speaking to the first point, notice that the elaboration in A will translate to a *definitional* relation. This particular definition *qua* description will allow the causal connection expressed by the move-directive, 'because,' to be detected with less non-textual inferencing. That is, the connection between Houston's economy and oil prices is facilitated by this definitional coherence.

As noted, the intentional form will represent, among other things, the goals and plans associated with the utterance. Still the most elusive aspect of this level is the representation of mutual belief, the 'common ground' between the speaker and the hearer. Speaking in terms of what is presupposed and inferred by a listener, we will distinguish between:

1.   those clauses that are asserted;
2.   those clauses presupposed by the lexical structure of an utterance;
3.   those clauses presupposed on the basis of the syntactic structure of the utterance; and
4.   those clauses presupposed as a result of convention, by which we understand the mutual beliefs of the participants in the discourse.

In short, presuppositions are triggered by different elements in different environments (Karttunen, 1973, 1974).

Now we ask, at what levels are the various presuppositions derived or computed? Lexical presuppositions, we claim, accompany the LF structure into DR; that is, they are already computed. Structural presuppositions, on the other hand, are computed from LF and feed into DR. Conventional implicatures will be computed from DR itself, making use of information associated with clue words and other 'conventional implicature triggers,' while the presuppositions associated with beliefs and common ground will be computed at IF. IF feeds into itself, indicating that inferencing is spawned as a result of these conventional inferences. The inferencing is kept local to the intentions and goals of the speaker/hearer, thus acting as a halting condition. In the next section we will outline our current implementation of a discourse inference system and how it manifests the theory of discourse analysis outlined above.

11.4. CICERO: inference controlling for discourse analysis

In this section I would like to describe the current capabilities of a system being designed at the University of Massachusetts. This project is part of a large natural language understanding system, COUNSELOR, currently under development. I will first describe the scope of the research involved and how the various components interact. I will then give a detailed description of the discourse interpreter, CICERO, as well as the knowledge representation used by the system. At all times I hope to make it clear how this system's functioning relates to the model proposed in the previous section. For a more detailed view of the current implementation relating to design and control issues, see Pustejovsky et al. (1985).

11.4.1. A natural language interface for a case-based legal reasoning system

COUNSELOR is the combined effort of four separate projects to develop a case-based legal reasoning system with full natural language capabilities. The projected capabilities will allow a lawyer to input interactively the facts of a case, let the system analyze them, and propose the strongest arguments and counterarguments based on the given facts. The system that actually does the legal reasoning (HYPO) is the causal agent for the natural language front end, which consists of a parser, a generator, and a discourse interpreter.[18] The interaction of the systems is illustrated in Figure 1.

As an example of the text and discourse encountered by the system, consider the fragment below from an actual interactive session between an attorney, P, and the system, S.

P: I represent a client named HACKINC who wants to sue SWIPEINC and Leroy
        Soleil for misappropriating trade secrets in connection with software developed by

---

[18] We will not be concerned with the actual reasoning capabilities of HYPO. Cf. Ashley and Rissland (1984) for details of the argumentation process involved in the system.

my client. HACKINC markets the software, known as AUTOTELL, a program
to automate some of a bank teller's functions, to the banking industry.

S: Did Soleil work for HACKINC?
P: Yes, he did.
S: Did he then later work for SWIPEINC?
P: Yes.
S: Was Soleil an employee on the AUTOTELL project?
P: Yes, in fact, he was a key employee.

This example illustrates two aspects of the understanding process: (1)
fact and plan recognition (the opening paragraph); and (2) a question-
answer interaction soliciting facts for the express purpose of formulating an
argument.

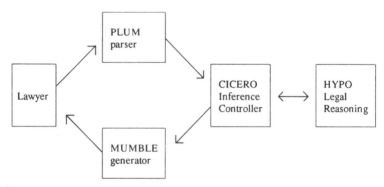

Figure 1. The structure of COUNSELOR.

11.5. Managing the discourse

The discourse component of COUNSELOR is the program called CICERO,
which can be viewed as essentially two subsystems. The first tracks and
predicts the structure of a discourse based on conversational moves, interpreted through keywords and a discourse grammar. The other subsystem
manages and controls the representation of the deeper semantic relations
between discourse entities and predicates.

The basic components of the system are:

(1)   A knowledge base defined in terms of *clusters*; and
(2)   a best-first control strategy generating and recognizing plans of the
        speaker and the hearer, respectively.

A *cluster* is a particular way to represent both the objects in the world and
mental objects such as plans and goals that operate over them. It is a frame
representation language with inheritance properties (cf. Minsky, 1975,
Bobrow and Winograd, 1977).

The ontology consists of the following types: [19]
1. *objects:* frames representing real-world objects with associated role-goal pairs.
2. *states:* predicates over the objects.
3. *events:* functions from one state to another.
4. *scripts:* prototypical event sequences.

Using examples from the dialog above, let us examine what structure these clustered objects have, and what role they play in the interpretation of the discourse.

Under the current implementation,[20] at the start of a session, the discourse tracking component of CICERO has already set the system mode to expect a case facts summary from either a layman or an attorney. That is, CICERO is expecting a particular kind of speech act; namely an *inform.*[21] This top-down expectation is represented in the current discourse frame under the slot *:discourse-mode*, along with the contextual parameters, *:participants*, *:speaker-goal*, and *:hearer-goal*.

After the parse of the initial sentence, CICERO's task is to confirm any expectations it has, concerning the speaker-goal, as well as to form a coherence representation of the semantic content of the proposition. The parse output for this sentence is a *legal-representation* frame, and passes this knowledge to CICERO that the speaker is an attorney. This in turn satisfies the precondition for the instantiation of the discourse script shown in (27) — the coherence representation — and confirms the system's expectation for what the speaker's goal is; viz. to inform about a case.

```
(27)      (define-cluster accept-information-about-case-script
            :participants ((hearer)
                       (speaker))
            :props ((lawsuit))
            :preconditions (((speaker '(:type attorney)))
            :events ((t0 '((:optional)
                           (:code (establish-relationship-of-lawyer-to-party))))
                     (t1 '((:head)
                           (:code (action-taken-by-the-plaintiff))))
                     (t2 '((:head)
                           (:code (elaboration-of-case-perspective))))))))
```

The script illustrated in (27) clusters together the rhetorical moves associated with presenting information about a case for this particular situation. Each speech act of *inform* is represented as a separate action in the *:events*

---

[19] In this implementation we assume a standard temporal logic, such as Allen's (1984), for interpreting and reasoning about the tense-based objects.
[20] The clusters including scripts have been implemented as flavors in Zetalisp on a Symbolics. For implementation details see Pustejovsky et al. (1985).
[21] *Inform* is one of about five distinct speech act types, which include *Request, Promise, Suggest,* etc.

190   *James Pustejovsky*

field, and this defines part of the larger textual structure of this preamble in the dialog.

In addition to the instantiation of the discourse script above, the semantic representation of the 'desire to sue,' the *lawsuit* frame from the parser, is bound as the value of the *:conceptual-frame* for this discourse space, and in particular, it is of type *misappropriation.* The state of the discourse at this point (after the first sentence) is represented by the following discourse-frame and bindings:

```
(28)     (define-cluster legal-discourse-frame discourse-frame
         :participants ((hearer 'COUNSELOR)
                (speaker '((:type attorney)
                (:infer from legal-rep attorney))))
         :hearer-goal()
         :speaker-goal ((inform 'legal-rep))
         :discourse-mode ((mode 'expect-inform))
         :discourse-script ((script 'accept-information-about-case script))
         :conceptual-frame ((lawsuit '(:type $misappropriation))))
```

At this point the system operates in a top-down expectation-driven mode, triggered by the value for the *conceptual-frame* slot. That is, *$misappropriation* is itself a script, and the best-first control strategy used by CICERO chooses to instantiate the script as a partial result of its inferencing about the potential coherence relations in the (upcoming) text.

```
(29)     (define-cluster $misappropriate script
         'legal concept'
         :participants
                ((plaintiff-corporation '((:type corporation)
                (:inherit thru parent lawsuit *)))
                (defendant-corporation '((:type corporation)
                (:inherit thru parent lawsuit *))) )
         :props
                ((plaintiff-product '((:type product)
                (:infer from plaintiff-corporation product)))
                (defendant-product '((:type product)
                (:infer from defendant-corporation product)))
                (misappropriated-knowledge '((:type knowledge-about-a-product))))
         :preconditions
                ((t0 '((:code '(produces plaintiff-corporation plaintiff-product))))
                (t1 '((:code 'used-in plaintiff-product misappropriated-knowledge)))))
         :events ((t2 '((:code $illegitimate-access-to-knowledge)))
                (t3 '((:code (equal misappropriated-knowledge
                        get-value defendant-product
                        :knowledge-used))
                (t4 '((:code $competitive-advantage))))
```

This representation provides us with the logical arguments for a relation, with the entailments and with a large set of presuppositions that will direct the inferencing to establish the deep coherence in later processing.

The discourse frame in (28) keeps a dual representation of the information streaming in from the parser. For structural bookkeeping purposes, the $misappropriate frame is bound to action-taken-by-the-plaintiff, in that it satisfies a particular structural property of such preamble paragraphs.

For deeper semantic coherence, however, the same frame is bound to :type of a lawsuit, and carries the complex of information shown above in (28).
There are two interesting aspects in the representation shown in (29):

1. Any inferences due to the presupposition-set of an utterance are computed by CICERO rather than by the expert system.
2. The exact same representation is used for understanding text as for generating text.

11.6. Conclusion

This chapter presents a very rough model of discourse analysis based on a level hypothesis, wherein the conflating factors of discourse interpretation have been teased apart. A working system, CICERO, was outlined, which is 'aware' of these levels at specific stages of text analysis. The system, however, is still incomplete at this point, in that it fails to model the speaker's belief space.

Acknowledgements

I would like to thank Sergei Nirenburg, Wendy Lehnert, Kevin Gallagher, Sabine Bergler, John Brolio, Penni Sibun, and Dave McDonald for fruitful discussion on this topic. The work was supported in part by a grant from the Defense Advanced Research Planning Agency contract No. N00014-85-K-0017.

12   Natural language generation: complexities and techniques

DAVID D. MCDONALD

The success of any machine translation (MT) system is measured in terms of the quality of its output. A good MT system must be able to appreciate the nuances of the word choices in the target language (TL) and the inferences that are invited by alternative syntactic phrasings. If such choices are not made deliberately, with an appreciation of their consequences, then the sense of the original text will be distorted. This fact is not well appreciated by the bulk of the MT community, which is evidenced by the fact that the generation programs that they employ are based largely on old-fashioned template-driven designs. Such programs have intrinsic limitations. They deal with language in fixed chunks, with minimal possibilities for variation and thus only the shallowest capacity to accommodate to their context. Large texts built from such rigid pieces have an awkward, mechanical style.

Such limitations do not pose a problem for those of the MT systems that do not demand a high prose style or sophisticated knowledge of nuance. Still, improving capacities in language analysis and representation will soon make it possible to deal with sophisticated texts such as newspapers or contracts, and the need for equal sophistication in generation will follow. The generators in MT systems will have to know how to judge whether a piece of information is new or old, whether it can be communicated tacitly by inferences from the choice of wording or phrasing or must be spelled out explicitly. There must be effective models of the choices a given language offers and their consequences if used. There must be ties to inference systems and to models of the commonsense expectations of a reader of TL. Above all, there must be a rich understanding of the grammatical capacity of the language, of the dependencies between the alternatives it offers and how they may be navigated by the procedures of the generator as it constructs the output text. Simple generation systems do not have such abilities.

Artificial intelligence (AI) research in generation independent of MT has taken considerable strides. It is in a position now to supply the generation capacities that strong MT systems will need. There is now a relatively sophisticated appreciation of alternative designs for a generator and of their consequences. Generation systems have been developed that are capable of quite delicate decisions of phrasing and content flow. Large syntactic grammars have been developed and are being exercised. Theories of the organization and construction of large texts and dialogs are being tried out. Text planning, rather than syntactic realization, has become the research frontier: What model should a conceptual-level program have of the linguistic resources a language puts at its disposal? In what kind of theoretical vocabulary should it do its 'linguistic reasoning'?

This chapter examines the nature of generation systems today, the problems they have been designed to deal with, their strengths and their weaknesses. Its goal is to give the MT community a sense of what has been accomplished, and indirectly to show where MT researchers could consider adopting or adapting some of the AI work in generation. At the same time, MT research can influence the work in AI. As an application, MT can provide more linguistically demanding sources for generation than almost any of today's expert systems. Translation, just like conversation, is a normal human ability, and a considered comparison of the generation process in both contexts should tell us more about the nature of generation as a module within the human mind than could either by itself.

12.1. Introduction

The circumstances in which generation takes place during MT are different from those in a natural language (NL) interface. For an NL interface, the purpose of generation is to deliberately construct a fluent and grammatical text that meets the communicative goals that the underlying AI program has specified. An MT system has no access to the goals the author of its source text may have had, and must either infer them or do without. In the interface, the generator works from a clean slate: it can choose whatever words, whatever syntactic constructions, it believes will accomplish the goals. It also has a relatively free hand with stylistic matters such as sentence length or the complexity of the clause structure. The generator for the MT program, on the other hand, has the option of carrying over the wording and phrasing choices from the source text, and can follow the sentence length and complexity of the source as closely as is plausible.

12.2. Generation versus comprehension

As a field, computational linguistics has far more experience in language comprehension than in generation. There is a tendency to look at generation as a problem similar to comprehension; this tendency should be discouraged, since to understand the issues in language generation one must learn to see it as a problem of construction and planning rather than analysis.

As a process, generation has its own organizational basis. Computationally, language comprehension typically follows the traditional stages of a linguistic analysis: morphology, syntax, semantics, pragmatics/discourse, moving gradually from the text to the intentions behind it. Generation has the opposite information flow: from intentions to text, content to form. What information is already known and what must still be discovered is quite different from comprehension. The known is the generator's awareness of the underlying program's intentions, its plans, and the structure of any text the generator has already produced. Coupled with a model of the audience, the situation, and the discourse, this information provides the basis for making choices among the alternative wordings and constructions that the language provides — the primary effort in constructing a text deliberately.

With its opposite flow of information, it would be reasonable to assume that the generation process can be organized like the reverse of the comprehension process. To a certain extent this is true. In generation, goal selection typically precedes consideration of discourse structure and coherence, which usually precede semantic matters such as the matching of concepts to words. In turn, the syntactic context of a word must be fixed before its morphological form is chosen. One must, however, avoid taking this as the driving force in a generator's design, since to emphasize this ordering of linguistic levels would be to miss generation's special character, namely that *generation is above all a planning process*. Generation entails realizing goals in the presence of constraints and dealing with the implications of limitations on resources, e.g., the specific expressive capacities of the devices a given language happens to have, or the limited space available in a sentence or paragraph for expressing ideas given the constraints of the prose style that has been chosen.

Once one accepts the view that generation is planning, it becomes natural to design a generation system to facilitate making decisions about using certain words or syntactic constructions, and constraining later decisions. The criteria for the division of the process into components now follow from the character of the decision-making involved, which will vary along the following three dimensions:

(1)   What information does the decision draw on: properties of lexical items? Conceptual attributes? Details of planned but not yet realized rhetorical structures? Details of the text's surface structure?

(2)   What other generation decisions, if made differently, would force a change in this decision? If the generation process is to be indelible (i.e., never retracting its decisions), then these relations among decisions will determine the order in which individual decisions are made.

(3)   How should the conclusion(s) be represented? Does a conclusion dictate linguistic actions or just constrain other decisions? Can it

be acted on immediately, or must it be scheduled for execution at a later moment and if so, which moment?

The decision-making perspective as an organizational criterion for generation yields an ordering of events based principally on what dependencies govern a given decision and what representations will supply any needed reference information. In most cases this tends to reinforce a breakdown into stages like the ones identified by linguists.

12.3. Terminology

It is important to establish a working vocabulary for describing the parts of the generation process. There is a fairly consistent temporal orientation in terminology that generation researchers have informally adopted, and a corresponding spatial orientation, though it is less established. Intentions and concepts, the starting point for generation in an interface, are 'earlier' and 'higher;' linguistic matters are 'later' or 'down' from the concepts, with the conventional linguistic levels: discourse, semantics, syntax, morphology, and phonetics, running from higher to lower in that order when they are discussed as a linear progression. Higher entities are more abstract, lower ones more concrete.

The question of what goes into a generation 'system' or a 'generator,' or of where to draw the boundaries between components has, as many answers as there are research groups. Usually the answer reflects the aspects of the problem that the research group has decided to tackle. Some projects maintain that the 'generator' encompasses all of the processing that is not domain-specific reasoning (Mann and Moore, 1981), others are comfortable restricting the term to cover only the linguistic processing, omitting the establishment of goals and the planning of content and large-scale organization (McDonald, 1983).

The rest of this section briefly introduces the processing elements that take part in generation, proceeding from early to late in the process. All references to the 'generator,' when not otherwise specified, will be to the linguistic processor that is responsible for realization.

When a generation system is part of a man-machine interface it will have some relationship to the other major component in that interface, the language comprehension system. Some kind of bridge between the two, a representation of the discourse as a whole, must be maintained to insure that the information is available to support coherent linguistic choices and interpretations across the turns of a dialog. Managing this representation and directing the overall communication activity should be some kind of discourse controller (see for example Bruce, 1975; Wilensky et al., 1984; or Woolf, 1984). In most ordinary cases, however, this controller will not be a separate module but just the executive portion of the underlying program, the non-linguistic, domain-oriented program for which the interface was built. This program can be a cooperative database, an expert diagnostician, an intelligent tutor, etc.

MT systems will have no counterparts to any of these 'supra-generation' modules. They do have the pragmatic equivalent of the 'urge to speak' by which those modules set the process in motion; the question is whether what ensues involves processing of the same kind, and then whether it is broken down into the same kinds of stages.

Within an interface, the generation process starts when some event within the underlying program leads to the need for it to speak: perhaps, to answer a question, to give an explanation or pose a question of its own. Once the process is initiated, three activities take place:

(1)   identifying the goals the utterance is to achieve

(2)   planning how the goals may be achieved by evaluating the situation and available communicative resources, and

(3)   realizing the plans as a text.

Goals, in a computer-related task, would usually be to impart certain information to the audience or to prompt them to some action or reasoning. Planning involves the selection (or deliberate omission) of the information to be conveyed directly in the text (e.g., concepts, relations, individuals). A coordinating rhetorical framework or schema for the utterance as a whole must also be adopted (e.g., temporal progression, compare-and-contrast). Particular perspectives may be imposed to aid in detecting intended inferences.

The non-linguistic plan or specification is typically called a message. The simple mental image evoked by the term 'message' is of written notes passed from one person to another. However, this is much too simple. Researchers who study both planning and realization continually make the point that there is no clean boundary between the two activities (see for example Appelt, 1980 or Danlos, 1984b). Planning proceeds by progressive refinement and must appreciate the linguistic consequences of its decisions. The realization of the largest, most encompassing relations in the message creates a grammatical context that imposes constraints on what can be planned for their arguments. Goals may emerge or change in priority opportunistically as planning and even realization proceeds. Thus though it is usually profitable to think in terms of an abstract 'message' that defines and controls what the later linguistic processing is to produce, one must be careful not to presume from that that the generation process is divided into two distinct stages or even that the message is constructed all at one time before any actual text production has begun.

Realization is the process of representing the planner's directives as actual text. This process has a counterpart in every MT system, since the equivalent of these directives will be the system's model of the source text being translated. Realization depends upon a sophisticated knowledge of the TL grammar and rules of discourse coherency; most realization components typically maintain a syntactic representation of the text as it is being assembled. Usually it is only the realization process that has any direct knowledge of a language's grammar. The form this knowledge takes is one of the greatest points of difference between generation projects, though all projects largely agree on the function it should serve. In generation the function of a grammar is to define and constrain linguistic choices. Choices are dependent on the goals and situation; consequently the information in the grammar must be tied to some kind of model of language use. Generation researchers ask what circumstances lead to the choice of one alternative over another — what functions the various constructions of the language serve that will make them able to achieve a given goal or fit a given discourse situation.

12.4. Why does generation seem to be a simple process?

A generation system cannot be better than the underlying program it is working for. If the program has only simple thoughts, the generator will only be able to say simple things. Measured in terms of the inferential content and structural relations that would make a text interesting linguistically, nearly all current candidate underlying programs 'think simple thoughts.' It is then no accident that until the early 1980s generation was considered by most people in AI to be a relatively simple problem. The level of skill that generators had to exhibit was minimal because only minimal demands were made on them. Taking a statement in an internal representation of the sort people used in the middle 1970's, say *(#supports :block6 :block3)*, coupling it with attributes stored separately for the individuals, and producing 'The big red block supports a green one' requires such a simple computational apparatus (typically a technique known as 'direct replacement,' see below) that the design is usually not worth publishing today.[1]

When generation researchers have the opportunity also to develop the underlying program and thereby to insure that it can supply interesting perspectives and intentions, a considerable level of sophistication can be

---

[1] This example comes from Winograd (1972). In his system the code for generation commanded only about 2% of what went into comprehension, and was not supported by a model of grammar. (Pronouns were introduced into output by reparsing the output and doing substitutions.)

achieved in the text. Figure 1 shows examples of the output from two such cases, both of them developed around 1974. Davey's Tic-Tac-Toe program was a player as well as a commentator. It had a rich conceptual model of the game, and consequently could use terms like 'block' or 'threat' with assurance. Its heuristics for grouping the descriptions of moves together into complex sentences were based on notions of salience and tactical consequences. Clippinger's emulation of one paragraph of speech by a psychoanalytic patient was the result of a computationally complex model of the patient's thought processes: from the first identification of a goal, through planning, criticism, and replanning of how to express it, and finally linguistic realization. Clippinger's program had a multiprocessing capability — it could continue to think and plan while talking. This allowed him to develop a model of 'restart' phenomena in generation including the motivation behind fillers like 'uh' or dubitives like 'you know.'

> 'The game started with my taking a corner, and you took an adjacent one. I threatened you by taking the middle of the edge opposite that and adjacent to the one which I had just taken but you blocked it and threatened me. I blocked your diagonal and forked you. If you had blocked mine, you would have forked me, but you took the middle of the edge opposite of the corner which I took first and the one which you had just taken and so I won by completing my diagonal.'

Figure 1. Output from Davey's program Proteus, commenting on a game of Tic-Tac-Toe that it played with a user.

> 'You know for some reason I just thought about the bill and payment again. (You shouldn't give me a bill.) <Uh> I was thinking that I (shouldn't be given a bill) of asking you whether it wouldn't be all right for you not to give me a bill. That is, I usually by (the end of the month know the amount of the bill), well, I immediately thought of the objections to this, but my idea was that I would simply count up the number of hours and give you a check at the end of the month.'

Figure 2. The monolog produced by Clippinger's program Erma modeling an actual psychoanalytic patient talking to her therapist. Text segments in parenthesis are what Erma was planning to say before it cut itself off and restarted. This is an actual paragraph from a transcript of the patient reproduced in every detail.

But such 'double work' in a research effort is unusual, and work on generation has suffered as a result of the high costs of getting a research effort started. In working on parsing it is clear what one begins with — the words of a text — and one can choose to recover as little or as much of the text's semantic and pragmatic structure as one likes. Generation on the other hand requires one to take a stand on the nature of conceptual representation and intention before one can even begin. To start from anything less abstract, for example to take the input to be a hierarchical structure of verb-like relations over noun-like objects (such as one might get from a compositional semantic interpretation component), is to see generation as just a matter of linearization plus local grammatical realization rules.[2]

When one considers the human generation capabilities, it becomes difficult to believe that the process or its input could be that simple. Consider the versatility the native human speaker can make use of in our simple example. There was no grammatical requirement to say 'a green one' instead of 'a green block:' a contextual influence determines this alternation, taking into account the possible ambiguity of the pronoun on the one hand and the cohesion effect that it brings on the other. More obviously, we can ask why the sentence should be couched as a statement about the red block (its subject) rather than as a statement about the green block. This decision cannot be made in isolation from the context of the intentions behind it — it can require reasoning. Since the option to use either active or passive is not available with every verb or set of adjuncts, this choice can influence other, more abstract choices that feed it.

Native speakers have knowledge about the uses to which phrases can be put that is beyond the ken of simple generators. Consider the use of a 'support' assertion as an attribute of the green block: '...the green block that's supported by the big red one.' How does the generator represent the fact that the relative clause is available as one of the realizations of the assertion? What gives the planner that feeds the generator assurance that such a usage is possible in this case? Can the generator use its representation of the syntactic structure of the declarative form of the assertion in producing the relative clause, or should it have an independent linguistic origin? These are not simple questions to answer.

Furthermore, it is not even possible to begin without adopting an anchoring framework for the generation process as a whole by which to coordinate the individual answers. Yet the 'startup' costs on any such framework are

---

[2] One of the earliest efforts in generation, that of Simmons and Slocum (1972), saw the problem in just those terms. The input to their system was a semantic network structured by case-frame relationships such as 'theme,' 'locus' or 'mood;' its output was single, simple sentences like 'What did the merry widow dance?' As pointed out by Webber (1971), the surface form of the output was already latently present in the linguistic vocabulary that they used in their input representation; all that remained was to read the structure out and make the necessary morphological adjustments. For this to be a reasonable general approach, the underlying program must use these same case-based networks in the internal representation that it uses for reasoning, in effect 'thinking in English.' If that is not the case (and it rarely is), some kind of planning and selection facility must mediate between the internal representation and the input language to the generator. Goldman (1975) did just this as he generated paraphrases of expressions in the conceptual dependency representation: he used a set of discrimination nets to choose lexical heads and subcategorization frames, which he then expressed in Simmons and Slocum's notation for realization by their generator.

high: the peculiarities of information and decision making flow make generation very different in intrinsic character from other language processes one might look to for inspiration. When coupled with the further difficulty of finding a strong underlying program to work with, the net effect has been that until recently very little work on generation has in fact been done.

Few people worked on generation during the last decade (or stayed with the problem for more than a year or two) either because they found the task too simple to be interesting (because of the peculiarities of the underlying systems), or because they found it too difficult to make any headway (because of the complexities of actual texts produced by humans). Today there are underlying programs, available from other research efforts, that are sophisticated enough in their reasoning to need sophisticated generators to voice their thoughts. As a result, the startup costs of good research on generation became lower, and more people are entering and staying with the area. This same increase in program sophistication is making other researchers in AI more appreciative of the need for careful generation because they see the difference that a slight change in wording can make and realize that perspective and context need to be considered in what their program says. They are looking for new approaches to generation to replace their template-based standbys. Before looking at the new work, however, it is important to have a clear understanding of how the old technique works.

12.5. The direct replacement technique

'Direct replacement' is the name that generation researchers have given to the informal, 'natural' technique for text generation from internal representations that non-generation researchers tend to use (see Mann et al., 1982). It is a more informative term for what is commonly known as 'using templates,' and has been independently rediscovered countless times. One of its major benefits, often overriding its deficiencies in grammar and text construction, is that it allows the programmer to use expressions directly from the internal representation of his program, thereby eliminating any need for a text planner or explicit representations of goals. Good descriptions of how the technique has been used in specific projects can be found in Swartout (1981), Chester (1976), or Forbus and Stevens (1981).

In examining any approach to realization — the part of generation most concerned with linguistic matters — there are three things to be considered:

(1)   What is the knowledge of natural language grammar: how is it represented; how is it brought into play during the processing?
(2)   What is the control structure: what determines what action these systems will take next; what possibilities for variation are there, and how are they embodied?
(3)   How does the approach organize the knowledge of how to realize specific objects (relations, attributes, etc.) from the underlying

program: how is it embodied; how is it incorporated into the control structure?

As an example, we can look at what was involved in the production of the sentence below, which is extracted from the standard dialog of Winograd's SHRDLU program (1972). Because of its use of pronouns, SHRDLU was more fluent than most direct replacement generators are programmed to be, but it is otherwise quite typical. (Said in answer to the question 'How did you do it?', which referred to an earlier directive to 'stack up both of the red blocks and either a green cube or a pyramid:')

> SHRDLU: 'By putting a large red block on the table; then letting go of it; then putting a large green cube on it; then letting go of that cube; then putting the red cube on that cube; then letting go of that cube.'

SHRDLU's generation knowledge, like the rest of its linguistic knowledge, was represented procedurally. Specialist programs or code fragments would be associated with terms in the internal representation by attributes indicating what they were to be used for. Special data-driven interpreters would dynamically combine these fragments into full programs as the situation warranted. SHRDLU's generation knowledge, like the rest of its linguistic knowledge, was represented procedurally. Specialist programs or code fragments would be associated with terms in the internal representation by attributes indicating what they were to be used for. The generation program for the event type *#puton*, for example, is this fragment of Lisp code:

```
(append (vbfix 'put) obj1 'on obj2)
```

While inelegant by today's standards because it calls Lisp functions directly ('append') instead of employing an abstract schema, this specialist program is none the less illustrative of the genre. The underlying message for the example text is the list below of events extracted from SHRDLU's model of its history. This list is taken directly from the model; the individual assertions are in the very same representation that the system used for its internal reasoning.

```
(#puton :B6 :table)
(#ungrasp :B6)
(#puton :B3 :B6)
(#ungrasp :B3)
(#puton :B1 :B3)
(#ungrasp :B1)
```

To produce the text, each of the assertions in the message is interpreted as though it was an instruction in a special kind of program. The term *#puton* thus becomes, in effect, a function call whose arguments are the objects *:B6* and *:table*. The specialist generation program just shown is the *#puton*'s definition, and the arguments will be bound to the program's formal parameters *obj1* and *obj2*. The Lisp function *vbfix* ('verb fix') is one of SHRDLU's internal routines. It is responsible for attuning the form of the verb to the grammatical context. The model of context that SHRDLU used was incredibly simple: when answering a 'how' or a 'when' question use the ending ' + ing;' when answering 'why' questions use the infinitive.

The generation process consists simply of the interpreter scanning the message as a stream, replacing expressions and subexpressions with the values returned by their generation functions. No intermediate representations mediate between the internal expressions and the words — hence the name 'direct replacement.' For example, when the generation process has finished evaluating the second element of the first expression in the list, the latter will look like this:

```
(append '(putting)
        '(a large red block)
        'on  ← next expression to evaluate
        :table )
```

Literals like 'on' are already words and are unchanged by the process; the initial preposition 'by' is introduced directly in the same way. Terms from the model like *:B6*, and *:table*, are replaced by lists of words assembled by the specialized generation program the programmer has associated with them. Embedded function calls like the one to 'vbfix' are executed as they are reached, and are expected to return words. A generation interpreter like this is easy to write: with a good programming environment a competent Lisp or Prolog programmer can turn one out in an afternoon.

Returning now to the original questions about the knowledge of grammar, of control structure, and the realization of specific object types, we can see that with direct replacement there is no explicit model of natural language grammar. Grammatical relations are manifested in the output text in an *ad hoc* manner by specialist routines that are incorporated into the replacement stream explicitly whenever they are needed. This piecemeal approach to grammar is effective enough in the construction of simple sentences, but breaks down as the complexity of the grammatical relations increases.

The difficulties of embodying the grammatical situation in a program state without the mediation of an explicit linguistic representation eventually require a programming *tour de force* to overcome and lead to a design that is unwieldy and awkward to extend. The pragmatic limit in grammatical complexity is using a subordinate clause: the effort required to transform a sentence into a relative clause within another, or to form 'Harry wants to go home' from a composite internal expression like *wants(Harry, gohome(Harry))* is too much for generators without proper grammars.

Control is exercised directly by the conceptual representation. As just illustrated, messages are built from expressions in the underlying program's internal representation and are treated as executable generation programs. The natural structure of the expressions defines the order in which their elements will be evaluated and the phrases of the text will appear.

This control technique is convenient and immediate. There are no wasted actions, and no need to define a control structure somewhere else in the generator's design. Its drawback is that the organization of the output text is in lock-step with that of the message. This enforced isomorphism is an inescapable consequence of the design. It is not troublesome if the underlying program's internal representation has been designed with natural language in mind (see for example Swartout, 1981). However it is problematic in two cases: (1) where the same internal expression can be viewed from several different perspectives depending on the situation, with a different organization of the text appropriate in each case; and (2) when it would be best stylistically to combine several independent expressions into one cohesive linguistic unit.

The knowledge of how to choose words to realize individual objects or relations is distributed among a set of specialist programs, usually one for each expression type. SHRDLU's generation specialist for blocks is typical. It was organized as a function from an individual block (say *:B6*) to a list of words, and used a simple algorithm that is the model for many other systems: start with the common noun that names the kind of the object ('block'); add enough of the object's attributes to distinguish it from all the other such objects in the scene. Attributes that can be realized as a single adjective like size or color are placed before the common noun; relations like support are placed afterwards; the determiner 'the' is placed at the front of the word list to indicate that the phrase refers to an individual object. The list returned as the realization of *:B6* would be roughly as shown below.

('the (#size :B6 (200 200 600)) (#color :B6 #red) 'block)

In fact SHRDLU's actual list was more *ad hoc*, since its generation procedure had no way to distinguish the occurrence of an assertion like *(#color :B6 #red)* that was intended as a description of *:B6* (and consequently should be realized as just an adjective) from one intended as an independent statement (and realized as a clause). This is an endemic problem in direct replacement systems, and stems from the central aspect of their design, namely that realization goes directly from the conceptual representation to words without employing any intermediary structure.

If an annotation were added to the block specialist's output list giving the perspective under which the two assertions were to be viewed, then it could serve as the basis for distinguishing the adjective realization from the clause. Annotating an expression in order to describe to the generator its intended use provides a context for its realization. Without a distinguishing context any generator will be forced to realize a given object in the same way each time (barring deliberately random variations). The relation that triggers the reference to an object, for example, the *#puton* event with its reference to the objects *:B6* and *:table*, also introduces a context that can be relevant in deciding the object's realization, one that the generation process should not overlook.

A subtle deficiency of typical implementations of direct replacement is that they bar any possibility of representing this context because of the time they realize a relation compared to the time they realize its arguments. A practically automatic design choice in building any special purpose evaluation function is to follow the protocol used by Lisp and other main-stream functional programming languages, namely the 'applicative order.' In this protocol, the arguments to a relation (function call) are evaluated before the relation is. In the present case this can mean, for instance, that the forms of the noun phrases are chosen before the linguistic form of the verb can be known. This is one of the reasons why all but the simplest grammatical forms can be difficult for a direct replacement generator to produce, since the generator is committed to the wording for embedded elements before it can know what grammatical constraints the embedding relation is going to impose. We will return to this issue later in the section on description-directed generation, where an alternative, 'normal order,' evaluation protocol makes this sort of context available in a natural way.

12.6. Modern approaches to generation

Natural language generation is becoming an increasingly popular research topic. There have been a significant number of Ph.D. theses presenting artifical intelligence approaches to generation in recent years (McDonald, 1980; Appelt, 1981; Tait, 1982; Conklin, 1983; Hoenkamp, 1983; Kukich, 1983; Jacobs, 1985) as well as some closely related theses on problems involving text planning (Swartout, 1981; Woolf, 1984; McCoy, 1985).

Generation is emerging as a recognized research area. The intellectual climate within the generation community is not unlike that of the language understanding community around 1974, with a roughly similar number of players and a similar feeling in the air that significant things are happening. Unfortunately, as with understanding in 1974, it is presently very hard to sort the different research efforts on generation into coherent schools of thought. This is in part because even now there are not so many researchers following any given approach that it can be properly called a 'school' (as for example the use of transition networks versus lexically activated daemons typify different schools in language understanding research). Individual generation systems are unusually hard to compare, mostly because generation starts with an empirically unknown representation: the thoughts, conceptualizations, and intentions of the human mind. Different projects inevitably work from different representations and focus on different technical problems. This lack of a common starting point has made it hard for researchers to build on each other's work, or even to replicate each other's examples. Nevertheless the commonalities are there, and can be expected to be more salient in the future.

The common ground is an overriding concern with the diversity of forms in natural languages, and with the control problem for generation. Diversity of form is a matter that is easily overlooked in studies of language comprehension. There, two ostensibly synonymous alternative forms will end up converted to the same 'canonical representation' because the differences between them will play no role in the reasoning of the underlying program. To the generation researcher, however, it is a nagging concern. Whenever the grammar defines an alternative, as for example between active and passive versions of the same clause, between the quantifiers 'some' and 'any,' between expressing references to natural kinds as bare plurals ('whales') versus generics ('the whale') versus prototypes ('a whale'), and so on, the realization procedure must make a choice. Omitting the alternatives is both dull and inappropriate, since no surface alternatives are truly synonymous in all contexts, and crucial distinctions can be lost if some alternatives are arbitrarily not made available. The generation researcher's problem is to learn when and in what way(s) differences are consequential and how they are governed by situation and the speaker's intent.

Approaches to the question of choice are inexorably tied up with approaches to control. Which of two alternatives the generator picks has obvious consequences for what actions it takes next, and the way in which linguistic knowledge is represented has consequences for how alternatives are defined and when they are considered. Every surface text, however small, is the result of dozens of choices, and it is not reasonable, at least not from an engineering standpoint, to combine these choices into massive single discriminations. This leads to the question of how to order choices and how to represent the intermediate results. What awareness does the generator have of the dependencies between choices? How are these dependencies represented and made to influence the control algorithms?

These will be the themes for the rest of this chapter as we look at the different approaches that are now being taken to the representation of grammar and the organization of the realization process. The earlier stages of generation, the identification of goals and the planning of what should be said, will not be discussed here, partly because there is not nearly as much commonality in the approaches or even the themes of approaches in text planning as there is in realization, but more because it is difficult to discuss goals or planning techniques separately from the underlying program being worked with; a proper treatment thus would take the discussion too far afield.

12.7. Mixing control with the statement of the grammar

The first question to be asked when looking closely at a particular approach to grammar in generation is the relationship of the grammar to the rest of the realization process. Logically, it would seem that dealing with the information content of the message should take priority over accommodating the stipulated regularities of a grammar. This is the stance taken in the direct replacement approach, where realization routines call grammatical functions when they need them (recall 'vbfix'), but this approach has severe limitations in its capacity for linguistic expression. By the same token, many of the details that make a text grammatical arguably do not and should not be expected to have any counterparts in the thoughts of any underlying program and thus must be independently supplied. Such details must come from somewhere other than the message, and some aspect of the realization process must supply the representations and control resources to insure that they are used correctly. One plausible desideratum for the design of generation grammars is thus that they express the linguistic relations while minimizing their intrusion into the process of realizing the information and rhetorical goals given by the message.

12.7.1. Augmented transition networks in generation

Almost immediately after Woods defined the augmented transition network (ATN) formalism for language parsing, it was applied to generation by Simmons and Slocum (1972). The ATN was a natural approach to the representation of a grammar at that time. For the types of texts Slocum and Simmons considered it satisfied the condition of supporting the production of linguistic relations without adding any complications to the realization process.

ATNs for generation (see also Shapiro, 1982) have essentially the same organization as their parsing counterparts, with the obvious exception that where a parser will scan a word from the input text as an action on an arc, these generators will produce one. Their network organization mimics the recursive and sequential phrasal constituent patterns of the language: there is a network for clauses, one for noun phrases, etc.; the clause network first looks for conditions in the message affecting whether there is an initial complement (as in questions or relatives), then determines and produces the subject, the verb and its auxiliaries, the verbal complements, and so on in left to right surface order. Grammatical words like 'to' or 'the' are produced by arcs that are taken automatically once the grammatical character of the phrase has been determined. Subordinate clausal morphology is supplied by optional arcs under the control of registers that are set by push operations in the dominating network where the grammatical function of the clause is defined.

With respect to control, the determination of which alternative path is taken is done by tests on the arcs, which apply predicates to the message structure. Depending on the state of the message (as defined by the tests) a particular sequence of arcs is traversed, and thus a particular text is produced with the word choice and ordering given by the associated arc actions. This control technique is the opposite of the more common 'message as program' design (e.g., direct replacement), where initiative rests with the structure of the message rather than of the grammar. Its benefit is to simplify the statement of grammatical constraints (stated implicitly by the restrictions on possible next states imposed by the network structure), since they fall out directly from the enumeration of surface forms that the ATN supplies.

The ATN control protocol has two shortcomings: the tests tend to proliferate and must be very closely tied to the conceptual representation of the particular underlying program. The number of tests seems excessive because most tests will turn out to be false: only one of the arcs coming out of any node is going to be the correct one to take. With a reasonably high branching factor (reflecting the large number of alternative surface sequences that a language like English provides), it is unlikely that the correct arc will always happen to have been ordered early in the arc set. The coupling of predicate definitions to the particulars of the underlying program's conceptualizations is a consequence of the ATN design having placed responsibility for determining the surface form of the text (i.e., the network path) within the grammar, rather than as a separate part of the realization component. To move an ATN-based generator to an underlying program other than the one for which it was originally developed, one with a different representational formalism or even just a different world view, will force changes in almost all of the predicate definitions. (To this author's knowledge no ATN generator has ever been moved between programs; it is easy to see why.)

One final point about the ATN as a generation formalism is the unusual fact that the generation ATNs do not ever backup (Shapiro, personal communication, 1979). They make no use of the nondeterminism that the ATN formalism provides. This means that they have no need for the indeterminacy of categorization that parsers need when scanning the words of a text and predicting its structure. This should not be unexpected — generation is a matter of planning rather than analysis; its information flow is the addition of constraints and the progressive refinement of a completely identified intention and content, not the tentative increase in the specificity of identification that characterizes parsing.

12.7.2. Systemic grammars

The ATN approach to generation places control of the generation process squarely within its grammar. This drastically simplifies the programming effort required to define the procedures for constructing grammatically complex linguistic forms over what a direct replacement approach would have required, and makes it practical to use these procedures in generation systems. However, when viewed as planners, ATN generation systems suffer from too tight a coupling between perception and action: for instance, as soon as a conceptual source of the subject noun phrase is found in the message it is passed through the NP network of the grammar and realized as a stream of words. This hinders efforts to plan in progressive stages, determining and propagating sets of constraints or partial descriptions of what is to be generated, which is a more controllable technique than working directly in terms of surface forms that are constructed in detail as soon as they are selected.

By contrast, the linguistic school known as systemic grammar views surface forms as the consequences of selecting a set of abstract, functional features. The interpolation of an intermediate, abstract level of representation between the message and the output text allows the specification of the text to accumulate gradually, giving constraints an opportunity to propagate and influence later decisions, as is customary in modern planning designs. As this is not general planning, the constraints are quite specific: they are features that describe the possible functions that texts can serve, based on determining intentional and communicative goals.

It is this concern for directly representing the choices a language provides and their functional consequences that has given systemic grammar its special significance in generation research. It is the only well-known linguistic formalism that has this special focus, the only one that makes the specification of possible choices the core of its notation. The founder of the systemic tradition, M.A.K. Halliday, believes that language function has been neglected in linguistic theory in favor of the classification of language structures. While structure is more accessible to study, explanatory theories of the structure that a language can have are arguably of little consequence without companion theories of the functions the structures can serve. Without theories that attempt to capture the criteria that govern when particular structures are used — the situational and intentional factors that contribute to the decisions made during generation — one cannot be sure that the modularity proposed in structural theories is in fact well founded.

As in an ATN, grammaticality of the text is insured by forcing the generation process to stay within predefined paths in the systemic network; however here the paths do not define surface phrasal sequences but dependencies between abstract text characteristics. Individual features are selected independently, subject only to the dependencies defined by 'systems' that group the features into networks of disjoint classes (see Figure 3). Choice systems are given either as conjuncts (leading curled brace), where one choice must be made from each of the systems named on the right, or as disjuncts (leading square bracket), where only one of the alternative features listed may be selected. The selection of a feature opens the system that it names (this feature will be the label on the horizontal line projecting leftwards from the system), which means that a choice from that system must be made at this point. Specific feature choices early, leftward, in the network force later choices to be made among the feature systems to the right that are dependent on them (as indicated by the connecting lines). Other sets of choices are rendered irrelevant.

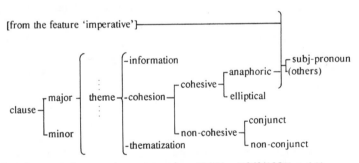

Figure 3. A fragment of a systemic grammar, from Halliday (1969/1981) p. 141.

Two important generation systems have been based on systemic grammar, Proteus (Davey, 1974), and Nigel (Mann and Matthiessen, 1985). Nigel is the largest systemic grammar in the world and very likely one of the largest machine grammars of any sort. Besides the quite important contribution simply of articulating a systemic grammar so thoroughly, Mann and Matthiessen have developed a technique for formalizing the usage criteria that govern the choices the grammar defines, which they term 'inquiry semantics' (Mann, 1983). For each choice system in the grammar a set of criterial predicates (tests) known as a 'chooser' is defined. These tests are given as functions from the internal state of the planner and underlying program to one of the features in the system the chooser is associated with.

The generation process consists of starting at the leftmost entry system of the network and evaluating successive choosers to determine the path through the network (i.e., the feature set) that best captures the speaker's intentions.

Davey's Proteus employed a very similar control protocol. The systems and dependencies of the grammar are arranged into connected networks whose modularity matches the large-scale structural options of the language. There is a network for clauses, one for noun phrases, adjective phrases, and adverbials — all of the major phrasal categories of English. (In Davey's published grammar, the clause network includes alternatives for verb structure and prepositional complements, and incorporates the differences between major, subordinate, and relative clauses.) Sentences are constructed recursively from the large structural elements downward. A sweep through the choice systems of the clause level network selects a specific subset of the concrete functional features given at the network's rightmost edge. These features collectively specify the structural form of the clause, and impose functional constraints on the conceptual elements it embeds. The realization of this feature set (done by an independent module) yields a sequence of grammatically and functionally marked words and embedded elements not unlike the lists found in the intermediate stages of a direct replacement generator. The functional analysis then applies recursively to the now constrained elements, making the decisions required by the connectivity of the systems in order to specify the form of the noun phrases, the subordinate clauses, etc. that the elements will become. The process of specifying functions and realizing them continues until all the conceptual elements referred to in the message have been realized as words, whereupon the accumulated word string is printed out. Careful attention to how much functionality is encoded at each successive system of alternative features in the network allows dependencies to propagate consistently (the presence of disjunctive systems means that several loci of decision-making will be operating simultaneously in a network). The result is that all decisions can be made indelibly, i.e., without ever needing to backup to an earlier system to remake the decision, and the generation process as a whole can operate in time proportional to the depth of its networks.

12.8. Stating the constraints of the grammar independently

In their overall design, the ATN and systemic grammar approaches to generation differ only in the kind of information they encode in their networks: ATNs specify choices between alternative surface structure patterns while systemic grammars specify choices between alternative sets of abstract functional features. Both use their networks as their control structure, making the definition of the grammar and the definition of the actions the generator can take inseparable. Both presume that it is simpler to state the realization rules for underlying program objects by having tests in the grammar look back to the message (which is most likely just to be the unsorted state of the underlying program at the time the generator is called), than to organize the rules around the message objects and have them project forward to linguistic structures. Consequently, both designs impose on their underlying programs the specific world view — a set of conceptualizations — that is implicit in their grammars. This is not necessarily bad: the hypothesis that one's language shapes one's thought has a long and serious history in linguistics (cf. the Sapir-Whorf hypothesis). It does however carry the pragmatic implication that compatibility at the conceptual level must be carefully considered when either approach to generation is used in a man-machine interface.

World view and grammatical model are decoupled in other modern designs, designs which, as it happens, are also message-driven rather than controlled from their grammars. We will look first at functional unification grammars, where a general purpose weak method for control has been adopted, and then at the description-directed approach, where control resides in the message and especially also in a model of the text syntactic surface structure acting as an intermediate representation. In both cases a key question is how the design insures that all of the grammatical dependencies between decisions about form will be respected when this is no longer automatically guaranteed by the control structure.

12.9. Functional unification grammars

General principles of parsimony suggest that a grammatical representation that can be employed both for generation and understanding should be preferred to one that cannot. The grammars of theoretical linguists are not specific to either direction, but by the same token they are also not grammars for processing: they capture only the abstract capacities and interior relations of a language, and not its relationships to the uses that a speaker might put it to or how it would enter causally into the psychological processes by which generation, comprehension, or learning are accomplished in specific situations. The models of language use that have been developed are almost without exception strongly directional: one cannot take a typical grammar for comprehension and 'reverse' it to supply a grammar for generation. Functional unification grammar (FUG), a representation developed by Kay (1979, 1984), is specifically put forward as a reversible model, where the rules of the grammar may be employed in either direction without changing the way that they are represented. The best known syntactic-level FUGs are the TELEGRAM grammar developed by Appelt (1985) for his generator, and the realization component developed by Bossie (1981) for use with the text planning system of McKeown (1985). Figure 4 shows a fragment of a FUG taken from Appelt's grammar (1985, p. 108). It defines the possible constituent roles for the components of noun phrases. The enclosing brackets define systems of features and values. Square brackets define conjunctive sets: a noun phrase must specify a value for each of their features. Curly brackets define disjunctive sets: the noun phrase must meet any one of the listed feature-values.

```
┌ CAT = NP                                                                    ┐
│ PAT = (... <DET> <PREMODS> <HEAD> <POSTMODS> ...)                            │
│ AGR =  <HEAD AGR>                                                            │
│ ⎧  ⎡HEAD =  [ CAT = N ]                             ⎤ ⎫                       │
│ ⎪  ⎢    ⎧  ⎡TYPE = PROPER⎤ ⎫                        ⎥ ⎪                       │
│ ⎪  ⎢    ⎨  ⎣DET = NONE   ⎦ ⎬                        ⎥ ⎪                       │
│ ⎪  ⎢    ⎩ TYPE = COMMON    ⎭                        ⎥ ⎪                       │
│ ⎨  ⎢  ⎡ ⎧HEAD = [ CAT = PRO ]  ⎫  ⎤                 ⎥ ⎬                       │
│ ⎪  ⎢  ⎢ ⎩HEAD = [ CAT = SCOMP ]⎭  ⎥                 ⎥ ⎪                       │
│ ⎪  ⎢  ⎢ DET = NONE               ⎥                 ⎥ ⎪                       │
│ ⎪  ⎢  ⎢ PREMODS = NONE           ⎥                 ⎥ ⎪                       │
│ ⎩  ⎣  ⎣ POSTMODS = NONE          ⎦                 ⎦ ⎭                       │
│ ⎧PREMODS = NONE          ⎫                                                   │
│ ⎩PREMODS = [ CAT = ADJP ]⎭                                                   │
│ ⎧POSTMODS = NONE          ⎫                                                  │
│ ⎨POSTMODS = [ CAT = PP ]  ⎬                                                  │
│ ⎩POSTMODS = [ CAT = SREL ]⎭                                                  │
└                                                                             ┘
```

Figure 4. A fragment of the functional unification grammar for noun phrases, from Appelt (1985).

The structure of a FUG — sets of equations that define feature-value pairs — suggests no immediate procedural interpretation beyond the 'outer versus inner' segmentation of the hierarchical groupings; this absence of procedure in the representation's interpretation is a requirement of any potentially bidirectional formalism. The computational role of the FUG is that of a set of constraints that any independently defined text construction procedure must meet. This makes it not a source of control but a filter on the control options of some other source or sources: in this instance, the weak method known as nondeterministic unification.

The focus of Appelt's work on generation is on the planning process, and relatively few details of how his planner initiates and regulates the realization process are available. However, it seems fair to characterize those aspects of his design as message-directed, in the sense that it is objects and relations selected by the planner that initiate realization, under the direction of concept-specific specialist programs as in direct replacement designs.[3]

---

[3] Appelt's KAMP planner feeds the linguistic levels of processing incrementally, specifying additional conceptual information for realization, as well as where it should appear, whenever the decision to include that information is made during the planning process. Given this, it

The specialists invoked by the text planner begin the process by building skeletal descriptions of the constituents that the text is to include, for example, that there is to be a clause with a certain main verb and two NPs with certain lexical heads. (The referents of these phrases will be indicated by pointers back into the underlying program model that can be referred to as needed.) The FUG is then used to extend such skeletal descriptions with the additional linguistic features that are required for the text to be grammatical.

The extension of the specialists' descriptions is done by merging them with the grammar constituent by constituent. This works because the grammar is effectively a maximal description of the possible constituents, functional relationships, and constraints of the language. It defines the linguistic resources that the specialists can draw on, and specifies the grammatical details that no conceptual-level planner would be concerned about. The merger of the initial, partial description of what the specialists want said with the grammar's description of what the language permits is so organized that only extensions consistent with the grammar will occur. The grammar supplies the constraints that proposed functional descriptions must meet, and, through its disjunctive feature sets, supplies the choice sets from which many of the extensions will come. The merger is governed by the semantics of the unification operator: features from the grammar may be added if they contradict none that are already present or if they subsume them.

The specialist's partial descriptions will prompt the addition of the features from the grammar that are tied to those in the description by functional links (see Kay, 1984 for details). This instantiation of previously unspecified features then has a ripple effect throughout the whole system: Other features that are dependent on a just instantiated feature force further unifications cyclically until a grammatically complete description has been formed. During the process feature values in the description will force selections among the disjunctive specifications in the grammar. For example, specifying a verb will force the grammatical subcategorization feature to take a compatible value, which in turn will impose constraints on the selections available to the noun phrases that the subcategorization pattern governs. The completed description will amount to a rooted tree of feature specifications as defined by the 'pat' (pattern) feature that dictates the sequential order of constituents at each level. The actual production of the text is performed by scanning this tree and reading out the words in the lexical features of each constituent.

---

makes no sense to say that there is ever an explicit 'message' in the sense of a structure planned as a unit and then realized without further intervention by the planner.

From the point of view of grammar development, FUGs are a satisfying treatment because they allow one to state the facts of the language compactly, i.e., interactions between statements need not be explicitly spelled out in the notation since they will come about automatically through the action of unification. However, from a processing point of view, this convenience comes with a price, since one must be willing to live with the tacit control structure that does the 'behind the scenes' merging of descriptions and grammar. In the present implementations, this is *nondeterministic unification*. If efficiency of execution is not relevant then this of course is no problem; however, there are indications (Ritchie, personal communication, 1986) that the computational properties of FUGs make general operations over them NP-complete. Since language is a very specific phenomenon, one would hope that equally specific, more computationally efficient processing schemes would suffice, rather than having to rely on such a general, and therefore such a powerful, mechanism. The next approach to be discussed, description-directed generation, was designed with such efficiency concerns in mind.

Recent work by Patten (1985) uses a systemic grammar in very much the same way that FUGs are used. In Patten's approach, operations at a semantic level (of the same kind as performed here by planning level specialists) specify a set of output features within the systemic grammar, i.e., features at the rightmost edge of the network. These are the equivalent of the initial functional description that drives a FUG. A backwards and then forwards chaining sweep through the system network determines what additional linguistic features must be added to the specification for a grammatical text to result, just as unification does with the FUG. This points out that systemic grammars can be viewed just as reference constraint sets and need not dictate the total control flow as is usually done.

12.10. Multi-level, description-directed generation

The major shortcoming of the direct replacement approach is the awkwardness of maintaining an adequate representation of grammatical context, or of carrying out grammatically mediated text-level actions such as producing the correct syntactic form for an embedded clause. At the same time, the message-directed control flow that drives direct replacement has a great deal to recommend it. Compared with grammar-directed control schemes, message-directed control is more efficient, since every action will contribute to the eventual production of the text. Message-directed control also gives a planner a very clear semantic basis for its communication with the realization component, since the message can be viewed simply as a set of instructions to accomplish specific goals. The question then becomes: is there a way of elaborating the basic, message-directed framework so as to overcome the deficits that plague direct replacement approaches while still keeping the computational properties that have made it attractive?

A number of researchers have independently chosen the same solution: to interpose a level of explicitly linguistic representation between the message and the words of the text (McDonald, 1975, 1984; Kempen and Hoenkamp, 1982; Jacobs, 1985; Swartout, 1981). They believe that employing a syntactic description of the text under construction is the most effective means of introducing grammatical information and constraints into the realization process, in particular, that it is a better locus for grammatical processing than a separately stated, active grammar.

The specifics of their individual treatments differ, but a common thread is clearly identifiable: realization is organized as a sequence of choices made by specialists, where the form of the choice — the output of the specialist — is a linguistic representation of what is to be said, i.e., a structural annotation of the syntactic relations that govern the words (and embedded conceptual elements) to be said, rather than just a list of words. These representations are phrase structures of essentially the same kind that a theoretical linguist would use.

It will be convenient to restrict the present discussion to only one system that uses this approach, the one developed by this author (cf. McDonald 1984; McDonald and Pustejovsky 1985b; McDonald, Pustejovsky and Vaughan 1986). As it is the historical outgrowth of a direct replacement system, it will be useful to organize the discussion in terms of how it extends that approach and addresses its deficiencies. We will also include the description of how it deals with the three general concerns one should have in examining a generation system: how it organizes its knowledge of grammar; what its control structure is; and its approach to realization.

Referring to our approach as 'multi-level, description-directed generation' emphasizes specific features of its architecture and control protocols that we consider important; it is, however, too large a phrase to use conveniently. The name of the computer program that implements the design, MUMBLE, will serve as a compact, agentive reference. Characterizing MUMBLE as multi-level draws attention to the fact that it carries out operations over three explicitly represented levels of representation simultaneously: message, surface structure, and word stream. Description-directed is the name we have given to its control protocol, which is a specialization of the common programming technique known as data-directed control. Under this protocol, the data in the representations at the three levels is interpreted directly as instructions to the virtual machine that constitutes the generator proper. Since each of these representational structures is also a valid description of the text, at its own level of abstraction, this characterization of the protocol emphasizes the fact that the particulars of how the

person developing messages or syntactic structures chooses to design them
have immediate consequences for the generator's performance (McDonald,
1984). The feedback that this gives a developer has proven to be invaluable
in refining the notations and their computational interpretations in all parts
of the system.

MUMBLE's virtual machine is the embodiment of our computational
theory of generation. It consists of three interleaved processes that manage
and carry out the transitions between the representational layers.

(1)   Phrase structure execution: this interprets the surface structure,
        maintaining an environment that defines the grammatical con-
        straints active at any moment, and producing the word stream as its
        incremental output.
(2)   Attachment: this interprets the message, transferring its component
        units to positions within the surface structure according to the func-
        tional relationships between them and their role in the message.
(3)   Realization: this takes the individual elements of the message into
        surface structure phrases by selecting from linguistically motivated
        classes of parameterized alternative forms.

A minor fourth process, operating over the word stream, morphologically
specializes individual words to suit their syntactic and orthographic contexts
(e.g., the 'a' going to 'an' before vowels).

To the developer of a text planner that would pass messages to MUMBLE
for the latter to produce texts from, the virtual machine appears as a very
high level, task-specific language, with its own operators and intermediate
representations. To a lesser extent this is true also with respect to the
linguist writing generation-oriented grammars for MUMBLE to execute,
since the virtual machine includes no presumptions as to what specific syntactic categories, functional relations, or syntactic constructions the natural
language includes. Instead it supplies a notation for defining them in terms
of primitive notions including: the *dominates* and *precedes* relations of
phrase structure, bound thematic relations, configurational regularities such
as head or complement from the X-bar theory; or the tree combination
rules of Tree Adjoining Grammars (Kroch and Joshi, 1985).

MUMBLE is best discussed by reference to a concrete example message,
situation, and resulting output text. Our illustration is an abstraction of a
real representation, in which many technical details have been omitted.
Figure 5 shows a generated output paragraph describing a legal case from
the Counselor project (McDonald and Pustejovsky, 1986) in which MUM-
BLE is used for generation. The structure below it is the message responsible for its second sentence, which details the events that were relevant to the
court's decision. Using this example, we will look at MUMBLE's knowledge
of grammar: how it is made manifest, and how it has its effects, interleav-
ing discussion of realization and control at convenient places.

> In the Telex case, Telex was sued by IBM for misappropriating trade secrets about its product Merlin. One of the managers of the Merlin development project, Clemens, left IBM to work for Telex, where he helped to develop Telex's competing product, the 6830. The key fact in the case was that Clemens brought a copy of the source code with him when he switched jobs. The court held for IBM.

> (temporal-sequence
>   (left-to-work-for (# <role # <project-manager Merlin> > # <name Clemens>)
>   (named-company # <IBM>)
>   (named-company # <Telex>))
> (helped-to-develop (named-person # <Clemens>)
>   (# <kind product>
>   # <competition-by # <Telex> >
>   # <name '6830' >)))

As previously discussed, one of the features of a message-directed approach is that items[4] directly from the underlying program are part of the messages. (These are indicated in the display above by enclosing angle brackets, # < ... >.) Once in a message, such items become instructions to the generator, and as such need interpretations, i.e., associated functions from the item, and the linguistic and pragmatic environment, to the surface specification of some text or text fragment. However, considered in terms of the space of texts that might realize them, real program objects are large and vague: they stand in many different relationships to other objects and to the underlying program's state, and consequently can have many different interpretations depending on the context and the speaker's intent.

We take it to be part of the job of a text planner to choose among these relationships and to indicate in the message the perspective from which an object is to be viewed. (The perspective on the first occurrence of Clemens, for example, is indicated to be his role as (former) manager of the Merlin project.) Adopting a specific perspective often amounts to selecting a specific wording (often just of the lexical head, e.g., 'manager;' but also entire conventional phrases such as 'leave <employer1> to work for <employer2>'). These examples indicate that many of the terms in a message are surface lexical relations (e.g., 'helped to develop') rather than a more abstract conceptual vocabulary; this has the obvious corollary that syntactic realization will usually occur after key words have been chosen. The text planner must therefore understand a good deal about how alternative word choices cover the semantic fields of the situation it is trying to communicate, and what emphasis and presupposed inferencing by the

---

[4] The word 'item,' and at other times the word 'object,' is intended as a general term that denotes representational data structures in an underlying program without regard to the kind of real-world entity that they model: individuals, kinds, relations, constraints, attributes, states, actions, events, etc.

audience a given choice of wording will convey. This appears to us to be a choice that is best made at a conceptual level (i.e., during message construction), since it does not depend in any crucial way on the details of the grammatical environment, the arguments of Danlos (1984b) notwithstanding (cf. McDonald et al., 1986).

Even though the key lexical choices for an item will have occurred before it has been syntactically realized, these message-level lexical decisions can draw on the grammatical context in which the text is going to occur. In particular, grammatical constraints imposed by syntactic relations will filter out grammatically inconsistent possibilities from the planner's choice set.[5] This is possible because the realization of messages is hierarchical, following the message's compositional structure from the top down. In other words, the message is interpreted much as a conventional program would be. The surface syntactic realization of the higher, dominating conceptual elements of the message is thus available to define and constrain the interpretations (i.e., linguistic realizations) of the lower, more embedded elements. This protocol for evaluation of arguments is known as *normal order*, and is in direct contrast with the previously discussed applicative order protocol used in most direct replacement designs.

The perspective that the text planner chooses to impose on an item from the underlying program is represented at the message-level by designating the realization class to be used for it. Realization classes are MUMBLE's equivalent of the 'specialist programs' in direct replacement. They are linguistic rather than conceptual entities, and are developed by the designer of the grammar using control and data structures defined in the virtual machine. New underlying programs are interfaced to MUMBLE by developing a (possibly very minimal) text planner and assigning program items (or item types) to predefined realization classes. A relatively self-contained example of a class, 'locative-relation,' developed originally for use with Conklin's program for describing pictures of house scenes (see Conklin, 1983) is shown below.

---

[5] This filtering is automatic if the relevant parts of the text planner are implemented using the same abstract control device as MUMBLE uses for its own decisions, i.e., parameterized, pre-computed annotated choice sets of the sort employed for realization classes (see text). The descriptions of the linguistic character and potential of the choices that the annotation provides are the basis for filtering out incompatible choices on grammatical grounds, just as occurs at the syntactic level in selections within a realization class. This technique is proving convenient in our own work with some simple text planners; however we can see a point where the requirement that the full set of alternatives be pre-computed may be unnecessarily limiting or possibly psychologically unrealistic, in which case an alternative design, presumably involving dynamic construction of the choices, will be needed and an alternative means of imposing the grammatical constraints will have to be found. For a discussion of another planning-level control paradigm that has been used with MUMBLE, see Conklin (1983).

```
(define-realization-class LOCATIVE-RELATION
    :parameters (relation arg1 arg2)
    :choices
        ( (Arg1-is-Relation-Arg2)
            'The driveway is next to the house'
          clause focus(arg1) )
        ( (Arg2-has-Arg1-Relation-Arg2)
            'The house has a driveway in front of it'
          clause focus(arg2) )
        ( (There-is-a-Arg1-Relation-Arg2)
            'There is a driveway next to the house'
          root-clause shifts-focus-to(arg1) )
        ( (Relation-Arg2-is-Arg1)
            'Next to the house is a driveway'
          root-clause shifts-focus-to(arg1)
          final-position(arg1) )
        ( (with-Arg1-Relation-Arg2)
            '...with a driveway next to it'
          prepp modifier-to(arg1) ))
```

The choices grouped together in a realization class will all be effective in communicating the conceptual item assigned to the class, but each will be appropriate for a different context. This context-sensitivity is indicated in the annotation accompanying the choice, for example 'focus,' which will dictate the grammatical cases and surface order given to the arguments, or the functional role 'modifier-to,' which will lead to realization as a post-nominal prepositional phrase. These annotating characteristics indicate the context(s) in which a choice can be used. They act both as passive descriptions of the choice that are examined by other routines, and as active test predicates that sample and define the pragmatic situation in the text planner or underlying program. This is the basis of MUMBLE's model of language use — the effects that can be achieved by using a particular linguistic form; as such they play the same kind of role as the 'choosers' in Mann's Nigel.

The surface structure level, the source of grammatical constraints on realization, is assembled top-down as the consequence of the interpretation and realization of the items in the message. In the example message the topmost item is a 'sequence' of two steps, each of which is a lexicalized relation over several program objects on which a particular perspective has been imposed.

One of the goals of a multi-level approach is to distribute the text construction effort and knowledge throughout the system so that no level is forced to do more of the work than it has the natural capacity for. For example, in the interpretation of the first item in the above message, *temporal-sequence*, MUMBLE is careful to avoid taking steps that would exceed the intentions in the message. As a message-level instruction, *temporal-sequence* says nothing about whether the items it dominates should appear as two sentences or one; it says simply that they occurred one after the other in time and that their realizations should indicate this. Since there is no special emphasis marked, this can be done by having them appear in the text in the order that they have in the message. The decision about their sentential texture is postponed until a linguistic context is available and the decision can be made on an informed basis.

This delay is achieved by having the attachment process (which moves items from the message to the surface structure according to their functional roles) delay the positioning of the second item of the sequence until the first has been realized. Only the first item will be moved into the surface structure initially, and it will appear as the contents of the second sentence as shown below. Note that a message item is not realized until it has a position, and then not until all of the items above it and to its left have been realized and the item has been reached by the Phrase Structure Execution process that is traversing the surface structure tree and coordinating all of these activities. By enforcing this discipline one is sure that all the grammatical constraints that could affect an item's realization will have been determined before the realization occurs, and consequently the virtual machine does not need to make provisions for changing an item's realization after it is finished.

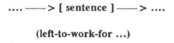

Figure 5. The first item of the message in a toplevel position of the surface structure annotated as a 'sentence.'

Considered as a function, a realization class such as 'left-to-work-for' specifies the surface form of a grammatically coherent text fragment, which is instantiated when the class is executed and a specific version of that phrase selected. Given its lexical specificity, such a class is obviously not primitive. It is derived by successive specializations of two linguistically primitive subcategorization frames: one built around the verb class that includes 'leave' (shown below) and the other around the class containing 'work for.' The specialization is done by a definition-time operation wherein arguments to the subcategorization frames are bound to constants (e.g., the verb 'leave'), producing new realization classes of reduced arity. On its face, a class built around variants on the phrase '<employee> leaves <company1> to work for <company2>' is more appropriate to a semantic grammar (cf. Burton, 1976) than to a conventional syntactic phrase structure grammar. This choice of linguistic modularity does however reflect the actual conceptual modularity of the underlying program that drives the example, [6] and we believe this is an important benefit methodologically.

```
(define-phrase subject-verb-locative (subj vb loc)
   :specification (clause
                   subject subj
                   predicate (vp
                              verb vb
                              locative-complement loc )) )
```

Comparing MUMBLE's organization of grammatical knowledge with that of the two grammar-directed approaches discussed above, we see that it resembles an ATN somewhat and Nigel hardly at all. ATN designs are based on procedurally encoded surface structures, which are executed directly. MUMBLE represents surface structure explicitly and has it interpreted. ATNs select the surface form to be used via a recursive, phrase by phrase, top-down and left-to-right consideration of the total set of forms the grammar makes available, and queries the state of the underlying program to see which form is most appropriate. MUMBLE also proceeds recursively, top-down and left to right, but the recursion is on the structure of an explicitly represented message. Conceptual items or item types control the selection and instantiation of the appropriate surface forms directly, through the realization classes that the planner associates with them.

MUMBLE packages linguistic relations into constituent phrases; it does not provide a feature-based representation as a systemic grammar does. It cannot, for example, reason about tense or thematic focus apart from a surface structure configuration that exhibits them. This design choice is deliberate, and reflects what we take to be a strong hypothesis about the character of linguistic knowledge. This hypothesis is roughly that the space of valid feature configurations (to use systemic terms) is smaller, less arbitrary, and more structured than a feature-heap notation can express (see McDonald et al., 1986 for details). Since our notation for surface structure incorporates functional annotations as well as categorial, and especially since it is only one of three representational levels, we believe that organizing linguistic reasoning in terms of packaged, natural sets of relations will provide a great

---

[6] As it happens, *leave-to-work-at* is a primitive conceptual relation in the legal reasoning system that serves here as the underlying program (Ashley and Rissland, 1986). The causal model that the phrase evokes in a person, i.e., that working for the new company is the reason why the employee is leaving (cf. 'John washed his car to impress his girlfriend') is encapsulated in this relation, and suppresses the causal model from consideration by the legal reasoner's rules. This encapsulation is deliberate. Reasoning systems should function at the conceptual level best suited to the task. This does however imply that some component of the natural language interface must now bridge the conceptual ground between the internal model and the lexical options of the language; see Pustejovsky (this volume) for a discussion of how this may be done.

deal of leverage in research on text planning and computational theories of language use and communicative intention.

Nowhere in MUMBLE is there a distinct grammar in the sense of a set of rules for deriving linguistic forms from primitive features. Rather it manipulates a collection of predefined linguistic objects — the minimal surface phrases of the language and the composite phrases derived from them. The phrases are grouped into the realization classes, the projected linguistic images of different conceptual types and perspectives. When selected and instantiated to form the surface structure, they take on an active role (through interpretation by the three processes), defining the order of further actions by the generator, defining the constraints on the realization of the embedded items from the message now at some of its leaf positions, and defining the points where it may be extended through further attachments from the message level. Figure 6 below shows a snapshot of the surface structure for the first part of the text in the example, and can illustrate these points. At the moment of this snapshot, the Phrase Structure Execution process has traversed the structure up to the item # < *telex* > and produced the text shown; its next action will be to have that item realized, whereupon the realizing phrase (an NP like the one for # < *IBM* >) will replace # < *telex* > in the surface structure and the process will traverse it and move on.

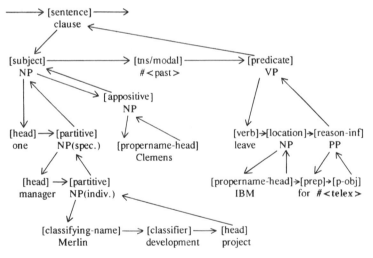

Said so far:
'...One of the managers of the Merlin development project, Clemens, left IBM to work for Telex //'

Figure 6. Snapshot of surface structure.

The first thing to consider is the difference in the details of this surface structure representation compared with the more conventional trees used by generative grammarians. Two of these are significant in this discussion. One is the presence of functional annotations over each of the constituents (indicated by labels inside square brackets). Terms like 'subject' or 'prep-complement' are used to summarize the grammatical relations that the constituents are in because of their configurational positions, which makes these labels the source of most of the grammatical constraints on message item realizations. The functional annotations also play a role in the dynamic production of the word stream. In the example this includes providing the access to the subject when the morphological process needs to determine the person/number agreement for tensed verbs, and supplying grammatical words like 'of' or 'to' directly into the word stream.

Formally the representation is not a tree but a sequential stream (as indicated by the arrows): a stream of annotated positions that are interpreted as instructions to the Phrase Structure Execution process. The grammar writer defines the interpretation an annotating label is to have, e.g., specifying control of morphological effects or function words, constraints to be imposed on realizations, or establishing salient reference positions (like the subject). Various useful technical details are expedited by defining the surface structure as a stream rather than a tree (see McDonald and Pustejovsky 1985b). The stream design provides a clean technical basis for the work of the Attachment process, which extends the surface structure through the addition of successive items from the message. The extensions are integrated into the active grammatical environment by breaking interpositional links in the stream and knitting in the new items along with any additional covering syntactic nodes or functional constituent positions needed to characterize correctly the linguistic relationship of the new material to the old.

In the present example, the second item of the message's temporal sequence item, the lexicalized relation 'helped-to-develop,' remains unattached — its position in the surface structure unknown — until enough linguistic context has been established for a reasonable decision to be made about stylistic matters, e.g., whether the item should appear as an extension of the first item's sentence or start its own. Since the functional constraints on a temporal sequence's realization prohibit embedding the second item anywhere within the first, the only legal 'attachment points' for it (i.e., links it could be knit in at) are on the trailing edge of the first item's sentence or as a following sentence.

In terms of our theory of generation, attachment points are grammatical properties of phrasal configurations: places where the existing surface structure may be extended by splicing in 'auxiliary' phrases (i.e., realizations of message items), for example adding an initial adjunct phrase to a clause or embedding the NP headed by 'manager' inside the selector 'one of.' Every phrasal pattern (as indicated by the annotating labels) has specific places where it can be extended and still be a grammatically valid surface structure; the grammatical theory of such extensions is developed in studies of Tree Adjoining Grammars (Kroch and Joshi 1985). What attachment points exist is a matter determined by the grammatical facts of the language; which points are actually used in a given situation is a matter of stylistic convention (see McDonald and Pustejovsky 1985a). In this case there is a very natural, compactly realized relationship between the first and second events: the final item in the realization of the first event, the Telex company, happens to be where the second event occurred. As neither clause is particularly complex syntactically, the attachment point that extends the final NP of the first event with a relative clause is taken and the second event knit into the surface structure there, to be realized when that position is reached in the stream.

12.11. Relating modern generation approaches to MT

One cannot expect to be able to take a generator design 'off the shelf' and use it without modification in an MT system. The latter do not have the information about intention and conceptual perspective that the AI designs presume is available to guide decisions. Conceivably this information could be deduced as the source text is parsed, but only at the cost of including a deep conceptual model of the subject matter of the text.

Once the parsers are made sensitive to the concerns that drive the rhetorical decisions of generators, then the output of MT may be made not so mechanical in texture. Nearly any generation system can reproduce the case frame information that standard parsers recover, but the best ones use information about the pragmatic situation and the speaker's intent to communicate whether that information is new, salient, conventional, etc. When parsers can notice these perspectives in source texts and associate them with the generation decisions that could have led to them, then we can expect that MT output should be able to be every bit as good as any text produced from an interface.

Acknowledgement

Preparation of this article was supported in part by contract number SU353-9023-3 from Rome Air Defense Center, and contract number N00014-85-K-0017 from the Defense Advanced Research Development Agency, monitored by the Office of Naval Research.

13 The research environment in the METAL project

JOHN S. WHITE

13.1. Introduction

As linguistic, software, and mechanical capabilities converge to increase the feasibility of industrial natural language products, there arises an accompanying awareness of the need for tools to assist in the development of such large-scale systems. In the course of its evolution, a system destined for product development must acquire a flexibility among its components, for at least three reasons.

The product prototype will have to contain a large data structure, and (where distinct) a large program for providing the linguistic coverage expected by a product. These data and program modules will have to be modified and tested to assure the most efficient coverage with the most consistent interaction among the components.

The software itself will have to be maintainable by field engineers when the product is on the market. Tools must be developed for of easy and flexible diagnostics and correction procedures. Such tools will also be of use in development, and will likely arise out of the devices used in the development environment.

The overall system must be delivered in such a way that the non-expert users who will be ultimately responsible for operating the system can interface to the data portion of the programs in a useful way. Tools must be developed that permit this, and again, these tools will also be useful in the development environment.

This description of the research and development environment of the METAL project shows something of the requirements for support tools in an undertaking of this magnitude. It also aims to show how these tools reflect simultaneously something about the theoretical underpinnings, the developmental approach, and the product goals.

13.2. History of development

The Linguistics Research Center (LRC) of the University of Texas has been involved in the development of machine translation projects since the early 1960s. From the beginning, the Center maintained the commitment to pursue machine translation by use of analysis of natural language syntactic structures, rather than by direct word-word manipulation which was more

225

in vogue among MT researchers at the time. Funded from various sources, at times sporadically, the METAL system evolved to take advantage of innovations in both programming tools and in linguistic theory. At any given point in its history, METAL possessed properties of the contemporary approaches in both.

13.2.1. Grammar-software distinction

Quite early in the development of the LRC machine translation model, a course of development was established which enabled the linguist to develop descriptive grammar rules in a shape similar to common linguistic formalisms. A higher-level Lisp dialect was developed for this purpose, allowing the linguist to write grammar rules in a form which portrays the APSG (below) logic of the grammar in a linguistically straightforward way. These rules are compiled into pure Lisp arrayed in a grammar database as <pointers> to functions. This decision had two very important consequences, namely that the grammar can be manipulated without knowledge of how the parser works, and the parser software can be maintained quite independently of the grammar. It is extremely fortunate (or farsighted of the early developers) that METAL had such a segregation at its beginning. It is easy to lose sight of the potential coverage requirement of a system when work is just beginning; consequently it is an easy error to build linguistic description into the programs of the system software. This of course leads to extreme difficulty in maintaining the linguistics apart from the software, and makes it difficult to increase grammatical coverage without significant changes to the parsing and generating programs. However, it would not be accurate to say that METAL escaped entirely: we have recently rewritten the automatic lexical-entry generator ('defaulter') in order to extract explicit morphological string tests from the program code.

13.2.2. Parser studies

The intrinsic separation of linguistic facts from parsing strategy has resulted in the capability to develop new parsing strategies without affecting the corpus of grammar rules in any way. The same grammar rules could be employed as the test environment for evaluating parser efficiency, as was done by Slocum (1981). The results of studies such as these have led to an enhancement of the original Cocke-Kasami-Younger parser to what is referred to as the Prioritized Chart Parser (PCP).

13.2.3. METAL *in a standalone environment*

Before METAL was converted to Lisp in the mid-1970s, the system ran on a CDC 6600 in FORTRAN. This environment did not allow time-sharing, and indeed only emulated interaction in its minimal operating system. Upon conversion to Lisp a genuine time-sharing operating system had to be employed to take advantage of the capabilities of interpretive-compiled programming environments. METAL ran in UCI-Lisp, and then in Interlisp, on a DEC-10 and later on a DECsystem-20 computer. This provided an improvement over a purely batch environment, yet was insufficiently optimized for development work in a large multi-user load. Also, thoughts of a delivery vehicle for an MT product had to be entertained; obviously a dedicated large system was not the answer.

The advent of standalone Lisp machines both answered the question of delivery vehicle and optimized development environment. The device is architecturally designed for the performance optimization of Lisp programming concepts. The application, operation, and system software environments are essentially the same (below). Both development work and translation performance are greatly accelerated.. The METAL system presently runs on Symbolics computers of the LM-2 and 36X0 class, and may be local area networked with office microprocessors for pre- and post-editing tasks. In this way, the METAL system may be delivered in a package feasible for integration into industrial office settings.

13.3. The METAL system

Problems that developers may face in building, adapting, or augmenting a system will be in part dependent upon general problems in natural language processing, of course, but will also depend upon the underlying design of the system itself. The ability to capture a natural linguistic phenomenon in a natural way, for example, is related to the inherent modularity of system design, and to both the module interfaces and human interfaces. A brief description of the METAL system is therefore warranted; the reader is encouraged to refer to other general descriptions (Slocum et al., 1984; White, 1985) for greater detail.

METAL translates text in one language into another by using automatic analyses of the morphological, syntactical, and 'semo-syntactic' relationships expressed in the source language. By the criteria of Hutchins (1982), METAL qualifies as somewhere between a second and third generation machine translation system, in that it uses some semantics in conjunction with a principally syntactically oriented system. The analyzed source-language unit is converted to a uniform syntactic representation, which is converted into the appropriate surface shape for the target language. Lexical translation occurs in conjunction with this conversion process. Translation algorithms of this sort are known as 'transfer' systems (Slocum, 1984).

METAL uses an all-paths chart parsing strategy to 'drive' an augmented phrase structure analysis grammar. The grammar rules, which perform the tasks of inflectional and derivational morphology as well as syntactic interpretation, constrain application to a string via sequences of tests and node-building instructions. Constituent tests check certain facts about the individual members of the candidate string. For example, an English rule that builds noun phrases from determiners and nouns may want to constrain against applying to 'abstract' nouns like *truth*. After constituent tests, the members of the string are tested with respect to possible interactions with each other. For example, the German version of the noun phrase rule just mentioned will constrain application to depend on gender agreement between the determiner and the noun.

If all tests succeed, the rule will apply, but it is still constrained to apply in a certain way, i.e., to build a new node with certain special characteristics. Generally, the new node will selectively inherit characteristics of its constituents, along with new characteristics computed from interactions among the constituents.

Each node built by the parser has attached to it the body of the rule that built it. Facts about the rule are therefore accessible to anything that is capable of accessing the node; among the consequences of this design is the fact that specific information about the transfer requirements for the node can be located on the node itself. Accordingly, each grammar rule has a transfer portion, named after the target language, which may effect three distinct types of operations on the node: it may send information down to sons, it may recursively transfer those sons, and it may send information back up the tree after transfer to assist in the transfer of brother nodes.

For the purposes of the grammar writer, then, the grammar rule represents snapshots of the state of the node at several different times in the derivational history of a translation. In general, such information is relatively easy to keep in mind with respect to one rule or a class of similar rules. Much more difficult is keeping track of potential rule interactions up the tree, down the tree and even back up the tree. The grammar writer must be in a position to know whether a rule in question performs the appropriate operations on all and only the strings intended. Specifically, the grammar writer must know whether a rule is of the correct form to compile; whether a rule applies when it is intended to apply; whether a rule fails to apply when it is intended to fail; whether the rule builds the correct node with the correct properties; and whether the rule correctly interacts with other rules (i.e., permits/blocks the application of rules which use the new nodes as constituents).

13.4. METAL software development tools

In this discussion we focus on the development tools used by the linguist, primarily because these are likely to be the ones that will have to be developed as applications in any natural language project environment. In any but the most primitive operating systems or programming environments, pure software maintenance and development can more likely take advantage of native tools. This is certainly the case in METAL, hence the relative lack of description of the programming tools herein. However, a certain description of the Lisp programming environment is certainly warranted, as a background to the more linguistic issues discussed.

Any Lisp environment will allow the developer certain advantageous tools for referring to cumbersome expressions, repeating or modifying previous commands, and so on. For example, the Lisp user can simply bind a variable to a lengthy function call frequently used in that session, and evaluate the variable instead of retyping. The user can pass parameters to the function call bound to that variable by writing very simple, *ad hoc* functions.

The Lisp Machine environment is an improvement over a general-purpose Lisp environment because of both the increased ease of manipulating often-used expressions (by using edit commands to access and modify previously used expressions), and because of the fact that the application environment, the command language environment, and the operating system environment are, in effect, one and the same. Calls to application, command language, and low-level internals can be mixed in programs in a straightforward and obvious way, and, indeed, system definitions may be easily changed for the life of a particular program run.

These attributes of Lisp and Lisp Machines are, of course, likely well-known by the reader. But their usefulness in a development environment cannot be overemphasized. The ability to manipulate cumbersome expressions of natural language structures with ease must be present in any MT system. Projects whose native programming environments do not have these capabilities must develop them, resulting in expenditures of resources.

13.5. Grammar development tools

As we discussed above, METAL uses a linguistic component composed of an augmented phrase structure grammar of a fairly classic form (cf., for example, the Winograd 1983 description). In such a grammar, a rule applies if the structural description is met AND if certain conditions on the constituents and functions among constituents are also met. If successful, the rule builds a left-hand side (lhs) node which has certain specified characteristics, usually feature-value pairs passed between superordinate and subordinate constituent nodes. One of the basic actions of tree-building, from the linguistic point of view, is the passing of relevant feature-value pairs from sons to fathers (via copying of intrinsic characteristics of the son node or via new facts computed along the way), and from father back to son during transfer. Thus diagnosis of the linguistic performance of translation must include the capability to determine whether the transfer of feature-value pairs has proceeded as intended.

13.5.1. TRANSLATE-SENTENCE

It is expected that the normal production environment translates texts, that is, reads sentences from an input file and writes translations to an output file. In the linguistics development environment, however, the developer must be in a position to perform tests immediately on grammar or lexical phenomena. Thus in the development environment the TRANSLATE-SENTENCE function is more immediately useful. In this mode, a 'sentence' (a translation unit, possibly a sentence fragment) is typed to the terminal, and the system responds by displaying any of a set of preset diagnostic data, the number of interpretations, and the translation of the most preferred interpretation.

The example in Figure 1 below is a request to translate the German sentence *Ein alter, verheirateter Mann hat dieses Programm niemals geschrieben,* perhaps an odd sentence semantically, construed to highlight such things as strong-inflection agreement and interpretation of deverbal adjectivals.

```
<1> (translate)
<2> Sentence: (Ein alter, verheirateter Mann hat dieses Programm
    niemals geschrieben)
<3> 1 interpretation in 25314 milliseconds.
    286 PHRASES: 250 REJECTED.
<4> Transfer plus generation time: 14538 milliseconds.
<5> (|an| |old| |married| |man| |has| |never| |written| |this| |program|)
```
Figure 1. Example of sentential translation.

In this example, <1> the call is given to the function TRANSLATE (in this case from the pure Lisp environment; could also be called from the application window with a somewhat different syntax); <2> the sentence is prompted, and given as a list; <3> the number of interpretations, along with performance and number of rule attempts ('PHRASES') is given for parsing diagnostics; <4> transfer and generation performance facts are given; <5> the translation of the most highly preferred interpretation (or only interpretation, in this case) is produced.

13.5.2. PTREE

Viewing the translation with the default diagnostics is the first step toward linguistic development work on a particular natural language phenomenon. Beyond these, though, the developer must know the exact circumstances in parsing and transfer which has led to this state of affairs. The developer must know which rules applied, which rules were rejected, and whether the successful rules did what they were intended to do.

PTREE is the form of interpretation display which is most commonly used by developers. It provides a means of viewing a parse tree, an analysis ('source') tree, or a target tree with respect to the values for any list of features. Fundamentally, this form of interpretation display allows not only examination of whether a certain rule correctly applied or failed, but also an inspection of the features intended to be passed up (or down) the phrase structure. In this respect it has an advantage over the 'Draw Tree' option, in that the latter has graphic limits to the amount of detail it can display about a node. PTREE displays each node in the tree depth first, using indentation to display domination.

PTREE takes two mandatory arguments and any number of optional arguments. The first mandatory argument is a number corresponding to the interpretation. The second is the tree-type, namely, analysis, parse, or target tree.

There is a difference between what is called the analysis, or source, tree, and what is referred to as the parse tree. The analysis tree displays the shape of the phrase structure after all nodes are built and all instructions (such as transformations) are applied to that phrase structure. Typically, deep trees reflecting recursive rule applications (as with ditransitive clauses, multiple adjective modification, etc.) may be 'pruned' in the traditional linguistic sense to result in fairly shallow structures. This process enhances later feature passing and case-role analysis. Consequently the analysis tree shown by PTREE will appear to be relatively shallow, in contrast to the parse tree.

The remaining arguments, if any, of PTREE are a string of features whose values the developer wishes to display. This capability makes it possible to see whether a particular feature correctly arrived at a particular node on the tree. The preference weight of the nodes can be viewed in this way also, which can assist in determining why one interpretation was favored over another in a translation.

Figure 2 shows a call to the analysis tree for the interpretation of our example sentence. In this call, the values for the features CAN (dictionary-form), EXPR (compiled-rule index), CA (grammatical case), NU (number), GD (gender), and TY (semantic type) are solicited. The resulting display gives the value at every node for each of these features. In addition, of

course, the relationship among constituents at this snapshot in the derivation is displayed, including, for example, the fact that the adjectival
verheirateter was correctly analyzed as a verb phrase built to a participial.

```
(ptree 1 s expr can cu nu gd ty)
S (EXPR PCP-F426)
   $
   CLS (EXPR PCP-F157)                        (TY HUM)
      (CAN |schreiben|)                       ADJ-LCL (EXPR PCP-F43)
      PRED (EXPR #:G0333)                        (CAN |verheiraten|)
         (CAN |schreiben|)                       (NU SG)
         (NU SG)                                 (GD M)
         HABEN (CAN |haben|)                     AST-LCL (EXPR PCP-F73)
            (NU SG)
         NFPRED (EXPR PCP-F234)                     (CAN |verheiraten|)
            (CAN |schreiben|)                       VB (EXPR PCP-F480)
            VB (EXPR PCP-F479)                          (CAN |verheiraten|)
               (CAN |schreiben|)                        (NU)
               (NU)                                      VST (CAN |verheiraten|)
               GE (CAN |ge|)                             V-FLEX (CAN |et1|)
               VST (CAN |schreiben|)               NO (EXPR PCP-F508)
               V-FLEX (CAN |en1|)                     (CAN |Mann|)
      NP (EXPR PCP-F302)                             (NU SG)
         (CAN |Mann|)                                (GD M)
         (NU SG)                                     (TY HUM)
         (GD M)                                      NST (CAN |Mann|)
         (TY HUM)                                       (NU SG)
         DET (CAN |ein|)                                (GD M)
            (NU SG)                                     (TY HUM)
            (GD M)                             NP (EXPR PCP-F302)
         NO (EXPR PCP-F246)                        (CAN |Programm|)
            (CAN |Mann|)                            (NU SG)
            (NU SG)                                 (GD N)
            (GD M)                                  (TY ABS DUR)
            (TY HUM)                                DET (CAN |dieser|)
            ADJ (EXPR PCP-F32)                         (NU SG)
               (CAN |alt|)                             (GD N)
               (NU SG)                              NO (EXPR PCP-F508)
               (GD M)                                  (CAN |Programm|)
               AST (CAN |alt|)                         (NU SG)
               A-FLEX (CAN |er3|)                      (GD N)
                  (NU SG)                              (TY ABS DUR)
                  (GD M)                              NST (CAN |Programm|)
            PNCT (CAN |comma|)                         (GD N)
            NO (EXPR PCP-F251)                         (TY ABS DUR)
               (CAN |Mann|)                    PRT (CAN |niemals|)
               (NU SG)                       $
               (GD M)                        NIL
```

Figure 2. PTREE analysis structure.

```
(ptree 1 p)
S (EXPR PCP-F426)
$
CLS (EXPR PCP-F157)                          (CAN |Mann|)
  (CAN |schreiben|)                          (NU SG)
  NP (EXPR PCP-F302)                         (GD M)
    (CAN |Mann|)                             (TY HUM)
    (NU SG)                                  NST (CAN |Mann|)
    (GD M)                                     (NU SG)
    (TY HUM)                                   (GD M)
    DET (CAN |ein|)                            (TY HUM)
      (NU SG)                          RCL (EXPR PCP-F416)
      (GD M)                             (CAN |schreiben|)
    NO (EXPR PCP-F246)                   HABEN (CAN |haben|)
      (CAN |Mann|)                        (NU SG)
      (NU SG)                           NFCL (EXPR PCP-F230)
      (GD M)                              (CAN |schreiben|)
      (TY HUM)                           NP (EXPR PCP-F302)
    ADJ (EXPR PCP-F32)                     (CAN |Programm|)
      (CAN |alt|)                          (NU SG)
      (NU SG)                              (GD N)
      (GD M)                               (TY ABS DUR)
      AST (CAN |alt|)                      DET (CAN |dieser|)
      A-FLEX (CAN |er3|)                     (NU SG)
        (NU SG)                              (GD N)
        (GD M)                             NO (EXPR PCP-F508)
    PNCT (CAN |comma|)                       (CAN |Programm|)
    NO (EXPR PCP-F251)                       (NU SG)
      (CAN |Mann|)                           (GD N)
      (NU SG)                                (TY ABS DUR)
      (GD M)                               NST (CAN |Programm|)
      (TY HUM)                               (GD N)
    ADJ-LCL (EXPR PCP-F43)                   (TY ABS DUR)
      (CAN |verheiraten|)              NFCL (EXPR PCP-F218)
      (NU SG)                            (CAN |schreiben|)
      (GD M)                             PRT (CAN |niemals|)
      AST-LCL (EXPR PCP-F73)            NFCL (EXPR PCP-F219)
        (CAN |verheiraten|)              (CAN |schreiben|)
        VB (EXPR PCP-F480)              NFPRED (EXPR PCP-F234)
          (CAN |verheiraten|)            (CAN |schreiben|)
          (NU)                           VB (EXPR PCP-F479)
          VST (CAN |verheiraten|)          (CAN |schreiben|)
          V-FLEX (CAN |et1|)               (NU)
        A-FLEX (CAN |er3|)                 GE (CAN |ge|)
          (NU SG)                          VST (CAN |schreiben|)
          (GD M)                           V-FLEX (CAN |en1|)
    NO (EXPR PCP-F508)              $
                                     NIL
```

Figure 3. PTREE parse structure.

Note that the tree structure specifies a CLS dominating a PRED, an NP, an NP, and a PRT. This would seem to imply that there is some rule of the form CLS → PRED NP NP PRT, but this is not the case. The configuration of sons will often be different from the phrase structures of the rules that applied to them, and indeed whole nodes (and their rule histories) may be missing at this point. When it is important to view the actual phrase structures of the rules that applied, the 'p' option is employed, as shown in Figure 3. The 'p' option of PTREE demonstrates that the actual phrase-structure (as if not augmented with transformations) is CLS → NP RCL.

Both PTREEs show the status of the requested features at each of the nodes. This will ordinarily be sufficient to verify whether a feature-value pair was percolated up as intended. In order to verify whether the appropriate inheritance of features occurred, as well as to determine whether the proper grammatical relations obtain for the target language sentence, the 't' option for PTREE is employed. Figure 4 shows the transfer tree for our sentence. Note the depth to which lexical transfer occurs, as indicated by the nodes which have new CAN values.

13.5.3. DRAW-TREES

A rather more graphic display of an interpretation may be obtained through the 'draw-trees' function recently implemented. This allows a quick, mnemonic view of the tree structures arrayed in the form of a phrase-structure tree. Format limitations prevent DRAW-TREES from having the full functionality of PTREE; basically it can be used to portray the nodes and CAN values. Figures 5 and 6 show the draw-trees for the parse and the transfer, respectively.

13.5.4. Grammar-rule access devices

13.5.4.1. PGR ('print German rule')

This command displays, in the current window, the German source rule or rules specified by the arguments given to the command. A rule may be identified in various different ways as an argument to PGR, but typically it is identified by a specification of its left side and right side constituents. Thus the command

    (pgr (lhs np rhs (det no)))

will display the rule whose lhs is an NP, and whose right-hand side (rhs) is the string DET NO.

```
(ptree 1 t)
S (EXPR PCP-F426)
  $                                              (CAN |man|)
  CLS (EXPR PCP-F157)                            (NU SG)
    (CAN |schreiben|)                            (GD M)
    NP (EXPR PCP-F302)                           (TY HUM)
      (CAN |Mann|)                               NST (CAN |man|)
      (NU SG)                                      (NU SG)
      (GD M)                                       (GD M)
      (TY HUM)                                     (TY HUM)
      DET (CAN |a|)                     PRED (EXPR #:G0328)
        (NU SG)                           PRED (EXPR #:G0333)
        (GD M)                              (CAN |schreiben|)
      NO (EXPR PCP-F246)                    (NU SG)
        (CAN |Mann|)                       HAVE (CAN |have|)
        (NU SG)                              (NU SG)
        (GD M)                             PRT (CAN |never|)
        (TY HUM)                           NFPRED (EXPR PCP-F234)
        ADJ (EXPR PCP-F32)                   (CAN |schreiben|)
          (CAN |old|)                        VB (EXPR PCP-F479)
          (NU SG)                              (CAN |write|)
          (GD M)                               (NU)
          (TY HUM)                             TO
          AST (CAN |old|)                      BE
            (NU SG)                            VST (CAN |write|)
            (TY HUM)                             (NU)
      NO (EXPR PCP-F251)                       PRFX
        (CAN |Mann|)              NP (EXPR PCP-F302)
        (NU SG)                    (CAN |Programm|)
        (GD M)                     (NU SG)
        (TY HUM)                   (GD N)
        ADJ-LCL (EXPR PCP-F43)     (TY ABS DUR)
          (CAN |verheiraten|)      DET (CAN |this|)
          (NU SG)                    (NU SG)
          (GD M)                     (GD N)
          (TY HUM)                 NO (EXPR PCP-F508)
          AST-LCL (EXPR PCP-F73)     (CAN |program|)
            (CAN |verheiraten|)      (NU SG)
            VB (EXPR PCP-F480)       (GD N)
              (CAN |married|)        (TY ABS DUR)
              (NU)                   NST (CAN |program|)
              TO                       (NU SG)
              BE                       (GD N)
              AST (CAN |married|)      (TY DUR)
                (NU)          $
              PRFX            NIL
      NO (EXPR PCP-F508)
```

Figure 4. PTREE target-language structure.

13.5.4.2. EGR ('edit German rule')

This command allows the developer to revise an existing German source rule or rules, by deleting the rules from the grammar database into a temporary file, and then entering an edit window containing that file. The edit session makes possible any ordinary editing function using the Symbolics native editor. Thus an incorrect rule may be revised, new ones created, duplicates or ill-considered rules removed, and so on. After the edit session, the revised version of the temporary file is loaded into the grammar database, and deleted from the file system.

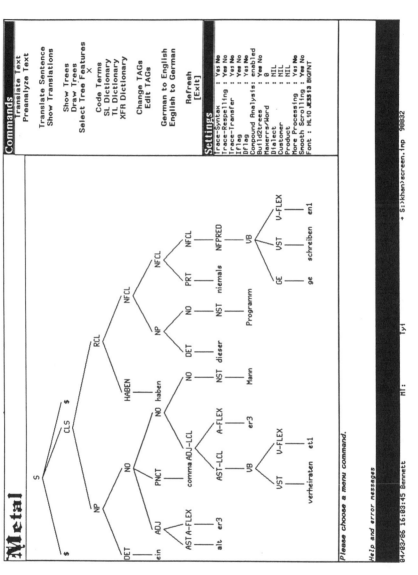

Figure 5. The draw-tree for the parse.

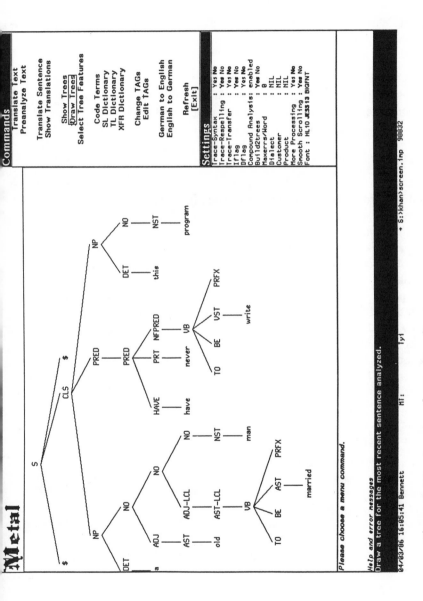

Figure 6. The draw-tree for the transfer.

The arguments to EGR are the same as for PGR; thus the command

(egr (lhs np rhs (det no)))

allows the editing of the same set of rules that the PGR example above displays.

13.5.4.3. DGR ('delete German rule')

Rules may be deleted through the edit process, of course, but frequently it is convenient to use a straightforward means of deleting a set of rules. DGR uses the same argument structure as PGR and EGR.

13.5.5. TRACE-SYNTAX

PTREE will show, for each interpretation (or phrase), the rules that applied and the provenience of the feature-value pairs requested. If, however, the developer needs to know why a rule intended to apply does not, or why a rule believed to be blocked keeps applying, it is useful to watch the application attempts as they occur, noting the exact conditions along any interpretation that cause a rule to fail. The variable TRACE-SYNTAX controls the display of rule applications as they are attempted. Each message displays the phrase-structure portion of the attempted rule, along with the phrase number (i.e., the nth rule attempt). The EXPR value (rule database pointer index) of the rule is given, followed either by the indication that the rule is rejected (and the constraint that caused its failure is given), or by the indication that the rule succeeds (by a numerical index).

Figure 7 is a highly abridged syntax trace, showing the basic message form, along certain special characteristics, particularly that every possible construal of the phrase that can be attempted is attempted. In the extreme example, note the attempt to build the article *ein* from *Ei*, which is a noun meaning 'egg.'

```
(setq trace-syntax t)
T
(translate)
...
Entering Analysis Phase...
NO:1 — > NST[Programm]  (PCP-F508)  99090
NO:2 — > NST[Programm]  (PCP-F507)  REJECTED: (1 REQ CL P-01 P-02)
VB:3 — > HABEN[hat]  (PCP-F484)  90001
NO:4 — > NST[Mann]  (PCP-F508)  99090
NO:5 — > NST[Mann]  (PCP-F507)  REJECTED: (1 REQ CL P-01 P-02)
...
NO:10 — > NST[Alter]  (PCP-F508)  REJECTED: (1 OR (OPT OR * LC) (REQ
ABB))
...
ADJ:13 — > AST[alt]  (PCP-F24)  90001
ADJ:14 — > AST[alt]  (PCP-F6)  REJECTED: (1 REQ DG COM)
ADV:15 — > AST[ein]  (PCP-F45)  REJECTED: (1 NRQ NUM)
ADJ:16 — > AST[ein]  (PCP-F24)  REJECTED: (1 REQ CL PP-0 PA-0)
```

```
ADJ:17 —> AST[ein]  (PCP-F6)   REJECTED: (1 REQ DG COM)
NO:18 —> NST[Ei]  (PCP-F508)   REJECTED: (1 REQ WF)
...
ADJ:29 —> AST[alt] A-FLEX[er]  (PCP-F32)   90000
...
VB:34 —> VST[verheirat] V-FLEX[et]  (PCP-F480)   90000
...
NP:47 —> DET[dieses] NO:1  (PCP-F302)   98441
NP:48 —> DET[dieses] NO:1  (PCP-F258)   REJECTED:
                            (1 REQ CAN eine Reihe von)
...
AST-LCL:53 —> VB:34  (PCP-F73)   90001
...
ADJ-LCL:58 —> AST-LCL:53 A-FLEX[er]  (PCP-F43)   90002
ADJ-LCL:59 —> AST-LCL:53 A-FLEX[er]  (PCP-F43)   90002
ADJ-LCL:60 —> AST-LCL:53 A-FLEX[er]  (PCP-F43)   90002
...
NO:63 —> ADJ-LCL:60 NO:4  (PCP-F251)   94546
...
NO:66 —> ADJ:31 PNCT[,] NO:63  (PCP-F246)   91515
...
NP:69 —> DET[ein] NO:66  (PCP-F302)   97359
...
PRED:73 —> VB:3  (PCP-F384)   90002
...
RCL:76 —> PRED:73  (PCP-F405)   90003
...
RCL:78 —> RCL:76 NP:47  (PCP-F422)   94221
RCL:79 —> RCL:78 PRT[niemals]  (PCP-F419)   92814
...
NP:88 —> NO:63  (PCP-F283)   98182
...
VB:196 —> GE[ge] VST[schrieb] V-FLEX[en]  (PCP-F479)   46250
...
NP:236 —> DET[ein] ADJ:31  (PCP-F301)   90000
...
NP:246 —> NP:236 PNCT[,] NP:88  (PCP-F281)   92727
...
AST-LCL:262 —> VB:196  (PCP-F73)   46251
...
PRN:267 —> DET[dieses]  (PCP-F399)   45000
PRN:268 —> DET[ein]  (PCP-F399)   45000
...
NP:270 —> PRN:268  (PCP-F305)   45001
...
NFPRED:277 —> VB:196  (PCP-F234)   46251
...
NFCL:279 —> NFPRED:277  (PCP-F219)   86562
NFCL:280 —> PRT[niemals] NFCL:279  (PCP-F218)   68125
NFCL:281 —> NP:47 NFCL:280  (PCP-F230)   89115
RCL:282 —> HABEN[hat] NFCL:281  (PCP-F416)   85522
CLS:283 —> NP:69 RCL:282  (PCP-F157)   95811
...
S:286 —> '$' CLS:283 '$'  (PCP-F426)   95968
```

Figure 7. A syntax trace.

13.5.6. ENGLISH n

Multiple interpretations, i.e., situations in which more than one path successfully builds to S, are quite frequent in translation of technical texts. It is particularly troublesome to have an incorrect translation of a text sentence, only to discover that a less-preferred interpretation, which was the linguistically correct one, actually succeeded but was not output because of the preference scheme. For the purposes of tuning the interaction among rules, rule-preferences, and lexical preferences, there is a convenient device for invoking transfer on a less-preferred interpretation.

The command '(english n)' transfers the nth interpretation in order to view the translation resulting from a less-preferred parse path. It is sometimes the case, as in the example below, that a lesser preferred interpretation actually produces the right translation. In these cases the developer uses this tool along with PTREE, the rule examination functions, and the lexical examination functions, to determine the best way to promote this interpretation to prominence, without adversely affecting the preferences of other sentences. More often, however, the developer wants to limit the number of interpretations produced, in order to enhance system performance. In these cases the tool is used along with PTREE to determine further constraints on rules.

Figure 8 shows a sentence containing a syntactic ambiguity concerning the governing of the prepositional phrase. The first interpretation takes the prepositional phrases to modify the NP (*the man*) therefore staying with it. This is the incorrect interpretation, even though it is the more preferred by METAL. The developer enters the command (english 2) to view the translation of the other interpretation, which is the correct one.

> (translate)
> Sentence: (Nach dem Krieg war der Mann in Muenchen)
> 2 interpretations in 9589 milliseconds: 4794 msecs/interp.
> 59 PHRASES: 37 REJECTED.
>
> Transfer plus generation time: 5988 milliseconds.
> (|the| |man| |in| |Munich| |was| |after| |the| |war|)
>
> (english 2)
>
> Transfer plus generation time: 1040 milliseconds. after the war, the man was in Munich

Figure 8. Viewing multiple interpretations.

13.6. Text translation tools

We have discussed above the usefulness of interactive translation capability for diagnostic and development purposes. The TRANSLATE and PTREE calls can be of use to the user-level lexicographer as well, in testing coding decisions, especially of verbs. However, the principal translation activity intended for the user of a METAL system is the batch translation of texts. In connection with that, METAL development has always borne an interface to unique automatic pre- and post-processing programs which, for example, can strip text from a wide variety of formats, and restore the translation to those same formats. In order for these interfaces to be maintained, MT output texts are producible in certain forms amenable to the reconstitution and post-editing processes. These forms happen also to be useful to the development effort. Additionally, one output form is of special use in development.

Text translation begins with a menu prompting for runtime parameters (such as subject area of the text). If desired, 'dribbles' and run-logs are generated which note the times of execution and the parameters set, along with information about number of interpretations and rule attempts on each sentence.

Upon completion of text translation, the output file may be examined as a set of translation units, or reconstituted into the original text format; more often for development purposes, however, the output is examined in the form of interlinear translations, so that each sentence may be compared with its translation. On a diagnostic-test text which has been run before, a comparison may be produced which gives the source sentence, the older translation, and the newer translation for only those sentences whose translation has changed since the last run.

A word about test texts is warranted here. An obvious, common-sense approach to testing syntactic phenomena in translation would seem to be the use of strictly diagnostic sentences which reflect the phenomenon. This is, indeed, a fruitful method employed particularly in the translate-sentence routines. But we have found from often painful experience that frequent tests with 'real' (industrial documents written by technical writers) texts are the only way to assure progress. Such texts invariably bring out problems which had not occurred to the developer, leading to solutions which attempt to address in a unified way both the expected and the unexpected problems. And real test texts are the best way to determine degradation, a situation which can occur despite the developer's most carefully thought-out predictions about possible rule-interactions.

So it turns out that the translate-text functions are quite useful in the research environment, particularly for use with real texts. They are, of course, also used for phenomenon-specific tests, as when a particular linguistic solution involves a distribution of several behaviors over a variety of phrase structures. In these cases, a file of test forms is frequently kept, as a convenience over individually typing each of the units in sentence-mode.

13.7. Lexicon development tools

13.7.1. *INTERCODER*

The official interface between METAL and hands-on end-users is the means of coding and modifying lexicon. The development environment has two systems, one of which, while somewhat 'Lispy,' avoids the strictures of windows and menus and can be operated either in batch or interactive processes. This one is the principal method used by research and development. The other system is the one offered as the official interface, being a menu-driven window system which presents queries in a form readily understandable to a translator, and which is safe (in the sense that it will not allow the user to exit from an entry until it is legally coded or cancelled). When called, the INTERCODER prompts for a source-language term, its subject area, and its part of speech. If the word does not already exist in the lexicon the INTERCODER will create a 'guess' entry (see the discussion of the defaulting mechanism below) and show the user a menu of what guess it made. The user may then alter any parameter. If the word does exist in the lexicon, the user is so informed and is allowed to alter it with just the same menu as with the unknown word. Figure 9 shows the source language entry for *schreiben.* The INTERCODER then prompts for the corresponding target word, repeats the above process, then creates a 'default' transfer lexicon entry, if unknown, or the actual entry if known, which the user may alter.

13.7.2. Development lexical functions

The development environment of METAL requires access to the lexical database that is different from the 'advertised' version. Such access needs less in the way of 'help,' and more in the way of fast insertion of quantities of lexical items in the database. The product-level, interactive coding system is safe and efficient for the entry of terminology in technical subject areas. But creation and installation of general terminology sets, or recoding whole databases when new enhancements are added to the grammar, require a form of access which trades a certain measure of safety for power, and which may be executed in a batch mode. The lexical functions covered by the defaulter, preanalyzer, and validator exist for the batch lexical DBMS as well as for the interactive coder. Additionally, the batch DBMS has access functions and completeness checking which are specifically suited to the needs of the lexical development environment.

13.7.2.1. VALIDATOR

This program checks to see whether a created entry is legal, that is, whether the features given actually are specifiable for that part of speech, and that the values given for those features are legal values. Beyond this, of course, the validator cannot guarantee that an entry is coded 'correctly.' The validator reports the perceived coding error, and the severity of the error. Certain errors are reported as warnings and ignored; others are reported upon rejecting the entry.

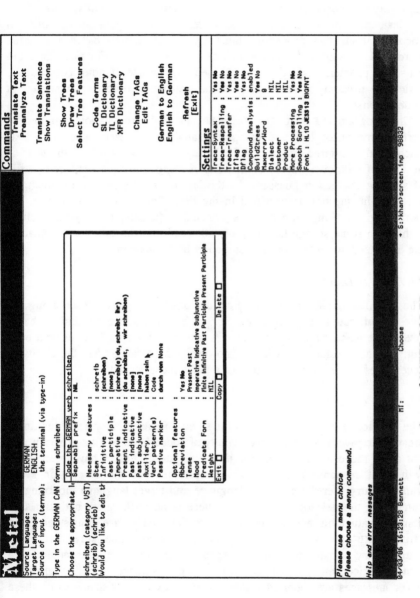

Figure 9. Screen dump of INTERCODER.

13.7.2.2. PREANALYZER

Both the user version and the development version require an automatic capability to determine which words in a text are not presently contained in the lexicon. For the sort of industrial texts typically generated as internal documentation, this procedure must try to distinguish between genuine words not covered and misspellings of covered words. For German input texts, the problem is further complicated by the use of noun compounds, which the preanalysis program (and the translation routines) must attempt to decompose.

The program PREANALYZE uses a subset of the translation grammar to perform morphological and compound analysis on each word in a text. Each word is entered either in a file listing the known words in the text, or in a file of unknown words, or in a file of compound 'guesses,' or in a file of spelling correction guesses. In the last three, the sentence context for the form in question is provided in the file. For the compounds file, the word is given along with a guess translation (usually part-by-part, left to right, with some special handling possible); if that translation is acceptable, the user need not enter the full compound in the lexicon.

13.7.2.3. DEFAULTER

The defaulter creates a full entry on the basis of a guess, made along the lines of suffixation, capitalization, etc. In both the intercoder and the batch DBMS, the defaulter makes the entries available for proofreading and editing. In the development version, however, the defaulter has the ability to access files containing lexical lists of a fairly loose format.

13.7.2.4. CHECK-LEXICAL-CONSISTENCY

The interactive user-coder assures the safety of entries, along various lines, most notably with respect to the legality of coded features (the program will not allow the user to exit unless all the required choices have been made with legal responses) and to the completeness of the entry (for every transfer entry there is a source language and target language monolingual entry). In the development version, there is no such safety net, and as a result certain tools are needed to assure that entries are consistent. The CHECK-LEXICAL-CONSISTENCY program checks to make sure that every source entry is matched to a transfer entry, and that every target-side in a transfer lexicon entry is matched with a target language monolingual entry. Error messages are reported if there is any lack of consistency along these lines.

13.7.2.5. PGW ('print German word')

PGW displays the entry or entries requested by an intersection of lexical feature-value-pairs. The display is in the standard lexical entry form. Frequently, the word is accessed by the value for CAN (the dictionary-entry form); consequently, there is a shorthand version of the print-function. PGW and the short version are accessed as follows:

```
(pgw (can |schreiben|))
(schreiben        CAT (VST)
   ALO   (schreib)
   PLC   (WI)
   SNS   (1)
   TAG   (GV)
   AX    (haben)
   CL    (IMP-1 INF-EN PRI-1 PRS-1)
   PV    (durch von)
   PX    (NIL)
   TT    (DT T)
   ARGS  ((1 A PP) (2 D (CP TH)) (3 D A) (4 A)
         (5 (CP TH)) (6 PP) (7 D) (8))   )

(g |schreiben|)
(schreiben        CAT (VST)
   ALO   (schreib)
   PLC   (WI)
   SNS   (1)
   TAG   (GV)
   ...
```

These examples show the long-form of the print function (by which a word can be accessed via one or several feature-value pairs) and an abridged display of the short-form, which prints on the value of CAN.

The functions PEW (print English word) and E are called in the same way as PGW and G, respectively.

The print function PXW has a difference, in that the feature must be addressed with a pseudonym referring to the language requested. In the following, *schreiben* is referred to as the value of the feature GCAN. If the entry is to be accessed only by the source or target CAN, the short-forms XG and XE are used.

```
(pxw (gcan |schreiben|))

(schreiben (VST GV) 0    !  write (VST GV) 0   )
(    T                    !  T                  )
(    *                    !                     )
(    PP-TO-PP auf on      !                     )
(    PP-TO-PP an on       !                     )
(    NP-TO-PP D to        !                     )
(                         +                     )

(xg |schreiben|)
(schreiben (VST GV) 0    !  write (VST GV) 0   )
(    T                    !  T                  )
(    *                    !                     )
```

```
( PP-TO-PP auf on      !              )
( PP-TO-PP an on       !              )
( NP-TO-PP D to        !              )
(                      +              )
```

13.7.2.6. EGW ('edit German word')

GW allows the development user to edit a German monolingual lexical entry. The entry is deleted from the database, dumped into a temporary file, and, after editing, which may include the deletion or addition of whole entries, as well as modification of entries, the contents of the temporary file are loaded back into the database. The syntax is exactly the same as that for the print functions, and the function EEW for the English corresponds appropriately for English and transfer.

13.7.2.7. DGW ('delete German word')

DGW allows the development user to delete a German monolingual entry from the DBMS. Even though deletion is possible from EGW, this is faster and of course more appropriate in the case of a specification of a large number of entries. In the following, every German entry which is both CAN *ein* and CAT ADV is deleted from the database.

    (dgw (can |ein| cat adv))

13.8. Conclusion

Research associated with METAL has been done with an awareness of the scale that the system would have to have in order to do industrial translation. For this reason, there has been a concentration upon the tools which enable linguists and programmers alike to perform their work in an efficient manner. Tools have been implemented which allow linguists to manipulate language structures in a linguistically familiar format, to add, delete, or modify these structures easily for heuristic experimentation, and to build these structures into the stable system. Aspects of the native programming environment have contributed both to the underlying ease of this sort of development, and to the ease of implementing the more direct linguistic tools. The fundamental segregation of linguistic fact from software statement has allowed research into profound modifications of METAL without having to rewrite data modules. Some of the effort in research and development tools has a fortuitous side effect, in that some version of these tools gets 'technology-transferred' along with the linguistic data and translation software, into the end-user environment. But beyond this, the tools remain to allow the creation of new language pairs and, indeed, new NLP systems, to be developed in the most efficient environment possible.

14 Knowledge resource tools for accessing large text files

DONALD E. WALKER

14.1. Introduction

This chapter provides an overview of a research program under development at Bell Communications Research.[1] The objective is to develop facilities for working with large document collections which provide more refined access to the information contained in these 'source' materials than is possible through existing information retrieval procedures and yet stop short of the processing required to identify their full meaning. The current technology supports search strategies that depend on matching index terms, which constitute a general characterization of the subject matter of a document, or on the application of pattern templates, which match specific sequences of words in the text. In contrast, most long-range research efforts in computational linguistics and artificial intelligence are trying to understand the meaning of individual sentences by analyzing their syntactic, semantic, and discourse structures. Our own efforts can be described most simply as addressing an intermediate goal based on capturing the semantics of words and phrases in the documents.

The tools being used for this purpose are machine-readable dictionaries, encyclopedias, and related *resources* that provide geographical, biographical, and other kinds of specialized knowledge. An increasing number of these kinds of materials are becoming available in machine-readable form, primarily as a byproduct of the use of computer-driven photocomposition techniques. In our research, we are identifying and extracting the information contained in these *resources* so we can apply them more effectively to text. However, it is clear that in their present form they are not wholly adequate for our objective. As an example, consider the use of a current dictionary for understanding a newspaper story — a relationship to which we will return below. The central elements of such stories are people, places, institutions, and events, few of which are included in the dictionary. Because of this kind of mismatch, a central element of our research program is exploring the interactions between *sources* and *resources*, that is

---

[1] This research is a continuation of work begun at SRI International in collaboration with Robert A. Amsler, who also joined Bellcore to participate in this effort. His contributions — and often his words as well — are reflected throughout this chapter.

between the structural features of texts and organized bodies of knowledge. While other knowledge *resources* can supplement the dictionary entries, analyses of the texts themselves can provide additional data, for example, candidate terms for proper nouns and recurrent phrases. In addition, dictionary information can be used to help identify the topical focus of a text, and, given that focus, the text can be analyzed to reveal features that should be incorporated into the dictionary to increase its coverage.

The techniques we are developing are intended for use in a workstation environment by experts who organize and use information from documents in the course of their work. In contrast to the research in artificial intelligence on 'expert systems' in which the goal is to extract the knowledge from an expert and embody it in a system, our concern might be said to be with 'systems for experts,' that is, with systems that support specialists in their search for knowledge. Two systems under development will illustrate our approach: one providing capabilities for full-text subject assessment; the other for concept elaboration while reading text.

In the next two sections, we consider some of the *sources* and *resources* we have been gathering. Following that, we present the two systems we have been building. At the end, we consider some of the directions for our work and their implications for information retrieval and machine translation.

14.2. Sources

Over the years we have been acquiring a large number of text files for our research. The following list indicates the range and variety of *sources* so far collected. However, with the increasing use of computer-generated phototypesetting and word-processing, we will be limited only by our capacity for storing items and our ability to get permission to use them.[2]

- *The Brown University Corpus*: 1,000,000 words of text gathered in 1963 and 1964 in samples of 2,000 words and intended to provide a representative cross section of reading material from 15 different subject areas (Kucera and Francis, 1967). The collection was motivated by an interest in getting frequency statistics for English, the results of which are referenced in the next section.

- *New York Times News Service*: over 90,000,000 words collected over a period of more than two years, beginning in 1983. The Times also contains a broad range of subject matter and a variety of different prose styles.

- *Associated Press News Service*: we receive releases at a rate of 1,500,000 bytes a day, and have accumulated more than a year's worth of material.

- *The Handbook of Artificial Intelligence*: a comprehensive survey of the field compiled during the period 1975 to 1980 and issued in three volumes edited by Barr,

---

[2] Some publishers, in recognition of the possible market value of their documents in digital form, have made it more difficult to gain access to them for research purposes. We are particularly grateful for those companies that have made their products available to us.

Feigenbaum, Cohen (1981, 1982). In addition to its broad coverage of the field, the *Handbook* provides an example of text formatted in TeX, a language designed for use with computer-based printers.

- *Understanding Expository Text*: a scientific monograph by Britton and Black (1985) that both provides an opportunity to examine a full-length book and is at the same time a 'handbook for analyzing explanatory text.'

- *Unix Manuals*: five volumes of manuals for using, managing, and programming in Unix (1979, 1984). In addition to text, they contain a wide variety of material in many different formats.

- *Moby Dick* and *Pride and Prejudice*: two novels that illustrate two quite different English prose styles.

- *LATA Switching Systems Generic Requirements*: a 5,000,000 byte file that contains the official definition of the telephone central office switch.

14.3. Resources

The *resources* we have collected can be grouped in five categories: word frequency lists, machine-readable dictionaries, derivative dictionary data, reference works, and databases. Each will be considered in turn.

Word Frequency Lists : as the name indicates, they contain information on the relative frequency of occurrence of words in text:

- *Computational Analysis of Present-Day American English*: statistics on the 1,000,000 word Brown University Corpus described in the previous section (Kucera and Francis, 1967). Over 50,000 different graphic word types are present, arranged both in order of frequency and alphabetically. For each entry, information is provided about its relative occurrence in the 15 different subject areas and 500 samples. A wide range of distributional analyses have been made of the data.

- *The American Heritage Word Frequency Book*: statistics on 5,000,000 words of text gathered in 500 word samples from the kinds of reading children in grades 3 through 9 were likely to encounter in the late 1960's (Carroll, Davies, and Richman, 1971). The 87,000 graphic word types were derived from 22 different kinds of materials, mostly different curriculum levels. They are grouped both alphabetically and by frequency, distinguishing both grade level and category.

- *New York Times News Service Corpus*: statistics on an 8,300,000 word sample of stories corresponding to three months of material distributed in the last three months of 1983 (Walker and Amsler, 1986). The database in which this material has been stored has been designed to accumulate information about case and punctuation as well as by frequency according to day, month, and year.

Machine-Readable Dictionaries : Each contains a large variety of different kinds of information for an entry: spelling form, syllabification, pronunciation, part-of-speech, inflections, etymology, sense distinctions, definitions, usage notes, example sentences, and synonyms. We have at various times been working with the following machine-readable dictionaries:

- *Merriam-Webster New Collegiate Dictionary* (Seventh Edition): one of the classic collegiate dictionaries and probably the first available in machine-readable form (G&C Merriam, 1963). It contains over 70,000 entries and represents more than 15.5 million bytes of data. It has been widely used in research because of its extensive distribution following its computerization in the mid-1960's.

- *Merriam-Webster New Pocket Dictionary*: an abridged version of the 'Seventh' (G&C Merriam, 1964). It contains almost 23,000 entries and consumes 4.5 million bytes of storage.

- *Longman Dictionary of Contemporary English*: a dictionary designed for people learning English as a second language (Procter, 1978). It contains over 55,000 entries and occupies 14 million bytes of storage. It is distinctive in a number of respects: the defining vocabulary is limited to 2,000 words; it has a very refined set of grammatical codes; and the computer tape provides detailed semantic information and a set of subject codes to characterize specialized senses of words.

- *Oxford Advanced Learner's Dictionary*: another 'Learner's' dictionary (Hornby, Gatenby, and Wakefield, 1963), it contains 35,000 entries and occupies 6.5 million bytes of storage. It is distinctive in containing an unusually large number of example sentences.

Derivative Dictionary Data : Two sets are available; they represent the taxonomic relationships among the 24,000 different noun senses and the 11,000 verb senses in the *Merriam-Webster Pocket Dictionary* (Amsler, 1980, 1981). The kernel terms in the definitions of each noun and verb sense were identified and disambiguated with respect to the appropriate word sense in their definitions. Relationships among the resulting pairs of words were calculated and a set of tangled hierarchies generated. Processing of this kind is intended to provide a more comprehensive lexical semantic classification of the language, demonstrating the complex interrelationships among words.

Reference Works : The first two items are of particular significance for our research.

- *The World Almanac & Book of Facts 1985*: one of the classic reference works for factual information (Newspaper Enterprise Association, 1984). It contains text, tables, illustrations, and time-lines to summarize encyclopedic information about science, history, geography, biography, and related categories of information. The source file, still being extracted from its phototypesetting matrix, occupies 10 million bytes of storage.

- *Academic American Encyclopedia*: one of the first encyclopedias to be available in machine-readable form (Grolier, 1984). It has more than 29,000 articles and tables and incorporates material online that is not in the printed edition.

- *INSPEC*: citation data for 6 months of the Computer and Control Section from 1980; about 10,000 items and 2 million bytes of storage.

- *Psychological Abstracts*: citation data plus abstracts for 2 years of material published in 1982 and 1983; 5-10 million bytes of storage.

Databases : Material under this heading is not in text form. The set below is primarily geographical in emphasis, but that reflects in part an interest in maps in our Division. A large variety of other types of databases would be easy to acquire.

- ZIP-Code List (5-digit): contains all the towns in the United States with ZIP-code assignments, including street name and address breakdowns for cities with multiple ZIP-codes.

- Name and Address List: for 1.25 million people living in Kansas; about 60 million bytes of data.

- Telephone Yellow Pages: for two major US area codes from 1980 and 1984; approximately 6 million bytes.

14.4. FORCE4, a system for full-text content assessment

The first system we developed to demonstrate the interaction between *sources* and *resources* is *FORCE4*, a procedure for full-text content assessment.[3] It makes use of a set of subject codes assigned to specialized word senses in the *Longman Dictionary of Contemporary English* (*LDOCE*), applying them to stories from the *New York Times News Service* (*NYTNS*). The result is an identification of the primary subject content of those stories.

14.5. How FORCE4 processes text

To understand how *FORCE4* works we first need to consider the *LDOCE* subject codes in more detail. There are 120 two-letter field codes that mark, for example, areas like medicine (MD) and political science (PL). These field codes are divided into 212 subfield categories; for example, physiology is represented as MDZP and diplomacy as PLZD, the Z being used in the third position exclusively as an indicator of subcategorization. The field codes can also be combined so that the designation for meteorology (ML) together with the one for building (CO), that is MLCO, is used to mark the entry *lightning conductor*. Similarly, MLGO (meteorology plus geography) marks *temperate* and *torrid*, while GOML (the same fields in the reverse order) marks *permafrost* and *drift ice*. In addition, there are 38 locality codes that identify major geographical areas and countries or distinguish areas within them. Thus, U represents Europe and F represents France; combined with meteorology, the code MLUF is applied to *mistral*, a distinctive wind that is characteristic of southern France. The word *typhoon* is marked MLX, meteorology and Asia. There are over 2600 realized combinations of two, three, and four-letter codes. Out of the 55,000 entries in the dictionary, 18,000 are marked as having specialized subject senses.

The following weather report will be used to illustrate the operation of *FORCE4*.

> Heavy rainfall and high winds clobbered the California coast early today, while a storm system in the Southeast dampened the Atlantic Seaboard from Florida to Virginia.
>
> Traveler's advisories warned of snow in California's northern mountains and northwestern Nevada. Rain and snow fell in the Dakotas, northern Minnesota and upper Michigan.
>
> Skies were cloudy from Tennessee through the Ohio Valley into New England, but generally clear from Texas into the mid-Mississippi Valley.

---

[3] This work was actually done at SRI International; the system was designed by Robert Amsler, and much of this description can be found in Walker and Amsler (1986). The system was implemented on a DEC/20 computer. The name *FORCE4* reflects the currency of *Star Wars* when we began the project.

The *LDOCE* subject codes for the first four content words in the report are as follows:

- *heavy*: FO-food, ML-meteorology, TH-theatre
- *rainfall*: ML-meteorology
- *high*: AU-motor vehicles, DGXX-drugs and drug experiences, FO-food, ML-meteorology, RLXX-religion, SN-sounds
- *wind*: HFZH-hunting, MDZP-physiology, ML-meteorology, MU-music, NA-nautical

FORCE4 works by applying the *LDOCE* codes to each successive word in the text. The frequency of occurrence of these codes is cumulated, and the codes themselves are arranged in order of frequency. We developed a display program to show how this process provides an assessment of stories. The program employs a full-screen display format with three windows that contain, respectively: (1) the text being processed; (2) the program's intermediate inferences regarding the syntactic and semantic properties of each content-bearing word in the text; and (3) a running tally of the frequencies of the top subject assignments made to the document on the basis of the cumulative set of content-bearing words that have been analyzed.

The text appears in *Window 1*, which occupies the major part of the screen, beginning at the upper left corner. For each content-bearing word in the text, the subject codes are looked up in the *LDOCE*. If the word fails to have a subject code, it is analyzed to determine whether it is the inflected form of some word with a set of subject codes. If subject codes are found, they are displayed together with their English descriptions in *Window 2* at the bottom of the screen. The subject codes identified for a word are merged into the set of subject codes established for the text so far, and the resulting array of revised frequencies is sorted and displayed in high-to-low order in *Window 3* at the upper right of the screen.

Window 1	*Window 3*
Heavy rainfall and high winds clobbered the California COAST early today, while a storm system in the Southeast dampened the Atlantic Seaboard from Florida to Virginia.	4 = ML 2 = FO 2 = NA
Travelers' advisories warned of snow in California's northern mountains and northwestern Nevada. Rain and snow fell in the Dakotas, northern Minnesota and Upper Michigan.	1 = AU 1 = MU
Skies were cloudy from Tennessee through the Ohio Valley into New England, but generally clear from Texas into the mid-Mississippi Valley.	1 = SN 1 = TH
Window 2	
coast = GOZG (geography) NA (nautical)	

Figure 1. Example of *FORCE4* processing, through the word *coast*.

Figure 1 shows *FORCE4* in the course of processing a weather report. The text has been analyzed through the word *coast* (capitalized here, but in inverse video in actual operation). The most frequent subject code is meteorology (ML) with 4; food (FO) and nautical (NA) both have 2; the rest all have the value 1. Completing the processing of the text yields the results shown in Figure 2. Meteorology (ML) is still the most frequent code with 10; geographical terms (GOZG) and drugs and drug experiences (DGXX) have 4; nautical (NA) has 3; and food (FO) and military (MI) have 2.

Window 1	Window 3
Heavy rainfall and high winds clobbered the California coast early today, while a storm system in the Southeast dampened the Atlantic Seaboard from Florida to Virginia.	10 = ML
	4 = GOZG
	4 = DGXX
Travelers' advisories warned of snow in California's northern mountains and northwestern Nevada. Rain and snow fell in the Dakotas, northern Minnesota and Upper Michigan.	3 = NA
	2 = MI
	2 = FO
Skies were cloudy from Tennessee through the Ohio Valley into New England, but generally clear from Texas into the mid-Mississippi VALLEY.	2 = GO
	1 = TH
Window 2	
Valley = GOZG (geography)	

Figure 2. Example of *FORCE4* processing, through the word *Valley.*

A set of more than 100 *NYTNS* stories (a 24-hour sample) was processed against the *LDOCE* codes to determine subject content. The results were remarkably good; *FORCE4* works well over a variety of subjects — law, military, sports, radio and television — and several different formats — text, tables, and even recipes.

14.5.1. A discussion of the FORCE4 approach

The *FORCE4* approach definitely merits further development. However, it is worthwhile to consider the weather example in a little more detail in order to point out some of the current limitations and, in general, to illustrate problems encountered in using machine-readable dictionaries.

First, it is appropriate to consider the words in the text that were marked with subject codes: *heavy, rainfall, high, winds, coast, storm, Southeast, Seaboard, Virginia, snow, mountains, northwestern, rain, snow, fell, Upper, skies, cloudy, Valley, New, clear, Valley.* Two of the words that were marked for meteorology, *heavy* and *high,* were actually being used as adjectives modifying the following nouns (*rainfall* and *winds,* respectively) and not in the coded sense. *Seaboard* should have been treated as part of a compound, *Atlantic Seaboard,* and not as a separate word, as should *Upper* with respect to *Michigan* and *New* with respect to *England.* The two *Valleys* may also be parts of compound expressions, since they denote areas quite different from the states they modify.

The following words did not have subject codes (function words and other general vocabulary items are excluded): *clobbered, California, early, today, system, dampened, Atlantic, Florida, Travelers,' advisories, warned, California's, northern, Nevada, Dakotas, Michigan, Tennessee, Ohio, England, generally, Texas, mid-Mississippi.* The obvious thing to note is the predominance of state names and other regional designations. The *LDOCE*, like most dictionaries, does not include many proper nouns. *Virginia* is actually coded for its tobacco sense. The rest of this set of terms probably do not have specialized subject senses, although it is a little puzzling for *Southeast* and *northwestern* to be included, while *northern* is not.

There are, of course, a number of conditions that have to be satisfied in order for FORCE4 to work well, even at its present, early state of development:

1.   The content-bearing words of the text must have entries in the *LDOCE*.
2.   The subject-codes for the content-bearing words must include the sense in which the word is being used in the text.
3.   The content-bearing words must not also be common function words, e.g., as *in* is in the sentence, 'The tide is in.'
4.   A sufficient quantity of text must be examined for the topmost subject-code assignments to stabilize (typically more than a sentence, but often less than two paragraphs).
5.   The text must be about a single topic, rather than a collection of different topics such as is found in a news summary of major headline stories.

The procedures that we have described for FORCE4 constitute only the first step in the development of its capabilities for content assessment. One extremely desirable extension entails *pruning* the spurious sense entries in the text. If we accept the principle that a word with multiple senses, and thus several subject codes, is likely to be used in the text only in one of these senses, then the following procedure can be applied. Take the code with the highest frequency — that would be meteorology (ML) in Figure 2 — and, for all the words so marked, eliminate from the cumulative frequency list all of the other codes they contained. The ordering there showed meteorology (ML) as the most frequent code with 10; geographical terms (GOZG) and drugs and drug experiences (DGXX) had 4; nautical (NA) 3; and food (FO) and military (MI) 2. After pruning, ML would still be 10, of course; GOZG would remain at 4; DGXX would be reduced to 1; NA would be reduced to 2; FO would be eliminated; and MI would become 1. Note that if a slightly more radical pruning strategy were invoked — that is, removing a subject code in the list if any instances of it were eliminated — DGXX, NA, and MI would all be 0, leaving only ML and GOZG, which is, of course, the desired *profile* for this weather report. It should be obvious that much more experimentation is needed to explore these issues.

To explore the significance of the discrepancy between words in text and dictionary entries, we compared our 8 million word sample of the *NYTNS* text with the *Webster's New Collegiate Dictionary* (*W7*).[4] Of the 119,630 different word forms present in the *NYTNS* sample and in the *W7*, 27,837 (23%) occurred in both; 42,695 (36%) occurred only in the *W7*; and 48,828 (41%) occurred only in the *NYTNS*. The fact that almost two-thirds of the words in the dictionary (61%) did not appear in the text is not surprising; dictionaries contain many words that are not in common use. That almost two-thirds of the words in the text were not in the dictionary (64%) is more problematic. A preliminary analysis of a sample of the *NYTNS* forms that were not in the *W7* reveals the following breakdown (expressing the values in fractional form is intended to show their approximate character): one-fourth were inflected forms; one-fourth were proper nouns; one-sixth were hyphenated forms; one-twelfth were misspellings; and one-fourth were not yet resolved, but some are likely to be new words occurring since the dictionary was published.

The inflected forms can be accommodated by performing a morphological analysis on the text entries. Hyphenated forms can also be handled, although some of the instances found in the *NYTNS* are more difficult to deal with; they also broach the issue of noun-noun compounds and phrases, a critical problem that will be discussed at more length below. Misspellings are less easy to detect and correct, but recent developments in spelling correction algorithms suggest that some progress is being made in this area (Durham et al., 1983). The missing proper nouns constitute a more serious problem. As noted in the analysis of the weather text, most dictionaries do not contain the names of people, places, institutions, trade-names, and similar items. Yet these entries are key features of newspaper text and essential for almost any class of documents. Geographical and biographical dictionaries can provide an initial base from which to develop such entries, but it would, of course, be necessary to assign subject codes to them and perhaps to establish new subject codes for them.[5]

Specialized technical dictionaries are one source for the additional vocabulary required. It is also possible to acquire entries from the texts themselves, although obviously at this stage of our understanding it would necessarily be a machine-aided operation. We have done some preliminary work toward this objective. Using the simple criterion of selecting all the words

---

[4] The *W7* was chosen for this study because it has a larger vocabulary; similar results would be expected for the *LDOCE*.
[5] It should be noted that both people and places can have sense distinctions that may be important to separate for given contexts. For example, a particular person may be noted as both actor and political figure; a state may be considered in relation to its location, its wine, and its ethos.

in the *NYTNS* sample that occur at least five times with initial capitals and never occur only in lower case, we were able to create a large file of entries that, while far from exhaustive, certainly contains many candidates for inclusion as proper nouns. Taking advantage of patterns in the text, we made some progress toward identifying cities in the United States as capitalized words preceding state names and followed by a comma. Similarly, the introduction of a name in a story is often followed by some explanatory information set off by commas. Consider some recent examples from the Associated Press:

- Edwin M. Joyce, president of CBS News, . . .
- Jesse Helms, R-N.C., . . .
- Winfield, Ill., about 20 miles west of Chicago, . . .
- Maryland Toleration Act, passed in 1649, . . .
- Prime Minister Margaret Thatcher, a staunch supporter of self-starting capitalists, . . .

In these remarks so far, we have been ignoring one of the major problems in using dictionary entries for content assessment: that is the relative scarcity of multiword entries in a dictionary. The problems of performing semantic analyses of noun-noun compounds are, of course, well known (Rhyne, 1976; McDonald, 1982). Equally difficult is the identification of aggregates of terms that should be treated as units in a 'phrasal lexicon' (Becker, 1975; Smith et al., 1982). As noted in discussing the weather text, *Atlantic Seaboard*, *Upper Michigan*, and *New England* should all have been treated as single entries. Working with the *NYTNS* text, we have made a beginning in attacking this problem by identifying groups of frequently recurring words, specifically those bounded by function words and sentence boundaries. The most frequent entries in the resulting lists are candidates for inclusion as multiword 'dictionary' entries.

With regard to augmentation of the current *LDOCE* subject codes, it is worth remarking that even those that currently exist may need refinement. Certainly, if the *FORCE4* procedure is to be extended to more technical text or even to more homogeneous text where greater discrimination is desired than that provided by the current coding, parameters will need to be developed that motivate the creation and assignment of additional categories. One potential source for them is the kind of taxonomic analysis entailed in the creation of the derivative dictionary data described in the *resource* section above (Amsler, 1980, 1981). These taxonomies establish relations among terms that can be exploited in making further dimensional analyses. For example, recognizing that *vehicle* includes *automobile, bicycle, carriage, locomotive, sled, tractor, truck*, and *wagon*, and noting that the definitions refer to parameters reflecting 'motive force,' 'objects transported,' 'surface medium,' and the like, one can begin to organize terms along these lines. The work by Evens et al. (1980) on semantic relations provides another direction for expansion. On a more technical level, it should be possible to take classification systems and thesauruses collected for a particular field of study and use them to help structure the vocabulary in that field.

14.6. THOTH, a system for concept elaboration

THOTH, the second system we are developing, makes it possible to model the conceptual connections among texts at semantic, logical, and rhetorical levels. One application we are exploring provides a user with a means of elucidating text during the course of reading it. In this form, *THOTH* makes it possible to identify concepts in stories from the *New York Times News Service,* the *Associated Press,* and other text *sources,* and then displays to the user elaborations of those concepts based on entries in the *World Almanac,* the *Academic American Encyclopedia,* and related *resources.* The system makes significant use of the kind of workstation environment provided by LISP machines, in our case, the *Symbolics 3670.*[6]

Setting up *THOTH* for concept elaboration entailed the following steps: (1) a set of windows was created on the display to provide space for scrolling the *text* and for displaying the *concepts* and the *elaboration;* (2) a set of stories from one of the news services was identified; (3) concepts considered relevant for consideration were selected; and (4) appropriate information from the *World Almanac* and other relevant *resources* was extracted and encoded. Using the system for this purpose is relatively simple. A person reads text on the screen; concepts that the system recognizes in the story are both highlighted in the text and listed in the *concepts* window; by moving the mouse to position the cursor on a concept, the user can determine what options are available and select from them. This operation is illustrated in Figures 3 and 4, which show how the information is displayed on the *Symbolics 3670* screen. The 'Einstein' menu in the *elaboration* window of Figure 3 is the result of selecting that concept from the text. Figure 4 presents the information associated with *Discoveries.*

Thus configured, *THOTH* provides a context within which we can begin to examine how concepts associated with particular terms are related to other data. The first research issue that we are addressing concerns how to extract and encode material contained in a *resource* so that it constitutes an

---

[6] George Collier is responsible for the design and implementation of *THOTH;* Robert Amsler has been processing the *World Almanac* to derive the material for concept elaboration. *Thoth* was the Egyptian god of wisdom and learning; the choice of that term for the system was further influenced by our use of ancient Assyrian names for our *Symbolics* computers: Eridu, Nippur, Kish, and Uruk (Samuel Epstein is responsible for that venue); unfortunately, we did not find an Assyrian name that so nicely conveyed the intent of the system and at the same time provided an allusion to the more common use (except in AI circles) of the word 'lisp.'

appropriate elaboration for a concept. We have been working primarily with the *World Almanac* for this purpose. A major problem is determining how the attributes and values are expressed in the format patterns contained in the text. For example, in the section on 'Nations of the World' each country begins with a centered boldface header containing the name in a larger font size. The major attributes, like *People, Geography, Government,* and *Economy,* begin paragraphs and are printed in boldface followed by a colon. Subordinate attributes within the paragraph are also in boldface followed by colons: for example, *People* contains *Population, Age distrib., Pop. density, Urban, Language, Ethnic groups,* and *Religions.* The values for these latter attributes — in Roman font — are variously expressed as numbers, percentages, text, or some combination, often with dates in parentheses to indicate the time that data item was collected. To complicate matters further, the colons themselves may be in bold face or roman, without regard for the hierarchical level. Consequently, to distinguish major from subordinate attributes, it is necessary to know whether one begins a paragraph or not. A brief history of the country usually concludes that section, most often without a specific heading bearing that name; however, for more complex entries, like the United Kingdom and the USSR (with their several constituencies), that attribute may appear in boldface, too, but usually followed by a period.

THOTH System for Concept Elaboration		
TEXT	*ELABORATION*	*CONCEPTS*
NEW YORK - A number of leading physicists are beginning to suspect that everything in the universe is made of strings.		EINSTEIN YANG SUNY-SB
The so-called 'superstring theories,' proponents say, offer the best hope of developing a unified theory accounting for all the particles of nature and the forces that control them, including gravity. By relating gravity, as defined by ALBERT EINSTEIN, to the electromagnetic and nuclear forces controlling atoms, molecules and subatomic particles, super-string theories could realize the unfulfilled dream of EINSTEIN and his successors.	**EINSTEIN** Personal Data *DISCOVERIES* Awards References	
As a cautionary note, however, Dr. C.N. YANG of the STATE UNIVERSITY OF NEW YORK AT STONY BROOK insists that there is as yet 'not a single experimental hint' that the string theorists are on the right track.		

Figure 3. Illustration of *THOTH* with a concept menu.

As the preceding characterization is meant to imply, the different attributes and their values are not neatly compartmentalized. In addition, not every country contains every attribute; nor are all the values consistently rendered. As a result, this first extraction is requiring a substantial amount of 'hand' editing for coherent results. One consequence, though, is that we should be in a position to advise the editors of the *World Almanac* on how to create a database from which entries in the printed version could be more systematically generated. In any case, the attribute/value structures do lend themselves well to realization in THOTH, and we are making substantial progress in identifying the ones in the *World Almanac* and organizing them for appropriate use.

THOTH System for Concept Elaboration		
TEXT	*ELABORATION*	*CONCEPTS*
NEW YORK - A number of leading physicists are beginning to suspect that everything in the universe is made of strings. The so-called 'superstring theories,' proponents say, offer the best hope of developing a unified theory accounting for all the particles of nature and the forces that control them, including gravity. By relating gravity, as defined by ALBERT EINSTEIN, to the electromagnetic and nuclear forces controlling atoms, molecules and subatomic particles, superstring theories could realize the unfulfilled dream of EINSTEIN and his successors. As a cautionary note, however, Dr. C.N. YANG of the STATE UNIVERSITY OF NEW YORK AT STONY BROOK insists that there is as yet 'not a single experimental hint' that the string theorists are on the right track.	Explained Brownian motion and the photoelectric effect, contributed to the theory of atomic spectra, and formulated the theories of special and general relativity.	EINSTEIN YANG SUNY-SB

Figure 4. Illustrating the result of menu selection on *THOTH*.

14.7. Discussion

Content assessment and *concept elaboration* are only two of the possible benefits flowing from our explorations of the interactions between document *sources* and reference *resources*. Our goal is to provide a more general set of tools that can be used by knowledge specialists for working with large text files. However, as the discussions of *FORCE4* and *THOTH* suggest, one of the steps is creating an appropriate set of workstation environments for our own research in order to cope with the vast amount of data that is entailed.

Machine translation is an area in which the results of this work certainly can be applied. If we establish effective procedures for content assessment, it will contribute to the problems of sense disambiguation that complicate translation. Identifying the subject matter of a document would make it possible to determine the senses for the terms it contains in the source language and, consequently, to restrict the senses that need to be considered for the corresponding terms in the target language. The work we have done so far on concept elaboration is only a beginning in the task of understanding the structural relations among lexical elements. However, it should lead toward a more effective characterization of meaning in the context of a lexical knowledge base. One of the critical challenges we face is identifying the terms and phrase collocations that constitute the set of lexical elements for a language. Translation efforts are significantly hampered by the lack of such a body of information. Our immediate focus is on English, but the tools we are developing can certainly be applied to many, if not most or all languages. In turn, it is possible that issues of meaning equivalence may be raised more directly in the context of translation than of information retrieval or information management. In any case, a fruitful interaction between our research and work in machine translation can be expected.

It is clear that progress will depend critically on developments in artificial intelligence, computational linguistics, and information science. Areas of particular interest are knowledge representation and knowledge acquisition; the lexicon, parsing, and text generation; and document analysis, abstracting, and indexing. However, effective realization of these expansions of the scientific base also depends on developments in technology. We need new software for handling both the sequential and structural features of texts, which can be viewed both as strings and as trees or tangled hierarchies. Storage and access for billions of words of text and for dictionaries that contain hundreds of thousands of entries require advances in database management techniques. The range and variety of the knowledge *resource* suggest a distributed systems design embodying server concepts. The massive movements of data entailed demand access through wideband networks, as does the accommodation of images and other 'nontextual' features that must eventually be included in a documentary data base.

Projecting the results of our efforts is clearly premature, but it is appropriate to note that, if we are successful, the 'systems for experts' that we are working toward will create an entirely new environment for knowledge workers, increasing their access to vast document collections and simplifying the procedures for working with the information contained in those files.

Acknowledgements

I wish to express my appreciation in particular to Robert Amsler for his many contributions to the work reported here. George Collier deserves special mention for his work on THOTH. I am also indebted to my colleagues in 21233, especially Robert Allen, David Copp, Stephen Hanson, and Patricia Gildea, and to Michael Lesk from Bellcore and George Miller from Princeton for their support and consultation.

It is appropriate to thank the people and organizations who have provided the *sources* and *resources* that we are using in our research. Special recognition is due the suppliers of the materials that have figured most prominently in our current activities: the Longman Group for the *Longman Dictionary of Contemporary English*, G. & C. Merriam Company for the *Webster's Seventh New Collegiate Dictionary*, the Newspaper Enterprise Association for *The World Almanac*, the New York Times Syndication Sales Corporation for the *New York Times News Service*, and the Associated Press for the *Associated Press News Service*.

The research on FORCE4 was supported in part by grants IST-8208578, IST-8209346, and IST-8300940 from the National Science Foundation, grant LM 03611 from the National Library of Medicine, a contract funding SRI International Project 5383, and Internal Research and Development funds from SRI International.

15 Role of structural transformation in a machine translation system

MAKOTO NAGAO

15.1. Necessity of structural transformation

When two languages belong to the same or a neighboring language family, what we want to say in a particular situation is often expressed in these two languages by using very similar words and sentential structures. This is hardly to be expected between two languages from different language families, like English and Japanese. Translation, therefore, requires a complete understanding of the sentential meaning, contextual situation, and social customs associated with each of the two languages. The human professional translator possesses and uses this.

The computer, on the other hand, cannot easily grasp the sentential meaning in a given context. It is much more successful with more local links, and the syntactic analysis of a sentence is done in this way. Syntactically speaking, MT is essentially the process of repetitive transformations of local sentential subtrees from one language to another, according to the 'compositionality principle.' In the case of MT of two languages belonging to the same language family, even such a local subtree transformation may be unnecessary, let alone a big structural change at the sentential level. The EUROTRA project aims at simplifying the structural transformation at the transfer stage within pairs of European languages.

When simplification of the transfer stage reaches its limit, the system becomes the pivot (or interlingua) method. The idea of the pivot method was proposed and studied by several groups over fifteen years ago, and all the efforts were unsuccessful even for translating between two European languages. The process of language analysis is, to some extent, a process of losing, or rather 'undergetting' information. We can analyze a sentence to a certain depth of abstraction rather easily. But beyond that point, the discovery and recording procedures become very complicated and difficult, so that in practice much valuable information remains inaccessible.

At the present level of linguistic theory and MT technology, a great deal of information is lost on the way to a pivot representation. Thus, word order formation, which often provides clues that help distinguish between the old and new information within a sentence, is typically lost in the pivot representation. The focus concept of a sentence will be lost as well, and so

262

on and so forth. Generally speaking, the speakers' attitudes and the information related to a discourse will be lost because at present we do not have a good linguistic theory to extract them.

Another difficulty is that various sophisticated structural transformations are required to lead to the same pivot representation from different sentential expressions of the same meaning in different languages. A similar problem will arise for the generation of a sentence from the pivot representation.

A third difficulty of the pivot method is that all the ellipses must be recovered in pivot representation. The transfer approach which we have taken, includes a structural transformation at the sentential level which helps to circumvent the ellipsis problem.

The pivot approach in MT essentially presupposes a perfect language understanding. If this can be realized, the translation will be perfect. Unfortunately, we are not able to achieve such an ideal situation at present. At the present state of research, therefore, we might be better off adopting the transfer approach. The transfer stage should be rich enough to lead to good translation results. Our transfer approach is improved by the addition of proper structural transformation and word selection rules. The machine translation system is really never complete, so it is important to design an open system which will grow infinitely through the continuous addition and improvement of grammatical rules and dictionary information.

15.2. General principles of our machine translation system

The MT system which we are constructing now has the following characteristics (Nagao, Tsujii, & Nakamura 1985):

a. The system has three priority levels in the application of grammatical rules. The first priority is word-specific rules which are stored in the entry of a word in the dictionary. The second priority is the general grammatical rules which check not only syntactic structures but also semantic relations. The last priority is the default grammatical rules which check only syntactic relations. Natural language has large numbers of exceptional expressions which cannot be covered by standard grammatical rules. These expressions are always word-specific and must be treated by the dictionary. The system first tries to apply the word-specific rules, and then the ordinary grammatical rules. Therefore our system can be described as a lexicon driven MT system.

b. Grammatical rules are represented by annotated trees. Tree-to-tree transformation is performed in all the stages of analysis, transfer, and synthesis. Each node of a tree can have any number of property-value pairs which are used mainly to check on the word semantics represented by about fifty semantic primitives.

c.   The translation process is enriched and reinforced by the introduction of such artificial intelligence techniques as feedback analysis and synthesis, recursive usage of grammatical rules, and the principle of most probable rule applied first.

d.   Varieties of structural transformations are applied at different stages of the translation process to fill in the structural gaps between Japanese and English. The introduction of extra stages such as pre-transfer and post-transfer structural transformations (see Figure 1) will be useful to facilitate the interface with other machine translation systems. For example, we can hand over the results of Japanese analysis to the generation stage of the EUROTRA system, in which case the pre-transfer structural transformation alone can be adjusted for the connection without changing the other parts.

e.   Word selection in a target language can be made on the basis of information not only on the syntactic structures but also on the word semantics.

f.   The translation system is robust enough in the sense that the system produces an output even if the sentence has unknown words, imperfect structural analysis parts, and many ellipses.

g.   The grammatical rules are designed to handle telegraphic expressions, long noun compounds, and complex sentential and phrasal conjunctions.

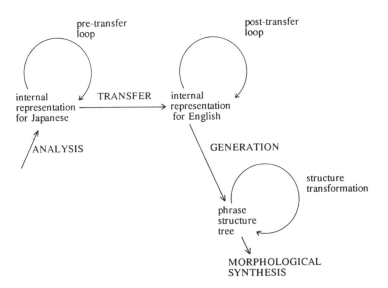

Figure 1. Processing flow for the transfer and generation stages.

15.3. Structural transformation at the transfer stage

15.3.1. Structural transformation at pre-transfer loop

The intermediate representation we adopted as the result of analysis in our MT system is the annotated dependency structure (Nakamura et al. 1984). Each node has a certain number of features, such as part of speech, surface case, deep case, number, tense, semantic codes, and so on. This tree representation is powerful and flexible for sophisticated grammatical and semantic checking, especially when the completeness of semantic analysis is not assured and trial-and-error improvements are required at the transfer and generation stages.

We have three conceptual levels for grammar rules in the transfer and generation phases as well as in the analysis phase (Nagao, Nishida, and Tsujii 1984).

Topmost Level: A heuristic grammar which attempts to obtain elegant translation for the input. Each rule is heuristic in the sense that it is word-specific and it is applicable only to some restricted expressions which are found by a strong pattern matching function of GRADE, the grammar writing system of our MT system (Nakamura, Tsujii, & Nagao 1984).

Kernel Level: Main grammar rules which choose and generate a target language structure according to semantic relations among constituents which are determined at the analysis stage.

Lowest Level: Default grammar rules which guarantee the output of the translation process. The quality of the translation is not assured. Rules of this level apply to those inputs for which no higher-level grammar rules are applicable.

The application of these rules is organized along the principle that 'a better rule is applied first.'

We use deep case dependency structure as a semantic representation. Theoretically, we can assign a unique case dependency structure to each input sentence. In practice, however, the analysis phase may discover several alternative structures because of syntactic and semantic ambiguities. Therefore, we use as an intermediate representation a structure which makes it possible to annotate multiple possibilities as well as multiple level representation. (An example is shown in Figure 2.) Properties at a node are represented as a vector, so that this complex dependency structure is flexible in the sense that different interpretation rules can be applied to the structure.

彼の仕事
his work

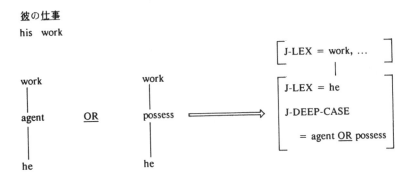

Figure 2. An example of complex dependency structure.

Some heuristic rules are activated just after the standard analysis of a Japanese sentence is finished, to obtain a more neutral (or target language oriented) analyzed structure. We call this stage the pre-transfer loop (Figure 1). Semantic and pragmatic interpretations are done in the pre-transfer loop. The more heuristic rules are applied at this stage, the better the result. (Examples are shown in Figures 3 and 4.)

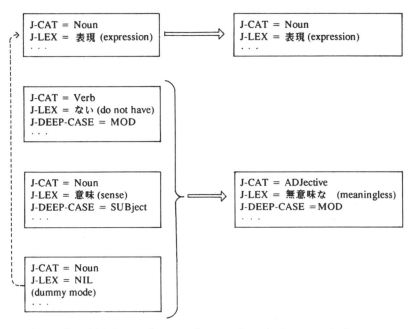

'expression which does not have sense' ⟶ 'meaningless expression'

Figure 3. An example of a heuristic rule used in the pre-transfer loop.

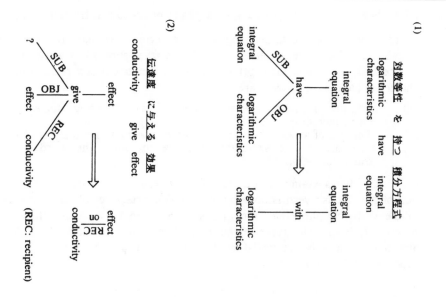

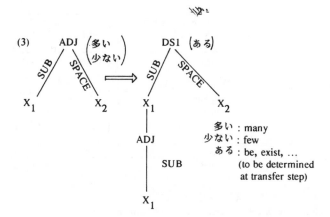

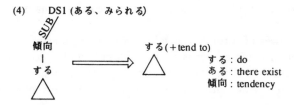

Figure 4. Examples of pre-transfer rules.

15.4. Word selection and structural transformation at transfer stage

Word selection in the target language is a serious problem for machine translation. There are varieties of choices of translation for a word in the source language. The main principles of the facilitation and restriction of choice adopted in our system are:

(1)   The use of a field code, such as electrical engineering, nuclear science, medicine, etc.
(2)   The use of a semantic code attached to a word at the analysis phase
(3)   The use of the sentential structure to which the word to be translated belongs.

Table 1 shows examples of a part of the verb transfer dictionary. Selection of the English verb is done by the semantic categories of nouns related to the verb. In the table, the number i attached to verbs like form-1, produce-2, is the i-th usage of the verb. When the semantic information attached to nouns is not available, the column indicated by φ is applied to produce a default translation.

生ずる	Xが生ずる	X	non-living substance structure	form-1	form X(obj)
			social phenomena	take place	X take place
			action, deed, movement reaction	occur-1	X occur
			standard, property state, condition relation	arise-1	X arise
			φ	produce-2	produce X
	XがYを生ずる	Y	non-living substance structure	form-1	X form Y
			phenomena, action	cause-1	X cause Y
			φ	produce-2	X produce Y
上げる	XがYを上げる	Y	property	improve-1	X improve Y
			measure	increase-2	X increase Y
			φ	raise-1	X raise Y

Semantic marker for X/Y

Table 1. Word selection in target language by using semantic markers.

In most cases, we can use a fixed format for describing word selection rules for lexical items. We developed a number of dictionary formats specially designed for ease of dictionary input by computer-native expert linguists.

The expressive power of format-oriented description is, however, insufficient for a number of common verbs such as 'SURU' (make, do, perform, ...), and 'NARU' (become, consist of, provide, ...), etc. In such cases, we can represent transfer rules directly by tree structures. An example is

shown in Figure 5. Every usage of a verb is listed with its corresponding
English sentential structures and semantic conditions.

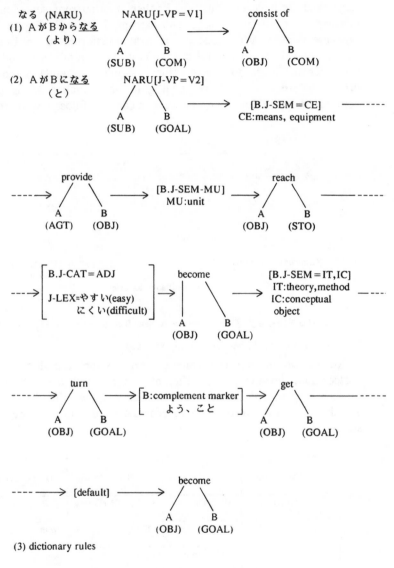

(3) dictionary rules

Figure 5. An example of dictionary transfer rules of popular verbs.

This transfer stage mechanism bridges the gap between Japanese and English expressions. Many odd structures still, however, remain after this stage, and we have to adjust the English internal representation. We call this part the post-transfer loop. An example is given in Figure 6, where a Japanese factitive verb, SASERU, is first transferred to an English word 'make,' and then a structural change is made to eliminate it and to provide a simpler and more direct expression. Another example is shown in Figure 7, where a term corresponding to 'the number of' is inserted in between 'increase' and 'car,' because 'a car' itself does not 'increase.'

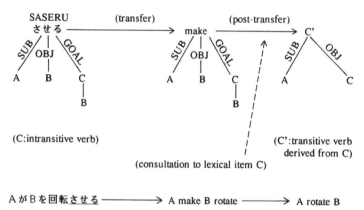

Figure 6. An example of post-transfer rule application.

Postpositions in Japanese generally express the case slots for verbs. A postposition, however, has different usages, and the determination of English prepositions for each postposition is quite difficult. The outcome also depends on the verb which governs the noun phrase having that postposition.

J-SURFACE-CASE	J-DEEP-CASE	E-DEEP-CASE	Default Preposition
に = (ni)	RECipient	REC, BENeficiary	to(REC--to,BEN--for)
	ORIgin	ORI	from
	PARticipant	PAR	with
	TIMe	Time-AT	in
	ROLe	ROL	as
	GOAl	GOA	to
	...	...	...

Table 2. Default rule for assigning a case label of English to a Japanese postposition 'NI.'

Table 2 illustrates a part of a default table for determining deep and surface case labels when no higher-level rule applies. Such tables are defined for all case combinations. In this way, we guarantee at least a literal translation to be given to an input. A better choice of a preposition depends on the usage of a verb, so that every usage of a preposition for a particular English verb is written into the lexical entry of the verb, and is used in the selection of preposition prior to the application of Table 2.

15.5. Structural transformation at generation stage

Global sentential structures of Japanese and English are quite different, and correspondingly the deep structure—as we set it up—of a Japanese sentence is not the same as that of English. The fundamental difference between Japanese internal representation and that of English is absorbed at the (pre-, post-) transfer stages. But at the stage of English generation, some structural transformations are still required in such expressions as embedded sentential structures and complex sentential structures.

We classify the embedded sentential structures into four kinds:

(1) A case slot of an embedded sentence is vacant, and the noun modified by the embedded sentence comes to fill in the slot.

(2) The form like 'N_1 GA V NA N_2' = '(N_2 NO N_1 GA V) NA N_2.' In this case the noun N_1 must have semantic properties such as parts, attributes, and action.

(3) The third and fourth classes are particular embedded expressions in Japanese, which have connective expressions like 'BAAI' (in the case of), 'HOHO' (in the way that), ' ... YOYUU' (in that), and so on.

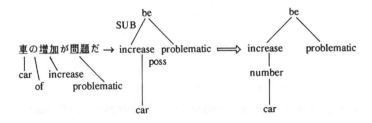

Increase of car is problematic.

The increase of the number
of cars is a problem.

Figure 7. An example of structural change at the post-transfer loop.

An example of the structural transformation is shown in Figure 8. The relative clause 'why ...' is generated after the structural transformation.

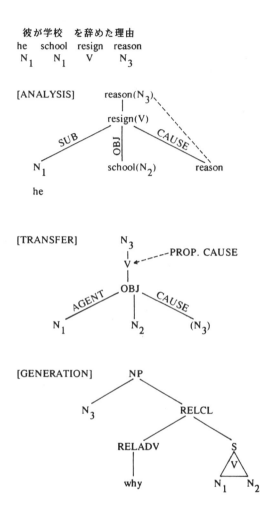

Figure 8. Structural transformation of an embedded sentence of type 3.

The way two sentences are connected in compound and complex sentences is illustrated in Figure 9.

The process of sentence generation in English is as follows. After the transfer is done from a Japanese deep dependency structure to an English one, conversion is done from the English deep dependency structure to a phrase structure tree with all the surface words attached to the tree. The processes explained above are involved at this generation stage. The conversion is performed step by step from the root node of the dependency tree to the leaf as a top-down process. Therefore, when a governing verb demands a noun phrase expression or a to-infinitive expression in its dependent phrase, which may be a verbal phrase or a noun phrase, a proper structural change of the phrase must be performed. The noun to verb transformation, and noun to adjective transformation are often required due to the difference of expressions in Japanese and English. When we cannot find a verb or a noun corresponding to a noun or a verb respectively in the dictionary, we can think of the process that makes the reference to a synonym word and see if it has a verb or a noun derived from the word. If there exists such a word, then we can use it for the constructing of a sentence. The generation goes down in this way from the root node until all the leaf nodes are converted to a phrase structure tree.

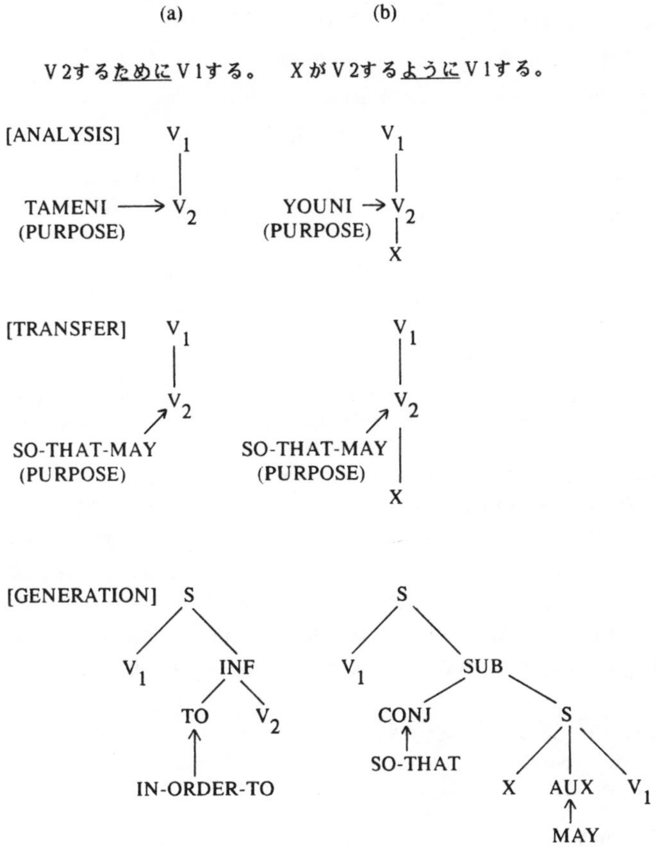

(a) (b)

V 2 する*ために*V 1 する。 X が V 2 する*ように*V 1 する。

Figure 9. Structural transformation of embedded sentence.

After this process of phrase structure generation, some sentential transformations are performed:

(1) When an agent is absent, the passivization transformation is applied.

(2)   When the agent and object are both missing, the predicative verb is
        nominalized and placed as the subject, and such verb phrases as 'is
        made,' and 'is performed' are supplemented. An example is
        shown in Figure 10.
(3)   When a subject phrase is a big tree, the anticipatory subject 'it' is
        introduced to avoid the top-heavy structure.
(4)   Pronominalization of the same subject nouns and the change of
        pronouns including deletion are performed.
(5)   Duplication of a head noun in the conjunctive noun phrase is elim-
        inated, such as, 'uniform component and non-uniform component
        → uniform and non-uniform components.'

There are many such structural transformations.

[Japanese Input]

実験　と　比較し、　良い　一致を　見た。
experiment　compare　good　coincidence　see

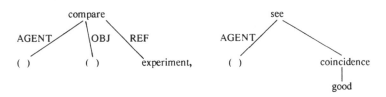

[English Translation]

The comparison is made with experiments, and good coincidence is obtained.
Nominalization of 'compare' is performed. 'See' is changed to 'obtain' by the consultation of the lexical entry of 'coincidence.'

Figure 10. An example of a sentence without subject and object.

Another serious structural transformation which is required results from
the essential difference between a DO-language (English) and a BE-language
(Japanese). In English the case slots such as tools, cause/reason, and some
others can often occupy the subject position, while in Japanese they never
can. This transformation is incorporated in the generation grammar as
shown in Figure 11, and produces more natural English expressions.

地震　で　建物　が　壊れた。
earthquake　building　collapse

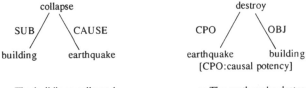

= The buildings collapsed   = The earthquake destroyed
  due to the earthquake.   the buildings.

Figure 11. An example of structural transformation in the generation phase.

15.6. Conclusion

MT does not, in practice, necessarily require understanding of the sentential meaning as it is assumed by the AI community. To achieve deep under-standing we must have sophisticated mechanisms of inference with a large amount of general knowledge of the real world. Even so, we cannot guarantee correct inferencing by the computer. For example, phrases like the following frequently occur:

SHOGAIKOKU TONO BOEKIMATSATSU NI JYORYOKU SURU
foreign   countries   with   conflict   in   trade help do

which is a kind of abbreviated expression. We have to recover a much more precise Japanese expression to get a proper English translation. If the mental attitude of the speaker of the sentence is in favor of the improvement of foreign relations, the insertion of KAISHO (resolving) should be done as

(We) help resolve the conflict in trade with foreign countries.

But if the speaker's attitude is quite contrary, the insertion of JYOCHO (accelerate) will be done as

(We) help accelerate the conflict in trade with foreign countries.

It is difficult to establish the speaker's attitude in a 'natural language understanding system.'

The sophisticated interpretations can often be left to the human being who reads the translated text. If the computer makes excessive inference in the wrong direction, that will be worse than doing nothing. In this sense, the MT should not make too many extra linguistic inferences. We have to make an effort to find much more solid and reliable linguistic and non-linguistic information from the text itself before going for general 'knowledge,' which is too vague and hard to use for MT purposes.

15.7. Appendix
Outline of mu MT project

In 1982, the Japanese Government initiated a MT project which aimed at the quick dissemination of scientific and technical information between Japanese and English. The project ended in March 1986.

The project was advanced as a result of the close cooperation between the following four organizations. (1) We at Kyoto University have the respon-sibility of developing the software system for the core part of the MT system (a system for grammar writing as well as its execution), grammar systems for analysis, transfer and generation; detailed specifications of the informa-tion to be written in the word dictionaries (analysis, transfer and generation dictionaries of all parts of speeches); and manuals for construction of these dictionaries. (2) Electrotechnical Laboratories (ETL) has the responsibility for input and output of texts for machine translation, for morphological analysis and synthesis, and for the construction of a dictionary of verbs and adjectives according to the working manuals prepared at Kyoto. (3) The Japan Information Center for Science and Technology (JICST) is in charge of the noun dictionary and accumulation of terminological words in science and technology. The Research Information Processing System under the Agency of Engineering Technology is in charge of completing the total MT system by assembling the componential results of the other three participating organizations, and by adding man-machine interfaces for editing, updating grammatical rules, and dictionary information.

The Japanese texts to be translated are abstracts of scientific and technical documents which are produced at JICST as the monthly journal *Current Bibliography on Science and Technology.* Only the fields of electronics and electrical engineering, including computer science, are treated at present in our project. The English texts to be translated into Japanese are the abstracts in INSPEC in the same fields. Sentential structures in abstracts are quite complicated compared to ordinary sentential structures, with long nominal compounds, noun phrase conjunctions, mathematical and physical formulae, embedded long sentences, and so on. The analysis and translation of these sentential structures present far more difficulties than do ordinary sentences, but we did not introduce a pre-editing stage as we wanted to know how far it was possible to handle such difficult structures.

At the moment there are about sixty subgrammars for analysis and about 900 rewriting rules in total. Sentence regeneration is also composed of a subgrammar network. The number of rewriting rules for transfer and generation processes is around 800, and it will be increased in the coming few months.

The dictionary contains about 16,000 items at present, and will be increased to 100,000 items at the end of the project. Among these 16,000 items, there are about 2,000 verbs and adjectives and about 400 adverbs—the rest are mainly special terms. The information to be written in the dictionary entry varies from one part of speech to another, but generally includes such features as head word, number of characters of the word ending, Chinese character part, reading in Kana, variant, derivational words, related words, morphological part of speech, conjugation, prefixal information, area code, syntactic part of speech, subcategorization of part of speech, case patterns, aspect, modal, volition, semantic primitives, thesaurus code, co-occurrence information (adverb, predicative modifier), idiomatic expressions, degrees of nominality, etc. One important kind of information is the case patterns for verbs and nouns. We have distinguished more than thirty cases. Each case slot in a case pattern of a verb usage has semantic information about the nouns which can occupy that slot. The nouns have the corresponding semantic codes in their entry. We have distinguished more than fifty such semantic codes. The noun dictionary also has information about specific verbs which co-occur with nouns. The specific information of these categories is checked prior to the standard rule applications, and the default rules are applied last. The evaluation of the translation result is given elsewhere (Nagao, Tsujii, & Nakamura 1985), and was fairly satisfactory.

16 An experiment in lexicon-driven machine translation

RICHARD E. CULLINGFORD and BOYAN A. ONYSH-
KEVYCH

16.1. Introduction: lexicon-driven machine translation

Systems designed for the Machine Translation (MT) of texts between
languages have traditionally relied upon explicit grammars of both the
source and target languages, in order to analyze the source text and produce
well-formed target-language sentences (cf., e.g., Tucker and Nirenburg,
1984). Grammar-based systems have been reasonably successful at
production-quality MT. The nature of grammatically driven processing
leads to certain problems, however.

First of all, an explicit grammar tends to make the system's computation
excessively *top-down*. Thus, it is usually not particularly robust under devi-
ant (e.g., ungrammatical, telegraphic or ellipsed) input. Moreover,
explicit-grammar approaches tend to be overly concerned with the *form* of
the language, rather than its content. Issues of preservation of meaning
between source and target texts tend to get downgraded.

In this chapter, we shall argue for an alternative style of MT in which the
focus of processing for both input and output texts is at the level of the *lexicon*, i.e., the words and phrases of a language, rather than its grammar.
No extensive experimentation in MT has been performed within this paradigm (but see, for example, Wilensky and Morgan, 1981; Lytinen, 1984).
We shall suggest, however, that the approach very naturally allows for
meaning-preserving MT, and provides solutions for difficult problems such
as word-sense disambiguation, anaphora resolution, the need for circumlo-
cution when lexical equivalents of source words are not available, etc.

Language analysis, in particular, has a very strong *bottom-up* nature in
the approach to be described. Such analyzers tend to produce fragmented
meaning structures for ungrammatical or ellipsed inputs. Thus, there is
the possibility of *diagnosis* of the fragments, in order to determine a reasonable reading of the input (e.g., Booth et al., 1985; Booth and Cullingford,
1985).

We illustrate the approach with a toy MT system which translates
Ukrainian texts into English. The overall methodology for designing
language interfaces in this paradigm is detailed in Cullingford (1986).

278

16.2. Goals and methodology

We wish to make it clear at the outset that the systems we have in mind *retell* or *paraphrase* the source text in the target language. We have not been concerned with modeling the professional translator's expertise in preserving the form, tone, and rhetorical flourishes of the speaker, but rather with his basic bilingual, meaning-preserving translation capabilities. We have argued elsewhere (Carbonell et al., 1981) that even this capability requires access to numerous, often culture-specific, knowledge structures representing what the translator knows about mundane reality, the plans and goals of motivated people, special-purpose rules for specialized domains of knowledge, and the like. As was noted long ago (Bar-Hillel, 1960), these structures, and their reflections in natural language, will need to be modeled effectively before fully-automatic high-quality MT will be possible.

Our methodology is derived from the *Conceptual Information Processing* approach to natural language processing (e.g., Winograd, 1972; Wilks, 1973, 1975; Schank, 1975; Cullingford, 1986). Here we will present only a brief summary of it.

We are assuming that an *interlingua can be designed which models the conceptual level of* understanding that people possess independently of any natural language. We assume, also, that this interlingua can be encoded in terms of a relatively small number of *primitive* meaning units, and that the meanings of words in a language can be represented by structures drawn from this interlingua. For effective use by an intelligent system, the primitive units for a knowledge domain must be selected on the basis of *coverage, economy,* and *orthogonality of inferencing.* The meaning structures assigned to sentences are to be composed from the meanings of the individual words in such a way as to provide *unique* and *unambiguous* representations of paraphrase-equivalent sentences (in whatever language). The representation scheme is to be *continuous* : small changes in sentence meaning should not cause large changes in the underlying representation. That is, the scheme should support the evolution of a 'semantic field' of words having related meanings (cf., e.g., Miller and Johnson-Laird, 1976).

Some simple principles for deriving representations for sentences have been described in Cullingford (1986). The representation scheme is based on notions of *bottom-up design,* the *maximal inference-free paraphrase,* the *model corpus,* and *continuous deformation* of meaning structures. We will illustrate the first two of these concepts for the following simple English sentence:

(1)   Olivia punched Muhammed in the nose.

A meaning representation for a given sentence is normally derived from what is called a *maximal inference-free paraphrase* (MIFP) of the sentence.

MIFPs express the meaning of the sentence in a verbose or circumlocuted form, by expanding it through the process of inferencing. None of the clauses should, however, involve a *substantive inference* from the meaning of the sentence. They should only represent what is derived from the lexical contents of the sentences themselves. This level of meaning we call *surface semantics*.

A substantive inference is an assertion drawn from the real-world context surrounding the utterance, or an auxiliary concept formed from the hearer's mental model or belief system. 'Surface semantic' inferences based on the meanings of lexical items in the input text are, however, legitimate parts of a MIFP. An example of a necessary, non-substantive inference will be the process of determining anaphoric antecedents. Thus, on accepting

> Ronald took an aspirin from the bottle and ate it

the system is entitled to conclude, on surface-semantic grounds, that 'it' refers to 'aspirin' rather than 'bottle.' This claim is based on the default meaning of 'eat,' which demands an ingestible object; and aspirins are ingestible while bottles are not. On the other hand, concluding that Ronald did this because he had a headache is a substantive inference. Facts about causality and counterfactual reasoning need to be involved in order to draw such a conclusion. (The two classes of inferences resemble, though do not exactly correspond to, the 'necessary' and 'invited' inferences of Geis and Zwicky, 1971; cf. also Chaffin, 1979.)

Having formed the MIFP, the system selects the clause that expresses the 'main' or most important component of the event being described as the *kernel* of the representation. The other clauses function as *nuances* serving to distinguish this particular event from others of the same type. Obviously, the point of maximizing the number of nuances formed from a given sentence is to maximize the total number of assertions that can be distinguished.

Thus, in (1) the clauses:

(1a)   The female person named Olivia propelled a hand into physical contact with a nose.
(1b)   This event was forceful.
(1c)   The event transpired in the past.
(1d)   The hand was in the form of a fist.
(1e)   The hand was part of Olivia.
(1f)   The nose was part of Muhammed.
(1g)   Olivia was facing Muhammed, and was within arm's reach when this event took place.

all seem to be reasonable components of an exact paraphrase of (1). However, assertions such as:

(2a)   Olivia was mad at Muhammed.
(2b)   Muhammed had done something to make Olivia punch him.
(2c)   Both parties were wearing clothes when the event took place.

are clearly *substantive inferences* from the described behavior.

Of the parts of the exact paraphrase of (1), the first, (1a), can be taken to be *basic*, since it is the one from which the most interesting consequences flow. Looking at (1a), one can begin to speculate on the likely reasons for such an episode, how Muhammed might react, how relations between the two may change, etc.

The kernel assertion for (1), 'Olivia propelled a hand into contact with a nose,' can be represented by the (conceptual dependency) primitive *propel*, which means that a causal actor applies a force to an object, with the possibility of a physical state change to it and/or another object. The verb 'punch,' in this sense of the word, designates a human hand as the object to which the force is applied, and clearly indicates that the hand came into *contact* with another object. (There are other possibilities: the verbs 'swing at' and 'throw at' are neutral about contact.)

Working on the representation of (1) from the bottom up, we need representations for the entities 'Olivia,' 'Muhammed,' 'fist' and 'nose.' [1] In a role-filler formalism (e.g., Charniak, 1981), these would respectively be:

        HUM0   (person gender (fem) persname (Olivia))
        HUM1   (person gender (masc) persname (Muhammed))
        BP0   (bpart bptype (grasper))
        BP1   (bpart bptype (proboscis))

based on the primitive types *person* and *b(ody)part*. The symbols HUM0, etc., name the meaning structures, allowing them to be reused. The (not entirely serious) choice of 'grasper' and 'proboscis' for the *bptype* fields of BP0 and BP1 was made to emphasize that the representation should not contain words, only indicators of function or form which are true of many entities simultaneously. Monkeys, elephants, people and robots, for example, all have functional grasping parts.

One can now propose a simple representation for (1a) as follows:

        EVNT0 (propel actor HUM0 object BP0 to (physcont part BP1))

In the role-frame of a *propel*, the (actor) path is expected to be animate and the (obj) path is filled with a physical object. The filler of the (to) path in a propel-concept is required to be a primitive type expressing a relationship of *physical configuration* (e.g., location, orientation or contact) between two objects.

---

[1] The primitive types used in this chapter are drawn from the ERKS (Eclectic Representations for Knowledge Structures) system, an amalgam of Conceptual Dependency, Preference Semantics and Commonsense Algorithms used for illustrative purposes in Cullingford (1986).

Of the nuance assertions, the first two, (1b) and (1c), clearly function to modify or comment on the event expressed in the kernel assertion. Assertion (1b) allows us to distinguish (1) from a sentence like 'Olivia tapped Muhammed on the nose.' To avoid complexities with representing relative time and physical quantities, one can simply incorporate (1b) and (1c) into the representation as follows:

> EVNT0 (propel actor HUM0 obj BP0 to (physcont part BP1)
> time (PAST) quantity (FORCEFUL))

The assertion 'hand was in form of a fist,' (1d), is an example of an *attributional* concept, one in which an intrinsic state or attribute of an object (such as color, weight, extent, etc.) is described. The attribute *partform* (i.e., 'form of a part') is used to express the state of an object that is 'malleable' in some sense, that is, it can take on several forms. A version of an attributional concept expressing (1d) is:

> STATE0 (s-attr actor BP0 attr (partform val (fist)))

The primitive type *s-attr* is used in STATE0 to encode a *stative attributional* assertion about the object in the (actor) path, along the attribute dimension in the (attr) path. The (attr val) filler specifies the particular 'value' of the attribute for this object. In STATE0, the filler 'fist' is *not* an English word, but represents a selection from the contrast-set for the *partform* role, when expressed in conjunction with a particular object which is an intrinsic part of another, in this case a hand. (Other choices might include 'flat,' 'cupped,' 'pointing,' etc.) Note that this nuance allows us to distinguish verbs such as 'slap' and 'poke' from 'punch.'

Assertions (1e) and (1f) are typical examples of *physical configurational* concepts. Configurational concepts express a relationship between two or more entities. In this case, the relation is 'physically part of': that is, one object is attached to another in such an integrated way that a severe negative change in the physical state of health (for animate entities) or usability (for artifacts) is likely to occur if the two are separated. A representation for (1e) is as follows:

> STATE1 (p-config con1 BP0 con2 HUM0 confrel (partof))

Here, the *confrel* slot contains the particular *config*urational *re*lationship encoded by the form 'partof.' This nuance allows us to distinguish (1) from such statements as 'Olivia hit Muhammed with a rock.'

Example (1f) features the same type of confrel as the above. Example (1g) is a *composition* of physical confrels.

Once the MIFP has been encoded in this way, one can form 'the' representation of sentence (1) in the following ERKS structure:

> (3)   Olivia punched Muhammed in the nose
>   (ms kernel EVNT0 nuance1 STATE0 nuance2 STATE1 nuance3 ...)

This is a form based on the special *m(eaning)* *s(tructure)* primitive, which is used in setting up dictionary entries for words in the analyzer and generator to be described. Note that the organization allows a search process looking, for example, for a word sense to express a concept to make increasingly fine-grain discriminations. First, one would look at the kernel form, then at (nuance1), (nuance2), etc. One can easily order the nuances by counting up the number of word senses that the associated form distinguishes from one another.

To make meaning structures such as the one in (3) easier to understand, we normally use a 'collapsed' form based on the kernel structure. The collapsed form for the meaning structure in (3) is:

(4)   (propel actor HUM0
              obj (bpart bptype (hand) partform (fist) partof HUM0)
              to (physcont part (bpart bptype (nose) partof HUM1)))

Here the stative *partof* and *partform* conceptualizations have been 'summarized' by making the associated *confrel* and *con2* fillers into a role-filler pair associated with the respective *con1* filler. For example, the filler:

    (bpart bptype (nose) partof HUM1)

is a shorthand for 'the nose which is part of Muhammed,' i.e., (1f). The role *partof* doesn't belong to the role-frame of *bpart*.

16.3. A lexicon-directed analyzer

The basic source of expectations for a surface-semantic analyzer comes from the words themselves. Certain words can predict that other meaning units are likely to occur in the sentence environment because of the semantic requirements of the meaning structure(s) they build. In sentence (1), for example, there are high-level predictions for an animate agent and a physical object, both found in characteristic places in the sentence. What is needed is a way of associating these predictions with the words in the system's dictionary, from which they can be summoned when the word is actually seen in the input stream.

A flexible and attractive means for accomplishing this is to organize the analyzer as a *production system* (e.g., Newell and Simon, 1972). The surface-semantic analyzer under discussion uses a system of productions, based on an extension of the notion of *requests* (Riesbeck, 1975), which represent positional/semantic predictions about concepts in the input stream. The productions, or test-action pairs, are maintained in a *production memory*. The test parts of the productions monitor a *working memory* which holds the current state of the concepts for words analyzed up to that point. The control of the system resides with an *interpreter*. This repeatedly selects the subset of productions which apply to the phrase or clause being currently considered, and whose test conditions match the current state of working memory. Then, by a process of *conflict resolution*, the interpreter selects one production out of the conflict set, and 'fires' it. The action portions of the productions generally add new concepts to the working memory, expand the concepts into greater specificity, or merge available concepts to form larger ones expressing the meaning of phrases or clauses. This cycle continues until no productions are applicable to the working memory, at which point the working memory contains the interlingual representation of the input concept.

16.3.1. *Analyzing English*

We will outline the production system cycle for (1). (See Cullingford, 1986 for an extensive discussion of this style of analysis.) Since the morphology of English is relatively simple, we shall defer discussion of morphology until the next section, which gives an example from Ukrainian.

The cycle begins with the dictionary look-up of words in the input stream. The look-up first attempts to find the word in the dictionary as it appears; failing that, a morphological parser attempts to strip the word to its root form, preceded by the morphemes. The dictionary look-up also attempts to match the input stream against phrases, i.e., for idiomatic or 'canned' expressions.

The analyzer enters *noun-group* mode at the start of (1), because the sentence begins with a personal name. The first item in the input stream, 'Olivia,' is found in its root form in the dictionary. (Actually, this process is managed with a 'named-person' macro form.) The production associated with 'Olivia' creates a concept which is a representation of the word — such as HUM0 above. The concept is placed on the *concept list*, or C-LIST, the working memory of available concepts. The analyzer then exits noun-group mode, because of the presence of the past/perfective fragment produced by the root-stripper. If the next word in the input stream had been 'Johnson,' it would have been adjoined to 'Olivia' (by productions) to form a firstname-lastname concept. The end of the noun group would be signaled, in this case, as soon as a non-name was encountered on the input stream. (Arrangements are easily made for titles, appositives, and the like.)

The next item in the input stream is 'punch.' The word's concept (assuming, for the moment, that it isn't ambiguous) is added to the concept list, in the form:

```
(5)      (propel actor (person)
              obj (bpart bptype (hand))
              to (physcont val (bpart partof (person)))))
```

The word also adds a number of productions to the production memory: a production which looks for a conceptual actor, and a set of productions which look for the object being punched, and the part of the object where contact was made. These productions reside in the production memory until their test parts fire. In the C-LIST, the concept for 'Olivia' satisfies the semantic test 'couldbe-person' and the positional/syntactic test for 'actor.' Thus, the production associated with the conceptual *actor* slot in (5) above is allowed to fire by the control and conflict-resolution mechanism. The action part of the production removes the 'Olivia' concept from the concept list, and inserts it in the *actor* slot in the concept for 'punch.' Since the test parts of the other productions do not test true (i.e., they are only predictions at this point), the control passes back to processing the input stream.

The next item on the input stream, 'Muhammed,' is analogous to 'Olivia' — (see HUM1 above). A conceptual representation is added to the concept list, and *end-of-noun-group* is signaled by 'in' from the input stream. The control selects a production from the production memory which fills in the 'person being punched' slot:

(6)   to (physcont val (bpart partof (person persname (Muhammed))))

The remaining production associated with 'punch' looks for a prepositional construction denoting proximity, governing a physical object constituent. The productions set up by 'in' can create any of a number of structures, including the locational or physical proximity relation required by 'punch.' Other constructions which 'in' needs to handle include temporal location ('in April'), a 'member of' relation ('in the army'), etc. When any of these productions fire, the rest of the production pool for 'in' is removed from the production memory.

Having exhausted all productions testing true, control gets the next word: 'the.' This word adds a 'definite concept' form to the c-list, and adds a production which awaits a following concept satisfying 'couldbe-entity.' The next word is 'nose.' It is placed on the C-LIST as a 'bodypart' type, then end-of-noun-group is signaled by the end-of-sentence marker, the period. The conflict resolution scheme selects the most-recently-added production which tests true to fire first. In this case, the production of 'definite concept' set up by 'the' fires, and marks the 'nose' concept as 'definite reference.'

(bpart ref (def) bptype (nose) partof (nil))

Next, the 'in' production for proximity to or location of a physical object tests true, and fires, picking up the 'definite nose' concept. This production creates a prepositional constituent. Now the remaining production associated with 'punch' tests true, and the action picks up the prepositional phrase, and merges 'the nose' with the *bpart* concept from (6). The preposition is not needed, and is discarded by the production. The end of the input stream has been reached, and all of the productions in the production memory are quiescent (test false); thus, the resulting concept (see (4)) is returned as the conceptual representation of the input.

This extremely flexible scheme allows for the analysis of all of the forms related to (1):

> Muhammed was punched in the nose by Olivia.
> Muhammed was punched.
> In the nose Olivia punched Muhammed.
> Muhammed Olivia punched in the nose.
> Punch!

The basic process needs to be modified only slightly in order to handle embedded uses of 'punch':

> Olivia wants to punch Muhammed
> Olivia likes Ronald's punching Muhammed
> Muhammed's having been punched was pleasing to Olivia

Finally, the all-or-nothing test-and-firing nature of requests is easily modified to allow for a notion of 'best fit,' as in Preference Semantics (Wilks, 1973; Dawson, 1985). Thus, we get the effect of grammatical analysis without the need for an explicit grammar. Since we are concerned with the meanings of words anyway, we include the grammatical processing (which is often idiosyncratic to the words) in the lexicon itself.

16.3.2. Analyzing Ukrainian

How does all of this apply to the analysis of other languages? Since all known languages build upon lexical units, it makes sense to consider lexicon-driven analysis of languages other than English. It turns out that the approach works very naturally for Ukrainian, a Slavic language.

In Ukrainian, extensive morphological information is conveyed by the heavy inflection of verbs, nouns, adjectives, and pronouns. Instead of relying on word order, as in more analytic languages like English, synthetic languages like Ukrainian rely on the morphological information for specifying much of syntactic structure.

It turned out that the bulk of the work involved in setting up the existing analysis scheme to handle Ukrainian involved the design of a morphological parser for the inflected parts of speech (mostly, nouns, adjectives, pronouns, and verbs).

The Ukrainian analysis scheme uses *exactly* the same production-system control mechanism as the English version, the only addition being the morphological processing component attached to the dictionary look-up procedure. After the grammatical morphemes are stripped off an inflected form, they are inserted into the input stream (as in the English case) preceding the root form which replaces the inflected input form. The grammatical morphemes have dictionary definitions very similar to the definitions of lexical items. The information derived from them is used for checking agreement, syntactic roles, etc.[2]

The following sentence will serve as an illustration of the process of root-stripping input forms, picking up morphological fragments, and the agreement/case checks. The English gloss is 'Ivan hit his horse with a stick':

(7)   konA vdaryv Ivan patykom.

Although 'horse' is the first item in the sentence, this is still an active voice sentence, because of the case marking.

The first word is read in from the input stream, and sent to the root-stripper, the morphological parser. The string returned is:

sgen$ sacc$ kin˘

The returned string is pushed back onto the input stream, and each component is marked as having already been stripped. The production associated with the Genitive-singular particle, sgen$, tests for a following nominal concept. The Accusative-singular particle does the same. Neither of the test parts fires until the nominal concept built by the root form is available. The production associated with the noun, as in the English example above, only places the noun concept on the C-LIST. At this point the case fragment productions fire, and the action portion, of the productions create a subfield of the case slot for the appropriate case, and fill the slots with the appropriate number — singular in this situation.

The verb *vdaryv* is the next item on the input stream. The morphological parser returns

perf$ past$ sing$ masc$

(No person information is available in this tense.) The productions for these fragments are similar to the noun fragments — they await a following verb-concept on the C-LIST. Once the verb root form, *vdar*, is reached, and the productions associated with it are placed in the active request pools, the (language-independent) conflict-resolution scheme considers one production test at a time. The first to be considered is the production which places the conceptual representation of 'hit' on the C-LIST. Now the morphology

---

[2] As the Ukrainian language uses the Cyrillic alphabet, it is necessary to have a systematic way of transliterating from the Ukrainian Cyrillic to a form usable on the machine. Direct use of the transliteration standard, the Library of Congress system, would complicate the morphological system substantially. The reason for this is that there are a number of single-letter phonemes in Ukrainian which need to be represented by dipgraphs in the Library of Congress transliteration system. In the experimental system to be described, we decided to set up a single-character transliteration standard.

fragment tests can fire, placing each of the fragments into the appropriate subfield of the *time* slot in the representation of the verb. The *perf$* fragment fills the aspect slot, *past$*, the tense slot, *sing$*, the number slot, and *masc$*, the gender slot.

The next productions considered are the ones which attempt to find the conceptual arguments for the case frame built by the verb root. As always, the test portion of the production which fills the conceptual actor slot considers the available concepts on the C-LIST, in order of their proximity to the verb-concept. When it looks at these concepts, it first checks that the nominal concept is in the Nominative case — that is to say, the 'casenom' subfield has either 'sing' or 'plur' as a filler. If so, then it takes that number filler, and checks its agreement with the number of the verb (the filler of the 'number' subfield of the *time* slot). Once these tests have been passed, the next condition considered is gender agreement — the syntactic gender of the noun definition associated with the concept on the C-LIST must match the filler of the 'gender' subfield of the verb *time* slot. The last test is the same semantic test as the English example, viz., is the proposed conceptual actor a 'person'?

An important difference between Ukrainian and English is that there need not be any grammatical checks on word order in Ukrainian. For example, since 'Olivia hit Muhammed' differs in meaning from 'Muhammed hit Olivia,' the production which fills the actor slot must find a noun preceding the verb (in the active voice), and the object must follow the verb. In Ukrainian the word order is not as important, since the object could easily precede the verb and actor (as in our example), since it is marked as Accusative, and the actor as Nominative.

At this point in the analysis of (7), the nominal concept available on the C-LIST is the concept for 'horse,' which is in the Accusative case. Thus, the actor slot-filling production fails on the first test, the case test. The production associated with the 'object being hit' slot only needs to test that the concept on the list is Accusative. Since the 'horse' concept is marked Accusative, and the semantics check out properly, the concept is removed from the C-LIST and inserted in the appropriate slot. The remaining productions associated with the verb which are in the pool do not find any concept at this point (i.e., they are *predictions*).

The next item in the input stream is the actor *Ivan*, which gets marked Nominative in the manner described above. The concept is put on the C-LIST, where the 'actor' production of the verb is able to test it. Since 'Ivan' is in the Nominative case, and all the other checks described above test positively, the concept is moved to the 'actor' slot of the verb.

The 'stick' concept is associated with the remaining word on the input stream, and is treated like the 'horse' above, except for the case being marked (by the stripped-off fragments) as Instrumental. The resulting concept is returned:

(8)   (propel actor (person persname (Ivan) gender (masc)
                    case (cases caseacc (sing) casenom (sing)))
              obj (artifact case (cases caseinst (sing)) artifname (stick))
              to (physcont val (animal animname (horse) case (cases caseacc (sing))))
              time (times time2 (:perf) time6 (:sing) time9 (:masc) time1 (:past)))

As we saw, the bulk of the modifications required for changing this system from one language to another involved the morphology. Since the analyzer being described is a lexically driven system, there need be no explicit syntactic rules. Ukrainian word definitions alone took care of the syntactic differences. While our consideration of Ukrainian sentence structure is not yet complete, all grammatical sentence constructions considered so far can be captured in the definition of the root verb or auxiliary verb: for example, predicate nominatives, passives, etc. Other analyzer systems are syntax-based, and would need to have the whole syntax module rewritten for each new language. With a lexicon-driven system, only the surface morphological routines need to be changed, and the definitions accommodated appropriately.

In the Ukrainian analysis system, the definitions for the morphological fragments (or the agreement check) account for constructions such as negative genitives, implicit subjects, possessive constructions, intransitivization, etc.

16.3.3. Pronominal reference

In the remainder of this chapter, we will be concerned with the translation of the following short passage:

(9a)   UriY Cumakuvav vozom. 'Uri (repeatedly) brought salt back from the salt flats in his cart, and sold it.'
(9b)   Vin skotyvsA z mosta. '(One day) the cart rolled off a bridge.'
(9c)   Rika zmyla viz. 'The river washed the cart away.'

This passage illustrates the analysis of pronouns and ambiguous words, as well as various generation problems to be described later.

Pronominal reference is a complex problem which puts the premises of our lexical approach to analysis to the test. We will illustrate the processing using the above passage. However, *exactly* the same process applies to the analysis of English pronouns.

A pronoun may be thought of as an ambiguous concept consisting of all the co-referent concepts previously seen which 'match up' with it in semantic terms. As an example, consider (9b). The possible referents of *vin* are either *UriY* or *viz* (the cart) — *viz* is masculine in Ukrainian. In this case, *vin* refers to *viz* because of the semantic requirements of *skotyvsA* (rolled off). However, if (9b) had the sense 'He retired after 30 years,' the pronoun *vin* would have *UriY* as the antecedent. That is, no purely syntactic process can guarantee that the correct anaphoric reference will be located.

The production associated with the definition of *vin* calls a function which finds the possible referents for the pronoun by applying a certain predicate function. In this case the predicate selects the concepts which satisfy the requirement 'masculine gender.' The reference function applies the predicate to concepts on a context list, called the NLP-context. In the simplest case, this list holds the concept names for all the 'substantive' concepts that the analyzer has formed. The 'substantive' concepts include the noun-group constituents, as well as clause and sentence-level concepts. How far back to look in the NLP-context during referent search is, of course, an open question.

When the list of possible referents is returned to the production for *vin*, the pronoun's concept is replaced with the concept of the antecedent if there is only one possible referent, or with a *vel* (Latin for 'non-exclusive or') of the possible referents if there are more than one. For the example of (9b), the resulting concept would be:

```
(vel v1 (person persname (UriY) gender (masc) sex (male))
     v2 (veh vtype (cart)))
```

The case information of the antecedents is irrelevant to the pronoun, and is dropped. The pronoun has case information of its own, in this case Nominative-singular, which is used to mark all of the disjuncts of the *vel*. When the pronoun is disambiguated by the verb, the *vel* is replaced with the concept of the one referent selected by the verb productions from the *vel*.

After the morphology fragments are picked up by the verb, it is in a position to pick up the actor concept. Both of the disjuncts of the *vel* satisfy agreement and case requirements — the disambiguation of the *vel* is up to the semantic restriction. The verb *skotytyvsA* (roll off) requires a wheeled vehicle or cylindrical object as actor in the reflexive. So the production picks up the *vel*, compresses it into the 'veh' concept only, and fills the actor slot of the verb with the result.

If the size of the disjunction is greater than one after the agreement checks and the verb selectional restrictions, the whole disjunction is used to fill the slot.

16.3.4. Prepositional constructions

This section will present an approach to the meaning of prepositions, and how other words can take advantage of these meanings. As an example, we shall continue with the analysis of (9b).

The prepositional phrase *z mosta* has the meaning 'from (off) the bridge.' However, the preposition *z* can take any of a number of meanings: 'from' and '(together) with,' among others. These two uses, however, take different case, for the following noun phrase. Thus, the productions can select between these two based on the case information associated with the noun phrase concept.

However, case alone is not able to distinguish among other meanings of the preposition. For instance, both the '(together) with' and 'at the time of' usages of the preposition *z* require arguments in the instrumental case. The semantic restrictions for the temporal reading require a time phrase such as 'New Year's' or 'Tuesday.' So in order to assert the 'at the time of' meaning of the preposition, the preposition's productions must pick up a 'time' concept as the argument.

In English, the first means of selecting the appropriate reading of the preposition does not apply. So the selection is achieved by the semantics alone. As an example, consider the readings of the preposition 'in' in English:

(10)   Olivia was in the house
(11)   Olivia was in the army
(12)   Olivia graduated in 1984.

It seems clear that prepositional phrases such as 'in the house,' 'in the army' and 'in 1984' have different readings. For example, 'in the house' contributes a meaning fragment that says something like: 'if someone (an event, for example) is looking for a particular kind of locational relationship, this phrase can build one.'

The word *mosta* (bridge) is marked as genitive case, so the meaning of the preposition is chosen to be 'from.' The conceptual definition of the verb 'roll off' seeks a 'from topof' argument; the prepositional construction indicates that it is a 'locational relation,' so the prepositional phrase's argument is the 'from' location. The argument of the prepositional phrase is inserted into the 'from topof' slot in the final concept:

```
(13)     (ptrans obj
             (veh case (cases casenom (:snom)) vtype (cart))
             from (topof part struc case (cases casegen (:sgen) caseacc (:sacc))
                   structype (bridge)))
             time (times time2 (:perf) time6 (:sing) time9 (:masc)
                   time7 (:intrans) time1 (:past)))
```

The primitive element *ptrans* is the conceptual dependency action rendering events in which an animate actor (here unmentioned) causes a physical transfer of the location of a movable object.

16.3.5. Word meaning disambiguation

The selection of the intended meanings of words in context is a key problem for any language analyzer. The best-known case of the meaning selection problem is *word-sense disambiguation*, the process of choosing the correct underlying representation for a word having several senses. A word-sense disambiguation scheme, therefore, will require a model of context consisting of both the meanings of surrounding words and higher level expectations.

In order for this selection process to proceed, an analyzer needs a means of making the alternative meaning structures of a word explicitly accessible. This is the motivation for the *vel* construction introduced in Section 16.3.3. Nominal words normally rely on requests of other words to compress the ambiguous structure down to a single meaning; the discussion of the pronouns illustrated the mechanism. Ambiguous nouns, such as 'ball' in English, are disambiguated in a similar manner.

Verbs, on the other hand, establish a set of productions to disambiguate themselves. (9c), for example, has the verb *zmyty*. The reading of the verb in this sentence is 'to wash away.' Other readings include the sense 'to wash off (something)':

(14a)   Rika zmyla berih. ('The river washed away its shore')
(14b)   UriY zmyv sil' z ruk ('Uri washed his hands of salt')
(14c)   Rika zmyla YuriYu sil' z ruk ('The river washed salt off Uri's hands')

When the verb concept is initially placed on the C-LIST, it sets up a *vel*, or disjunction of the different readings. The productions attempt to find surrounding constituents which allow a decision to be made. The first production looks for an animate entity in the actor spot. If it finds it, it *asserts* that the (14b) sense of *zmyty* may be the preferred reading. We say 'may be' because the consideration process for the productions gives *all* the requests a chance to perform a disambiguation. When all of the productions have had a chance to fire, the system packages up the result: a single concept if the word has been completely disambiguated, or another *vel*, if only a partial disambiguation is possible.

Note that what this requires is a means for saving and restoring the state of the analysis process just before a production is considered and just after it fires. Since the state of the working memory is completely described by the C-LIST, it suffices to remember the state of the C-LIST as a production pool starts, then remember the revisions to the C-LIST (i.e., the compressed *vel* subconcepts) caused by a production's firing. Before each production is considered, the analyzer restores the C-LIST to the saved state. The simplicity of the production system model makes the management of processes such as staged disambiguation very easy.

Returning to the *zmyty* example, one can see that the presence of a 'natural force' (the river) available on the C-LIST to fill the actor slot will allow either the (14a) or the (14c) readings. However, the (14c) reading requires an indirect object. (The gloss should be 'The river washed the salt off the hands for Uri.') The (14a) production finds the natural force subject, and the 'physical object' direct object it requires to be asserted. Thus, this reading of the verb is *asserted*, the *vel* is compressed to the meaning selected, and the analysis is able to be completed, resulting in the disambiguated concept:

(15) (ptrans
         actor (movingwater case (cases casenom (:snom)) mwtype (river))
         obj (veh case (cases caseacc (:sacc) casenom (:snom)) vtype (cart))
         time (times time6 (:sing) time9 (:fem) time1 (:past)))

16.3.6. Surface-semantic machine translation

In the rest of this chapter, we are going to discuss a simplistic model of MT in which the source analysis and target generation are done on the basis of surface semantics, i.e., literal word meanings, alone. Of course, we know perfectly well that access to detailed world knowledge is necessary in order to perform much of the inferencing that is needed to produce full understanding, and therefore high-quality MT. There is an important class of simpler inferences, however, which can be supported directly at the surface-semantic level. These include word meaning selection, many kinds of anaphoric reference resolution, and a process which we will call 'distributed target realization.'

A block diagram of a surface-semantic MT system is shown in Figure 1. As can be seen, a conceptual analyzer of the kind discussed in the last section creates a meaning structure for each of the input sentences, and passes it on to a module called a *surface-semantic annotator*. This slightly modifies the concept in order to allow for certain differences in the modes of expression available in the source and target languages, then hands it to a conceptual generator for expression in the target language.

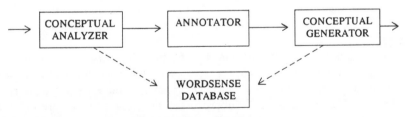

Figure 1. Surface-semantic machine translation system.

16.3.7. Surface-semantic generation

Conceptual generation is the process which performs the inverse mapping from a meaning structure into a NL string. This process has several distinctive features. First of all, the system begins with a concept to be expressed, and possibly an indication of a sub-concept to be 'said' first. The system is not told anything about the words or syntactic constructions to be used.

This is in contrast with most models of generation (e.g., Simmons and Slocum, 1972; cf. also Chapter 12) in which the program's input is a syntactic phrase structure of some sort, including some or all of the words to be used.

Secondly, the generation process need not in any way be the processing inverse of the analysis process. The system to be described starts with a complete, well-formed 'thought' to be 'said.' Thus, the generation process is *top-down*, in a way that analysis can never be. As we have seen, analysis has a very strong bottom-up flavor of recognition, as the listener attempts to match the fragments of meaning from the words that are being heard against his conceptual expectations. A corollary of these two ideas is that literally *everything* (words, syntax, focus, connectives, etc.) that a generator of this kind chooses in order to express the concept will be motivated by *conceptual features* of the given concept, its conversational context, or the goal-following activities of the overall system. In many cases, therefore, the generator algorithm to be described will not be able to 'say' the most fluent-sounding thing, because a conceptual reason for choosing the fluent construction is not apparent. This is the price one pays for a radically conceptual-level approach.

The generator to be described has data and control structures which are reminiscent of the analysis module discussed earlier. Just as in the analyzer, there is no explicit grammar; syntactic information is stored with the individual words of the lexicon. The generator's primary data structure is a short-term memory, called the C-LIST, consisting of concepts intermingled with words and morphological fragments. The basic control structure of the generator accesses the C-LIST in an iterative process of *looking up* word(s) to express the meaning of a concept that is currently the focus of attention (at the 'front' or 'top' of the C-LIST); and second, of *inserting* left-over subconcepts in appropriate places around the chosen word(s) on the C-LIST.

The subconcepts may be accompanied by function words, such as prepositions or conjunctions, which serve to mark the conceptual case in the parent concept from which the subconcept came. From time to time during the basic iteration, 'daemon' subprocesses may intervene to prescribe a more economical means of expressing a concept than a dictionary entry may allow.

Initially, the C-LIST contains a single conceptual form to be expressed. The overall generation cycle can be described by the following rules:

Rule 1   If the front of the C-LIST is empty, then there is nothing to generate; return.

Rule 2   If there is a word or fragment on the front of the C-LIST, then after some preprocessing 'say' the word by saving it on a special list to be returned as the generator's result.

Rule 3   If there is a concept at the front of the C-LIST, check if any of the 'daemon' processes want to do anything to it. The daemons, called *sketchifiers,* are described in Cullingford (1986). If a daemon fires, go to Rule 1 and start over.

Rule 4   When none of the daemons fires, remove the concept from the front of the C-LIST, and try to find a word in the dictionary to express the concept. The dictionary entries are based on *word-senses,* associations between words and conceptual forms. The conceptual form of an entry which matches a C-LIST item is a *template* for the item: a pattern containing roles and fillers which must be present in the item if the dictionary entry is to be used.

Rule 5   If the current concept is completely 'spanned' by an entry, then replace it on the C-LIST by the word(s) of the entry.[3] Otherwise, insert the fillers not matched into the C-LIST using the positional constraints stored with the word-sense found.

It is worth noting that Rule 3, above, usually embodies a decision *not* to say something that the dictionary would normally want to say. Thus, the model of generation we're presenting can be thought of as an 'exhaustive' algorithm, Rules 1,2,4 and 5 being *restrained* by rules of type 3.

16.3.8. *Dictionary entries for English*

To outline how a lexicon-driven generator for English works, consider the dictionary entries needed to generate the passive form of example sentence (1) 'Olivia punched Muhammed in the nose,' from a concept, e.g., c55, produced by the analyzer. In ERKS format, this would be:

```
c55: (propel
        actor c27
        obj (bpart bptype (hand) partof c27)
        to (physcont val (bpart bytype (nose)
                           partof (person persname (Muhammed) gender (masc))))
        time (times time1 (:past))
        mode (modes mode1 (:t)))

c27: (person gender (fem) persname (Olivia))

focus path: (to val partof)
```

The first thing to note is that the generator, if it is working in the same language as the analyzer, can use many of the same word-senses as the analyzer did in order to arrive at c55 in the first place. Thus, for example, both the analyzer and generator definitions for 'punch' can be based on word-sense WSPUNCH1, as shown in Figure 2. The word-sense entry

---

[3] The pattern-matching operation implied here is implemented by a general-purpose knowledge base manager described in Cullingford and Joseph (1983).

provides a *structure-frame* (associated with 'ws-structure') from which to obtain instances of the concept associated with the sense such as: a set of *constraints* on fillers proposed for the slots of the concept; a specification (not needed here) of any irregular forms of the root word; and a *focus* field to give the generator a sentential focus, a subconcept to 'say first' if the concept supplied doesn't contain one. (The sentential focus in our example concept is on 'Muhammed.') The generator matches C-LIST items against the 'ws-structure' form, and if the entry is selected, uses the 'surface-form.'

```
;This is EXACTLY the same wordsense as the analyzer uses
(def-wordsense wsPUNCH1
   surface-form (punch)
   ws-structure
   (propel-f actor (nil)
            obj (bpart-f bptype (hand) partof (nil))
            to (physcont val (bpart-f bptype (nil) partof (nil))))
   equivs
   (((actor)(obj partof)))
   focus            ;default focus of the generator
   (actor))

(gdictdef wsPunch1
   (actor)          ;[1]    syntax for the active voice
   (((actor)        ;[2]    (actor) placement for (actor) focus (active voice)
     (pr)           ;the realization of the (actor) is to precede punch on the C-LIST
     (pr (to val partof))  ;to precede the realization of the (to val partof) filler
     (pr (to val)))        ;and to precede the filler of (to val)
    ((to val partof)       ;(to val partof) placement in active voice
     (fo)                  ;following punch
     (fo (actor))          ;following the (actor)
     (pr (to val)))        ;and preceding the (to val) filler
    ((to val)              ;(to val) placement
     (fo)                  ;following punch
     (fo (actor))          ;following (actor)
     (fo (to val partof))  ;following (to val partof)
     (fo in)))             ;and following the function word in

                    ;[3]    syntax for the passive voice
    (to val partof)
    (((to val partof)
      (pr) (pr (actor))(pr (to val partof)))
     ((to val)
      (fo) (fo (to val partof))(pr (actor))(fo in))
     ((actor)
      (fo)(fo (to val partof))(fo (to val))(fo by))))
```
Figure 2. Generator definition for *punch*.

The function *gdictdef* in Figure 2 adds the additional information necessary to make the word-sense wsPUNCH1 available to the generator. This function supplies the specification of syntax for sequencing words. These specifications are sensitive to the 'focus' property provided with the input concept, and all use the positioning predicates *pr* (precedes) and *fo* (follows). The dictionary definition for main verbs, such as 'punch,' contains pairs consisting of a path to a focussed-on subconcept, and a set of positional specifications for leftover fillers. At [1] in Figure 2, for example, are the specifications to be used when the conceptual *(actor)* path is to be the sentential focus. The specification is an association list (alist) consisting of a path into the C-LIST item, and a set of predicates for placing the filler found at the end of the path on the C-LIST. At [2], for instance, is the alist for the conceptual *(actor)* filler:

```
((actor) (pr)(pr (to val partof)) (pr (to val)))
```

What this says to do is: if the *(actor)* path in the C-LIST item matching the template is nonempty, then position it on the C-LIST *preceding* the word ('punch') spanning the item, *preceding* the filler of the *(to val partof)* path, and *preceding* the filler of the *(to val)* path. Similarly, the filler of *(to val partof)* is to *follow* the word 'punch,' *follow* the filler of *(actor)*, and *precede* filler of *(to val)*. The specification for the *(to val)* filler is:

```
((to val) (fo)(fo (actor))(fo (to val partof))(fo in))
```

This indicates that the *(to val)* filler is to follow the word, the *(actor)* filler, and the *(to val partof)* filler. It is also to follow the *function word* 'in,' which is simply inserted as a lexical entry on the C-LIST. Thus, the entry specifies the standard ordering of constituents for the active voice of the verb 'punch.'

The second association of focus and specification in a dictionary entry is assumed by the generator to correspond to the passive voice. At [3] in Figure 2, we see that the passive voice goes with the sentential focus on the *(to val partof)* filler. If c55 were expressed using the passive, the dictionary would specify an ordering of constituents on the C-LIST as follows:

```
(to val partof) 'punch' 'in' (to val) 'by' (actor)
```

To handle 'Olivia' and 'Muhammed,' one has the generator's analog of the analyzer's named-person macro viz., wsNAMED-PERSON1, as shown in Figure 3. The motivation is exactly the same: to be able to generate thousands of names with a single, concise definition.

Figure 3 contains several new things. First of all, the word in the word-sense is 'nil,' the 'empty' lexeme. It will have no direct realization in the sentence; it merely serves as a pivot to position the naming information. In the call to *gdictdef*, the empty path () indicates that there is no focus, as is typical of nominal concepts. The syntactic predicates position the *persname* filler preceding the empty lexeme, with the *surname* filler following it.

```
(def-wordsense wsNAMED-PERSON1
              ;word is the empty lexeme
    surface-form (nil)
    ws-structure
    (person-f persname (nil) surname (nil)))

(gdictdef wsNAMED-PERSON1
    ()
    (((persname)
```

```
(pr)(pr (surname)))
((surname)
(fo)(fo (persname))))
sempreds
(or (filledp '(persname))(filledp '(surname))))
```

Figure 3. Generator Definition for *named-person*.

We also have shown some 'semantic predicates' (sempreds), arbitrary Lisp code (however, without side-effects!) making special checks on the given item which are hard to encode with just the structural information in the template. (Any matching process, for NLP or anything else, needs a structured way to 'escape to Lisp' to look for things that are difficult to represent.) The predicates here use *filledp* to demand that at least one of the name slots in the input be filled. (Entries without such a sempred would allow the realization of unnamed persons, such as 'a man,' 'he,' etc.)

The dictionary entry for 'nose' is contained in the following function call:

```
(gdictdef wsNOSE1)
```

Since there are no imbedded concepts to be expressed (at least in the simple cases), one just needs to declare the word-sense defined earlier.

The generator's dictionary lookup routines are responsible for selecting the word or words that span as much of the current concept as possible. Sometimes information in the concept does not map into a complete word, but is expressed by morphological changes in a root form, or by the addition of auxiliary items. Examples in English are the ''s' fragment indicating possession, and the 'to' that signals the infinitive form in the phrase 'to graduate is my heart's desire.'

When the concept sent to the dictionary contains temporal or modal information, a surface verb kernel must be built to express the *time* and *mode* slots of the concept, and the verb form must be made to agree in person and number with the focus of the sentence. Temporal and modal information is like sentential focus information in that it is not an integral part of the meaning of the concept but expresses auxiliary information. The *time* information expresses the temporal relationship of the action or state to the time of the speech act ('now'), and possibly to the time of some other event. (Our scheme for representing time is based loosely on the theory discussed in Bruce, 1972.) Modal information expresses the ability, intent, obligation, etc. of the speaker and/or hearer to participate in the expressed action or state. This processing is handled in our generator by the *verb kernel routines* (see Cullingford, 1986).

A generator of English also needs to be able to create 'advanced' syntactic constructions such as infinitives, gerunds, coordinated forms, etc. Most often, the availability of these realizations is signaled by characteristic *redundancies* in the concept to be 'said' or in its surrounding context. Creating these forms is the responsibility of the sketchifier daemons

16.3.9. Annotating surface-semantic forms for output

The conceptual representation of the source input meaning still has some traces of the source language — in Ukrainian, for example, the tense/case information. These fields must be adjusted for the generator as the intermediate step between analysis and generation in the translation process.

The case information is never used directly by the target language, since the case of each nominal position is specified by the generator word definitions, if needed. The seven cases in Ukrainian, for instance, are discarded by the intermediate process, the Annotator, since the generator knows what cases are needed in what positions in English (for determining pronoun cases). For the reverse translation process, i.e., from English to Ukrainian, the definitions of the verbs would have the case for each argument explicitly made available to the generator.

Other intermediate annotations need to be performed on the verb tense information. Much of the tense information in Ukrainian is superfluous or unnecessary for English generation. The person and number fields can be extracted from the 'subject' position information. The gender agreement slot is also not necessary for English generation; in a language like French, the gender for agreement would be extracted from the subject. When there is no explicit subject in the source language, as is often the case with first and second person conjugation, and the target language needed gender for agreement, the annotator would have to mark the 'implicit subject' with the gender of the agreement slot from the source language, if it were available.

In our Ukrainian-to-English example the annotator discards most of the tensing information, leaving only time and aspect. Since the tenses do not match exactly, the annotator adjusts the Ukrainian tenses to the most nearly equivalent English ones.

One of the strengths of an intermediate-language approach to MT is that the analyzer is not target-language specific, and that the generator does not know about the source language. Thus if we were to expand our system to handle Ukrainian to French translation, and the French generator were available, the analyzer would not be changed at all, only the minimal intermediate annotator would need to be added.

16.3.10. Distributed target realization

The lexically driven nature of the analyzer and generator suggest interesting advantages over syntactic (e.g., transfer) schemes. Among these is the possibility for handling a distributed target instance — a one-word concept in the source language can be translated into a multi-word or multi-clause realization just as easily and naturally as into a single-word realization. The fact that there is a meta-representation, which gets created by the analyzer, allows a number of more complex constructions to be analyzed.

An example of such a situation is demonstrated by a sentence from our example passage, repeated below:

UriY Cumakuvav vozom.

The English translation of this sentence would be: 'UriY (repeatedly) brought salt back from the salt flats in his cart, and sold it.' A simple version of the conceptual form corresponding to the verb 'Cumak' (which does not contain the content implied by 'repeatedly') is:

```
(sequel
    con1 (ptrans actor (hianimate)
            obj (hianimate)
            from (locrel)
            to (inside part (geofeat geoname (nil) geotype (saltflats)))
            inst ($drive actor (hianimate) veh (veh))
            time (times) mode (modes))
    con2 (atrans actor (hianimate)
            obj (ingobj phase (granular) ingtype (salt))
            to (poss part (hianimate)))
    con3 (ptrans actor (hianimate)
            obj (ingobj ingtype (salt))
            inst ($drive actor (hianimate) veh (veh))
            to (locrel)
            from (inside part (geofeat geoname (nil) geotype (saltflats))))
    con4 (dual con1 (atrans actor (hianimate)
            obj (ingobj ingtype (salt))
            from (poss val (hianimate)))
        con2 (atrans actor (hianimate)
            obj (money)
            to (poss val (hianimate)))))
```

This conceptual representation of the verb captures much of the nature of the verb; e.g., the '$drive' fillers of the 'inst' slots represent a *script* for the activity of 'driving,' that is a whole sequence of events which is captured by the one verb. Many of the slots of the representation refer to the same concept. For example, the actor of the 'driving down to the salt flats' (con1) is the same as the actor of the 'driving back from the salt flats' (con3). These equivalences can be specified in the definition explicitly, so that instead of having a copy of the same concept in the multiple slots, the same actual concept appears in as many places in the concept as necessary.

Sentence (9c) is analyzed into the following concept:

```
(16)    (sequel con1
            (ptrans actor (person persname (UriY) gender (masc)
                    case (cases caseacc (:sacc) casenom (:snom)))
                obj c54
                from (locrel)
                to (inside part (geofeat geoname (nil) geotype (saltflats)))
                inst ($drive actor c54 veh (veh case (cases caseinst (:sinst)) vtype
        (cart)))
```

```
                    time (times time2 (:imprf) time1 (:past) time6 (:sing) time9 (:masc))
                    mode (modes mode1 (:t)))
        con2
        (atrans actor c54
                    obj (ingobj phase (granular) ingtype (salt))
                    to (poss part c54))
        con3
        (ptrans actor c54 obj c54
                    inst ($drive actor c54 veh c120)
                    to c69 from c70)
        con4
        (dual con1 (atrans actor c54 obj (ingobj ingtype (salt)) from (poss val c54))
              con2 (atrans actor c54 obj (money) to (poss val c54))))
```

Here any concepts specified merely as 'c##' are subsequent references to concepts already expanded in full. For instance, the actors of all the sub-concepts are the same concept — c54.

As we see, the power of a lexically driven analysis is such that there is minimal language-specific information encoded, yet the range of analyzable sentences includes many examples of very troublesome syntactic constructions and lexical meaning.

16.4. Conclusions

We have argued that lexicon-directed MT is a viable alternative to standard explicit-grammar approaches. As our simplistic experimental system suggests, many difficult problems in meaning preserving translation are very naturally approached in this style of analysis/generation. Since the interface does create/map out of interlingual forms, it can easily be adapted to work with an expert reasoning/database system containing models of world knowledge and MT expertise, which will be needed for the fully automatic high-quality MT systems that we really would like to build.

17   Integrating syntax and semantics

STEVEN L. LYTINEN

17.1. Introduction

It has long been realized by MT researchers that semantics[1] must be used to resolve many of the lexical and structural ambiguities that occur in natural language. The correct resolution of ambiguities is often critical to the translation process, since often ambiguities which occur in one language cannot be preserved in other languages. Bar-Hillel's 'the box is in the pen' example (Bar-Hillel, 1960) illustrated that even simple English sentences could contain ambiguities that would require extensive semantic analysis to resolve. Thus, interest has risen in recent years to adding semantic analysis to MT. Efforts have ranged from adding domain-specific semantic features to syntactic analysis, such as in METEO-TAUM (Chandioux, 1976), to analyzing the syntactic parse tree for logical relations between constituents, as in ARIANE (Boitet and Nedobejkine, 1981), to a full-blown semantic analysis of the input text such as Wilks' system (Wilks, 1973).

If one accepts the premise that semantics should be added to the analysis techniques used in MT, what is the way in which it should be added? This chapter will argue for an *integrated* approach to semantic processing. By that, I mean that syntactic and semantic processing should take place at the same time, rather than in separate stages. If syntactic and semantic processing are performed separately, with the results of a syntactic parse passed to a semantic interpreter, this must result in the inability to resolve many ambiguities during the syntactic analysis stage, thus dramatically increasing the number of syntactic interpretations that must be considered during the parse.

An integrated approach to parsing has been argued for before (e.g., Riesbeck and Schank, 1976; Schank and Birnbaum, 1980). However, previous integrated parsers, such as ELI (Riesbeck and Schank, 1976) and Wilks' parser (Wilks, 1975) have been integrated in *representation*, as well as processing. That is, these parsers have not maintained separate syntactic representations of the input text apart from the text's semantic representation. This, I will argue, also leads to trouble, making it difficult to resolve

---

[1] By semantics, I mean the traditional linguistic concept of semantics, or knowledge about the meanings of words, as well as *pragmatics*, or knowledge about the world and about how language is used.

syntactic ambiguities without requiring an inordinately large number of parsing rules.

To remedy the difficulties of syntax-first parsing and of previous integrated parsers, this chapter will present an alternative approach to integrated parsing. The approach is implemented in a machine translation system called MOPTRANS, which parses short (one to three sentences) newspaper stories about terrorism and crime, in English, Spanish, French, German, and Chinese. Translations are produced for these stories in English and/or German. Enough vocabulary, linguistic knowledge, and semantic knowledge have been encoded in the parser to enable it to parse 25 to 50 stories for each input language. The MOPTRANS system produces translations for all of the stories into English, and for some of the stories into German.

The MOPTRANS parser is integrated in the sense that syntactic and semantic processing take place at the same time. However, MOPTRANS does maintain a separate syntactic representation of the input text during parsing, and it uses a largely autonomous set of syntactic rules. Unlike syntax-first parsers, however, these syntactic rules are driven by the system's semantic analyzer. Thus, syntactic attachments are only considered when the semantics of the system judges the potential attachment to be semantically meaningful.

This chapter will not include a discussion of MOPTRANS' semantic analyzer (for a detailed description, see Lytinen 1984). Instead, this chapter will focus on the way in which the semantics of the system is integrated with syntactic processing, and why this integration is desirable.

Nothing in the argument for the way in which syntax and semantics are integrated in the MOPTRANS parser is specific to MT *per se*. The argument is based on examples of ambiguities which are problematic for nonintegrated approaches to parsing and for previous integrated approaches. Thus, in any natural language system in which ambiguities that require semantic processing must be resolved, the arguments presented in this chapter are relevant.

17.2. Why syntax needs semantics

Consider the following sentences:

> The cleaners dry-cleaned the coat that Mary found at the rummage sale for $10.
> The cleaners dry-cleaned the coat that Mary found in the garbage for $10.

On the basis of syntactic information alone, these two sentences are both ambiguous. In both sentences, the prepositional phrase *for $10* could be attached to either verb, or to the last NP (*the rummage sale* or *the garbage*). However, due to the semantics of the sentences, their syntactic structures are not the same. In the first example, the preferred attachment of *for $10* is to the verb *found*, although it could be argued that the sentence is still ambiguous, even after semantic interpretation. However, in the second example, the attachment of *for $10* is definitely to the verb *dry-cleaned*.

Examples like these illustrate that semantics must be used in order to resolve some syntactic ambiguities. It is very difficult to write syntactic rules to resolve the ambiguity in these examples. Obviously the syntactic structure of these sentences gives no clue, since the structure up to the point of the ambiguities is the same. There is no way that selectional restriction rules could help either, since the same verbs, *dry-cleaned* and *found*, appear in both sentences. The ambiguity can be resolved only after inferring the different meanings of the word *found* in these two sentences. In the first sentence, since finding an article at a rummage sale usually entails purchasing the article, *for $10* can, and does, attach itself to this meaning of *found*. However, in the second sentence, since finding an article in the garbage does not involve any sort of purchase, *for $10* cannot be attached to *found*. Thus we see that the syntactic ambiguities in these two sentences cannot be resolved until a semantic analysis is performed on them which enables the inference to be made that *found* in the first sentence refers to a purchase.

If one accepts the premise that all syntactic ambiguities should be resolved during syntactic analysis, then this example argues for the integration of syntactic and semantic processing. The only way that this ambiguity could be resolved during syntactic analysis would be to perform an extensive amount of semantic analysis during the syntactic analysis stage. However, the argument could be made that syntactic analysis need not resolve all syntactic ambiguities. Unresolvable ambiguities could be passed on to the semantic analysis stage, where they would be resolved after semantic analysis provided the necessary information.

If syntactic ambiguities are not resolved immediately, though, there is a computational price to pay. This is because an unresolved syntactic ambiguity can affect the remainder of the syntactic analysis. Consider the following sentence:

> The cleaners dry-cleaned the coat that Mary found in the garbage for $10 while she was away in New York.

If semantics is used immediately to resolve the attachment of 'for $10' to the verb *dry-cleaned*, then the clause *while she was away in New York* must also be attached to *dry-cleaned*, since the clause containing *found* is already closed by the attachment of *for $10* to a constituent prior to *found*. However, if the attachment of *for $10* is not resolved immediately, then the syntactic analyzer must consider other attachments of this clause. Since *for $10* could possibly attach to *found*, this means that the clause could also be attached there. This 'artificial' ambiguity cannot be resolved syntactically, either. Thus, a syntactic parser would find this sentence to be (at least) 3-way ambiguous. The additional ambiguity could be completely avoided if semantics were used immediately to resolve the original ambiguity.

Carrying forward unresolved ambiguities in syntactic analysis can result in a combinatorial explosion in the number of syntactic ambiguities that must be considered as the parse continues. For example, consider the following sentence:

> The stock cars raced by the spectators crowded into the stands at over 200 mph on the track at Indy.

This sentence is highly ambiguous syntactically, but if semantic processing proceeds in parallel with syntactic processing, many of the ambiguities can be resolved along the way, reducing drastically the number of possible interpretations that must be considered. Let us compare the complexity of a left-to-right parse of this sentence, with and without the use of semantics to resolve ambiguities. The verbs *raced* and *crowded* could both be either past active or past participle. Syntactically, these ambiguities cannot be resolved. Thus, the part of the sentence up to *into the stands* has four possible syntactic interpretations: one in which *raced* is past active, one in which *crowded* is past active, one in which both *raced* and *crowded* begin reduced relative clauses which modify *cars,* and one in which the second relative clause modifies *spectators* instead. However, semantics can provide the information that *spectators* are not likely to race stock cars. Therefore, semantic information can determine that *raced* must be a past active verb. This determination eliminates all but one of the four interpretations.

As the parse continues, *at 200 mph* could be attached in many ways without considering semantics: to *cars, raced, spectators, crowded* or *stands.* Because of the combination of the possible PP attachments and the possible interpretations of *raced* and *crowded* as active or passive, a syntax-first parser would be faced with thirteen possible parses of the sentence up to this point.[2] However, with semantics, there are only three possible attachments: to *raced, crowded,* or *stands.* Since semantics could supply the additional information that spectators cannot be on the track in a race, two of these choices can be eliminated, leaving *raced* as the only possible attachment.

The number of possible attachments for the next two PP's continues to grow combinatorially without the use of semantics. These PP's could

---

[2] There would be twenty possible parses, due to the four possible interpretations from before, multiplied by the five possible attachments of the prepositional phrase, but seven of these parses are not possible due to the fact that some constituents are closed by previous attachments. For example, if *crowded* is interpreted to be active, *on the track* cannot be attached to anything before *crowded.*

conceivably be attached to all five of the constituents to which the previous PP could attach, as well as to *200 mph*. Given six different possible attachments, thirteen possible parses thus far, and two prepositional phrases, we have 156 (6 x 13 x 2) potential interpretations to consider. Selectional restrictions could probably eliminate some of these attachments, and some attachments are not possible in some of the thirteen interpretations, due to the closure of some constituents by previous attachments, but we can see that the number of combinations becomes quite large. However, since semantics would have been able to eliminate all but one of the thirteen interpretations thus far, the last two PP's could only conceivably be attached in two places, *raced* or *200 mph*. This is because the attachment of *on the track* to *raced* eliminated the possibilities of attachment anywhere else.

As this example demonstrates, the price for separating syntactic and semantic processing can be quite expensive computationally. Unresolved syntactic ambiguities can build on each other, resulting in the need to consider many syntactic attachments which would be eliminated if semantic processing were done in parallel. Therefore, it seems that semantic and syntactic processing should indeed be integrated, to control the combinatorial explosion that can take place in syntax-first parsing.

17.3. Why semantics needs syntax

Syntactic and semantic processing have been integrated in many previous parsers; for example, ELI (Riesbeck and Schank, 1976), and Wilks' parser (Wilks, 1975). However, in these previous parsers, the assumption has been made that a full-blown, separate syntactic analysis is not needed in order to build a semantic representation of text. Instead, many past conceptual analyzers have relied on 'local' syntactic checks for the syntactic information needed.

To illustrate, let us consider some of the syntactic rules which were used in the Conceptual Analyzer (CA) (Birnbaum and Selfridge, 1979), a descendant of ELI. CA's parsing rules were encoded in the form of *requests*, which were test-action pairs stored mainly in the parser's lexicon. A request could be in one of two states: active or inactive. A request was activated when the parser encountered a word whose dictionary entry contained it. Once active, a request stayed active until it *fired*, or was executed; or until it was explicitly deactivated by another request. A request fired if it was in the active state and the conditions of active memory satisfied the test portion of its test-action pair.

Requests were responsible for making most of the decisions that took place during parsing, including the resolution of syntactic ambiguities. For example, consider the following sentence, which was parsed by CA:

A small plane stuffed with 1500 pounds of marijuana crashed.

The word *stuffed* can function as either a past participle or a past active verb. In this context, it functions as a past participle, signaling the beginning of a reduced relative clause.

To resolve this ambiguity, CA used three requests. One looked for the presence of a form of 'to be' to the left of *stuffed*. If it was found, then *stuffed* was passive, and a representation was built of *stuffed* with the NP to the left of *stuffed* (in this case *plane*) assigned to the OBJECT being stuffed. A second request looked for the word *with* appearing after *stuffed*. If it was found, *stuffed* was again treated as passive, and again the NP to the left was the OBJECT being stuffed. This request, if it fired, also activated another request which looked for another verb further on in the sentence, marking the end of the relative clause. Finally, the third request looked for something which was of the semantic class CONTAINER to the right of the word *stuffed*. If this request fired, the CONTAINER was the OBJECT being *stuffed*, and the NP to the left of *stuffed* was the ACTOR. This request fired for sentences like *John stuffed the plane with marijuana.*

In more precise terms, the requests required for this sentence were the following:

REQUEST	TEST	ACTION
1:	A form of 'to be' appears to the left of *stuffed*.	Fill the ?PART position of the conceptualization built by *stuffed* with the conceptualization to the left of the form of 'to be,' and deactivate requests 2 and 3.
2:	The word *with* appears after *stuffed*.	Fill the ?PART position of the conceptualization built by *stuffed* with the conceptualization to the left of *stuffed*, remember all the conceptualizations in active memory to the left of *stuffed*, load REQUEST 2A, and deactivate request 3.
2A:	A verb has been found.	Reset active memory to the state remembered in the ACTION of REQUEST 2.
3:	A conceptualization which can function as a container has been found after *stuffed*.	Fill the ?PART position of the conceptualization built by 'stuffed' with the container conceptualization, fill the OBJECT slot with the conceptualization to the left of stuffed, and deactivate request 2.

These three requests used 'local' syntactic information in order to disambiguate the word *stuffed*. In other words, only words in the immediate neighborhood of *stuffed* were checked for particular syntactic properties, or for their presence or absence. For example, the preposition *with* appearing directly after *stuffed* signaled that *stuffed* was part of an unmarked relative clause.

The advantage of using only local syntactic checks in requests was that it was not necessary for the parser to keep track of a separate syntactic analysis. Syntactic ambiguities were resolved by examining short-term memory to see what *semantic* constituents had appeared in the sentence. However, it is not always the case that local checks are enough. Consider the following examples:

    The soldier called to his sergeant.
    I saw the soldier called to his sergeant.
    The slave boy traded for a sack of grain.
    I saw the slave boy traded for a sack of grain.

In these cases, the appearance of a preposition after the verbs *called* and *traded* does not guarantee that the verbs are passive. This is because both verbs can be used either transitively or intransitively. Instead, the information that must be used to determine whether the verbs are active or passive is whether or not there is another verb in the sentence which functions as the main verb.

The requests needed to handle these examples would be more complex. First, a request would be required which looked to the left to see if another verb was already on the active list. If so, then *called* would have to be unmarked passive. But the absence of a verb would not guarantee that *called* was active, since the main verb of the sentence could also come afterwards, as in the following example:

    The soldier called to his sergeant was reprimanded.

Thus, the requests required to disambiguate *called* would be the following:

REQUEST	TEST	ACTION
1:	A form of 'to be' appears to the left of *called.*	Fill the OBJECT slot of the MTRANS built by *called* with the conceptualization to the left of the form of 'to be,' and deactivate requests 2-4.
2:	A verb is in active memory to the left of *called.*	Fill the OBJECT slot of the MTRANS built by *called* with the conceptualization to the left of the verb, and deactivate requests 1, 3, and 4.
3:	An active verb has been found to the right of *called.*	Fill the OBJECT slot of the MTRANS built by *called* with the conceptualization to the left of the verb, and deactivate requests 1,2, and 4.
4:	The end of the sentence has been found, and no active verbs are to the left or the right of *called.*	Fill the ACTOR slot of the MTRANS built by *called* with the conceptualization to the left of the verb, and fill the RECIPIENT slot of the MTRANS with the conceptualization after the verb, or after the word *to.*

Even with these additional requests, however, many sentences could still not be handled:

The soldier called to the sergeant shot in the arm.
The soldier called to the sergeant shot three enemy troops.

In these examples, the verb which appears later in the sentence is also syntactically ambiguous. So the appearance of a verb after *called* does not always guarantee that it is a past participle.

To handle examples like these, a special set of requests would be needed for the case in which another syntactically ambiguous verb is in the sentence. First, an additional request under *called* would have to look for a verb which could either be past active or past participle. If such a verb was found, then other requests would have to be activated which would look for the appropriate clues around the second verb to determine whether it was active or passive, thus also determining if the first verb was active or passive. These requests would be the following:

REQUEST	TEST	ACTION
5:	A verb appears after *called* which could either be past active or past participle.	Activate special requests for that verb which determine whether that verb is past active or past participle
SPECIAL REQUESTS FOR 'SHOT': 6:	A form of 'to be' appears to the left of *shot* (indicating that *called* was an unmarked passive, as in *The soldier called to his sergeant was shot*).	Fill the OBJECT slot of the conceptualization built by *shot* with the conceptualization to the left of the form of 'to be,' fill the OBJECT position of the MTRANS built by *called* with the conceptualization to its left, and deactivate requests 7 and 8.
7:	The word *in* appears after *shot* (indicating that *called* was the main verb of the sentence, as in *The soldier called to the sergeant shot in the arm*).	Fill the OBJECT slot of the conceptualization built by *shot* with the conceptualization to its left, fill the ACTOR slot of the MTRANS built by *called* with the conceptualization to its left, and deactivate request 8.
8:	A conceptualization which is a PHYSICAL-OBJECT has been found after *shot* (indicating that *shot* is the main verb of the sentence, and *called* was an unmarked passive, as in *The soldier called to the sergeant shot three enemy troops*).	Fill the OBJECT slot of the conceptualization built by *shot* with the PHYSICAL-OBJECT, fill the ACTOR slot with the conceptualization to the left of *shot*, fill the OBJECT slot of the MTRANS built by *called* with the conceptualization to its left, and deactivate request 7.

There are still examples for which even this complex set of requests would not be enough:

The soldier called to the sergeant shot in the arm was reprimanded.

In this sentence, even though *shot* is part of a relative clause, *called* is still not the main clause verb, since *was reprimanded* follows later in the sentence. Thus, the above requests will fail to parse this sentence correctly.

In general, then, it appears that some syntactic ambiguities cannot be resolved without great difficulty using only local syntactic checks. This is because the resolution of syntactic ambiguities sometimes requires more global knowledge about the syntax of a sentence, such as whether a particular verb functions as the main clause verb. Information like this cannot be determined so easily by rules which examine only immediate context. Thus, although we would like syntactic and semantic processing to be integrated, as it was in ELI and CA, it seems that a separate syntactic representation must still be built during the analysis process in order to resolve these ambiguities.

17.4. A parser which satisfies both constraints

I shall now describe the MOPTRANS parser, and demonstrate how it overcomes the difficulties outlined in the last two sections. The MOPTRANS parser is an integrated parser, in the sense that syntactic and semantic processing take place in tandem. However, it is different from previous integrated parsers, in that it uses a largely autonomous set of syntactic rules, and a syntactic representation of the input text is built during parsing.

The MOPTRANS parser utilizes two largely separate bodies of rules, which encode its knowledge about syntax and semantics. Semantic rules are responsible for determining what attachments or slot-fillings are semantically desirable; as well as for making inferences which must be made in order to understand the input text properly. The semantic rules which MOPTRANS uses will not be discussed in detail here, except when necessary to illustrate the interaction between these rules and syntactic processing.

MOPTRANS' syntactic knowledge is encoded in terms of PARSIFAL-like parsing rules (Marcus 1978), which specify how sequences of syntactic constituents in the input text can be attached to each other. As in Marcus' parser, the MOPTRANS parser does not always account for every new constituent immediately, as is the case in an ATN parser (Woods 1970). If no syntactic pattern is matched by the input, the parser continues reading on until a rule does match. However, unlike PARSIFAL and other syntactic parsers, syntax rules in MOPTRANS are only considered and applied if the syntactic attachments that they make are judged by the parser's semantic analyzer to be semantically appropriate. In this way, syntactic and semantic processing are completely integrated.

As MOPTRANS parses a piece of text. the semantic and syntactic representations that it builds are kept in its active memory. During parsing, new constituents are added to active memory as each new word is read. As new constituents are added, semantics is asked if anything in active memory 'fits together' well; that is, if there are any semantic attachments that could be made between the elements in active memory. If so, MOPTRANS' syntactic rules are consulted to see if any of these semantic attachments are syntactically legal. In other words, semantics proposes various attachments, and syntax acts as a filter, choosing which of these attachments makes sense according to the syntax of the input. The interaction between syntax and semantics is displayed graphically in Figure 1.

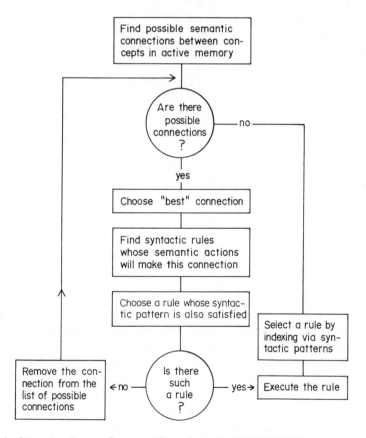

Figure 1. Interaction Between Syntax and Semantics in the MOPTRANS Parser

To make this clearer, consider how the following simple sentence is parsed by MOPTRANS:

John gave Mary a book.

MOPTRANS' dictionary definitions contain information about what semantic representation the parser should build when it encounters a particular word. Thus, *John* causes the representation PERSON to appear in the parser's active memory. At the same time, since *John* is a proper noun, the syntactic class NP is also activated.

When the word *gave* is processed, MOPTRANS' definition of this word causes the Conceptual Dependency representation (Schank 1972) ATRANS (transfer of possession or control) to be placed in active memory. At this point, MOPTRANS considers the two semantic representations in active memory, PERSON and ATRANS. The semantic analyzer tries to combine these representations in whatever way it can. It concludes that the PERSON could be either the ACTOR or the RECIPIENT of the ATRANS, since the constraints on these roles are that they must be ANIMATE. It also concludes that the PERSON could be the OBJECT of the ATRANS (that is, the thing whose control or possession is being transferred). However, since this role is expected to be a PHYSICAL-OBJECT rather than an ANIMATE, the match is not as good as with the ACTOR or RECIPIENT roles.[3]

This is the point at which the MOPTRANS parser utilizes its syntactic rules. Semantics has determined that two possible attachments are preferred. Now the parser examines its syntactic rules to see if any of them could yield either of these attachments. Indeed, the parser's Subject Rule will assign the PERSON to be the ACTOR of the ATRANS. The Subject Rule looks like this:

Subject Rule

Syntactic pattern:	NP, V (active)
Additional restrictions:	NP is not already attached syntactically
Syntactic assignment:	NP is SUBJECT of V, V is indicative (V-IND)
Semantic action:	NP is ACTOR of V (or another slot, if specified by V)
Result:	V-IND

This rule applies when an NP is followed by a V, and when the NP can fill the ACTOR slot of the semantic representation of the V. The NP is marked as the SUBJECT of the V, and the V is marked as indicative (V-IND). As dictated by the RESULT of the rule, the V-IND is left in active memory, but the NP is removed, since its role as subject prevents many subsequent attachments to it, such as PP attachments. In addition to these syntactic assignments, the semantic representation of the NP *John* is placed in the ACTOR slot of the ATRANS representing the verb.

<hr>

[3] The way in which the semantic analyzer reaches these conclusions is not discussed in this chapter. For more details, see Lytinen 1984.

The rest of the sentence is parsed in a similar fashion. To determine how *Mary* should be attached to *gave*, semantics is asked for its preference. It determines that the RECIPIENT slot of the ATRANS is the best attachment.[4] Syntax is consulted to see if any syntactic rules could make this attachment. This time, the Dative Movement Rule is found:

Dative Movement Rule

Syntactic pattern:	V-IND, NP
Additional restrictions:	V-IND allows dative movement
Syntactic assignment:	NP is (syntactic) INDIRECT OBJECT of V-IND
Semantic action:	NP is (semantic) RECIPIENT of V-IND (or another slot, if specified by V-IND)
Result:	V-IND, NP

When applied, this rule assigns *Mary* as the indirect object of *gave*, and places the PERSON concept which represents *Mary* into the RECIPIENT slot of the ATRANS.

The final NP in the sentence, *the book*, is attached to *gave* in a similar way. Semantics is asked to determine the best attachment of *book*, which is represented as a PHYSICAL-OBJECT, to other concepts in active memory, which at this point contains the ATRANS as well as the person representing *Mary*. Semantics determines that the best attachment is to the OBJECT role of the ATRANS. The syntactic rule which can perform this attachment is the Direct Object Rule, which is similar in form to the Dative Movement Rule above. This rule is applied, yielding the final semantic representation (ATRANS ACTOR PERSON OBJECT PHYSICAL-OBJECT RECIPIENT PERSON), and the syntactic markings of *John* as the subject of *gave*, *book* as its direct object, and *Mary* as its indirect object.

One important thing to note about the parsing process on this sentence is that although the Direct Object Rule could have applied syntactically when *Mary* was found after the verb, it was never even considered. This is because the semantic analyzer preferred to place *Mary* in the RECIPIENT slot of the ATRANS. Since a syntactic rule was found which accommodated this attachment, namely the Dative Movement rule, the parser never tried to apply the Direct Object Rule.

The MOPTRANS parser is able to resolve syntactic ambiguities that proved difficult for previous integrated parsers. For the sentence discussed earlier, *I saw the soldier called to his sergeant*, MOPTRANS has no trouble determining that *called* is an unmarked passive, because according to its syntax rules,

---

[4] Just as earlier, *Mary* could either be the ACTOR or RECIPIENT of the ATRANS, but *John* has already been assigned as the ACTOR.

another indicative verb at this point is not possible. The rule which is applied instead is the Unmarked Passive Rule:

Unmarked Passive Rule

Syntactic pattern:	NP, VPP
Additional restrictions:	none
Syntactic assignment:	NP is (syntactic) SUBJECT of VPP, VPP is PASSIVE, VPP is a RELATIVE CLAUSE of NP
Semantic action:	NP is (semantic) OBJECT of S (or another slot, if specified by VPP)
Result:	NP, VPP

Called is represented by the Conceptual Dependency primitive MTRANS, which is used to represent any form of communication. Since *soldier* can be attached as either the ACTOR or the OBJECT of an MTRANS, semantics would be happy with either of these attachments. However, the Subject Rule cannot apply at this point, since *soldier* is already attached as the syntactic direct object of *saw*. Thus, this restriction on the Subject Rule prevents this attachment from being made. Instead, the Unmarked Passive Rule applies, since it semantically attaches *soldier* as the OBJECT of the MTRANS, and since *called* is marked as potentially being a past participle (VPP).

Unlike syntax-first parsers, the MOPTRANS parser can immediately resolve syntactic ambiguities on the basis of semantic analysis, thereby cutting down on the number of syntactic attachments that it must consider. We have already seen this in the example *John gave Mary the book*, in which the parser does not even consider if *Mary* is the direct object of *gave*. Let us return now to two examples discussed earlier:

The cleaners dry-cleaned the coat that Mary found at the rummage sale for $10.
The cleaners dry-cleaned the coat that Mary found in the garbage for $10.

MOPTRANS parses the relative clause *that Mary found* with the following rule:

Clause Rule for Gap After the Verb (CGAV Rule)

Syntactic pattern:	NP, RP (relative pronoun) (optional), V-IND
Additional restrictions:	V-IND is not followed by an NP
Syntactic assignment:	V-IND is a RELATIVE CLAUSE of NP
Semantic action:	NP is the semantic OBJECT of the V-IND
Result:	NP, V-IND (changed to CLAUSE-VERB)

The Subject Rule assigns *Mary* to be the subject of *found*, since *Mary* is not yet attached syntactically to anything before it. Then, since no NP follows *found*, and since the attachment of *coat* (a PHYSICAL-OBJECT) as the OBJECT of the ATRANS is semantically acceptable, the CGAV rule applies, assigning *that Mary found* as a relative clause.

When the parser reaches *for $10*, the first S, *The cleaners dry-cleaned the coat*, as well as the relative clause, are both still in active memory. The NP *$10* is represented as MONEY. The preposition *for* also has a semantic representation, which describes the possible semantic roles that a PP beginning with *for* can fill. One of these roles is called IN-EXCHANGE-FOR. *Dry-cleaned* is represented by the concept PROFESSIONAL-SERVICE, which expects to have its IN-EXCHANGE-FOR role filled with MONEY, since most professional services are done for money. ATRANS, on the other hand, does not explicitly expect an IN-EXCHANGE-FOR role. Thus, semantics prefers to attach the PP *for $10* to PROFESSIONAL-SERVICE and the verb *dry-cleaned*.

In the second example, on the other hand, when the PP *at the rummage sale* is attached to *found*, this triggers an inference rule that the ATRANS representing *found* must actually be the concept BUY, since *rummage sale* is a likely setting for this action. BUY, like PROFESSIONAL-SERVICE, expects the role IN-EXCHANGE-FOR to be filled with MONEY. Thus, semantics has no preference as to which verb to attach *for $10* to. To resolve the ambiguity, a syntactic recency preference is used, thereby attaching *for $10* to *found*.

Because of this resolution of ambiguity, the MOPTRANS parser does not have to consider ambiguities further on in the sentence that it might otherwise have to. For example, in the sentence, *The cleaners dry-cleaned the coat Mary found in the garbage for $10 while she was away in New York*, the PP attachment rule which MOPTRANS uses removes the relative clause *that Mary found in the garbage* from active memory, since the PP attaches to something before this clause. Therefore, when the parser reads the clause *while she was away in New York*, there is only one possible verb, *dry-cleaned*, to which this clause can be attached.

17.5. Conclusion

In this chapter I have argued that semantic and syntactic analysis should be integrated. By this, I mean that syntactic and semantic processing must proceed at the same time, relying on each other to provide information necessary to resolve both syntactic and semantic ambiguities. Non-integrated, syntax-first parsers must leave some syntactic ambiguities unresolved until the semantic analysis stage. This can result in a highly inefficient syntactic analysis, because the failure to resolve one syntactic ambiguity can lead to other, 'artificial' syntactic ambiguities which would not have to be considered had the original ambiguity been resolved with semantics. These new ambiguities may also be unresolvable using only syntax. If several of these ambiguities are encountered in one sentence, the combinatorics of the situation can get out of hand.

316   *Steven L. Lytinen*

Previous integrated parsers have avoided these inefficiencies, but have suffered from problems of their own. Because of the lack of a separate representation of the input text's syntactic structure, it is difficult to write 'local' syntax-checking rules to resolve some types of syntactic ambiguities. Attempts to resolve these ambiguities result in a proliferation of rules.

To solve both of these problems at the same time, the MOPTRANS parser is integrated, in that syntactic and semantic processing proceed in parallel, but MOPTRANS has a separate body of syntactic knowledge, and builds a representation of the syntactic structure of input sentences. This enables it to use semantics to resolve syntactic ambiguities, and to easily resolve ambiguities that cause difficulties for local syntax-checking rules.

The MOPTRANS parser relies heavily on its semantic analyzer during the parsing process. Therefore, its ability to parse is only as good as its semantic theory. Obviously no semantic theory presently exists which can allow for correct semantic analysis of arbitrary texts, or even for a broad domain of texts. However, in limited domains, the prospects for mapping out the necessary semantic knowledge are higher. In any case, given the present desire to use semantics in MT systems, an integrated approach to the use of semantics with syntax appears to be advantageous to the approach of syntax-first analysis followed by a semantic interpreter.

Acknowledgement

This research was conducted at the Artificial Intelligence Laboratory of Yale University, and was supported in part by the Advanced Research Projects Agency of the Department of Defense and monitored by the Office of Naval Research under contract No. N00014-82K-0149.

References

Aho, A.V., and J.D. Ullman. 1972. *The Theory of Parsing, Translation and Compiling*. Englewood Cliffs, NJ: Prentice-Hall.

Allen, J. 1984. Towards a general theory of action and time. *Artificial Intelligence* 23:123-154.

Allen, J.F., and C.R. Perrault. 1980. Analyzing intention in utterances. *Artificial Intelligence* 15:143-178.

ALPAC. 1966. *Language and Machines: Computers in Translation and Linguistics*. A report by the Automatic Language Processing Advisory Committee (ALPAC). Division of Behavioral Sciences, National Academy of Sciences, National Research Council Publication 1416. Washington:NAS/NRC.

Alterman, R. 1985. A dictionary based on concept coherence. *Artificial Intelligence* 25:153-186.

Amsler, R.A. 1980. The Structure of the Merriam-Webster Pocket Dictionary. Ph.D. Dissertation, University of Texas at Austin, Texas.

Amsler, R.A. 1981. A taxonomy for English nouns and verbs. In: *Proceedings of ACL-81*. pp.133-138.

Anderson, R.C., R.E. Reynolds, D.L. Schallert and E.T. Goetz. 1977. Frameworks for comprehending discourse. *American Educational Research Journal* 14:367-381.

Appelt, D. 1980. Problem solving applied to language generation. In: *Proceedings of ACL-80*. pp.59-63.

Appelt, D. 1981. Planning Natural Language Utterances to Satisfy Multiple Goals. Ph.D. dissertation, Dept. of Computer Science, Stanford University.

Appelt, D. 1985. *Planning English Sentences*. Cambridge: Cambridge University Press.

Arnold, D.J., and R.L. Johnson. 1984. Robust processing in machine translation. In: *Proceedings of COLING-84*. pp.472-475.

Arnold, D.J., L. Jaspaert, and L. des Tombe. 1985. EUROTRA ELS-3 *Linguistic Specifications (1985)*, DGXIII, CEC, Luxembourg.

Arnold, D.J., S. Krauwer, M. Rosner, L. des Tombe, and G.B. Varile. 1986. The <C,A>,T framework in EUROTRA: a theoretically committed notation for MT. In: *Proceedings of COLING-86*. pp.297-303.

317

Arnold, D.J., L. Jaspaert, R.L. Johnson, S. Krauwer, M. Rosner, L. des Tombe, G.B. Varile, and S. Warwick. 1985. A MU1 View of the <C,A>, T Framework in EUROTRA. In: *Proceedings of the Conference on Theoretical and Methodological Issues in Machine Translation of Natural Languages*, Colgate University, Hamilton, NY. pp.1-14.

Ashley, K., and E. Rissland. 1984. Toward modeling legal argument. In: *Proceedings of the Second International Congress Logica Informatica, Diritto Automated Analysis of Legal Texts*, Florence, Italy. pp. 97-108.

Austin, J. 1962. *How to Do Things with Words.* New York-London: Oxford University Press.

Bach, E. 1985. The algebra of events. *Linguistics and Philosophy.* 9:5-16.

Bach, K., and R. Harnish. 1982. *Linguistic Communication and Speech Acts.* Cambridge, MA: MIT Press.

Bar-Hillel, Y. 1960. The present status of automatic translation of languages. In: F.L. Alt (ed.) *Advances in Computers* (Volume 1). New York: Academic Press. pp.91-163.

Barr, A., E.A. Feigenbaum, and P.R. Cohen. (eds.) 1981, 1982. *The Handbook of Artificial Intelligence* (3 volumes). Stanford, CA: HeurisTech Press; Los Altos, CA: William Kaufmann.

Barwise, J., and J. Perry. 1983. *Situations and Attitudes.* Cambridge, MA: MIT Press.

Becker, J. 1975. The phrasal lexicon. In: R.C. Schank and B.L. Nash-Webber (eds.) *Theoretical Issues in Natural Language Processing.* Menlo Park, CA: Association for Computational Linguistics. pp.60-63.

Bennett, W.S. 1982. *The Linguistic Component of METAL.* Working Paper LRC-82-2. Linguistic Research Center, The University of Texas, Austin.

Bennett, W.S., and J. Slocum. 1985. The LRC machine translation system. *Computational Linguistics* 11:111-121.

Birnbaum, L., and M. Selfridge. 1979. *Problems in Conceptual Analysis of Natural Language.* Technical Report 168. Yale University Department of Computer Science, October 1979.

Birnbaum, L., and M. Selfridge. 1981. Conceptual analysis of natural language. In: R.C. Schank and C. Riesbeck (eds.) *Inside Computer Understanding.* Hillsdale, NJ: Lawrence Erlbaum Associates. pp.318-372.

Bobrow, D.G., and T. Winograd. 1977. An overview of KRL, a knowledge and representation language. *Cognitive Science* 1:3-46.

Bobrow, R., and B.L. Webber. 1980. Knowledge representation for syntactic/semantic processing. In: *Proceedings of AAAI-80.* pp.316-323.

Boitet, Ch. 1976. Problèmes actuels en TA: Un essai de réponse. In: *Proceedings of COLING-76.*

Boitet, Ch., and N. Nedobejkine. 1981. Recent developments in Russian-French machine translation at Grenoble. *Linguistics* 19:199-271.

Boitet, Ch., and N. Nedobejkine. 1983. Illustration sur le développement d'un atelier de traduction automatisée. Paper presented at *Colloque "l'informatique au service de la linguistique"*, Université de Metz, France, June 1983.

Boitet, Ch., P. Guillaume, and M. Quézel-Ambrunaz. 1985. A case study in software evolution: from ARIANE-78.4 to ARIANE-85. In: *Proceedings of the Conference on Theoretical and Methodological Issues in Machine Translation of Natural Languages*, Colgate University, Hamilton, NY, August 1985. pp.27-58.

Booth, S.L., and R.E. Cullingford. 1985. How to make a natural language interface robust. In: *Proceedings of 1985 IEEE International Conference on Cybernetics and Society*, Tuscon, Arizona, November 1985. pp. 229-236.

Booth, S.L., R.E. Cullingford, and N.H.White. 1985. DESI, A robust natural language interface to a decision support system. In: *Proceedings of the IEEE/ACM Conference on Software Tools*, New York, pp. 741-745.

Bossie, S. 1981. *A Tactical Component for Text Generation: Sentence Generation Using a Functional Grammar.* University of Pennsylvania, TR MS-CIS-81-5.

Brachman, R., and J. Schmoltze. 1985. An overview on the KL-ONE knowledge representation system. *Cognitive Science*, 9:171-216.

Bresnan, J. (ed.) 1982. *The Mental Representation of Grammatical Relations.* Cambridge, MA: MIT Press.

Britton, B.K., and J.B. Black. 1985. *Understanding Expository Text.* Hillsdale, NJ: Lawrence Erlbaum Associates.

Brown, G. and G. Yule. 1983. *Discourse Analysis.* Cambridge: Cambridge University Press.

Bruce, B. 1972. A model for temporal references and its application in a question answering program. *Artificial Intelligence* 3:1-25.

Bruce, B. 1975. Generation as social action. *Proceedings of the TINLAP-1 Conference, ACM.* pp. 74-78.

Bruderer, H. 1977. *Handbuch der maschinellen und maschinenunterstützten Sprachübersetzung.* Munich: Verlag Dokumentation.

Burton, R. 1976. *Semantic Grammar: An Engineering Technique for Constructing Natural Language Understanding Systems.* BBN Technical Report 3453, Cambridge, MA.

320 *References*

Carberry, M.S. 1985a. A pragmatics-based approach to understanding intersentential ellipsis. In: *Proceedings of ACL-85*. pp.188-197.

Carberry, M.S. 1985b. Pragmatic modeling in information system interfaces. Ph.D. dissertation, University of Delaware. (Unpublished.)

Carbonell, J.G., and P.J. Hayes. 1983. Recovery strategies for parsing extragrammatical language. *American Journal of Computational Linguistics* 9:123-146.

Carbonell, J.G., R.E. Cullingford, and A.V. Gershman. 1981. Steps towards knowledge-based machine translation. *IEEE Transactions on Pattern Analysis and Machine Intelligence*, 3:376-392.

Carbonell, J.G., W.M. Boggs, M.L. Mauldin, and P.G. Anick. 1985. First steps toward an integrated natural language interface. In: S. Andriole (ed.) *Applications in Artificial Intelligence*. Princeton, NJ: Petrocelli Books Inc. pp.227-243.

Carlson, L. 1983. *Dialogue Games*. Dordrecht, Holland: Reidel.

Carroll, J.B., P. Davies, and B. Richman. 1971. *The American Heritage Word Frequency Book*. Boston, MA: Houghton Mifflin.

Cecchi, C., R.L. Johnson, S. Krauwer, J. Mcnaught, D. Petitpierre, M. Rosner, and G.B. Varile. 1985. EUROTRA ETS-6. *Final Report (March 1985)*, DGXIII, CEC, Luxembourg.

Chaffin, R. 1979. Knowledge of language and knowledge about the world: a reaction-time study of invited and necessary inferences. *Cognitive Science* 3:311-328.

Chandioux, J. 1976. METEO: An operational system for the translation of public weather forecasts. FBIS Seminar on Machine Translation. *American Journal of Computational Linguistics* Microfiche 46, pp.27-36.

Charniak, E. 1972. Towards a Model of Children's Story Comprehension. (Ph.D. Diss.) AI Laboratory TR-266, Massachusetts Institute of Technology, Cambridge, MA, 1972.

Charniak, E. 1981. A common representation for problem-solving and language comprehension information. *Artificial Intelligence* 12:225-255.

Charniak, E. 1983. Parsing, how to. In: K. Sparck Jones, and Y.A. Wilks (eds.) *Automatic Natural Language Parsing*. Chichester, England: Ellis Horwood. pp.156-163.

Cherry, L.L., and W. Vesterman. 1980. *Writing Tools: The STYLE and DICTION Programs*. Technical Report 9. Murray Hill, NJ: Computing Science, Bell Laboratories.

Chester, D. 1976. The translation of formal proofs into English. *Artificial Intelligence* 7:262-278.

Chomsky, N. 1965. *Aspects of the Theory of Syntax.* Cambridge, MA: MIT Press.

Chomsky, N. 1981. *Lectures on Government and Binding.* Dordrecht, Holland: Foris.

Church, K., and R. Patil. 1982. *Coping with Syntactic Ambiguity or How to Put the Block in the Box on the Table.* Technical Report MIT/LCS/TM-216, Laboratory for Computer Science, Massachusetts Institute of Technology, April, 1982.

Clancey, W. 1979. Tutoring rules for guiding a case method dialog. *International Journal of Man-Machine Studies* 2:25-49.

Clippinger, J. 1977. *Meaning and Discourse: a computer model of psychoanalytic speech and cognition.* Baltimore, MD: Johns Hopkins University Press.

Cohen, R. 1984. A computational theory of the function of clue words in argument understanding. In: *Proceedings of COLING-84.* pp.251-258.

Cohen, P.R., and C.R. Perrault. 1979. Elements of a plan-based theory of speech acts. *Cognitive Science* 3:177-212.

Colmerauer, A. 1971. *Les* SYSTEMES-Q: *un formalisme pour analyser et synthetiser des phrases sur ordinateur.* Groupe TAUM, Université de Montréal.

Conklin, E. 1983. Data-Driven Indelible Planning of Discourse Generation Using Salience. Ph.D. dissertation, Department of Computer Science, University of Massachusetts.

Cullingford, R.E. 1977. Script Application: Computer Understanding of Newspaper Stories. Ph.D. dissertation, Yale University, September 1977.

Cullingford, R.E. 1979. Pattern matching and inference in story understanding. *Discourse Processes* 2:319-334.

Cullingford, R.E. 1986. *Natural Language Processing: A Knowledge Engineering Approach.* Totowa, NJ: Rowman and Allanheld.

Cullingford, R.E., and L.J. Joseph. 1983. A heuristically 'optimal' knowledge base organization technique. *IFAC Automatica* 19:647-654.

Cullingford, R.E., and M.J. Pazzani. 1984. Word meaning selection in multimodule language processing systems. *IEEE Transactions on Pattern Analysis and Machine Intelligence* 6:493-509.

Cullingford, R.E., M.W. Krueger, M. Selfridge, and M.A. Bienkowski. 1981. Towards automating explanations. In: *Proceedings of IJCAI-81.* pp.432-438.

Danlos L. 1984a. Génération automatique de textes en langues naturelles. Thèse d'Etat, Université de Paris 7.

Danlos, L. 1984b. Conceptual and linguistic decisions in generation. In: *Proceedings of COLING-84.* pp.501-504.

Davey, A. 1974. *Discourse Production.* Published in 1978 by Edinburgh University Press.

Dawson, B. 1985. A Preference-Based Conceptual Analyzer, Department of EE&CS Research Report (M.Sc. thesis), University of Connecticut, Storrs, CT.

Dijk, T. van. 1980. The semantics and pragmatics of functional coherence in discourse. *Versus* 26.

Durham, I., D.A. Lamb, and J.B. Saxe. 1983. Spelling correction in user interfaces. *Communications of the Association for Computing Machinery* 26:764-773.

Eastman, C.M. and D.S. McLean. 1981. On the need for parsing ill-formed input. *American Journal of Computational Linguistics* 7:257.

Evens, M.W., B.E. Litowitz, J.A. Markowitz, R.N. Smith, and O. Werner. 1980. *Lexical Semantic Relations: A Comparative Survey.* Carbondale, IL, and Edmonton, Canada: Linguistic Research, Inc.

Eynde, F. van, A.L. des Tombe, and F. Maes. 1985. The specification of time meaning for machine translation. In: *Proceedings of ACL-85* (European Chapter). pp.35-40

Fass, D., and Y.A. Wilks. 1983. Preference semantics, ill-formedness, and metaphor. *American Journal of Computational Linguistics* 9:178-187.

Fillmore, C.J. 1971. Verbs of Judging. In: C.J. Fillmore and D.T. Langendoen (eds.) *Studies in Linguistic Semantics.* New York: Holt, Rinehart, and Winston. pp. 273-289.

Forbus, K., and A. Stevens. 1981. *Using Qualitative Simulation to Generate Explanations.* BBN Technical Report No. 4490, prepared for Navy Personnel Research and Development Center, 1981. Also in *Proceedings of Third Annual Conference of the Cognitive Science Society.* pp.219-221.

Gazdar, G., E. Klein, G. Pullum, and I. Sag. 1985. *Generalized Phrase Structure Grammar.* Oxford: Basil Blackwell.

Geis, M., and A. Zwicky, 1971. On invited inferences. *Linguistic Inquiry* 2:561-566.

Gerber, R. 1984. Etude des possibilités de coopération entre un système fondé sur des techniques de compréhension implicite (système logico-syntaxique) et un système fondé sur des techniques de compréhension explicite (système expert). Thèse de 3ème cycle, Grenoble, January 1984.

Gershman, A.V. 1979. *Knowledge-Based Parsing.* Research Report No. 156, Department of Computer Science, Yale University, New Haven, CT.

Goldman, N. 1975. Conceptual generation. In: R. Schank (ed.) *Conceptual Information Processing.* Amsterdam: North-Holland/Elsevier. pp.289-372.

Granger, R.H. 1983. The NOMAD system: Expectation-based detection and correction of errors during understanding of syntactically and semantically ill-formed text. *American Journal of Computational Linguistics* 9:188-198.

Granville, R. 1984. Controlling lexical substitution in computer text generation. In: *Proceedings of COLING-84.* pp.381-384.

Grice, H.P. 1968. Utterer's meaning, sentence-meaning, and word-meaning. *Foundations of Language* 4:225-242.

Grice, H.P. 1969. Utterer's meaning and intentions. *Philosophical Review* 78:147-177.

Grice, H.P. 1971. Meaning. In: D.D. Steinberg and L.A. Jacobovits (eds.) *Semantics: An Interdisciplinary Reader in Philosophy, Linguistics and Psychology.* Cambridge: Cambridge University Press. pp.53-59.

Grice, H.P. 1975. Logic and conversation. In: P. Cole and J.L. Morgan (eds.) *Syntax and Semantics, Volume 3: Speech Acts.* New York: Academic Press. pp.53-59.

Grishman, R., and R. Kittredge. (eds) 1986. *Analyzing Language in Restricted Domains.* Hillsdale, NJ: Lawrence Erlbaum Associates.

Grishman, R., T.N. Ngo, E. Marsh, and L. Hirschman. 1984. Automatic determination of sublanguage syntactic usage. In: *Proceedings of COLING-84.* pp.96-100.

Grolier Electronic Publishing. 1984. *Academic American Encyclopedia.* New York, NY: Grolier Electronic Publishing.

Grosz, B. 1978. Focusing in dialog. In: *Theoretical Issues in Natural Language Processing-2,* Association for Computational Linguistics, University of Illinois at Urbana-Champaign, July, 1978. pp.96-103.

Grosz, B. 1981. Focusing and description in natural language dialogs. In: A. Joshi, B. Webber, and I. Sag (eds.) *Elements of Discourse Understanding.* Cambridge : Cambridge University Press. pp.84-105.

Grosz, B. and Sidner, C. 1985. *The Structures of Discourse Structure.* BBN Technical Report No. 6097, Cambridge, MA.

G. & C. Merriam Company. 1963. *Webster's New Collegiate Dictionary* (Seventh Edition). Springfield, MA: G. & C. Merriam Company.

G. & C. Merriam Company. 1964. *The New Merriam-Webster Pocket Dictionary.* Springfield, MA: G. & C. Merriam Company.

Hajičová, E. 1983. Topic and focus. *Theoretical Linguistics* 10:268-276.

Halliday, M.A.K. 1969. Options and functions in the English clause. In: Halliday and Martin (eds.) 1981. *Readings in Systemic Linguistics.* Batsford Academic Press. pp.138-145.

Halperin, I.R. (ed.) 1972. *New English-Russian Dictionary.* Moscow: Sovetskaja Enciklopedija.

Harris, Z. 1963. *Discourse Analysis Reprints.* The Hague: Mouton.

Harris, Z. 1968. *Mathematical Structures of Language.* New York: Wiley-Interscience.

Hayes, P. 1979. The naive physics manifesto. In: D. Michie (ed.) *Expert System in the Microelectronic Age.* Edinburgh, Scotland: Edinburgh University Press.

Hayes, P.J. 1984. Entity-oriented parsing. In: *Proceedings of COLING-84.* pp.212-217.

Hayes, P.J., and J.G. Carbonell. 1981. *Multi-Strategy Parsing and its Role in Robust Man-Machine Communication.* Technical Report CMU-CS-81-118, Carnegie-Mellon University, Computer Science Department, May, 1981.

Hayes, P.J., and R. Reddy. 1979. *An Anatomy of Graceful Interaction in Communcation.* Technical Report, Carnegie-Mellon University, Computer Science Department.

Hayes, P.J., A.G. Hauptmann, J.G. Carbonell, and M. Tomita. 1986. Parsing spoken language: a semantic caseframe approach. In: *Proceedings of COLING-86.* pp.587-592.

Heim, I. 1982. The Semantics of Definite and Indefinite Noun Phrases. Ph.D. dissertation, University of Massachusetts. (Unpublished).

Hendrix, G., E. Sacerdoti, D. Sagalowicz, and J. Slocum. 1978. Developing a natural language interface to complex data. *Association for Computing Machinery: Transactions on Database Systems* 3:105-147.

Hintikka, J. 1969. Semantics for propositional attitudes. In: J.W.Davis et al. (eds.) *Philosophical Logic.* Dordrecht, Holland: Reidel. pp.21-45.

Hobbs, J. 1979. Coherence and coreference. *Cognitive Science* 3:67-90.

Hobbs, J. 1982. Towards an understanding of coherence in discourse. In: W.G. Lehnert and M.H. Ringle (eds.) *Strategies for Natural Language Processing.* Hillsdale, NJ: Lawrence Erlbaum Associates. pp.223-243.

Hoenkamp, E. 1983. Een Computermodel van de Spreker: Psychologische en Linguistische Aspecten. Ph.D. dissertation, Department of Psychology, Catholic University, Nijmegen, The Netherlands.

Hornby, A.S., E.V. Gatenby, and H. Wakefield. 1963. *The Advanced Learner's Dictionary of Current English.* London, England: Oxford University Press.

Hundt, M.G. 1982. Working with the Weidner machine-aided translation systems. In: Lawson (ed.) 1982. *Practical Experience in Machine Translation.* Amsterdam: North Holland. pp.45-51.

Hutchins, W.J. 1978. Machine translation and machine-aided translation. *Journal of Documentation* 34:119-159.

Hutchins, W.J. 1982. The evolution of machine translation systems. In: V. Lawson (ed.) *Practical Experience in Machine Translation.* Amsterdam: North Holland. pp.21-37.

Hutchins, W.J. 1986. *Machine Translation: Past, Present, Future.* Chichester, England: Ellis Horwood Limited.

Isabelle, P. 1984. Machine translation at the TAUM group. Paper presented at The ISSCO *Tutorial on Machine Translation.*

Jacobs, P. 1985. *A Knowledge-Based Approach to Language Production.* Computer Science Department, University of California, Berkeley. TR 86/254.

Jensen, K., G.E. Heidorn, L.A. Miller, and Y. Ravin. 1983. Parse filling and prose fixing: getting a hold on ill-formedness. *American Journal of Computational Linguistics* 9:147-160.

Johnson, R.L., M. King, and L. des Tombe. 1985. EUROTRA: a multi-lingual system under development. *Computational Linguistics* 11:155-169.

Johnson, R.L., S. Krauwer, M. Rosner, and G.B. Varile. 1984. Design of kernel architecture of the EUROTRA system. In: *Proceedings of COLING-84.* pp.226-235.

Kamp, H. 1981. A Theory of truth and semantic representation. In: J. Groenendijik, Th. Janssen, and M. Stokoff (eds.) *Formal Methods in the Study of Language.* Part I, pp.277-322.

Kaplan, D. 1977. *Demonstrative: Essay on the Semantics, Logic, and Metaphysics and Epistemology of Demonstratives and other Indexicals.* Draft 2., ms. UCLA.

Kaplan, R.M., and J. Bresnan. 1982. Lexical functional grammar: a formal system for grammatical representation. In: J. Bresnan (ed.) *The Mental Representation of Grammatical Relations.* Cambridge, MA: MIT Press. pp.173-281.

Karttunen, L. 1973. Presuppositions of compound sentences. *Linguistic Inquiry* 4:169-193.

Karttunen, L. 1974. Presuppositions and linguistic context. *Theoretical Linguistics* 1:3-44.

Karttunen, L. 1976. Discourse referents. In: J. McCawley (ed.) *Syntax and Semantics 7.* New York: Academic Press. pp.363-385.

Kay, M. 1973. The MIND system. In: R. Rustin (ed.) *Natural Language Processing.* New York: Algorithmics Press. pp.155-188.

Kay, M. 1979. Functional grammar. In: *Proceedings of Fifth Annual Meeting of the Berkeley Linguistic Society.* pp.142-158.

Kay, M. 1980. *The Proper Place of Men and Machines in Language Translation.* Working paper CSL-80-11. Xerox PARC.

326   *References*

Kay, M. 1982. Machine translation. *American Journal of Computatio·al Linguistics* 8:74-78.

Kay, M. 1984. Functional unification grammar: a formalism for machine translation. In: *Proceedings of COLING-84.* pp.75-78.

Kempen, G., and E. Hoenkamp. 1982. Incremental sentence generation: implications for the structure of a syntactic processor. In: J. Horecky (ed.) *Proceedings of COLING-82,* Prague, July 1982. North Holland Linguistic Series No. 47. Amsterdam: North Holland. pp.151-156.

King, M. 1981. Design characteristics of a machine translation system. In: *Proceedings of IJCAI-81.* pp.42-46.

King, M. 1982. EUROTRA: An attempt to achieve multilingual MT. In: V. Lawson (ed.) *Practical Experience in Machine Translation.* Amsterdam: North Holland. pp.139-148.

King, M. 1985. EUROTRA *General System Description.* Report for contract ETL-6, DGXIII, CEC, Luxembourg, November 1985.

King, M., and S. Perschke. 1982. EUROTRA and its objectives. *Multilingua* 1:27-32.

Kittredge, R. 1982. Variation and homogeneity of sublanguages. In: R. Kittredge and J. Lehrberger (eds.) *Sublanguage: Studies of Language in Restricted Semantic Domains.* Berlin-New York: deGruyter. pp.107-137.

Kittredge, R. 1983a. Semantic processing of texts in restricted sub-languages. *Computers and Mathematics with Applications* 9:45-58.

Kittredge, R. 1983b. *Sublanguage-Specific Computer Aids to Translation: A Survey of the Most Promising Application Areas.* Government of Canada, Secretary of State Department.

Kittredge, R., and J. Lehrberger. (eds.) 1982. *Sublanguage: Studies of Language in Restricted Semantic Domains.* Berlin-New York: deGruyter.

Kittredge, R., L. Bourbeau, and P. Isabelle. 1976. Design and implementation of an English-French transfer grammar. In: *Proceedings of COLING-76.*

Knowles, F.E. 1982. The pivotal role of the various dictionaries in an MT System. In: V. Lawson (ed.) *Practical Experience of Machine Translation.* Amsterdam: North Holland.

Koskenniemi, K. 1984. A general computational model for word-form recognition and production. In: *Proceedings of COLING-84.* pp.178-181.

Krauwer, S. (ed.) 1986. EUROTRA *Reference Manual. Version 1.1.* DGXIII, CEC, Luxembourg, February 1986.

Krauwer, S. and L. des Tombe. 1984. Transfer in a multi-lingual MT system. In: *Proceedings of COLING-84.* pp.464-467.

Kroch, A.S. 1981. On the role of resumptive pronouns in amnestying island constraint violations. In: *The Proceedings of the 17th Regional Meeting of the Chicago Linguistic Society.* Chicago: Chicago Linguistic Society. pp.125-135.

Kroch, A.S., and A. Joshi. 1985. The Linguistic Relevance of Tree Adjoining Grammars. Technical Report MS-CIS-85-16, Department of Computer Science, University of Pennsylvania.

Kucera, H., and W.N. Francis. 1967. *Computational Analysis of Present-Day American English.* Providence, Rhode Island: Brown University Press.

Kukich, K. 1983. Knowledge-Based Report Generation: A Knowledge Engineering Approach to Natural Language Report Generation. Ph.D. dissertation, Information Science Department, University of Pittsburgh.

Kwasny, S.C., and N.K. Sondheimer. 1981. Relaxation techniques for parsing grammatically ill-formed input in natural language understanding systems. *American Journal of Computational Linguistics* 7:99-108.

Landsbergen, J. Isomorphic grammars and their use in the Rosetta Translation system. To appear in M. King (ed.) *Machine Translation: the state of the art.* Edinburgh : Edinburgh University Press.

Lavorel, B. 1982. Experience in English-French post editing. In: V. Lawson (ed.) *Practical Experience of Machine Translation.* Amsterdam: North-Holland. pp.105-109.

Lawson, V. (ed) 1982. *Practical Experience of Machine Translation.* Amsterdam: North Holland.

Lehmann, W.P., and R. Stachowitz. 1972. *Development of German-English Machine Translation System.* University of Texas at Austin, Linguistics Research Center.

Lehnert, W.G. 1978. *The Process of Question Answering.* Hillsdale, NJ: Lawrence Erlbaum Associates.

Lehnert, W.G. 1982. Plot units: a narrative summarization strategy. In: W.G. Lehnert and M.H. Ringle (eds.) *Strategies for Natural Language Processing.* Hillsdale, NJ: Lawrence Erlbaum Associates.

Lehnert, W.G., and M.H. Ringle. (eds.) 1982. *Strategies for Natural Language Processing.* Hillsdale, NJ: Lawrence Erlbaum Associates.

Lehrberger, J. 1982. Automatic translation and the concept of sublanguage. In: R. Kittredge and J. Lehrberger (eds.) *Sublanguage: Studies of Language in Restricted Semantic Domains.* Berlin-New York: deGruyter.

Lehrberger, J. 1986. Sublanguage analysis. In: Grishman, R., and R. Kittredge. *Analyzing Language in Restricted Domains.* Hillsdale, NJ: Lawrence Erlbaum Associates. pp.19-38.

Lenat, D., M. Prakash, and M. Sheperd. 1985. CYC: using common sense knowledge to overcome brittleness and knowledge acquisition bottlenecks. *AI Magazine* VI(4):65-85.

Litman, D.J., and J.F. Allen. 1984. A plan recognition model for clarification subdialogues. In: *Proceedings of COLING-84.* pp.302-311.

Locke, W.N., and A.D. Booth. 1957. *Machine Translation of Languages.* Boston, MA: Technology Press.

Lozinskii, E.L., and S. Nirenburg. 1982. Parallel processing of natural language and the locality phenomenon. In: *Proceedings of the Sixth European Meeting on Cybernetics and Systems Research.* Amsterdam: North Holland.

Lytinen, S. 1984. The Organization of Knowledge in a Multi-lingual Integrated Parser. Ph.D. dissertation, Yale University, Department of Computer Science. (Also available as Research Report No. 340, Department of Computer Science, Yale University.)

Lytinen, S., and R.C. Schank. 1982. *Representation and Translation.* Technical Report 234. Department of Computer Science, Yale University, New Haven, CT.

Maas, H.-D. 1984. The MT system SUSY. Paper presented at The ISSCO Tutorial on Machine Translation 1984.

Mann, W.C. 1982. *The Anatomy of a Systemic Choice.* ISI TR/RS-82-104.

Mann, W.C. 1983. *Inquiry Semantics: a Functional Semantics of Natural Language.* ISI TR/RS-83-8.

Mann, W.C. 1984. *Discourse Structures for Text Generation.* ISI Research Report 84-127.

Mann, W.C., and C.M.I.M. Matthiessen. 1985. Nigel: a systemic grammar for text generation. In: Freedle (ed.) *Systemic Perspectives on Discourse: Selected Theoretical Papers of the 9th International Systemic Workshop.* Norwood, NJ: Ablex.

Mann, W.C., and J. Moore. 1981. Computer generation of multi-paragraph English text. *American Journal of Computational Linguistics* 7:17-29.

Mann, W.C., and S. Thompson. 1983. *Relational Propositions in Discourse.* ISI Research Report 83-115.

Mann, W.C., M. Bates, B. Grosz, D.D. McDonald, K. McKeown, and W. Swartout. 1982. Text generation: the state of the art and literature. *American Journal of Computational Linguistics* 8:62-69.

Marcus, M. 1978. A Theory of Syntactic Recognition for Natural Language. Ph.D. dissertation, Massachusetts Institute of Technology, February 1978.

McCoy, K. 1985. Correcting Object-Related Misconceptions. Ph.D. disseration, University of Pennsylvania.

McDonald, D.D. 1975. A preliminary report on a program for generating natural language. In: *Proceedings of IJCAI-75*. pp.401-405.

McDonald, D.D. 1980. Natural Language Generation as a Process of Decision-Making under Constraints. Ph.D. dissertation, Dept. of Electrical Engineering and Computer Science, MIT.

McDonald, D.D. 1983. Natural language generation as a computational problem: an introduction. In: M. Brady and R. Berwick (eds.) *Computational Models of Discourse*. Cambridge, MA: MIT Press. pp.209-266.

McDonald, D.D. 1984. Description directed control: its implications for natural language generation. In: N.J. Cercone (ed.) *Computational Linguistics*. Oxford: Pergamon Press. pp.403-424.

McDonald, D.D., and J. Pustejovsky. 1985a. A computational theory of prose style for natural language generation. In: *Proceedings of ACL-85 (European Chapter)*. pp.86-94.

McDonald, D.D., and J. Pustejovsky. 1985b. TAGs as a grammatical formalism for generation. *Proceedings of ACL-85*. pp.94-103.

McDonald, D.D., and J. Pustejovsky. 1986. The UMass Counselor Project. *Computational Linguistics* Finite String Newsletter.

McDonald, D.D., J. Pustejovsky, and M. Vaughan. 1986. A measure of complexity for text planning and generation. In: *The papers from the 3rd International Workshop on Language Generation*. Dordrecht, Holland: Martinus Nijhoff Press. (In press.)

McKeown, K. 1985. *Text Generation*. Cambridge : Cambridge University Press.

Melby, A.K. 1978. Interactive translation. In: *Proceedings of COLING-78*.

Melby, A.K. 1981. Translators and machines — can they cooperate? In: META *Translator's Journal*, 26 (1), March 1981. pp.23-34.

Melby, A.K. 1982. Multi-level translation aids in a distributed system. In: J. Horecky (ed.) *Proceedings of COLING-82*, Prague, July 1982. North Holland Linguistic Series No. 47. Amsterdam: North Holland. pp.215-220.

Melby, A.K. 1984. Recipe for a translator work station. In: *Multilingua*, 3:225-228.

Miller, G.A., and P.N. Johnson-Laird. 1976. *Language and Perception*. Cambridge, MA.: Belknap/Harvard Press.

Minsky, M. 1975. A framework for representing knowledge. In: P. Winston (ed.) *The Psychology of Computer Vision*. New York: McGraw-Hill. pp. 211-277.

Montague, R. 1974. *Formal Philosophy*. New Haven: Yale University Press.

Morin, G. 1978. SISIF: *systeme d'identification, de substitution et d'insertion de formes.* Groupe TAUM. Université de Montréal.

Nagao, M. 1983a. On restricted sublanguage. In: *IPSJ Symposium on Natural Language Processing.* Information Processing Society of Japan (in Japanese).

Nagao, M. 1983b. A survey of Japanese language processing, 1980-1982. In: T. Kitagawa (ed.) *Computer Science and Technologies.* Amsterdam: North Holland. pp.64-70.

Nagao, M., T. Nishida, and J. Tsujii. 1984. Dealing with incompleteness of linguistic knowledge in language translation. In: *Proceedings of COLING-84.* pp.420-427.

Nagao, M., J. Tsujii, and J. Nakamura. 1985. The Japanese Government project for machine translation. *Computational Linguistics* 11:91-110.

Nakamura, J., J. Tsujii, and M. Nagao. 1984. Grammar writing system (GRADE) of Mu Machine Translation Project and its characteristics. In: *Proceedings of COLING-84.* pp.338-343.

Newell, A., and H. Simon. 1972. *Human Problem Solving.* Englewood Cliffs, NJ: Prentice-Hall.

Newmark, P. 1982. *Approaches to Translation.* New York: Pergamon Press.

Newspaper Enterprise Association. 1984. *The World Almanac and Book of Facts 1985.* New York, NY: Newspaper Enterprise Association.

Nida, E.A. 1964. *Toward a Science of Translating.* Leiden, Netherlands: E. J. Brill.

Nirenburg, S. (ed.) 1985. *Proceedings of the Conference on Theoretical and Methodological Issues in Machine Translation of Natural Languages,* Colgate University, Hamilton, NY, August 1985., August.

Nirenburg, S. 1986. Linguistics and artificial intelligence. In: P. C. Bjarkman and V. Raskin (eds.) *The Real-World Linguist: Linguistic Applications in the 1980's.* Norwood, NJ: Ablex.

Nirenburg, S., and Y. Ben Asher. 1984. HUHU, the Hebrew University Hebrew Understander. *Journal of Computer Languages* 9:161-182.

Nirenburg, S., V. Raskin, and A. Tucker. 1985. Interlingua design for TRANSLATOR. In: *Proceedings of the Conference on Theoretical and Methodological Issues in Machine Translation of Natural Languages,* Colgate University, Hamilton, NY, August 1985. pp.224-244.

Nirenburg, S., V. Raskin, and A. Tucker. 1986. On knowledge-based machine translation. In: *Proceedings of COLING-86.* pp.627-632.

Nirenburg, S., I. Nirenburg, and J. Reynolds. 1985. *POPLAR: a Testbed for Cognitive Modelling.* Research Report COSC7, Division of Natural Science, Colgate University. June, 1985.

Nishida, T., and S. Doshita. 1983. Application of Montague Grammar to English-Japanese machine translation. In: *Proceedings of Conference on Applied Natural Language Processing*. Santa Monica, CA. February. pp.156-165.

Patten, T. 1985. A problem solving approach to generating text from systemic grammars. In: *Proceedings of ACL-85 (European Chapter)*. pp.251-256.

Pereira, F.C.N. 1985. A structure-sharing representation for unification-based grammar formalisms. In: *Proceedings of ACL-85*. pp.137-144.

Polanyi, L., and R. Scha. 1984. A syntactic approach to discourse semantics. *Proceedings of COLING-84*, Stanford, CA, pp. 413-419.

Postal, P.M. 1970. On the surface verb *remind. Linguistic Inquiry*, 1:20-37.

Procter, P. (ed.) 1978. *Longman Dictionary of Contemporary English.* Harlow and London, England: Longman Group Limited.

Pustejovsky, J., K.Q. Gallagher, and S. Bergler. 1985. Clustered Objects as Knowledge Representation for Natural Language. Unpublished manuscript, University of Massachusetts.

Quine, W.V.O. 1960. *Word and Object.* Cambridge, MA: MIT Press.

Raskin, V. 1971. *K teorii jazykovyx podsistem [Towards a Theory of Sublanguages].* Moscow: Moscow University Press.

Raskin, V. 1974. On the feasibility of fully automatic high quality machine translation. *American Journal of Computational Linguistics* 11:3, Microfiche 9.

Razi, A.M. 1985. An Empirical Study of Robust Natural Language Processing. Ph.D. dissertation, University of Delaware. (Unpublished).

Reichman, R. 1985. *Getting Computers to Talk Like You and Me.* Cambridge, MA: MIT Press.

Reinhart, T. 1983. *Anaphora and Semantic Interpretation.* Chicago: Chicago University Press.

Rhyne, J.R. 1976. Lexical Rules and Structures in a Computer Model of Nominal Compounding. Ph.D. dissertation, University of Texas, Austin, Texas.

Riesbeck, C.K. 1975. Conceptual analysis. In: R.C. Schank (ed.) *Conceptual Information Processing*. New York, NY: North Holland.

Riesbeck, C.K., and R.C. Schank, 1976. *Comprehension by Computer: Expectation-based Analysis of Sentences in Context.* Technical Report 78, Yale University Department of Computer Science, October 1976.

Rooth, M. 1985. Associating with Focus. Unpublished Ph.D. Dissertation, Department of Linguistics, University of Massachusetts, Amherst, MA.

Rumelhart, D.E. 1975. Notes on a schema for stories. In: D.G. Bobrow and A. Collins (eds.) *Representation and Understanding*. New York: Academic Press. pp.211-236.

Sager, N. 1981. *Natural Language Information Precessing: A Computer Grammar of English and its Applications*. Reading, MA: Addison-Wesley.

Sager, N. 1982. Syntactic formatting of science information. In: *AFIPS Proceedings*, reprinted in R. Kittredge and J. Lehrberger. 1982. *Sublanguage: Studies of Language in Restricted Semantic Domains*. Berlin-New York: deGruyter.

Saito, H., and M. Tomita. 1986. On automatic composition of stereotypic documents in foreign languages. In: *Proceedings of 1st International Conference on Applications of Artificial Intelligence to Engineering Problems*. pp.179-192.

Sawai, S., M. Sugimoto, and N. Ukai. 1982. Knowledge representation and machine translation. *Fujitsu Science and Technology Journal (Japan)* 18:117-133.

Schank, R.C. 1972. Conceptual dependency: a theory of natural language understanding. *Cognitive Psychology* 3:552-631.

Schank, R.C. 1973. Identification of conceptualizations underlying natural language. In: R.C. Schank and K.M. Colby (eds.) *Computer Models of Thought and Language*. San Francisco: Freeman. pp.187-247.

Schank, R.C. (ed.) 1975. *Conceptual Information Processing*. New York, NY: North Holland.

Schank, R.C. 1982. Reminding and memory organization: An introduction to MOPs. In: W.G. Lehnert and M.H. Ringle (eds.) *Strategies for Natural Language Processing*. Hillsdale, NJ: Lawrence Erlbaum Associates. pp.470-485.

Schank, R.C., and R. Abelson. 1977. *Scripts, Plans, Goals and Understanding*. Hillsdale, NJ: Lawrence Erlbaum Associates.

Schank, R.C., and L. Birnbaum. 1980. *Memory, Meaning, and Syntax*. Technical Report 189, Yale University Department of Computer Science.

Schank, R.C., M. Lebowitz, and L. Birnbaum. 1980. An integrated understander. *American Journal of Computational Linguistics* 6:13-30.

Searle, J.R. 1969. *Speech Acts*. Cambridge: Cambridge University Press.

Shapiro, S. 1982. Generalized augmented transition network grammars for generation from semantic networks. *American Journal of Computational Linguistics* 8:12-25.

Shieber, S.M. 1985. Using restriction to extend parsing algorithms for complex-feature-based formalisms. In: *Proceedings of ACL-85*. pp.145-152.

Sidner, C.L. 1985. Plan parsing for intended response recognition in discourse. *Computational Intelligence* 1:1-10.

Simmons R., and J. Slocum. 1972. Generating English discourse from semantic networks. *Communications of the Association for Computing Machinery* 15:891-905.

Slocum, J. 1981. *A practical comparison of parsing strategies for machine translation and other natural language processing purposes*. Technical Report NL-41, Department of Computer Sciences, University of Texas Austin.

Slocum, J. 1984. Machine Translation: its history, current status, and future prospects. In: *Proceedings of COLING-84*. pp.546-561. Also Working Paper LRC-84-3, Linguistics Research Center, University of Texas, Austin.

Slocum, J. 1985. Survey of machine translation: its history, current status, and future prospects. *Computational Linguistics* 11:1-17.

Slocum, J. 1986. How one might automatically identify and adapt to a sub-language: an initial exploration. In: R. Grishman and R. Kittredge (eds.) *Analyzing Language in Restricted Domains*. Hillsdale, NJ: Lawrence Erlbaum Associates. pp.195-210.

Slocum, J., W. Bennett, J. Bear, M. Morgan, and R. Root. 1984. METAL: *The LRC machine translation system*. Working Paper LRC-84-2, Linguistics Research Center, University of Texas, Austin.

Smith, H.T., and T.R.G. Green. (eds.) 1980. *Human Interaction with Computers*. New York, NY: Academic Press.

Smith, R.N., D. Bienstock, and E. Housman. 1982. A collocational model of information transfer. In: A.E. Petrarca, C.I. Taylor, and R.S. Kohn (eds.) *Information Interaction: Proceedings of the 45th ASIS Annual Meeting, Volume 19*. White Plains, NY: Knowledge Industry Publications. pp.281-284.

Stalnaker, R. 1979. Assertion. In: J. McCawley (ed.) *Syntax and Semantics 7*. New York: Academic Press. pp.315-332.

Stewart, G. 1978. Specialisation et compilation des ATN: REZO. In: *Proceedings of COLING-78*.

Strawson, P. 1950. On referring. *Mind* 59:320-344.

Swartout, W. 1977. A digitalis therapy advisor with explanations. In: *Proceedings of IJCAI-77*. pp.819-825.

Swartout, W. 1981. Producing Explanations and Justifications of Expert Consulting Programs. Ph.D. dissertation, Dept. of Electrical Engineering and Computer Science, MIT. (Available as TR-251, MIT Laboratory for Computer Science.)

Tait, J. 1982. Automatic Summarising of English Texts. Ph.D. thesis, Cambridge University, Dept. of Computer Science.

TAUM-METEO. Description du système. Report from the University of Montréal, January 1978.

Thompson, B.H. 1980. Linguistic analysis of natural language communication with computers. In: *Proceedings of COLING-80*. pp.190-201.

Toma, P. 1977. SYSTRAN as a multi-lingual machine translation system. In: *Commission of European Communities: Overcoming the Language Barrier*. Munich: Dokumentation Verlag. pp.129-160.

Tombe, L. des, D.J. Arnold, L. Jaspaert, R.L. Johnson, S. Krauwer, M. Rosner, G.B. Varile, and S. Warwick. 1985. A preliminary linguistic framework for EUROTRA (June 1985). In: *Proceedings of the Conference on Theoretical and Methodological Issues in Machine Translation of Natural Languages*, Colgate University, Hamilton, NY, August 1985. pp.283-288.

Tomita, M. 1984. Disambiguating grammatically ambiguous sentences by asking. In: *Proceedings of COLING-84*. pp.476-480.

Tomita, M. 1985a. Feasibility study of personal/interactive machine translation systems. In: *Proceedings of the Conference on Theoretical and Methodological Issues in Machine Translation of Natural Languages*, Colgate University, Hamilton, NY, August 1985. pp.289-297.

Tomita, M. 1985b. An efficient context-free parsing algorithm for natural languages. In: *Proceedings of IJCAI-85*. pp.756-764.

Tomita, M. 1985c. *Efficient Parsing for Natural Language: A Fast Algorithm for Practical Systems*. Boston, MA: Kluwer Academic Publishers.

Tomita, M. 1986a. An efficient word lattice parsing algorithm for continuous speech recognition. In: *Proceedings of International Conference on Acoustics, Speech, and Signal Processing (ICASSP-86)*. pp.1569-1572.

Tomita, M. 1986b. Sentence disambiguation by asking. *Computers and Translation*. 1:39-57.

Tomita, M., T. Nishida, and S. Doshita. 1984. User front-end for disambiguation in interactive machine translation system. In: *IPSJ Symposium on Natural Language Processing*. Information Processing Society of Japan (in Japanese).

Trawick, D.J. 1983. Robust Sentence Analysis and Habitability. Ph.D. dissertation, California Institute of Technology, February, 1983. (Unpublished).

Tucker, A. 1984. A perspective on machine translation: theory and practice. *Communications of the Association for Computing Machinery* 27:322-329.

Tucker, A.B., and S. Nirenburg. 1984. Machine translation: a contemporary view. *Annual Review of Information Science and Technology* 19:129-160. American Society for Information Science.

Tucker, A., S. Nirenburg, and V. Raskin. Discourse, cohesion and semantics of expository text. In: *Proceedings of COLING-86.* pp.181-183.

UNIX. 1979, 1984. *UNIX User's Manual* (2 volumes), *UNIX Programmer's Manual* (2 volumes), *UNIX System Manager's Manual.* Berkeley, CA: University of California.

Vasconcellos, M., and M. Leon. 1985. SPANAM and ENGSPAN: Machine translation at the Pan American Health Organization (PAHO). *Computational Linguistics* 11:122-136.

Vauquois, B. 1975. *La Traduction automatique à Grenoble.* Paris: Dunod.

Walker, D.E., and R.A. Amsler. 1986. The use of machine-readable dictionaries in sublanguage analysis. In: R. Grishman and R. Kittredge (eds.) *Sublanguage: Description and Processing.* Hillsdale, NJ: Lawrence Erlbaum Associates. pp.69-84.

Waltz, D.L. 1978. An English language question answering system for a large relational database. *Communications of the Association for Computing Machinery* 21:526-539.

Webber, B.L. 1971. The case for generation. In: *Papers presented at the Seminar in Mathematical Linguistics, vol. XIII.* Aiken Computational Laboratory, Harvard University, Spring 1971.

Webber, B.L. 1978. A Formal Approach to Discourse Anaphora. Ph.D. dissertation, BBN Report No. 3761.

Weiner, J.L. 1980. BLAH, a system which explains its reasoning. *Artificial Intelligence* 15:19-48.

Weischedel, R.M., and N.K. Sondheimer. 1982. An improved heuristic for ellipsis processing. In: *Proceedings of ACL-82.* pp.85-88.

Weischedel, R.M., and N.K. Sondheimer. 1983. Meta-rules as a basis for processing ill-formed input. *American Journal of Computational Linguistics* 9:161-177.

Weischedel, R.M., W. Voge, and M. James. 1978. An artificial intelligence approach to language instruction. *Artificial Intelligence* 10:225-240.

Wheeler, P.J. 1984. Changes and improvements to the European Commission's SYSTRAN MT system, 1976-1983. In: *Proceedings of the International Conference on the Methodology and Techniques of Machine Translation.* Cranfield Institute of Technology, UK.

White, J. 1985. Characteristics of the METAL machine translation system at production stage. In: *Proceedings of the Conference on Theoretical and Methodological Issues in Machine Translation of Natural Languages,* Colgate University, Hamilton, NY, August 1985. pp.359-369. Also Working Paper LRC-85-4, Linguistics Research Center, University of Texas.

Wilensky, R. 1982. Points: A theory of the structure of stories in memory. In: W.G. Lehnert and M.H. Ringle (eds.) *Strategies for Natural Language Processing.* Hillsdale, NJ: Lawrence Erlbaum Associates. pp.345-374.

Wilensky, R., and M. Morgan. 1981. *One Analyzer for Three Languages.* UCB/ERL TR-M81-87, University of California, Berkeley.

Wilensky R., Y. Arens, and D. Chin. 1984. Talking to UNIX in English: An overview of UC. *Communications of the Association for Computing Machinery* 27:574-593.

Wilks, Y.A. 1973. An artificial intelligence approach to machine translation. In: R.C. Schank and K.M. Colby (eds.) *Computer Models of Thought and Language.* San Francisco: W.H. Freeman and Company. pp.114-151.

Wilks, Y.A. 1974. Natural Language Understanding Systems within the AI paradigm: A survey with some comparisons. AI Memo 237, AI Laboratory, Stanford University. (Also in A. Zampolli (ed.) 1977. *Linguistic Structures Processing.* Amsterdam: North Holland. pp.341-398.)

Wilks, Y.A. 1975. A preferential, pattern-seeking, semantics for natural language understanding. *Artificial Intelligence* 6: 53-74.

Wilks, Y.A., and J. Bien. 1983. Belief, points of view, and multiple environments. *Cognitive Science* 7:95-119.

Winograd, T. 1972. *Understanding Natural Language.* New York: Academic Press.

Winograd, T. 1983. *Language as a Cognitive Process. Volume 1: Syntax.* Reading, MA: Addison-Wesley.

Witkam, A.P.M. 1983. *Distributed Language Translation, Feasibility Study of a Multilingual Facility for Videotex Information Networks.* Utrecht, The Netherlands: Buro voor Systeemontwikkeling.

Witkam, A.P.M. 1984. Distributed language translation, another MT system. In: *Proceedings of the International Conference on the Methodology and Techniques of Machine Translation,* Cranfield Institute of Technology, UK.

Woods, W. 1970. Transition network grammars for natural language analysis. *Communications of the Association for Computing Machinery* 13:591-606.

Woolf, B. 1984. Context Dependent Planning in a Machine Tutor. Ph.D. dissertation, University of Massachusetts, Department of Computer Science.

Woolf, B., and D.D.McDonald, 1984. Building a Computer Tutor: Design Issues. *IEEE Computer* 17:61-73.

Zarechnak, M. 1979. The history of machine translation. In: B. Henisz-Dostert, R. Ross Mcdonald, and M. Zarechnak. *Machine Translation*. Trends in Linguistics: Studies and Monographs, Volume 11. The Hague, Holland: Mouton Publishers. pp.3-87.

Subject index

ALEX, 71
all-or-nothing test, 286
ALPAC, 69, 136, 317
ALPS, 13, 147, 148, 150
anaphora, 30, 93, 104, 171, 176, 180
   discourse, 185
   interpretation of, 181
   inter-sentential, 184
   resolution, 100, 278, 293
APSG, 226
artificial intelligence (AI), 1, 25, 41, 81, 247, 260
   approach, 6, 112, 335
   research in, 19, 168, 192, 200, 248
   techniques, 26
ATLAS/I, 25
Augmented Transition Network (ATN), 32, 34, 37, 38, 87, 206-210, 221, 310

bindings and coreference, anaphoric, 171, 172, 185

CA, a conceptual analyzer, 306-307
case role analysis, 231
CICERO, a discourse management system, 19, 168, 187-191
clue words (and phrases), 104, 163, 168, 172, 174, 179, 186, 309, 321
clusters, 91, 188-190

conceptual dependency (CD), 25-27
constraints,
   pragmatic, 159, 167
   semantic, 156, 159, 160, 167,
   syntactic, 167
context space, 171, 172
COUNSELOR, a legal reasoning system, 187-188, 190
Cyrillic alphabet 287

data-directed control, 215
dative movement, 313
dictionary,
   augmentation, 17
   automated update interfaces, 71
   bilingual, 3, 6, 17, 18, 25, 150
   bilingual transfer, 23
   biographical, 225
   collegiate, 249
   data, 249, 256
   English-Russian, 5
   entry, 31, 71, 93, 174, 248, 251, 255, 256, 283, 295, 298, 306
   frame, 93
   generation, 8, 275
   IL, 91, 92, 98, 105, 113
   learner's, 250
   local, 71
   look-up, 1, 13, 23, 148, 152, 284, 286, 298
   machine-readable, 20, 249, 253

338

Author index

Abelson, R. 75, 173, 332
Aho, A.V. 88, 317
Allen, J.F. 161, 168, 173,
175-176, 180, 189, 317, 328
Alterman, R. 174, 178, 317
Amsler, R.A. 247, 249-251,
256-257, 260, 317, 335
Anick, P.G. 320
Appelt, D. 196, 204, 212, 317
Arens, Y. 336
Arnold, D.J. 17, 33, 114,
123-124, 143, 317, 334
Ashley, K. 188, 221, 318
Austin, J. 56, 171, 318

Bach, K. 171, 318
Bar-Hillel, Y. 68-69, 260, 302,
318
Barr, A. 248, 318
Barwise, J. 176-177, 318
Bates, M. 328
Bear, J. 333
Becker, J. 256, 318
Ben Asher, Y., 4, 330
Bennett, W.S., 27, 31-33, 318,
332
Bien, J. 168, 176, 335
Bienstock, D. 333
Birnbaum, L. 27, 302, 318, 332
Black, J.B. 249, 319
Bobrow, D.G. 188, 318, 331
Bobrow, R. 161, 318
Boggs, W.M. 320
Boitet, Ch. 24, 75, 302, 319
Booth, A.D. 68, 328

Booth, S.L. 278, 319
Bossie, S. 212, 319
Bourbeau, L. 326
Brachman, R. 92, 319
Bresnan, J. 86, 127, 319, 325
Britton, B.K. 249, 319
Bruce, B. 195, 298, 319
Bruderer, H. 319
Burton, R. 220, 319

Carberry, M.S. 161, 165, 167,
320
Carbonell, J.G. 17, 25-26, 28,
68-69, 74-75, 86, 89-90,
156, 279, 320, 324
Carlson, L. 177, 181-182
Carroll, J.B. 249, 320
Cecchi, C. 114, 320
Chaffin, R. 280, 320
Chandioux, J. 302, 320
Charniak, E. 27, 156, 281, 320
Cherry, L.L. 159, 320
Chester, D. 200, 320
Chin, D. 336
Chomsky, N. 43, 50, 168, 182,
321
Church, K. 78, 321
Clippinger, J. 198, 321
Cohen, P.R. 168, 173, 175, 180,
318, 321
Cohen, R. 165, 321
Colmerauer, A. 30, 321
Conklin, E. 204, 218-219, 321
Cullingford, R.E. 74, 278-279,
281, 284, 295, 298, 321